JAN**GARBAREK:**

Deep Song

Other titles in the East**Note** series

Artie**Shaw**: Non-Stop Flight - John White
Sonny**Rollins**: The Cutting Edge - Richard Palmer

forthcoming

Bill**Evans**: - Keith Shadwick
Oscar**Peterson**: Discography - Arnold van Kampen

Series Editor Richard Palmer

JAN**GARBAREK:**
Deep Song

Michael Tucker

East**Note**

For Tom Bækkerud

and

to the memory of Stefan Bakke

EastNote

HULL STUDIES IN JAZZ

The University of Hull Press
Cottingham Road
Hull
HU6 7RX

A CIP catalogue record for this book is available from the British Library.

© **Michael Tucker**

Published 1998

Paperback ISBN 0 85958 684 7

Printed by Viking Press, Hebeden Bridge, England

A beautiful church bell means more to me than sermons and hymns.

Gunnar Ekelöf   'The Last Bell Toll', _Modus Vivendi_

You shall not think 'the past is finished'
or 'the future is before us'.

T. S. Eliot   _Four Quartets_

Can you sing me a song?

Lester Young

Study for Sea of Space and Time
Ian McKeever
(1998, watercolour on paper, c. 20 x 13 cms. collection of the artist)

Contents

Breathing in, breathing out: Jan Garbarek at the Barbican
(London, December 1997) Peter Symes

Acknowledgements

Initially, my gratitude goes to Glen Innes, of Hull University Press, and Dr. Richard Palmer, commissioning editor of the *Eastnote* Studies In Jazz at the Press, for suggesting the present work. I am particularly grateful to Richard, for his unfailing good humour and astute and patient editorial input. Parts of the text were read by Jon Christensen and Niels-Henning Ørsted Pedersen, while Manfred Eicher and Steve Lake of ECM read the whole manuscript: my gratitude to all for giving so generously of their time and expertise.

The University of Brighton, where I teach, gave me time towards research and writing and also helped to fund research trips to Munich, Oslo and Copenhagen. I am most grateful to Dr Paddy Maguire, Head of the School of Historical and Critical Studies, and Professor Bruce Brown, Dean of the Faculty of Arts and Architecture, for their support and encouragement.

I am no less indebted in this respect to Øystein Braathen, Minister Counsellor for Press and Cultural Affairs at the Royal Norwegian Embassy, London, and the Foreign Ministry of the Royal Norwegian Government: the cultural seminar on the west coast of Norway to which I was invited in summer 1998 proved extremely stimulating, enabling me to meet several people whose expertise was of assistance to me. Professor Harald Herresthal of the Norwegian State Academy of Music, Oslo, his colleague, Professor Olav Anton Thommessen, and the poet, dramatist and writer Jon Fosse were all particularly helpful.

Although Jan Garbarek has not collaborated directly on the present text, I wish to thank both him and Vigdis Garbarek for many hours of stimulating conversation, and for supplying various historical and technical information over the years. Many other people have also given generously of their time and expertise. My thanks to: Misha

Alperin, Arild Andersen, Ragnar Augland, Tom Bækkerud, Constantin Gonzalez Barros, Johs Bergh, Jon Christensen, Richard Cook, Lars Danielsson, Palle Danielsson, Peter Erskine, Lars Gundersen, Trilok Gurtu, Geoff Hearn, Roald Helgheim, Tor Hammerø, Jan Horne, Randi Hultin, Ken Hyder, Alfred Janson, Lars Jansson, Steinar Kristiansen, Karin Krog, John Marshall, Professor John Mayer, Palle Mikkelborg, Alison Minns, Knut Moe, Nils Petter Molvær, Rod Paton, Niels-Henning Ørsted Pedersen, Per Kleiva, Edith Roger, Bernt Rosengren, George Russell, Terje Rypdal, Gladyse Saul, Karl Seglem, Andy Sheppard, Hilbre Skinner, Tommy Smith, Theodosii Spassov, Tomasz Stanko, Bobo Stenson, John Surman, John Taylor, Margaret Tucker, Edward Vesala, Jan Erik Vold, Eberhard Weber, Bobby Wellins, Kenneth White and Frans Widerberg. Mike Fearey, of the University of Brighton, was of great assistance in the preparation of the book's visual material.

Eddie Cook, Editor of *Jazz Journal International*, kindly allowed me to trawl through the journal's archives. I am also grateful to Eddie for enabling me to review a good many ECM records over the past decade and a half, and to Mark Gilbert, Deputy Editor at the *Journal*, for much stimulating discussion. I am no less indebted to New Note Distribution, and in particular, Steve Sanderson and Kerstan Mackness. Over the years Steve, label manager for ECM in Britain, has given me considerable and much appreciated help with research material. My thanks go also to Alan Davie, who loaned me several important, now rare recordings of twentieth-century music and graciously gave permission for the reproduction of his work, as did Frans Widerberg – to whom I am grateful for too many things to mention here.

In the mid-1990s the musician and composer, writer and broadcaster Maxwell Steer invited me to speak at the two *Music and the Psyche* conferences which he organised at the City University, London. I am grateful to Maxwell for the considerable stimulus which these conferences provided. Over the past few years, Dr Rod Paton of the Chichester Institute, West Sussex has invited me to lecture to his music students on the work of Jan Garbarek. It has always been a distinct pleasure to work with Rod, whose many telling observations about both technical and emotional aspects of Garbarek's oeuvre have been especially helpful to me. I am equally indebted to Ian McKeever for the enthusiasm, creativity and care with which he executed the frontispiece for the book.

Manfred Eicher anwered a variety of questions with patience and perception during a research trip which I undertook to Munich in October 1997. That trip was made further memorable by the consideration shown to me by everyone at ECM. My thanks to Sarah Humphries, who did a great deal to expedite my research in the ECM archives; to Helga, for arranging accomodation, and to everyone in the ECM office, especially Heike and Mark, for their kindness.

Thanks to the kindness of John Cumming and John Ellson of Serious Productions, London, Fiona Alexander and Roger Spence of Assembly Direct, Edinburgh, and Veit Bremme and Peter Hohensee of Bremme/Hohensee Productions, Heidelberg, I have been able to see Garbarek in more contexts than might otherwise have been possible. Had it not been for the further generosity of spirit of several people, this book might never have seen the light of day. In London, John Cumming of Serious Productions set up several key contacts for me, while in Oslo, Tom Bækkerud and Hilde Hjulstad, Tor Hammerø, Knut Moe and Susie Juul, and Frans and Aasa Widerberg gave me indispensable encouragement, information and hospitality. Without Tom Bækkerud, who with his close friend Stefan Bakke (1946-93) first introduced me to Norwegian life and culture a quarter of a century ago, this book would never have been possible. It is a privilege to dedicate the book in friendship to such a man. And without Tor Hammerø, with whom I have shared many moments of mutual enthusiasm for jazz over the years, my knowledge of recent Norwegian jazz – and the pleasures of the Molde jazz festival – would have been considerably poorer.

With exceptional generosity, Jon Christensen lent me his personal photo-diaries, containing many rare newspaper clippings and photographs from the early 1960s onwards. Jon also offered invaluable historical insights in interview, lent me some rare, private recordings from the 1960s and gave me key telephone numbers. Thanks to Jon and his wife Ellen, I was introduced to the NRK film director Jan Horne. Jan's kindness was remarkable: he sent me video tapes of Garbarek in concert in the 1960s and 1970s and lent me some irreplaceable photographs of Garbarek from the 1960s. So did Steinar Kristiansen, who was considerate enough to supply the rarest of photographs of Garbarek and Don Cherry playing together at Sogn Jazz Club in Oslo in the late 1960s. Randi Hultin was equally kind, especially with regard to facilitating the reproduction of both her photographic and graphic work: so too was Ragnar Augland, who sent me some excellent selections of Garbarek on video tape. And George Ware, with whom I have spent many happy hours listening to music, kindly allowed me to use some of the fine photographs which he took during a tour of Norway in the summer of 1980. My thanks also to Wivi-Ann, daughter of Randi Hultin, for her help with accessing photographs.

At the Norwegian Jazz Archives, housed in the excellent Norwegian Music Information Centre in Oslo, Director Finn J. Kramer-Johansen was patience itself. Day after day, Finn not only pointed the way to many cassette and video recordings and newspaper articles for me to listen to and read, but also (as a fluent English speaker) tolerated – with unfailing good humour – my variously wayward attempts to navigate his native language. I am deeply grateful for all the considerable help which he gave me during the research for this book: *tusen takk* Finn.

My wife Louise has been an enormous support and encouragement to me, as she has always been during such periods of research and writing. Over the years, we have spent many hours listening to Jan Garbarek and her love of his music has played an essential part in the preparation and realisation of this book. Needless to say, its surviving shortcomings remain entirely my responsibility.

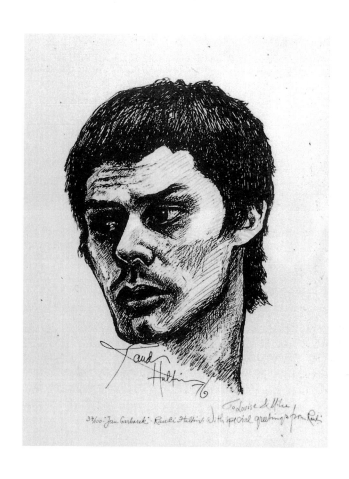

Jan Garbarek, portrait
(1976 serigraf, after a photograph by Jochen Mönch, private collection)
Randi Hultin

Portrait of the Artist as a Young Man
(c. 1968-70 collection of National Jazz Archives, Oslo)

Prelude

In his _Maxims and Missiles_ Nietzsche made known his belief that, without music, life would be a mistake. I tend to agree. Over the years, music has been a (more or less) constant companion of mine. Innumerable musicians and composers, from Ben E. King and Bob Dylan to Van Morrison and Léo Ferré, Louis Armstrong and Duke Ellington, George Russell and Arvo Pärt, J. S. Bach and Joe Zawinul, Janet Baker and Mari Boine, Mozart and Beethoven, Sibelius and Bartók, Don Cherry and Keith Jarrett, John Coltrane and Nusrat Fateh Ali Khan have all given me - what? The joy of music, yes ... but what does that joy signify?

As any student of the aesthetics of music - or enthusiastic, enquiring listener - will be aware, such a question invites a potential library of answers. The simplest answer that makes sense to me is that music - however ostensibly different or dissonant it may be - offers an infinite variety of journeys towards a simultaneously aural and imaginal experience of the poetics of integration: of creator and listener, sound and silence; melody and rhythm, scale and chord; the horizontal and the vertical, the linear and the cyclical - of part and whole. Again, as any student of comparative musicology - or aforementioned listener - will be aware, such a proposition begs a library of genre-crossing questions.[1]

There is one music this century which, more than any other, has been able to stimulate awareness of how much joy there is to be had in exploring - and perhaps revisioning - the relations that might obtain between such questions and answers. That music is jazz, a music which, in its many different forms, has radically redefined the notion of music as a journey to both known and previously unsuspected aspects of oneself. Think: once upon a time, jazz did not exist. Once upon a time, there was no Louis Armstrong, and no Duke Ellington; no Jelly Roll Morton, and no Fats Waller; no Coleman Hawkins or Lester Young, no Billie Holiday or Betty Carter; no Charlie Christian or Django Reinhardt, no Dizzy Gillespie or Charlie Parker; no Miles Davis or John Coltrane, no Thelonious Monk or Oscar Peterson; no

7

Clifford Brown or Stan Getz, no Bill Evans or George Russell; no Sonny Rollins or Ornette Coleman, no Joe Henderson or Wayne Shorter; no Milt Jackson or Gary Burton, no Sun Ra or Joe Zawinul. Beyond all questions of technical achievement, stylistic category or historical evolution, one might ask: what did (and do) such figures offer us that was not present in music before?

My answer would be: they offer the simultaneous presence and potentiality of the poetics of synthesis, understood on both a larger and more intimate scale than hitherto imaginable. I am aware that the twentieth century sometimes likes to pride itself on ambitions and achievements which were in fact present - in embryonic form, at least - many years previously. One thinks, for example, of Modernism's umbilical (yet often neglected) relation to Romanticism, or - to be more specific - of the anticipation of aspects of both nineteenth- and twentieth-century Orientalism in the improvisational achievements of a seventeenth-century composer such as the Venetian, Johannes Hieronymous Kapsberger.[2] However, in jazz, the question of synthesis - of gospel and blues elements, folk melody and popular song, improvisation and composition, melancholy and affirmation, individual and group, body and soul, heart and mind - really does take on extraordinary and new proportions. In particular, the synthesis of musical resource(s) and spiritual overtone(s) in the music is such as to make jazz one of the great potential vehicles to that state of transformed and transformative, devotional consciousness which has been the concern of so many artists, in so many media, this century.

Child of a century which, more than any other, has revealed the bottomless depths of the viciousness of which humanity is capable, jazz speaks of hope: the hope that we might yet learn to live with both ourselves and others, free of fanaticism and fear; the hope that we might yet transform the divisiveness of falsely politicised (or racist) consciousness into the healing wholeness of a broad-based poetic sensibility; the hope that, wanderers on earth as we are, we might yet sing the loneliness of existence into the pure joy - the ecstasy - of being.

In contrast to the B-movie cliché that always associates jazz with low life, the great bebop trumpeter Dizzy Gillespie believed there were strong connections between the practise of jazz and religious consciousness (which, given Gillespie's Bahai beliefs, one might fairly understand as ecumenical, spiritual consciousness). In his 1979 autobiography _To Be Or Not To Bop_ Gillespie argued that creative jazz musicians could - and should - be considered the people the most in tune with what Gillespie called "the Universe".[3] Perhaps this is what Louis Armstrong meant when he said that, in order to play jazz, you have to have love in your heart. Whatever, it is my belief - and that of many others - that it is in jazz that one finds some of the most inspiring stimuli to (re)consider the relations between self and others, self and world, world and "the Universe".

This century, few countries in the world have offered so much to the mind keen to consider such various relations of self and "whole" as the Nordic lands of Denmark, Sweden and Norway, Iceland and Finland. Combining a commitment to principles of democratic modernity with an ability (or compulsion) to chart the more visionary aspects of the human imagination, these Nordic lands have long produced not only some of the world's finest architecture and design, but also some of the most stimulating art and literature, music and film.

In particular, Norway - a country of barely four million people, stretching from its southern skerries (roughly parallel in latitude to the northern extremities of Scotland) to the Arctic Circle and beyond - has made an exceptional contribution to the culture of our century. While the historical novels of Sigrid Unset (1882-1949) remain some of the most accomplished and popular of their era, the achievements of Ibsen and Munch, Grieg and Hamsun have long been fundamental to twentieth-century avant-garde drama and painting, music and the novel. In recent decades, the legacy of such achievement has been developed by such creative Norwegian spirits as Tarjei Vesaas and Jon Fosse, Jakob Weidemann and Frans Widerberg, Arne Nordheim and Rolf Wallin, Axel Jensen and Jostein Gaarder. Two of the most important philosophical thinkers of our time are Norwegian: the architectural theorist Christian Norberg-Schulz, and Arne Næss, the father of "deep ecology". The names of Kjell Lund and Nils Slaatto, Sverre Fehn and Peter Opsvik, Bård Breivik and Marianne Heske, Annbjørg Lien and Truls Mørk, Benny Motzfeldt (1909-95) and Tone Vigeland should suffice to indicate the excellence of much of Norway's recent, internationally recognised contributions to art and design, sculpture and multi-media art, folk music and the classical repertoire, craft and design.[4]

In a variety of ways, the creative spark of jazz seems to have ignited a particularly rich field of responsive - and transformative - energy in this rugged, scenically compelling country, as renowned for the raking purity of its light as it is for the sublime majesty of its mountains and fjords. Norwegian jazz festivals, such as those at Molde, Kongsberg and Voss, have long been recognised as some of the best in the world - as have a good many Norwegian musicians. Few books can have captured the symbiotic relation between much of the most stimulating modern abstract art, lyric poetry and jazz as successfully as did the 1997 _Blåtoneboulevardene_ (The Blue-toned Boulevards) by (ex-AHA) graphic artist Magne Furuholmen and poet Henning Kramer Dahl.[5] And few recordings have revealed so beautifully the love which Louis Armstrong aroused around the world as the Norwegian double-bassist Bjørn Alterhaug's setting of his fellow countryman Harald Sverdrup's poem _Old Louis_, from the 1976 collection _Gamle Louis og andre dikt_ (Old Louis and other poems). Recorded in 1983, this moving homage to Armstrong (who played in Norway in 1952, 1955 and 1959) was interpreted by an ensemble which included Sverdrup himself, vocalist Karin Krog, trumpeter Åge Midtgård, alto and baritone saxophonist Jon Pål Inderberg, guitarist Frode Alnæs and drummer Svein Christiansen.[6]

I think it would be reasonable to say that, of these musicians, only Karin Krog has broken through to the sort of international recognition which leads to the winning of _Down Beat_ polls and regular invitations to appear at the world's most prestigious festivals. I think it would also be reasonable to suggest that such a fact is no true reflection upon the quality of the musicians accompanying Krog on this date, all of whom are considerable instrumentalists, with a sound and identity very much their own.

Gunnar Ekelöf (1907-68), the mystically-inclined Swedish poet whose work was translated into English (which Ekelöf spoke and wrote well, as he did several other European languages) by such distinguished contemporaries as W. H. Auden, Muriel Rukeyser and Leif Sjöberg, believed that, good as it was that the spread of English had facilitated a certain level of world-wide comunication, it was nevertheless regrettable that the increasing dominance of this language had also led to a considerable degree of cultural ignorance - if not active diminishing - of the achievements, or poetics, of other languages. The same point might be applied to jazz.

Wonderful music that jazz is, the idea that everyone playing it should strive to sound as much as possible like the American originals who first inspired them to take up an instrument strikes me as an infinitely depressing idea: not that far removed from the nightmare thought that, one day, anywhere in the world, there might be nothing but Big Macs and Coca-Cola to eat and drink. In his sleeve-note to **This Is Always**, a 1984 session by (the late) Norwegian tenor saxophonist Bjarne Nerem, producer Bjørn Petersen chose to address potential purchasers of this fine, modern mainstream music by saying that, "The only worry I have about this LP is that you dismiss it as an example of 'Norwegian jazz' before listening. Nothing could be more wrong.Take time to *listen* to Bjarne Nerem and you will find that his tenor saxophone playing is directly out of the American tradition."[7] By 1984 however, many a jazz enthusiast and critic - whether British or Norwegian, German or American, for example - had long come to listen to Norwegian jazz precisely because it *was* somehow 'Norwegian', and not directly imitative of the American tradition.

In fact, Norway has produced distinctive jazz musicians with an identity of their own for quite some time now. Bjarne Nerem, indeed, was one such: a musician who, steeped in the values of the modern American "cool school" as he was, contributed characterful solos to such outstanding documents of burgeoning Scandinavian identity as Swedish trumpeter Bengt-Arne Wallin's ground-breaking 1962 recording **Old Folklore In Swedish Modern** (on which the Norwegian-born but Swedish-domiciled drummer Egil "Bop" Johansen was also present).[8] Since then, such names as Karin Krog and Egil Kapstad, Terje Rypdal and Arild Andersen, Jon Christensen and Knut Riisnæs, Per Husby and Jon Balke, Sidsel Endresen and Nils Petter Molvær have come to signify the increasingly distinctive identity of contemporary Norwegian jazz, or jazz-related music.[9] One musician, above all, has created a body of work which exemplifies the achievement of such an identity: the saxophonist and composer, Jan Garbarek.

Some years ago, Ekelöf - a poet resolutely opposed to the shibboleths of official religion, but deeply spiritual in nature - asked: "Will it come, or will it not/ The day when the joy becomes great,/ The day when the grief becomes small?"[10] In the remarkable, wide-ranging oeuvre which Jan Garbarek has created over the past four decades, the relations between grief and joy, loneliness and ecstasy - and self and others, self, world and "the Universe" - have acquired increasingly fresh resonance. It is an essentially poetic resonance, born of the impulse to synthesise that has always fired the language that is jazz, and which takes aspects of that impulse and language into new realms of both musical and spiritual presence and potentiality.

Almost thirty years ago, the distinguished Afro-American composer and arranger, theorist, pianist and band leader George Russell described the young Garbarek as "just about the most uniquely talented jazz musician Europe has produced since Django Reinhardt."[11] The comparison can stand scrutiny today, as it could then. Just as there are both characterfully Gallic and more international elements in Reinhardt - consider, for example, the anticipation of the cultural patching in today's so-called "world music" which can be sensed in the 1937 *Bolero de Django* - so are there specifically Nordic and more international elements to be heard in the music of Garbarek. And just as Reinhardt was both a forward-looking modernist and a folk musician with fructifying roots (think of the transmuted traces of flamenco rhythms which can be heard within the virtuosity of his jazz improvisations) so does the mature Garbarek synthesise aspects of progressive jazz contemporaneity with historically distant, yet psychologically - spiritually - replenishing elements of folk-like phrasing, feeling and form.

As the British trumpeter and jazz specialist Ian Carr has observed, the music of Jan Garbarek offers us a very special type of affirmation: completely contemporary in its post-Coltrane technical authority, while at the same time "full of resonances from the past - echoes of Nordic folksong, old church music, half-forgotten things from long ago."[12] It is a music Garbarek has performed and recorded with jazz duo, trio, quartet and quintet, but also in various larger aggregations, as well as solo with strings; which has found him in acoustic and electric contexts, playing with church organist or avant-garde guitarist; and which has seen him improvising in response to the solo invocations of folk singers from the Far North, or weaving his way within and across the polyphony of Britain's Hilliard Ensemble.

Recently, I asked George Russell how he would now describe the work of the musician whose sound on tenor saxophone had meant something special to him as long ago as 1965. It was then that Russell sat in on piano at a jam session with Garbarek's quartet at the Molde Festival - a session that, as we shall see, was to have considerable consequences for both the young saxophonist and one of his playing companions, the Norwegian drummer Jon Christensen. Russell's response to my question was carefully weighed, but immediate: "Jan plays the Himalayas - that's how I would put it. It's a big, big concept of music that he has."[13]

Whatever its particular manifestation, that concept has been mostly very well received, by fellow musicians, critics and listening public alike. **Officium**, Garbarek's 1993 collaboration with the Hilliard Ensemble, has sold in extraordinary numbers, and the current Jan Garbarek Group - featuring Rainer Brüninghaus (piano, keyboards), Eberhard Weber (electric bass) and Marilyn Mazur (drums, percussion) - has long been one of the most popular attractions on the European jazz circuit. However, there have been those critics, especially in the jazz world, who have taken occasional issue with aspects of Garbarek's work. In particular, Garbarek has sometimes been accused of putting manner before matter, of cultivating too atmospheric an ambience in his music at the (alleged) expense of supposedly more red-blooded and swinging values. This is a criticism which has also been levelled at Manfred Eicher - the man who, ever since Garbarek's first recording for ECM in 1970, has produced all of his work on the independent, multi-award-winning, Munich-based label.[14]

Although I disagree with both the tenor and the detail of such criticism, I find it refreshing that the work of Garbarek (and Eicher) has prompted such a diversity of opinion. In today's world, where a good deal of so-called high culture is little more than an analgesic - and heavily subsidised - appendage to the various blandishments of the entertainment industries, genuine art should have the power to disturb: to fracture familiar expectations and offer fresh perspectives on matters of content and form, manner and meaning.[15]

To trace the development of Garbarek's music over the years - from his early days with Karin Krog and Jon Christensen, George Russell's various small groups and big bands and his own initial, pre-ECM quartets, to the extraordinary body of work he has created with Manfred Eicher - is to listen to the development of a singularly inspiring, yet multivalent musical mind. It is also to encounter the exceptional work of all the many musicians who - as Garbarek has always emphasised - have contributed so much to the development of his music. Exploring the poetics of Garbarek's music, and various reactions to it, will involve setting that music within contexts of recent

American, European and Nordic jazz activity, as well as those broader Nordic and international cultural contexts which may help to shed light on central aspects of the work.

In this regard, the present book eschews a straightforward chronology, preferring to mix over-arching thematic approaches with chronological detail. The book can be read straight through, but each chapter, I hope, can also be approached by the reader independently of the whole. If I have devoted particular historical attention to the early period of Garbarek's work, in the 1960s, this is not because I am unduly attached to that decade, but because, up to now, relatively little has been readily available in English about what remains a fascinating period in the history of Norwegian jazz.

Even so intelligent and sensitive a commentator as Ian Carr has stated in print that the 1970 **Afric Pepperbird** was Garbarek's first recording.[16] It was not. Together with such colleagues as singer Karin Krog, pianist Terje Bjørklund, guitarist Terje Rypdal, bassists Per Løberg and Arild Andersen, and - above all - drummer Jon Christensen, Garbarek created a considerable body of rewarding music in the 1960s, with two L Ps under his own name and many contributions to other artists' recorded work (including, especially, that of George Russell).

I have supplied selected discographies and bibliographical material for any reader who would like to pursue further some of the issues raised in the text. Also, since Garbarek has long been inspired by various aspects of twentieth-century, so-called "serious" or "art" music - and has contributed to that music on several recordings - I have supplied a selected discography in this area. With regard to the dates of those recordings which are given in both the text and discographies, the year noted is always, where possible, that of the actual recording rather than the date of release.

Listening to the music of George Russell - a key figure in Garbarek's development, as already indicated - has always made me think of what one might call painterly and poetic matters of hue and texture, gesture and overall "field" of both musical and spiritual aura. The same applies to the music of Jan Garbarek. As the Norwegian critic Torodd Karlsten chose to headline his March 1987 _Stavanger Aftenblad_ review of the 1986 solo album **All Those Born With Wings**, "Jan Garbarek paints with sound".[17] As we shall see, many a parallel might be drawn between aspects of the music that Garbarek has created and the work of such other wide-ranging, yet acutely focused poets of innovative artistic practice this century as Russell himself, Rainer Maria Rilke and Edith Södergran; Gunnar Ekelöf and Tomas Tranströmer, Edvard Munch and Frans Widerberg, Ingmar Bergman and Andrei Tarkovsky.

For the moment, the nature of such parallels - and the particular resonance of Garbarek's work - might best be intimated through the words of one of Garbarek's favourite authors: his late compatriot, the novelist, poet and dramatist Tarjei Vesaas (1897-1970). In the final chapter of the largely autobiographical _The Boat In The Evening_, Vesaas reflected that, face to face with the unfathomable mystery of what it means to live on earth, "One listens for what one does not understand, as always."[18] Precisely here, it seems to me, is the joy of music, the joy of life.

Distant Mountains
(Molde 1980) George Ware

Notes to Prelude

1. With the abandoning of linear or narrative concerns of tension and release in much "minimalist" music from the early 1960s onwards, the idea of the poetics of integration in music takes on a radically different aspect from that evident, for example, within the traditional development and resolution of sonata form in the Western classical tradition: see Mertens, W. *American Minimal Music: La Monte Young, Terry Riley, Steve Reich, Philip Glass* (trans. J. Hautekiet, with a Preface by Michael Nyman) Kahn & Averill, London 1994 passim. For aspects of Garbarek's work in relation to these issues, see Chapter Five below. For a general introduction to key aspects of the poetics of music see e.g. Storr, A. *Music And The Mind* HarperCollins, London 1992; Scruton, R. *The Aesthetics Of Music* Clarendon Press, Oxford 1997, and, for an especially cogent investigation of a number of key (post-Susanne Langer) questions in the aesthetics of music, Reid, L. A. *Meaning In The Arts* George Allen & Unwin, London 1969. On the diversity of "meaning-making" which may occur in music from the listener's - and record collector's - point of view, see Eisenberg, E. *The Recording Angel* Picador/Pan Books Ltd., London 1987.

2. On the relations of Modernism to Romanticism, see e.g. Wiedmann, A. *Romantic Roots In Modern Art: A Study In Comparative Aesthetics* Gresham Books, Unwin Brothers Ltd., The Gresham Press, Old Woking 1979. On Kapsberger, see (the Norwegian) Rolf Lislevand's notes to his own interpretations of Kapsberger's music: **Johannes Hieronymous Kapsberger: Libro Quarto D'Intavolatura Di Chitarone *Roma 1640*** (Astree E 8515).

3. Gillespie, D. (with A. Fraser) *To Be Or Not To Bop* W. H. Allen, London 1980 pp. 474-5. Gillespie offers some interesting thoughts on the origins and overtones of the word 'jazz', the relation of that art to painting, and the social importance of the music: " Jazz is an African word [from Malenke *jasi*, meaning to act out of the ordinary, thus to speed up, to excite, as a footnote to the text explains]. It doesn't detract from the importance, the seriousness, or the dignity of our music [...] In improvisation, the first thing you must have is the sight of a gifted painter. You've got to see colors and lines in music, and then you've got to be able to mix the colors and draw the lines [...] The role of music goes hand in hand with social reformation - the changing of society to make things right because music is a form of worship." Ibid. pp. 492-3.

4. For an intelligent and well-illustrated introduction to recent Norwegian cultural creativity, see Jerman, G. (ed.) *A Cultural Odyssey: Focus on Norwegian Art* Index Publishing, Oslo 1997.

5. *Blåtonenboulevardene* Grøndahl Dreyer, Oslo 1997. The book combines striking polychrome woodcuts and lyric poetry in a way which the authors themselves describe as being an "anti-digital" manifesto. Certainly, this superb book has something to it of the qualities (including smell) of a real, as opposed to a virtual, art gallery. See Marcussen, T. 'Jazzklang i trykk og tekst' (The sound of jazz in graphic print and text) *Aftenposten*, Oslo 16/8/97 p. 40.

6. Alterhaug, B. **Constellations** (Odin NJ 4035-2). Born in the Northern

town of Mo i Rana in 1945, Alterhaug is one of the several exceptional bassists that Norway has produced in recent years. He played briefly in a trio with Jan Garbarek and Jon Christensen in the late 1960s, and recorded with Garbarek on the 1975 Norwegian album **Østerdalsmusikk**. Since then he has distinguished himself not just as a bassist, but also as a fine composer. See e.g. the 1978 **Moments** (Arctic Records ARCX-2). For the poetry of Sverdrup, see e.g. _Samlede Dikt 1948-1982_ (Collected Poems) Aschehoug & Co. Ltd., Oslo 1987. In 1986 Sverdrup collaborated with the painter and graphic artist Frans Widerberg, a favourite of Garbarek's, on the artist book project _Øyeblikk_ (Blink of an Eye) Labyrinth Press, Oslo 1987.

7. Reissued as Nerem, B. **This Is Always** (Gemini Records GMCD 47). The Gemini/Taurus catalogue covers a fine range of modern Norwegian jazz, including musicians such as singer Laila Dalseth, tenor saxophonist Bjørn Johansen, pianist Egil Kapstad and drummer Egil "Bop" Johansen. The 1990 **Jazz På Norsk** (GMCD 70) is one of the catalogue's many gems: a charmingly atmospheric, nine-piece Norwegian equivalent of Jan Johansson and Georg Riedel's 1962-4 classic **Jazz På Svenska** (which has been reissued on CD as part of **Folkvisor**, Megafon MFCD 0410).

8. Reissued as **The Birth and Rebirth of Swedish Folk Jazz** (ACT 9254-2). On the historical importance of this record, see my review in _Jazz Journal International_, September 1998 pp. 45-6.

9. Further to notes 6 & 7, other important figures include singers Kari Bremnes, Berit Opheim and (the late) Radka Toneff, and the poet Jan Erik Vold; saxophonists Odd Riisnæs, Vidar Johansen, Jon Pål Inderberg, Guttorm Guttormsen, Bendik Hofseth, Tore Brunborg, Morten Halle and Karl Seglem; trombonist Torbjørn Sunde and trumpeters Torgrim Sollid, Per Jørgensen and Arve Henriksen; pianists and keyboardists Svein Finnerud (who played with Garbarek at the end of the 1960s), Dag Arnesen, Rune Klakegg, Jan Gunnar Hoff, Frode Fjellheim, Reidar Skår, Ketil Bjørnstad, Christian Wallumrød and Bugge Wesseltoft (who has played and recorded with Garbarek in the 1990s); (church) organist Iver Kleive and guitarists Jon Eberson, Frode Alnæs, Knut Reiersrud and Eivind Aarset; bassists Terje Venaas, Bjørn Kjellemyr, Sveinung Hovensjø, Terje Gewelt, Kåre Garnes and Sigurd Ulveseth; and drummers and percussionists Ole Jacob Hans(s)en, Espen Rud, Svein Christiansen, (the late) Svein-Erik "Atom" Gaardvik, Pål Thowsen, Finn Sletten, Tom Olstad, Audun Kleive, Terje Isungset, Hans-Kristian Kjos Sørensen and the Italian, but Norwegian-domiciled Paolo Vinaccia. See the contextual discography. For a brief introduction to the recent wealth of creative Norwegian jazz activity, including groups like Brazz Brothers, see Tucker, M. 'Magnetic North' in _Jazz From Norway_, Oris London Jazz FestivalSerious/Royal Norwegian Government, London 1996.

10. Quoted in Hammarskjöld, D. _Markings_ (trans. W. H. Auden & L. Sjöberg) Faber & Faber, London 1975 p 87.

11. Sleeve-note to 1970 recording **Trip To Prillarguri**.

12. Carr, I., Fairweather, D., Priestley, B. _Jazz The Essential Companion_ Grafton Books, London 1987 p. 180.

13. Personal communication, March 1998.
14. Some of the many awards which Manfred Eicher and ECM have received are: Producer of the Year (_Down Beat_ 1976); Outstanding Production (_Record World Jazz Award_ 1977); Innovating Design (_Record World Jazz Award_ 1977) Best Jazz Producer (_High Fidelity Magazine_, 1979); Record Label of the Year (_Down Beat Critics' Poll_ 1980); Ehrenpreis der Deutschen (_Schallplattenkritikk_ 1986); Record of the Year (_Deutsche Jahrespreis_ 1994); Record of the Year (_Down Beat Critics' Poll_ 1996); Record of the Year (_Deutsche Jahrespreis_ 1998). Since I shall be dealing with a fair portion of the negative criticism which Eicher and ECM have received, it is important to remember the extent of such recognition and success.Typical of the negative response to ECM is Matthew Bateson's May 1982 _Jazz Journal International_ review of Garbarek's 1980 **Eventyr** - which, besides Garbarek himself, featured the typically imaginative and cross-cultural personnel of American guitarist John Abercrombie and Brazilian percussionist Nana Vasconcelos: " [D]espite its arty packaging, superlative recording quality, generous playing time and enigmatic track titles, **Eventyr** is just another typical ECM release, with the sombre facade of great art but without the concomitant emotional depth." In the February 1984 _Jazz Journal International_ Record Of The Year Poll, Bateson found it necessary to give his own "golden turkey" award to Garbarek's allegedly "sententious" 1981 **Paths, Prints** recording: see my letter to _Jazz Journal International_ (March 1984) taking issue with this and other, similar points made by Barry McRae in his January 1983 _JJI_ review of **Paths, Prints**. See Chapter Four.
15. The fact that the diversity of critical response to ECM may be refreshing does not mean, of course, that it is not important to counter negative criticism when the reasoning that has informed such criticism is, in one's own judgement, flawed.
16. Carr, Fairweather, Priestley op. cit., new edition, _Jazz: The Rough Guide_ Rough Guides Ltd,, London 1995 p. 225 : "This [**Afric Pepperbird**] was a double debut - Garbarek and ECM's first album." This is a rough guide indeed: prior to **Afric Pepperbird**, six (highly diverse) albums had been recorded on ECM.
17. 'Garbarek maler med lyd': _Stavanger Aftenbladet_ 13/3/87. Unless otherwise indicated, translations throughout are my own.
18. _The Boat In The Evening_ (trans. E. Rokkan) Peter Owen, London 1971 p 183.

A Quality of Singing: Jan Garbarek,
Royal Northern College of Music
(Manchester, 1990) Sefton Samuels

By The Water, A Living Light
Frans Widerberg
(1974, oil on canvas, 105 x 140 cms. collection of the artist)

Open Channel

In the spring of 1978 I read in the jazz press about the forthcoming summer programme at the Molde festival on the west coast of Norway. One detail stood out from all the rest: the festival would feature two concerts by the Solstice Quartet of Ralph Towner (classical and 12-string guitars, piano), Jan Garbarek (saxophones, flute), Eberhard Weber (electric bass) and Jon Christensen (drums). This unusual group's first, eponymous ECM album, recorded in December 1974, had long been a favourite of mine, together with such other ECM releases as Ralph Towner's **Diary**, Eberhard Weber's **The Colours of Chloë** and **Yellow Fields,** and practically every ECM session on which Jan Garbarek and Jon Christensen had appeared.

Hearing Garbarek and Christensen live for the first time in the summer of 1976 – at Oslo's legendary Club 7, in the outstanding quartet which Garbarek co-led at the time with Swedish pianist Bobo Stenson, and which also featured the excellent Swedish bass player Palle Danielsson – had been a memorable experience, stimulating me to interview Garbarek and begin writing about his work. It was hardly surprising, therefore, that in that spring of 1978 it took a bare minute or so to decide to book tickets for the Molde festival there and then.

Undertaken in an old VW Beetle, with a fellow ECM enthusiast, the architect Maurice Acton, the first of what would become several trips to Molde remains one of the highlights of my life. The journey – *via* a North Sea ferry crossing, the Viking Ship and Munch Museums in Oslo, the snow-crested Hardanger-Vidda (or plateau) and the edges of Jotunheimen, Norway's spectacular mountain wilderness – had something of a fabulous quality to it: the weather was perfect, with the Molde fjord swimmable in parts, and the people at Molde as lovely as their mountain-encircled "town of roses". In the event, the Solstice group gave three concerts in all. Presented in the relative intimacy of Molde's *circa* 400 seat cinema, the blend of elements in the music – acoustic and electric, modal and harmonic, painterly and poetic – was both exquisite and immensely energising. Over the years, the details have faded a touch in the memory. However, one outstanding impression remains: this was organic, improvised but strongly "story-telling" music, as introspective and intense, as joyous and exhilarating as one could wish. Above all, it was music that flowed, that sang.

Around the same time that I was enjoying the initial memory of these Solstice Quartet performances, a young Norwegian trumpet player by the name of Nils Petter Molvær heard the classic **Belonging** quartet record on ECM which Garbarek, Danielsson and Christensen had made in 1974 under the leadership of pianist Keith Jarrett. Born in 1960, Molvær's earliest musical interests had embraced elements as distinct as Miles Davis (particularly the **Birth of the Cool** sessions), the Buddy Rich Big Band and rock'n'roll. Hearing **Belonging** confirmed Molvær's then-growing, late-teenage commitment to contemporary, jazz-inflected improvisation – a commitment which has continued to this day, resulting in an impressive variety of recordings.[1]

Why had **Belonging** been so important so Molvær? When I put this question to him in the summer of 1998, the trumpeter spoke of the quality of both the compositions and the group empathy evident throughout the 1974 session, but especially of Garbarek's contributions to the date: "He shows so much power – but above all, he's singing. He's not playing 'licks' – it's a much more considered way of playing, yet still sounding fresh and strong."[2]

It is this power of Garbarek, the quality of projection that he has in his sound, that first strikes many listeners. This is a sound which Garbarek has said he has always had somewhere in his head, ever since, as a young teenager, he first heard the music of John Coltrane and began to try to develop his own saxophone sound (initially on tenor, with the soprano instrument coming into the picture at the beginning of the 1970s). As the Scottish drummer Ken Hyder has remarked: "The first thing you notice about Jan Garbarek is his tone, his sound. It's what you start off with. The first time I heard the music of Tibetan monks I was knocked out first of all by the sound. It was the same for me with Albert Ayler, with Gaelic psalm singing, Bulgarian choirs, Tuvan singers, and Elvin Jones. If you've got a sound that's not only attractive, but distinctive, you start off with a big plus. Jan Garbarek has got such a sound."[3]

The sound that a saxophonist has is the result of many things: imagination, bone structure and breath control, for example. There is also the factor of work. There have been months upon months when Garbarek has practised relatively simple things, such as holding long tones, for anything up to six or seven hours a day. The result has been an extraordinary control of the dynamics of saxophone playing. For Eberhard Weber, who has been a constant colleague in Garbarek's groups since the early 1980s, Garbarek is "*the* player of dynamics – a completely non-stereotypical saxophone player, always looking for something fresh."[4] When the English pianist John Taylor toured with Garbarek and Weber in the late-1970s quintet (with Bill Connors and Jon Christensen) which made the **Photo With Blue Sky, White Cloud, Wires, Windows And A Red Roof** album, he was struck by the considerable care which Garbarek took with his sound: "Until then, John Surman was the only saxophonist I'd played with who'd paid a similar amount of attention to projecting his sound as he wanted it, night after night. Jan travelled with his own microphone and Lexicon [reverb] set-up; I remember that, before the sound-check of every concert, he would go through several handfuls of reeds, testing each of them out, very thoroughly."[5]

Projected with simultaneous laser-like clarity and atmospheric finesse, and equally expressive in the lower, middle and upper registers of both tenor and soprano, Garbarek's is a sound which, despite inspiring a good many epigones, remains unique. Penetrating and plangent, but also fully rounded and rich; sometimes subtly shaded, sometimes as exultant as it may otherwise be keening in nature, with a glowing warmth infusing its frosted edge, it is a sound which can carry the listener deep into the spaces of reflection, of reverie. In an age which has seen both saxophone sound and technique attain almost mass-produced levels of somewhat dry, hard-edged hyper-competence, Garbarek's is a sound which speaks in an utterly distinctive and deeply human voice.

That sound is set in the service of a uniquely poetic conception of melody and dynamics. Think, for example, of the beautifully floated soprano theme and subsequent improvisations on *Going Places*, from the 1977 album **Places**, the ascensional gravity of the tenor theme on the title track of the 1984 **It's OK to listen to the gray voice** recording, or the deep pedal or "bell" notes within the *pianissimo* obbligati which Garbarek supplies on *Primo tempore*, from **Officium**, his 1993 collaboration with the Hilliard Ensemble. In all such pieces, notes can be simultaneously eased across and etched into a subtly woven spectrum of group textures and space, the whole informed by an exceptional, song-like psychological sensibility. For me, to listen to Garbarek has always been to hear what Nils Petter Molvær heard in the **Belonging** session: a quality of singing.

This is singing so acutely focused, yet expansive in effect, that it can attain the impact of the best lyric poetry. It is no exaggeration to suggest that, at his finest, Garbarek – who has recorded several times with Jan Erik Vold, one of Norway's strongest poets – phrases melody in the way that a great lyric poet of our century, such as Rilke or Trakl, Ekelöf or Elytis, makes words sing. And, as Yeats knew in his bones, what is life, unless soul clap its hands and sing?[6]

Just as a successful lyric poem acquires its resonance as much by what is left out as by what is put in – and by the relations, most often taut, between word and space, individual line and total expression – so does the music of Jan Garbarek build upon silence, with the most carefully conceived accents and angles of melodic utterance. Exceptional improviser that he is, Garbarek's playing always carries the conviction of composition. As Ian Carr has observed, in a telling appraisal which both echoes and elaborates the estimate of Molvær, and which is focused on the work which the saxophonist has recorded for ECM: "Garbarek does not play 'licks' (preconceived or habitual patterns), but his improvisations sound like distilled thought – ideas conceived, edited and expressed on the spur of each moment. Underneath this icy clarity he burns with a feeling which is the more potent for being so tightly controlled. Every note, every phrase is meant; there is no rhetoric, only poetry."[7]

In 1992 the Czechoslovakian bass virtuoso Miroslav Vitous wrote a suite of compositions with the playing of Garbarek specifically in mind. Aware as I am of the poetic qualities in the work of Johnny Hodges or Lester Young, Stan Getz or Bobby Wellins, for example, the distilled beauty of Garbarek's playing on the resultant **Atmos** album led me to ask, in a _Jazz Journal International_ review of records of the year: "Has there ever been a finer poet of the saxophone than Garbarek?"[8] To speak of Garbarek in such terms is, of course, to make both a large and a problematic claim for his work. (This is so whether one takes the word "poet" in either its literal or metaphoric sense.) Large, because to call someone a poet – and in particular, a lyric poet – is to attribute to them what have traditionally been conceived as the highest qualities of feeling and imagination, expressed with the keenest sensitivity to matters of form and content, music (in both the literal and metaphoric sense) and meaning. Problematic, because – for a good deal of this century, at least – the very possibility of the creation of compelling lyric poetry has often been debated (in both poetry itself and music). Herein lies a considerable part of the importance of the oeuvre which Garbarek has developed over the years.

The Romantic Friedrich Hölderlin (1770-1843) once asked: who needs poets in a destitute time? We shall investigate the implications of Hölderlin's question in more detail in chapter two: for now, all we need to remember is how much poets this century have been aware of both the difficulties and the complexities of hymning the world in the manner in which another Romantic, William Wordsworth (1770-1850), was once able to do. As already indicated, this point applies as much to the realm of music (and all the arts, in fact) as it does to the specific practice of poetry. With the late string quartets and piano intermezzi of, respectively, Beethoven and Brahms, or Mahler's *Song of the Earth*, for example, what one might call the lyrical-philosophical impulse in music might seem to have reached heights unattainable (if not unthinkable) to succeeding generations.[9]

A relatively recent study of Wordsworth is entitled _Wordsworth and the Adequacy of Landscape_.[10] If the healing qualities of landscape were the chief focus of the Romantics' attention, for the twentieth-century (Western) Modernist that focus has usually shifted to the urban alienation often said to be omni-present in industrialised town or city: a recent overview of this theme is called, typically enough, _Unreal City_.[11] The complexities of T. S. Eliot's _The Waste Land_ (1922) constitute the most provocative, collaged example of the subsequent poetic tension between an impulse towards spiritualised, Romantic utterance and the world-weariness of a profane, Modernist self-consciousness. A further and particularly intriguing example of that tension is furnished by the Portuguese poet Fernando Pessoa (1888-1935).

Some of Pessoa's lines, such as the following from 1934, might almost seem to have been written in presentiment of the spiritually questing Garbarek of such records as **Dansere** (1975), **Aftenland** (1979) and **Paths, Prints** (1981): "Hills, and the peace in them, for they are far away .../Landscape – that is, no-one .../I have a soul made to be a monk's/But am not at ease."[12] In the fragmented reflections of Pessoa the would-be hymnal unity of the Romantic "I" collapses, leading to the assumption of a variety of poetic personae, or voices, by the author. Which, if any, of these voices should we believe, or privilege? Is one to infer that, at what Romanticism once considered to be the deepest level of the poet, his "true" self, a poet such as Pessoa – highly regarded this century – is unable to say anything of compelling, synthesising value?[13]

In the subsequent years of a century that has come to witness Auschwitz and Belsen, Hiroshima and Nagasaki, the issue becomes even more pointed. In 1963 John Coltrane recorded his deeply affecting composition *Alabama*, as a response to the death of four black children in a racist bombing of a church in that town. As I write these lines, three young boys in Northern Ireland have just been buried, following their death in an unprovoked arson attack upon the house in which they slept at night. In the light of such unspeakable horror, can the sentiment which inspires poetic utterance, no matter how diverse its voices may be, avoid the decline into sentimentality? I believe that it can – and must.

It is sometimes claimed that, after Auschwitz, poetry – or art – is no longer possible. I do not think that such a belief could be more wrong. And this is not just a matter of the fact that poets such as Paul Celan and Primo Levi, Pablo Neruda and Seamus Heaney have produced the most compelling and disturbing post-Auschwitz work.[14] It is, rather, a matter of the whole question of the particular, ongoing capacity of poetry – and art – to engage the often contradictory depths of a human being's attention and potentiality; to revitalise their sense of the (trans-human and replenishing) mystery which lies at the heart of existence, and perhaps to awaken thoughts of their creative responsibility – as much political as poetic in import, and *vice versa* – to that mystery.[15]

The Mexican writer Octavio Paz (1914-98) said that the prime duty of the poet this century was to rescue us from the false sorcery of history and numbers, and to restore to us our sense of the plenitude of life that may exist in the pure magic of a simple second, if that second is lived (or dreamed) deeply enough.[16] If Jan Garbarek is a (lyric) poet of the saxophone, then he is an artist who, first and foremost, has helped restore our sense of the many mysteries of existence. And these are mysteries rooted in the primal mystery of the human experience of time.

In _The Magic Mountain_ (1924), his multi-layered investigation of the dialectics of illness and health, Thomas Mann wrote that music "quickens time, she quickens us to the finest enjoyment of time."[17] Naturally, for Mann, to quicken or give life to time was not to help it pass more quickly. On the contrary: music can deepen, extend, intensify our sense of the rhythms – and mysteries – that may lie underneath the perpetual circling of the minute and second hands of our watches. In the world(s) of music, time may be simultaneously a matter of the mathematical, the magical and the mythical.[18] And in jazz, especially, time can be a matter of the pulsation peculiar to both town and country, urban highway and rural back-road.

Jazz is often taken to be a "hot" music, its sounds and rhythms redolent of nothing so much as the sexual promise of a crowded dance floor or the fugitive sweep of car headlights through the neon night. However, jazz can also be a "cool" music, its textures and tones suggestive of the poetics of reflection and reverie. If jazz speaks of the urban world, it can do so in tones both sexual (or, rather, sensuous) _and_ spiritual. And, no matter how urban the music may seem to be, much of the spiritual quality in jazz comes from its roots in the rural worlds of small-church gospel, field holler and country blues, worlds which themselves can be seen in the light of ancient African evenings, the rhythms of ritual ceremony, praise song and dance.[19]

In the best of jazz, there is a perpetual creative tension between the ancient and the new, the rural and the urban, the primal and the sophisticated. Garbarek is a musician who has developed what for him was the initial urban "charge" of modern jazz in his native Norway – a modern, industrialised country, but blessed with mile upon mile of exactly that magnificent landscape which once appealed so much to the Romantic taste for the sublime, or awe-inspiring. That tension has resulted in a provocative refashioning of the experience of time by Garbarek. Within music which is simultaneously "hot" and "cool", and where passages of _ad libitum_ creativity are particularly apparent, the lived factor of time is often returned to ancient, non-linear realms. This is particularly the case within the primal – archetypal – soundscape created by the tonally indeterminate, textured drones of much of **Dis** (1976), the reverie-rich, rhythmic suspensions of **It's OK to listen to the gray voice** or the propulsive, shaman-like energy in a good deal of **Legend Of The Seven Dreams** (1988), **I Took Up The Runes** (1990) and **Twelve Moons** (1992).

The Italian poet Eugenio Montale – winner of the Nobel Prize for Literature in 1975 – once commented on the fact that, the faster the business cycles of the modern world turn, and the more urgent the sense of that efficiency which is supposed to be quarried endlessly from the earth, the greater the sense of ennui or meaninglessness that has come to pervade life: "What we find in the so-called civilized world (something that has been developing ever since the end of the Enlightenment but is now accelerating at an ever faster pace) is a lack of interest in the sense of life. This has nothing to do with activity: on the contrary."[20] What is meant here by "the sense of life"?

Defending art's ability to transport us to other realms than those of history or politics, Montale himself answers: "What animates man? Biology or [Marxist-Hegelian, political] dialectics? Neither the one nor the other offers him consolation. Man is not particularly interested to know that one day he may well be able to create a facsimile of himself by artificial processes. He is far from interested in the discovery of new galaxies, and he is totally indifferent to the news that his mind contains a mechanism of theses, antitheses and a final entity about which we know nothing. But marvel, wonder, is the aim of all men, whether they are poets or not, and art is not a sum of figures to be added together: it is a leap, for quantities which do not belong together in the same order cannot be totalled up."[21]

What Montale is defending here is the psychic – or spiritual – terrain which so concerned a poet such as Paz, and which the scientist Einstein once celebrated in one of his most famous remarks: "The most beautiful experience we can have is the mysterious. It is the fundamental emotion which stands at the cradle of true art and science. Whoever does not know it and can no longer wonder, no longer marvel, is as good as dead."[22] This is exactly the experience which, over the past four decades, the music of Jan Garbarek has done so much to bring back into consciousness. And one of the most remarkable aspects of that music is the extent to which Garbarek has been able to combine an essentially Romantic concept of poetics (art understood as vehicle to and revelation of one's deeper self, a revelation usually rooted in the experience of landscape) with what some may wish to see as a post-Pessoa (if not Post-modernist) position. Here, the notion of any one "deeper" self is suspended, if not abandoned, and art seen, rather, as vehicle to and revelation of the multiplicity of "selves" which may co-exist at any one time (a revelation usually taken to be rooted in the complexities of post-Romantic urban experience).

The idea of the multiplicity of self-identity is exclusive to neither the Freudian theory of the psyche which emerged a century ago from the socio-sexual contradictions of Viennese society – a theory which divided the self into the three inter-related layers of ego, unconscious and super-ego – nor the (oh-so-urbane) Post-modernism and so-called "decontructionism" of our own time, with their various urges to de-stabilise any "essentialist" concept of the self. The poet Walt Whitman (1819-1892) knew all about contradiction and multiplicity, and many years before Whitman's immense, multiple "songs of himself", medieval Arabic philosophers were concerned precisely with the idea that every individual consciousness is but part of a far greater, pan-individual consciousness. Thus they could speak of "Man, the Great" – multiple, yet ultimately part of a mysterious, integrated totality.[23]

In the present century, it is the philosophy of Carl Gustav Jung (a thinker often dismissed, in my experience, by Freudians or Marxists who have read scarcely a word of him) which has been most concerned to transpose such ancient wisdom as that of the medieval philosophers and Renaissance alchemists (with their search for what Jung saw as the psychological or spiritual gold at the heart of life) into a contemporary psychological register. While Freud chose to focus his theory of the personal unconscious exclusively upon the idea of the sexual – or libidinous – energy which he took to be the power-house of our being, Jung was unable to accept that the spiritual impulse in humanity was nothing more than a sublimation of such energy.[24] Nor did Jung restrict his understanding of the unconscious to the purely personal level.

Through his central idea of the collective unconscious, with its rich store of archetypal images and energies underpinning the personal unconscious of each of us, and his faith in the creative wisdom of dreams, Jung (1875-1961) addressed the human experience of both psychic multiplicity and time in an especially intriguing and potentially illuminating way. In particular, Jung's ideas help to underline the psychic inadequacy of our current obsession with the idea that our identity is defined exclusively by our social self – a self often set adrift within the shallow, fast-moving currents of both advertising 'glamour' and so-called 'progressive' or linear, historico-political time.[25]

As Bettina L. Knapp has argued, in her excellent _Music, Archetype, And The Writer_, the Jungian perspective on the relations of conscious and unconscious life, dreamed and lived time has clear implications for the understanding of the potentially healing power of what Knapp calls "archetypal music."[26] This is music which "gets to one" on a variety of levels. The (overly) intellectual thinker or listener, for example, may be recalled to the sensate and feeling aspects of life through music which engages the unconscious on a profound level: music in which the colour or contour of a melody may draw one towards the more intuitive and nourishing channels of life, as that melody seeps into the soul, and perhaps replenishes its *élan vital* . One of Knapp's chief examples is the effect upon the character Roquentin in *Nausea*, Jean-Paul Sartre's classic 1938 novel of existential consciousness, of his repeated listening to a jazz vocal recording of a popular song. It is this music which, at the end of the novel, finally empowers the long-alienated Roquentin to hear his own "inner song" of life, and to experience a kind of healing, sensuous relatedness to the outer world.[27]

The Romantic Novalis believed that every illness is a musical problem. In the middle of the nineteenth century, the Danish thinker Søren Kierkegaard – who is usually regarded as the founding father of existentialist philosophy – had the intelligence to realise that, from the point of view of someone who wishes to develop life to the full, it is precisely intelligence (understood in its purely logical or analytical guise) which must be overcome: not dismissed as a factor in and of experience, which would be absurd, but rather integrated into the totality of life.[28] Unfortunately, the twentieth century has seen many a critic (and a good few artists) for whom the analytical capacity of intelligence has continued to reign supreme, in a kingdom constituted solely of the daily-driven worlds of history and politics. In such a domain, the healing properties of music can easily be forgotten.

In terms of musical criticism, the Marxist thinker Theodor Adorno (1905-69) furnishes a particularly clear example of this. First published in 1948, Adorno's *Philosophy of Modern Music* is not concerned with any archetypal, healing properties that music may have, but rather with music's place within the alleged development of 'H'istory. Adorno's approach to modern music is based upon the simple (but turgidly elaborated) principle that, like any Marxist, Adorno knows the socio-historically generated "inner necessity" of music's historical evolution. Thus, after the "historically inevitable" serialism of Schoenberg early this century, the tonality of the Classical and Romantic bourgeois era can no longer function as a component of any music that would have itself be taken seriously by the progressively-minded listener. From the modal harmonies of Sibelius to the recurrent harmonic patterns of jazz – a music which Adorno dismissed with both offensive and laughable ignorance – any continued engagement with the idea of tonality could only reveal to Adorno the onset of either sentimentality or barbarism. "It is not simply", he opined, " that these sounds [of tonal harmony] are [now] antiquated and untimely, but that they are false. They no longer fulfill their [once true, or historically appropriate] function."[29]

From the point of view of common sense (a faculty which Adorno was wont to malign) as well as today's Post-modernist ideas postulating the plurality of meaning available within the arts, the notion that any art form unfolds (and ultimately exhausts) its potentialities solely on the plane of socio-political consciousness – of linear history as understood in the Western intellectual tradition – is simply ridiculous.[30] After all, was not one of the greatest achievements of recent Western cultural history something we choose to call the Renaissance? And was not a large part of that Renaissance founded on the creative tension, as much cyclical as linear in nature, between the play of the (historically distant, yet intellectually – existentially – alive) forces and ideals of classical paganism and Christianity, mediated by the ideas of neo-Platonism?[31]

It is the exclusive emphasis upon a narrowly conceived concept of history – rooted only in the Western experience of time, but spelled, nevertheless, with a capital 'H' – which has led to the enervation of much thought and creativity this century.[32] From the point of view of the Jungian idea of the collective unconscious, the historically-inflected "surface" of art's presence and impact in the world is but one aspect of its total potential. From the Jungian perspective, this is a potential which only achieves maximum resonance when, as the Dadaist Tristan Tzara said, "The summit sings what is being spoken in the depths."[33]

How does one come to sing what is spoken of in the depths? In traditional societies, the rich fabric of mythology supplied the means whereby the individual voice accessed the deeper realms of life. Is this still possible today? In *A Coat*, from the 1914 collection _Responsibilities_, Yeats spoke in the persona of a poet who had once fashioned a coat for his song, covered from heel to throat with "embroideries out of old mythologies". However, the fools of the world had caught hold of this coat, wearing it as though they had wrought it. The poem concludes: "Song, let them take it,/For there's more enterprise/ In walking naked."[34] As the work of Samuel Beckett attests, such nakedness has become typical of our existentially-oriented century, so bleakly aware of finitude and death.

However, to walk naked is not necessarily to perish on the sands of despair – as, indeed, one might infer from at least some of Beckett, whose overall bleakness can be leavened by an absurdist, yet liberating sense of humour. In the work of Gunnar Ekelöf – some of whose ideas can at times seem close to Beckett, but whose work is in fact totally different in spiritual tenor – nakedness (or nothingness) often functions, as it did for the mystics of old, as the *via negativa* to a deepened and reverent sense of life.[35] To understand how this might be possible, it may be helpful to look a little deeper at the question of mythology.

Joseph Campbell, the late historian of religion and mythology, believed that the encounter with the mythic realm presents the human mind with two alternatives. One alternative is to encounter that realm as the arena of absolute, unchangeable and literal truth: while this is the immensely productive realm of "localised" traditional mythologies, it is also the breeeding ground of religious fanaticism, of the foolishness from which Yeats' poet wished to distance himself in "walking naked". The second alternative, suggests Campbell, is to approach the mythic realm as an infinitely rich reservoir of metaphor: metaphor which enables one to access the sort of poetic and psychic energies which lead, not to the false security of the pseudo-literalism of myth, but rather to that shape-shifting terrain where, walking naked, one is all the more open to the depths of life – all the more "transparent to the transcendent", as Campbell (1904-87) put it.[36]

Herein lies a great part of the poetic and psychic importance of Garbarek's music. Garbarek himself has said that, one of the most important things he learned in playing music was the necessity of weeding his garden, so to speak. Having stripped his art of everything cluttered, and having found the naked space from which he might begin to create that which was really resonant and meaningful to him, Garbarek has been able to approach questions of musical structure in the way in which Campbell suggested one might best approach the inner or metaphorical dimensions of mythology. Walking naked, Garbarek has come to shape an oeuvre rich in mythic overtones.

Far from the historically-driven imperatives of a good deal of Adorno-like musical ideology today, Jan Garbarek has shaped a world in which are to be found both healing melodic simplicity and chromatic sophistication, folk-like repetition and serial economy, the drama of tonal harmony and the measured moods of modality. Here, the summit can indeed sing of what is being spoken in the depths, within an oeuvre in which the play of conscious and unconscious factors, dream and desire is allowed maximum creative play. And it is no contradiction to observe that such creative play is often precipitated precisely by the sort of poetic sensibility whereby musical form – and "archetypal music" – is created with a maximum of control. Like many a Modernist before him, Garbarek – a master of musical space – is acutely aware that less can be more.

The concept of archetypal music implies that the concepts and colours, the rhythms and the relations of music are able to build a bridge from the worlds of politics and history to those of dream and myth, and from the realm of the personal to what both Jungian and other holistic thinkers call the world of the transpersonal. What is the world of the transpersonal? One might say that is is the world of all true art. Far from the pathetic narcissism of much of today's art world – as evinced by such a (largely) dispiriting spectacle as the aptly named *Sensation* show which took place at London's Royal Academy in 1997 – this is the world of (energising, not reductive) myth and metaphor, of embodied metaphysics and metamorphosis: the world which, ever since the first shamans – or visionary artists and healers – of aboriginal societies, has been the concern of any artist concerned to explore the deeper meaning(s) of our brief sojourn here on earth.[37]

In our century, for example, it is the world of Wassily Kandinsky and Paul Klee, Marc Chagall and Henri Matisse, Joan Miró and Joseph Beuys, Constantin Brancusi and Barbara Hepworth; of Jean Arp and Ted Hughes, Frida Kahlo and Georgia O'Keeffe; of Max Beckmann and Meret Oppenheim, Mary Wigman and Frans Widerberg. It is also the world of Jean Sibelius and Bela Bartók, John Coltrane and George Russell – and Jan Garbarek. No matter how different the details of their practice may be, the work of all such artists exemplifies the idea that, rooted in the intensely personal as it (initially) may be, art nevertheless can take one beyond the purely personal or symptomatic realm, as it comes into contact with the (transformative, transpersonal) terrain of both generative and sustaining artistic structure and form and psychological "meaning" and "myth".[38]

In Jungian terms, the move from the personal to the transpersonal world is the transition from individuality to individuation. Jung speaks of the prime need of the human being first to achieve individuality (breaking away from the family nest) and then, some years later, individuation. The latter, the key aspect of the total development of the self, often assumes particular importance in mid-life. Besides acknowledgement of what Jung calls the shadow side of ourselves which lies underneath our public persona, such development involves a creative awareness of not just one's capacity for rational analysis or intuition, thinking or feeling, but also the relation of the complementary contrasts of male and female drives within us which Jung called the *animus* and *anima*.

It is important to remember that, for Jung, there were no magic formulae to help effect the transition from individuality to individuation. Each individual has to find his or her own way towards the world of the archetype: and this journey can, initially, be as difficult and disturbing as it might eventually prove to be transformative and affirming. As Erich Neumann, one of Jung's chief disciples, has made evident in his _Art and the Creative Unconscious_, dream and art may suggest fruitful, if often challenging paths for the self to follow – but they never say "you must do this, you must do that." They are multivalent, ambiguous – demanding creative participation from anyone who would truly profit from them – and a descent into the relative chaos of the unknown may well be a necessary prelude to the generation of those new forms or orientations in life that are to prove lasting and meaningful.[39] The Swedish poet Tomas Tranströmer has summarised such matters well enough, in the Campbell-like beginning to his prose-poem *The Clearing*: "Deep in the forest there is a clearing, which can only be found by someone who has lost their way."[40]

What Neumann and Tranströmer say is especially relevant to the various musical journeys undertaken by an improvising jazz musician, or group of musicians. Although Garbarek, one of the most lucid of improvisers ever to have appeared in jazz, has spoken of not wanting to "get lost" during the course of an improvisation, his career as a whole manifests a refreshing ability to eschew the familiar and the well-trodden. Consider also how the variable play of the psychic drives which Jung outlined may help illuminate aspects of both the compositions and improvisations with which a musician such as Garbarek may become involved – and how what Jung says about the psyche has much in common with the old medieval idea of the four temperaments, or humours: with our capacity to feel "in our element" (or not, as the case may be) with earth and fire, wind and water.

One of the many things I love about the music of George Russell is the way in which that music is able to combine the earthy (the blues roots of jazz, evident throughout so much of Russell's work) with the celestial (the chromatic flights of such an explorative, yet richly realised work as **Jazz In The Space Age**, for example). Much of Garbarek's music can be seen in the same light. Combining "elemental" psychological principles, this is music which has the power to engage and perhaps deepen our capacity for reverie – that faculty of apprehending the world as if through the magical veils of an open-eyed dream. Gaston Bachelard, the great French philosopher of the imagination, believed one has never seen the world well if one has not dreamed it first, and that, dreaming the world, one might come to sense how "space, vast space, is the friend of being."[41]

Especially relevant here are Garbarek's compositions on the **Gray Voice** album, with tracks like *It's OK to telephone the island that is a mirage* soaked in the reverie that Bachelard regarded as crucial to a truly healthy psyche. And while Garbarek has had the courage to explore new paths and combinations of "elemental" expression – Manfred Eicher has observed to me that "Jan is always ready for surprises" – the resultant music has often tempered the sometimes overly "macho" aura of jazz with considerable elements of the female principle, or anima. Exemplary here is the tender, Taoist quality in such pieces as *Sart* (from the 1971 album of that name), *Footprints* and *Still*, from **Paths, Prints**, *Gentle* and *Spor*, from the 1983 **Wayfarer**, *Send Word*, from **Legend Of The Seven Dreams**, and *Star*, from the 1991 album of the same title.[42]

In the Jungian scheme of things, the transition from individuality to the more integrated self of individuation involves a re-appraisal of one's relation to the world. Whereas too long and continued an emphasis upon individuality can lead to feelings of isolation and estrangement, and even mental breakdown (or, less seriously, but more tediously, shows like the aforementioned *Sensation*) individuation awakens intimations of one's relation to the transpersonal and psychically loved, or cherished, world.[43] Here, the creative interplay of conscious and unconscious elements opens the psyche up to the impact of what Jung called archetypal images and energy from the collective unconscious of humanity, a collective unconscious which Jung understood as going back to the beginnings of human life on earth.[44]

One commentator on Jung has described the state of individuation – which, it should be noted, is never achieved by any parrot-like imitation of others – as consisting of "the awareness on the one hand of our unique natures, and on the other hand of our intimate relation with all life, not only human, but animal and plant, and even with inorganic matter and the cosmos itself. It brings a feeling of 'oneness' and reconciliation with life."[45] Jungians sometimes summarise this state – which is so reminiscent of central ideas of the European Romantics or, in our century, D. H. Lawrence – as the realisation of the Great or Cosmic Self within one. As I have argued at length elsewhere, such a state of psychological development suggests remarkable parallels with the exalted state of consciousness attained by the shamans – or visionary seers, or healers – of old. And the struggle – or quest – to achieve such a state reveals equally remarkable parallels with many aspects of avant-garde activity in the arts this century. This includes music – especially jazz music. For jazz offers a particularly rich image, or model, of the transmutative interplay of the forces of history and myth, consciousness and the unconscious, individuality and individuation: the singular and the collective voice.[46]

This book, which is primarily about Jan Garbarek, but which also investigates aspects of what (rightly or wrongly) has come to be known as "the ECM aesthetic" of producer Manfred Eicher, owes its title to a central idea, or image, developed by the Andalusian poet and painter, dramatist and essayist, Federico Garcia Lorca. It is an idea, or image, with a distinctly archetypal or transpersonal ring to it. Lorca first used the concept of *cante jondo* – "deep song" – in a lecture of the 1920s, when he reflected upon the spiritual qualities which for him lay in the Indian, or Gypsy, roots of flamenco music. The poetic overtones of this idea, or image, were in large part the means whereby Lorca sought both to clarify and intimate the depths of his feelings for the sheer mystery and wonder of existence. As assured as his creative grasp of metaphor and simile was, Lorca often expressed such feelings in the simplest, pared-down language. Concerned always to get to the cosmic heart of things, to sense the magical murmur of earth and sky, Lorca could state, for example, that "Only mystery makes us live. Only mystery."[47]

It is such fructifying mystery that I – and many other listeners, I would suggest – have heard in the music of Jan Garbarek. And this is the case whether that music involve the free jazz explorations of such albums as **Afric Pepperbird** (1970) and **Triptykon** (1972), the beautiful ballads of such lyrical quartet albums as **Belonging** and **My Song** (1977), the expansive, yet finely etched meditations of such "classically" inflected albums, with strings, as **Luminessence** (1974) and **Arbour Zena** (1976), the haiku-like distillations of such solo flute and soprano saxophone pieces as *Its Name Is Secret Road* and *Mirror Stone* (both from **Legend Of The Seven Dreams**) or the totalising grandeur of the five-part *Molde Canticle* (from the 1990 **I Took Up The Runes**).

Furthermore: in the many interviews about his work which Garbarek has given, there is much to suggest that he would agree with the propositions of Paz and Montale, Lorca and Einstein. And also Jung: Garbarek has read the Jungian-inflected novels of Hermann Hesse, for example, with a good deal of interest, and, like Jung, his oeuvre shows a considerable capacity to immerse himself in the rhythms and ideas of the East. At the end of a long and searching interview with jazz writers Pawel Brodowski and Janusz Szprot in 1984, Garbarek was asked if he might agree with the proposition that music is a mystery. His response was immediate: "I would say that everything is a mystery – and not least music."[48]

The ostensible simplicity of such statements by Garbarek and Lorca, Montale and Einstein may strike some as telling. To others, however, such simplicity may seem merely simplistic. In a moving – and simultaneously simple and complex – short story about a young man who goes out onto some Northern marshes early one morning, in order to experience the fleeting, beautiful presence of a flock of mysterious dancing cranes, Tarjei Vesaas could write of the longing for "An open channel, where we can search for the mystery we share while we walk in the marshes and on the earth."[49] If ours is an age in which such an (essentially mythic) urge towards the simple and the beautiful, the mysterious and the transcendent has been a major force in all the arts, it is also an age in which that urge has been countered by the historically-oriented cultivation of the (theoretically) complex.

There are critics today who cannot listen to a piece of music without asking themselves, in the manner of Adorno, whether the emotional content or musical structure of that piece reveals "progressive" or "reactionary" historical tendencies. And, in our so-called Post-modernist times, when many a "decontructionist" writer cannot wait to dissolve any seemingly "essentialist" question of mystery and meaning in the supposed acid bath of contextual criticism, there are plenty who would wish to deny the meaningfulness of either experiencing or talking about any such qualities as the simple, the beautiful and the mysterious.[50]

The open channel that so concerned Vesaas is thus first clogged up, and then the very possibility of its existence denied. And, as has already been suggested, this phenomenon is not restricted to critical commentary on the arts. In 1958 the American post-Schoenberg serialist composer Milton Babbitt wrote an Adorno-like article, entitled – "Who Cares If You Listen?". The tone and content of the article typify a tendency amongst some musicians, composers and critics this century to assume that their art has reached such a level of specialised historical development that any talk of its constituting an "open channel" between ostensibly discrete realms of experience is, at best, simply an irrelevance to the technical and creative matters at hand.

"The time has passed", asserted Babbitt, "when the normally well-educated man without special preparation could understand the most advanced work in, for example, mathematics, philosophy and physics. Advanced music, to the extent that it reflects the knowledge and originality of the informed composer, scarcely can be expected to appear more intelligible [...] I dare suggest that the composer would do himself and his music an immediate and eventual service by total, resolute and voluntary withdrawal [... to a world of ...] private performance and electronic media, with its very real possibility of complete elimination of the public and social aspects of musical composition."[51]

It would not be long before the intellectual snobbery and divisive nature of Babbitt's argument (which ends by contrasting "the whistling repertory of the man in the street" with the task of guarding the evolution of advanced music, as Babbitt understood this term) could be seen in the contrasting light of the ideas of such holistic thinkers as Fritjof Capra or Danah Zohar. Addressed to the "normally well-educated" person (and Garbarek, for example, has found much of interest in the work of Capra) their respective books _The Tao of Physics_ and _The Quantum Self_ suggest how "the most advanced work" in physics, for example, might be seen in relation to the poetics of both contemporary creativity and other forms of intellectual enquiry, including the ancient and synthesising Chinese philosophy of the Tao, or Way.[52] However, the fundamental sterility of Babbitt's argument had already been anticipated and countered earlier in the 1950s, by a composer whose work – *pace* Adorno – had long been distinguished by both its immense public appeal and formal rigour: Jean Sibelius.

Late in life, Sibelius (1865-1957) observed to Santeri Levas, his private secretary: "How endless a lot of well-composed music is – but nothing else than note-scribbling. The inner life is absent. They've built a huge shipyard – but where is the ship?"[53] On another occasion, Sibelius – who regarded Alban Berg as Schoenberg's greatest achievement – developed such thoughts while also looking forward to a resurrection of that "inner life" which meant so much to him: "The main thing with today's composers is cerebration. What they write is more mathematics than music – sometimes only mathematics. It is serious that it is often devoid of inner life. I can't imagine that the music of the future will be as contrived as it is today. It is inconceivable that ethics are entirely missing in what is written now. In the end these are the foundations of every valid art. But I can't believe that music will always be as it is now. What is written today is often no more than empty sound effects which are completely superfluous if the composer himself has anything to say – and that is all that matters. Personality can show itself in five notes. What is eternal sometimes lives in very modest form."[54]

One of the most cogent appraisals of the value of the music of Sibelius this century is to be found in Constant Lambert's *Music Ho!* First published in the mid-1930s, and subtitled 'A Study of Music In Decline', Lambert argued that Sibelius had always been a figure apart from the rest of modern music (which for Lambert's purposes typically embraced both Schoenberg and Stravinsky, Debussy and Satie, Hindemith and Bartók). In Sibelius, argued Lambert, content and form, orchestration and musical argument ("Like the colour in a Cézanne landscape, Sibelius's orchestration is an integral part of the form") attained a visionary integrity of utterance beyond the reach of those composers who had developed their work in too close a relation (either imitative or dialectical) with what they took to be the driving forces of immediate historical circumstance. Tired of the constant search for the new in music, Lambert argued thus: "There is nothing in music which has really lost its meaning, no device of rhythm, no harmonic combination which the composer of vision cannot reanimate. The music of the future, if it is to avoid the many psycholological cul-de-sacs which have been examined in this volume, must inevitably be directed towards a new angle of vision rather than to the exploitation of a new vocabulary."[55]

Another twentieth-century composer was singled out by Lambert for special approbation: Duke Ellington. Although Lambert's comments on jazz were often quite critical, and from today's perspective might appear patronising (if not racist) in the extreme, he was full of praise for the man whom he described as "a real composer, the first jazz composer of distinction". Ellington's command of orchestral colour and dynamics led Lambert to compare him favourably with both Ravel and Stravinsky. If Ellington was, according to Lambert, definitely a " *petit maître*", that did not make him any the less a stimulating figure in twentieth-century music.[56]

Had Lambert published his book a decade later, after the many triumphs of Ellington's Blanton-Webster aggregation, for example, he might have been able to see Ellington as the grand master of music that he in fact is. Nearly three decades after *Music Ho!* the American writer Henry Pleasants published a somewhat similar book with the provocative title *Death of A Music?* As one might infer from the book's subtitle – 'The Decline of the European Tradition and the Rise of Jazz' – Pleasants' goal here was to deliver a sustained critique upon what he saw as the enervation of so much "advanced" work of composers of so-called "serious music" this century, composers obsessed with avoiding, Adorno-like, the alleged clichés of an old-fashioned tonal and harmonic world. At the same time, Pleasants mounted a vigorous and intelligent defence of jazz as perhaps the most rewarding music of both the present and future.

Enthusiasts of "serious music", whether of this or previous centuries, were inclined, said Pleasants, to dismiss jazz for what they considered to be the lack of reflective substance in the music, "the obviousness and obtrusiveness of the beat, the apparent insignificance of the melodies and [..] the absence of structural extension based upon tonal modulation."[57] As Pleasants pointed out, while such criticisms may, at times, have had a point, they betray an essential ignorance of the evolving essence of jazz: namely, the flight of the spirit that is fired by the richness of the rhythmic pulsations of syncopated phrasing which swings – and a spirit which, in fact, has been able to accomodate (and transmute) more and more of the values of so-called "serious music".

The conclusion of Pleasants' (anti-Adorno) argument merits quoting at length: "What saves the jazz composer from the harmonic predicament of the serious composer is that he is not required to be harmonically original. Given a music of different character and purpose, he can use an inherited harmony in an original way, exploiting such unique resources as the jazz drummer, the jazz double-bassist and the ability of the jazz instrumental-virtuoso to excel within the framework of pulsative composition [..] If jazz continues in this direction we may anticipate a gradual narrowing of the gap which has for so long separated it from serious music. By this I do not mean to suggest that serious music will absorb jazz. It is the other way round. The inner pulsation of jazz is foreign to the character and objectives of serious music. There is nothing about the melodic forms and harmonic structures of serious music, however, that is irreconcilable with the character and objectives of jazz."[58]

"What counts in any music", Pleasants concluded, "is song. The jazz musician need only remember what the serious composer has long forgotten, namely, that the purpose of the musician is to sing [..]."[59] And what, for Pleasants, was the point of a musician singing his or her song? It was "the initiation of his [or her] listeners into an experience of the beautiful."[60] While Pleasants' terms here are so general as to beg definition, they supply a suitable launching pad for further consideration of the open channel which is the music of Jan Garbarek.

Rich in both reflective substance and pulsative energy, in that inner life which so concerned Jung and Sibelius, this is music which, as rooted in jazz as it may be, has progressively absorbed and refashioned a good deal of the worlds of both folk and so-called "serious music". It is also music which has not been afraid to pursue and embrace a quality which would almost seem to embarrass a good deal of the contemporary art world, so rigorous is the avoidance of any mention of it there: beauty.[61] Later, we shall elaborate upon the theme of the Nordic depths which might be discerned within Garbarek's oeuvre, and the particular beauty contained therein. For the moment, the following reflection from Garbarek can serve to remind us how much those depths have been stirred by currents and confluences from abroad. Speaking to *Down Beat* writer Michael Bourne in 1986, Garbarek remarked, "You might say that I live in a spiritual neighbourhood which is scattered geographically all over the world."[62]

One of Garbarek's neighbours in that world, Tomas Tranströmer, has characterised his poems as "meeting places", or "open frontiers" – fields of energy that may bring together aspects of language and life that conventional (politicised) languages and ideologies ordinarily keep apart, or suppress from consciousness.[63] In an age such as ours, which is increasingly threatened by one virulent variety of fanaticism or another – be it religious or economic, political or artistic – it is hard to think of more appropriate images with which to indicate the import of Garbarek's music than these from Tranströmer.

As we shall come to see, Garbarek has created music of both an expanded, contemporary vocabulary and ancient, archetypal vision: music which is open, essentially, to the poetics of space – to North and South, East and West; earth and fire, wind and water. Finely crafted, lucid music that it is, it remains music which has always revealed the courage necessary to engage the sometimes disturbing, sometimes fructifying energy of the unconscious, the better to intimate transcendent realms. Above all, it is music which has never neglected the impulse to sing: to hymn the beautiful – however unknowable, however simple, complex or mysterious it may be.

late-1970s publicity, Britain

Notes to Chapter One

1. See e.g. his work in the Davis-inspired Masqualero quintet; the duo **Hastening Westward**, an unclassifiable set of meditations with percussionist Robyn Schulkowsky, and the rhythmically tough, yet lyrical, electro-ambient **Khmer**. See the contextual Nordic & European discography.
2. Personal communication, July 1998.
3. Personal communication, June 1998.
4. Personal communication, May 1998. Substitute bass player for saxophone player and you have an excellent description of Weber himself, a musician able to supply lead melody, root figures and the subtlest of transitional textures within a few bars of space-conscious, yet highly energetic playing on his customised five-string instrument (with an additional treble C). Garbarek, who first heard Weber with Wolfgang Dauner and Fred Braceful in the early 1970s, has described his playing companion of the last sixteen years or so as, "not really a *bass* bass player at all, but a musician who happens to play the bass - which he does in all kinds of wonderful, fresh ways." Personal communication, November 1985. Apart from his work with Garbarek in a variety of quartets, quintets and special projects (such as his own 1984 **Chorus**) Weber has played the occasional duo sets live with Garbarek. For an overview of Weber's approach to the bass, see Tucker, M. 'Eberhard Weber', _Jazz Journal International_ January 1987 pp. 12-14.
5. Personal communication, July 1998. Taylor's lyricism, lovely touch and ability to weave a melodic line through unusual rhythmic groupings of notes made him an excellent contributor to Garbarek's music in the late 1970s. For his current work in Azimuth and Peter Erskine's trio (with Palle Danielsson), see the contextual discography.
6. W. B. Yeats 'Sailing To Byzantium', _Selected Poems_ (ed. A. Norman Jeffares) Macmillan, London 1970 p. 104.
7. Carr, I., Fairweather, D., Priestley, B. op. cit. p. 180 (new edition:_Jazz: The Rough Guide_ p. 225.)
8. _Jazz Journal International_ February 1994 p.20. The Scottish tenor saxophonist Bobby Wellins regards Garbarek as an outstanding player, with "a very poetic approach to music, and a lovely, deep and sometimes melancholy sound." Personal communication, October 1996. Although their music is (mostly) very different, particularly in its rhythmic qualities, parallels could be drawn between aspects of the emotional register of some of the work of Garbarek and Wellins. Both players phrase lines with a song-like sensitivity – and both have listened very closely to Billie Holiday.
9. Hölderlin's question appears in his elegy _Bread and Wine_ and, as we shall see in Chapter 2, was reiterated by the twentieth-century philosopher Martin Heidegger with reference to the work of Rilke. For three related but also contrasting perspectives on the question of the status, ambitions and achievements of the arts this century see Alsberg, J. _Modern Art and its Enigma_ Weidenfeld & Nicolson, London 1983; Gablik, S. _Has Modernism Failed?_ Thames and Hudson Ltd., London 1985 and Tucker, M. _Dreaming With Open Eyes: The Shamanic Spirit_

in Twentieth-Century Art and Culture Aquarian/HarperCollins, London 1992.

10. Wesling, D. *Wordsworth and the Adequacy of Landscape* Routledge & Kegan Paul, London 1970. See pp. 75-6 for Wesling's illumination of the complexities of the relation between the impact of the "outer view" of Nature and the sensibility of the solitude of the "inner eye" in Wordsworth.

11. Timmes, E. & Kelley, D. (eds.) *Unreal City: Urban Experience in Modern European Literature and Art* Manchester University Press, Manchester 1985.

12. *The Surprise of Being* (trans. J. Greene & C. de Azevedo Mafra) Angel Books, London 1986 p. 53. See also Lisboa, E. with Taylor, L. C. (eds.) *A Centenary Pessoa* Carcanet Press Ltd., Manchester 1997.

13. On this general theme see e.g. Bradbury, M. and McFarlane, J. (eds.) *Modernism 1890-1930* Pt. 2 Sect. 5 'The Lyric Poetry of Modernism'; Hamburger, M. *The Truth of Poetry: Tensions in Modern Poetry from Baudelaire to the 1960s* Methuen, London & New York 1982; Davies, L. 'The Death and Rebirth of an Art' in his *Paths To Modern Music* Barrie & Jenkins, London 1971 and Tippett, M. *Moving Into Aquarius* Paladin/Granada Publishing, St Albans 1974.

14. See e.g. Paul Celan *Selected Poems* (trans. M. Hamburger) Penguin Books, London 1990; Primo Levi *Collected Poems* (trans. R. Feldman & B. Swann) Faber & Faber, London 1992 ; Pablo Neruda *Residence on Earth* (trans. D. D. Walsh) Condor/Souvenir Press, London 1976; Seamus Heaney *North* Faber & Faber, London 1975.

15. See e.g. Skelton, R. *Poetic Truth* Heinemann Educational Books, London 1978 for formal and philosophical justification of the idea that "Poetry [..] does present itself as a kind of judgement of all other and more approximate modes of communication and decision [..] " (p.116) and, for an excellent defence of poetry's "otherness", Ward, J. P. *Poetry and The Sociological Idea* The Harvester Press, Brighton 1981.

16. 'Poetry and History' in *Octavio Paz: Selected Poems* (ed. C. Tomlinson) Penguin, Harmondsworth 1979 p. 15. For Paz, poetry should be "a Fiesta, a precipitate of pure time." Ibid.

17. *The Magic Mountain* (trans. H. T. Lowe-Porter) Penguin Books, Harmondsworth 1971 p. 114. Mann focuses on the theme of time at various points in the novel: see e.g. pp. 66 and 103-5.

18. See Hamel, P. M. *Through Music To The Self* Compton Press, Tisbury 1978 pp. 89-91. See also Stravinsky, I. *Poetics of Music* (trans. A. Knodel & I. Dahl) Harvard University Press, Cambridge 1970 pp. 28-32 and, for a cross-cultural approach to time, Fraser, J. T. (ed.) *The Voices of Time* Allen Lane The Penguin Press London 1968.

19. See Schuller, G. *Early Jazz: Its Roots and Musical Development* Oxford University Press, Oxford & New York 1986 chs.1 and 2; Jones, L. *Blues People: Negro Music In White America* William Morrow & Company, New York 1963 chs. 1-6 and Nanry, C. (with Berger. E.) *The Jazz Text* D. Van Nostrand Company, New York 1979 chs. 2 and 3.

20. *Poet In Our Time* (trans. A. Hamilton) Marion Boyars, London 1976 p.16.

21. Ibid. p. 67.

22. Quoted and referenced in Kuspit, D. & Gamwell, L. _Health and Happiness in Twentieth-Century Avant-Garde Art_ Cornell University Press, New York 1996, p. 68.

23. See the discussion of this point in Gustafsson, L. _Forays into Swedish Poetry_ (trans. R. T. Rovinsky) University of Texas Press, Austin & London 1978 pp. 40-44, with reference to Gunnar Ekelöf's poem _Each Person Is A World_, from his 1941 collection _Ferry Song_ .

24. Jung and Freud broke on this point. See Jung, C. G. _Memories, Dreams, Reflections_ (ed. A. Jaffé, trans. R. & C. Winston) Flamingo/Fontana Paperbacks, London 1988 p. 173 and, for a general comparison of Freudian and Jungian perspectives, Tucker 1992 op. cit. pp. 94-99.

25. For a representative example of the historical emphasis here, see Taylor, B. _Modernism, Post-Modernism, Realism_ Winchester School of Art Press, Winchester 1987.

26. _Music, Archetype, And The Writer: A Jungian View_ The Pennsylvania State University Press, University Park & London 1988 pp. 1-12. As Knapp clarifies, _arche_ means "beginning, origin, primal source and principle", while _type_ signifies a "blow, and what is produced by a blow, the imprint of a coin ... form, image, copy, prototype, model, order, and norm." For Jung - who felt that music should be "an essential part" of every analysis - the term archetype was not meant to denote "an inherited idea, but rather an inherited mode of psychic functioning [...] An archetype is to the psyche what an instinct is to the body. The existence of archetypes is inferred by the same process as that by which we infer the existence of instincts." Jung, quoted and referenced ibid. p. 3. For a thorough examination of the idea, see Stevens, A. _Archetype: A Natural History of the Self_ Routledge, London 1990; and for an introduction to esoteric traditions of understanding music, from Plato to Stockhausen - a good many of which exhibit parallels to Jungian ideas - see Godwin, J. (ed.) _Music, Mysticism And Magic: A Sourcebook_ Arkana/Routledge & Kegan Paul, London 1987.

27. Knapp op. cit. pp. 136-43.

28. See e.g. _The Journals of Kierkegaard_ (ed. & trans. A. Dru) Fontana Books, London 1967 p. 243.

29. _Philosophy of Modern Music_ (trans. A. G. Mitchell & W. V. Bloomster) Sheed & Ward, London 1973 p. 34. For Adorno's ill-informed assessment of jazz - 'Perennial Fashion - Jazz' see his _Prisms_ (trans. S & S. Weber) Neville Spearman, London 1967 pp. 121-32. One infers from the opening of this piece that it was either written or prepared for publication some time in the early 1960s. This makes doubly unacceptable both the tone of the text - e.g. "Jazz is the false liquidation of art - instead of Utopia becoming reality it disappears from the picture" - and the essay's lack of detailed reference to any specific players, groups or stylistic areas of expression. See also Rifkin, A. 'Down On The Upbeat: Adorno, Benjamin And The Jazz Question', _Block_ 15, 1989 pp. 43-47 and Chapter Two below.

30. For detailed consideration of this point, see Tucker 1992 op. cit. pp. 27-48.

31. For an introduction to the many complexities of this theme, see the classic account in Burckhardt, J. _The Civilization Of The Renaissance_ (rev. ed. I. Gordon, trans. S. G. C. Middlemore) Mentor, New American

Library, New York 1960, Pt. 4 'The Revival of Antiquity'.

32. See Lévi-Strauss, C. _The Savage Mind_ Weidenfeld & Nicolson, London 1972 ch. 9 'History and Dialectic' for a key critique of the irrationalities of the linear and 'progressive' approach to factors of time and history, irrationalities manifest within the 'coding' of the historical eras or time-frames within which such an approach places events. The impact which an event has within a framework of hours or days is obviously different from the one it would have were it placed instead in the framework of decades, centuries or even (as is the case with the writing of so-called pre-history) tens of thousands of years. Lévi-Strauss argues that the writing of history (particularly from the viewpoint of a committed Western and left-wing humanist such as Jean-Paul Sartre, with whose ideas Lévi-Strauss here took issue) is often irrational in the way in which it switches between these various frameworks. Thus, for Lévi-Strauss, there can never be a direct engagement with something called History, but rather an engagement with the questions: history how, and for whom?

33. 'Note on Art' (1917) in _Seven Dada Manifestos and Lampisteries_ (trans. B. Wright) John Calder, London/Riverrun Press, New York 1977/81 p. 59.

34. Yeats op. cit. p. 63.

35. _Via negativa_ : the way of negation, or renunciation, which in the mystical traditions of the world is usually held to lead to that experiential reversal, or transformation, whereby the greater whole, or totality of the mystery of life is revealed. The negation in Beckett, however, is usually seen as precisely that: negation, and nothing more. According to George Steiner, "There is no greater virtuoso of strangulation than Beckett, no master of language less confident of the liberating power of the word." _After Babel: Aspects of Language and Translation_ Oxford University Press, Oxford/New York 1998 p. 497. I agree, but with the important reservation that, bleak as it may be, Beckett's humour can be liberating. The Norwegian poet Jan Erik Vold has suggested that Gunnar Ekelöf is "poetry's Beckett, the North's Beckett". _Entusiastike Essays: Klippbok 1960-75_ Gylendal Norsk Forlag, Oslo 1976 p. 103. Here I can't agree. While some superficial parallels might be drawn between the two writers, there is a deeply mystical impulse in Ekelöf, a yearning for absorption in the larger scheme of the mystery of things, that distinguishes him utterly from Beckett. It is impossible to imagine Beckett writing (or publishing) a poem like Ekelöf's great _Euphoria_, from the 1941 collection _Ferry Song_ - just as it is impossible to imagine Beckett giving a book of his a title with such mythically expansive overtones. With the Garbarek/Stenson quartet, Vold offers a lovely tribute to Ekelöf, _Sommernatten_ (The Summer Night), on the September 1977 **Ingentings Bjeller** (Nothing's Bells) - a recording shot through with the positive spirit of the Nature-loving and (essentially) Taoist Ekelöf. For an introduction to Ekelöf, see Tucker 1992 op. cit. (_Dreaming_) pp.136-39. (When I put this point about Ekelöf and Beckett to Vold in October 1998, he replied that, if there is something of Beckett in Ekelöf, Ekelöf of course has many more aspects to him than that.)

36. See Cousineau, P. (ed.) _The Hero's Journey: Joseph Campbell on his Life and Work_ Harper and Row Publishers, San Francisco 1990 p. 40. Campbell took this term from the twentieth-century German psychologist Karlfried Graf Dürkheim. According to Campbell, Dürkheim thought that the whole problem (or potential) of life is to become "transparent to the transcendent"; to be able to live the divine life within oneself, "not as the final term but as a vehicle of consciousness and life". Dürkheim's phrase led Campbell to define myth as "a metaphor transparent to the transcendent." Ibid. For the painter Max Beckmann (1884-1950) it was essential to develop a new existentialism, or spiritually 'naked' authenticity in art, but an existentialism fructified by an archaic imagination: see Belting, H. _Max Beckmann: Tradition as a problem in Modern Art_ (trans. P. Wortsman) Timken Publishers, New York 1989 p.60 and Chapter 5 'Myth in Art or Art as Myth'.

37. See e.g. Campbell, J. _The Hero with a Thousand Faces_ Abacus/Sphere Books, London 1975; _The Masks of God_ (four volumes: _Primitive Mythology_/_Oriental Mythology_/_Occidental Mythology_/_Creative Mythology_) Penguin Books, Harmondsworth (various editions, 1970s-present) and Apostolos-Cappadona, D. (ed.) _Art, Creativity and the Sacred_ Continuum, New York 1996.

38. See e.g. Campbell, J. _The Masks of God: Creative Mythology_ Penguin Books, Harmondsworth 1976 and Cousineau, P. (ed.) op. cit.

39. _Art and the Creative Unconscious_ (trans. R. Mannheim) Harper Torchbooks/The Bollingen Library, Harper & Row Publishers, New York 1966. See Tucker 1992 op. cit. pp. 94-99 for the differences between Freudian and Jungian approaches to factors of dream and creativity, and the extent to which Neumann was able to apply Jungian insights within a more sympathetic and revealing analysis of modern art than that evinced by Jung himself (in such books as his _The Spirit In Man, Art and Literature_ , for example).

40. See _Collected Poems_ (trans. R. Fulton) Bloodaxe Books, Newcastle upon Tyne 1987 p. 118 for slightly different translation.

41. Bachelard, G. _The Poetics of Space_ (trans. M. Jolas) Beacon Press, Boston 1969 p. 208.

42. No gender stereotyping is intended in such a use of psychological principles, principles which make it perfectly possible to consider the extent to which female jazz artists, for example, may wish to - and do - play with great assertion and power.

43. In visual art, two of the best examples this century are furnished by the work of Meret Oppenheim and the later work of Edvard Munch - the content, structure and colour scheme of some of whose images, such as the 1934-35 _The Fight_ (Munch Museum, Oslo) lend themselves directly to Jungian ideas concerning the struggle to achieve individuation. See the discussion of Oppenheim and Munch in Tucker 1992 op. cit. pp. 9-12 and 151-7.

44. See Jung's description of the (now-famous) dream of the multi-storied house which confirmed his ideas here: Jung 1988 op. cit. pp. 182-4.

45. Fordham, F. _An Introduction to Jung's Psychology_ Penguin, Harmondsworth 1953 pp 61-3.

46. See Tucker 1992 op. cit. passim and Tucker, M. 'Music Man's Dream' in *Alan Davie* Lund Humphries, London 1992 pp. 71-92.

47. Written at the foot of one of his sketches. See Lorca, F. G. *Deep Song and Other Prose* (ed. & trans. Christopher Maurer) Marion Boyars, London 1980 p. ix .

48. 'Jan Garbarek: Mysterious Wayfarer' *Jazz Forum* no. 86 1/1984 p. 44. See the Romantic poet Keats' idea of "negative capability", as expressed in a letter of 1817: "that is, when a man is capable of being in uncertainties, mysteries, doubts, without any irritable reaching after fact and reason." Quoted and referenced in Ellman, R. & Feidelson Jr., C. (eds.) *The Modern Tradition: Backgrounds of Modern Literature* Oxford University Press, New York 1975 pp. 70-71. See also note 35 above.

49. *In the Marshes and on the Earth*, in Vesaas 1971 op. cit. p. 45. There is a key passage here in which the narrator wonders if the birds signify liberation to him: "Liberation is a big word. It doesn't suit me; what am I to be liberated from? On the contrary, I must be able to receive. To fill a void." (p. 41.) See also the concluding lines to Tomas Tranströmer's *Vermeer*, where "The clear sky has leant itself against the wall./It's like a prayer to the emptiness./And the emptiness turns its face to us/and whispers/'I am not empty, I am open.'" *Collected Poems* (trans. R. Fulton) op. cit. p. 150. The titles of Garbarek's **It's OK to listen to the gray voice** album were derived from Tranströmer: see Chapter 4 below.

50. For an extraordinary documentation of the thickets of musical/ psychological/ sociological theory which have developed here, see Shepherd, J. & Wicke, P. (eds.) *Music and Cultural Theory* Polity Press, Cambridge 1997. After presenting page after page of tortuous, post-Freudian theorising about the possibly determining or 'given' relations of signifier and signified, the unconscious and the conscious in music, the editors conclude with the following declaration: "*There is, in fact, nothing given in the relations possible between 'language' and 'music', the 'conscious' and the 'unconscious'.* Within the constraints evident in each instant of human life, constraints which facilitate its continuation, everything remains possible." (p. 217.) Unable to shake off the shackles of determinism as it is, such (relative) common sense is refreshing. It would have been even more so, had the editors had the open-mindedness to consider Jungian approaches to their subject matter. However - one is tempted to say, of course - Jung does not feature once in the book, any more than an author like Bettina L. Knapp. See also e.g. Connor, S. *Postmodernist Culture: An Introduction to Theories of the Contemporary* Basil Blackwell Ltd., Oxford 1991 (where the whole range of human endeavour signalled in notes 36-38 above is conspicuous by its absence); Lehman, D. *Signs Of The Times: Deconstruction and the Fall of Paul de Man* Andre Deutsch Ltd., London 1991 (a sustained critique of the various absurdities and hypocricies of the deconstructionists) and Donoghue, D. *The Arts Without Mystery* The British Broadcasting Corporation, London 1983. The last is a well-argued defence of the idea of mystery in the arts, such as is also to be found in Steiner, G. *Real Presences: is there anything in what we say?* Faber & Faber, London 1989. Although Steiner does not

mention jazz, he places great - and welcome - emphasis on music's key role in awakening us to dimensions of life beyond the grasp of logo-centric reason and language (the very reason and language which, ironically enough, dominate so much of the deconstructionists' attack upon what they consider logocentricity's impulse to establish and rationalise a world of essentialist meanings).

51. Girvetz, H. & Ross, R. (eds.) *Literature and the Arts: The Moral Issues* Wadsworth Publishing Company, Belmont 1971 pp. 27-8. The sociological contradictions of Babbitt's position are obvious: did this American think that, rather than the tax-paying public, a latter-day Renaissance prince would subsidise his every ivory-tower indulgence? See the (favourable) discussion of *All Set* - the serialist piece for jazz instrumentation which Brandeis University commissioned from Babbitt in 1957 - in Harrison, M. *A Jazz Retrospect* David & Charles/ Crescendo, Newton Abbott/ Vancouver 1976 pp. 183-4.

52. See Capra, F. *The Tao of Physics* Flamingo/Fontana Paperbacks, London 1983 (first published 1975) and Zohar, D. *The Quantum Self* Flamingo/HarperCollins, London 1991. On Taoism see Lao Tsu *Tao Te Ching* (trans. G-F. Feng & J. English) Gower Publishing, Aldershot 1996; Chang Chung-yuan *Creativity and Taoism: A Study of Chinese Philosophy, Art and Poetry* Wildwood House Ltd., London 1975 and Willis, B. *The Tao Of Art* Century/Rider, London 1987.

53. Levas, S. *Sibelius: a personal portrait* (trans. P. M. Young) J. M. Dent & Sons Ltd., London 1972 p. 75.

54. Ibid. p. 76. It is interesting to reflect upon the wisdom of Sibelius's words in the light of the work of such subsequent composers as Arvo Pärt, Peteris Vasks and Terje Bjørklund, for example. See the contextual discography.

55. *Music Ho! A Study Of Music In Decline* Faber & Faber, London 1966 p. 279. (For the comparison of Sibelius and Cézanne see p. 262.)

56. *Petit maître* : a master, but of relatively small scope. Ibid. pp. 187-8.

57. *Death Of A Music? The Decline of the European Tradition and the Rise of Jazz* The Jazz Book Club/Victor Gollancz Ltd., London 1962 p. 136. Lambert's and Pleasants' texts have both been criticised, by the British jazz and "serious music" critic Max Harrison, for what Harrison sees as their simplistic dismissal of much challenging and rewarding avant-garde music of our century. Harrison may have a point - but not the whole argument, by far. See his 'The Pleasures of Ignorance', *Wire Magazine* issues 34/35 December 1986/January 1987 pp. 58-63. Harrison is often an especially perceptive and rewarding critic. However, jazz enthusiasts are perhaps not the only listeners who will raise an eyebrow at his estimate of Milton Babbitt as "the greatest musician" involved with the 1957 **Brandeis Festival** LP recording, which also featured works by Jimmy Giuffre, Charles Mingus, George Russell, Harold Schapero and Gunther Schuller. See Harrison 1976 op. cit. p 183.

58. Pleasants op. cit. pp. 189-90.

59. Ibid. p. 191.

60. Ibid. The problematic aspect of Pleasants' position is that he insists that the discipline within which the creative jazz musician must work is "his

listeners' concept of song [..which..] requires a knowledge of and acceptance of the listener's language. The objective of the musician's song is communication, and it cannot be accomplished without giving the listener an even break." (p. 191) Note how, within a couple of sentences, listeners have become transformed into a single listener: what was perhaps a simple type-setting error underlines the impossibility of Pleasants' generalisations here. Why should not a degree of atonality (which Pleasants does not see as functioning productively within an evolving jazz context) inform song? As a listener, I look to a creative musician, or composer, to broaden my idea of song, not simply to confirm whatever musical language it is that others may wish to assume I am already familiar with. This is precisely the value of a good deal of Garbarek's work: a false, separatist dialectic of the old and the new is avoided, and a genuine synthesis of such elements evolved. See Chapter Five below.

61. See Raine, K. 'The Use of the Beautiful' (1966) in _Defending Ancient Springs_ Golgonooza Press, Ipswich 1985 pp. 156-75 and Gadamer, H-J. _The Relevance Of The Beautiful And Other Essays_ (trans. N. Walker) Cambridge University Press, Cambridge 1991.

62. 'Jan Garbarek's Scandinavian Design' _Down Beat_ vol. 53 no. 7, July 1986 p. 26. Those interested in the technical details of Garbarek's saxophones, mouth pieces and reeds will find a brief paragraph here. Garbarek played a specially made "straight neck" Yamaha tenor saxophone in the mid-1980s, but has since reverted to the (conventional neck) Selmer saxophone which he played before. Rico reeds are his preferred choice.

63. See Allnutt, G. 'Interview with Tomas Tranströmer', _The Fiction Magazine_ 1987 vol. 6 no. 4 pp. 27-8 and _Ironwood no 13 Tranströmer: A Special Issue_ Ironwood Press, Tuscon AZ 1979 passim. See also Chapters Four and Five below.

Tongue of Secrets: Jan Garbarek, Town & Country Club/Forum
(London, November 1988) Christian Him

Deep Song

The haunting blend of rhythmic power and lapidary meditation which is Garbarek's current signature has drawn upon – and refashioned – sources as diverse as minor-hued cattle calls and major-keyed Sami *joiks*, Slavic bi-tonality and Balinese pentatonic scales, Pakistani ragas and Brazilian polyrhythms, European serialism and Arabic modes, and both pre- and post-Gregorian chant and Renaissance polyphony.[1] Given such a breadth of resource in his music, it is understandable that Garbarek is often asked whether or not what he plays today can be called jazz.

Much of the innovative force of Garbarek's music has indeed lain in the development of fresh ways of inflecting the aesthetic of improvisation which lies at the heart of jazz. And, certainly, this has often generated music which some critics find hard to relate either to any earlier period of jazz history or whatever essentialist concept of jazz it is that they may carry around in their heads at times. However, no matter how fresh or diverse the music which Garbarek has played and recorded may be, it remains the case that he began his musical life playing jazz, inspired by the recordings of one of the most explorative, border-crossing artists of this or any other century: John Coltrane. And it is no less a fact that Garbarek developed his early (and in many respects, lasting) musical conceptions under the inspiration of another two such artists in the world of jazz: George Russell, with whom he studied and worked (on and off) from the mid-1960s to the beginning of the 1970s, and Don Cherry, with whom he played occasionally in the mid-to-late 1960s, and whose interest in folk forms was a key factor in precipitating Garbarek's own involvement with this area of music.

In interview after interview, Garbarek has said that, however one might wish to describe the music which he plays today, the development of that music would have been inconceivable without the initial stimulus which he received from the art which has given us, for example, Armstrong and Ellington, Hawkins and Young, Davis and Coltrane, Russell and Cherry.[2] Over the years, that art has meant many things to many people. When Jean Cocteau first heard American jazz in 1918, he felt it was "as fertilising to the artist as life itself."[3] A decade later, Hermann Hesse's Harry Haller, the alienated "Steppenwolf" of Hesse's multi-dimensional novel about the growth of an individuated consciousness, came to experience jazz as the healing music which finally led him into the organic, shape-shifting dreamworld of the Magic Theatre of his inner life.[4] In contrast, Theodor Adorno – that Marxist friend of the people, for whom the aim of jazz was "the mechanical reproduction of a regressive moment, a castration symbolism" (!) – could write in the early 1960s that jazz had only the effect "of strengthening and extending, down to the very physiology of the subject, the acceptance of a dreamless-realistic world [..]."[5]

That jazz could (and still does) inspire such extremes of response is surely testimony to its potency. As already indicated, I believe that jazz is both the most stimulating and inspiring of musics this century: or rather, the *spirit of jazz* is the most stimulating and inspiring of any such musics. When jazz becomes a matter of academicism – of preserving the spirit of the past in aspic, as it were – it can be as deadening as any other activity devoted to the proposition that, however they do things now, they did them better in the past. (This applies to the revivalist spirit of any inclination, from New Orleans good-time music to New York bebop and beyond.) By 'spirit of jazz' I mean the electric impulse to make the old new: to combine elements from previously separate areas of both music and life, in pursuit of new, pulsative syntheses of expression and experience.

Think of the 'sliding' or 'cracked' combination of pentatonic and diatonic scales in the pre-history of the music in America, as African slaves learned European hymns – a factor which many commentators believe led to the 'in-between' or 'blue note' so vital to jazz. Consider also how, in jazz, gospel elements of call and response, flowing rhythm and emotional directness – elements which the gospel world has usually wished to keep separate from the so-called 'devil's music' of the blues – are synthesised with the simultaneous directness and wryness, the world-weariness and the existential affirmation, the sensuality and the spirituality of the blues. As Sonny Rollins has said, a lot of times, jazz has meant no barriers.[6]

As such, jazz has offered humanity one of the great vehicles to that transformation of itself which, early this century, a poet like

Rainer Maria Rilke saw as essential if both humanity and the world were to survive: the replenishment of a spiritually charged, yet intensely sensuous relation of self and world.[7] This was precisely what Rilke's contemporary, Lorca, was to call the transformative power of deep song.

As Timothy Mitchell has pointed out in his excellent study _Flamenco Deep Song_, a good many of Lorca's remarks on this subject might be seen to be coloured by a sentimentalised primitivism, or rose-tinged looking to the past. Mitchell suggests, for example, that Lorca's remarks on the origins of flamenco, which are central to his discussion of deep song, have much in common with the nineteenth-century Romantic taste for ruins. Mitchell also maintains that the poet's veneration of the (alleged) purity of (supposedly) archetypal deep song blinded him to the liberating, socially grounded irony which is to be found in flamenco's _cante chico_ forms.[8] Nevertheless, Mitchell is sensitive to the fact that very real archetypes of pain, grief and catharsis lie behind the "bleeding heart" image of flamenco which Lorca's ideas may have helped to create.[9]

This is the key thing to note about Lorca on deep song: no matter how much one might wish (and need) to deconstruct various superficial, perhaps sentimental aspects of the idea, or image, the resonance of the concept of deep song carries way back beyond any Romantic taste for ruins, to generative well-springs of feelings and forms. And, as we shall see, these are well-springs which might be deemed essential to the development of both feelings and forms today. Although Lorca's ideas of deep song were illustrated by reference, not to jazz, but to flamenco, it is through further consideration of these ideas that we can best begin to approach the question of the emotional tenor and spiritual implication(s) of the spirit of jazz: to repeat, _not_ in terms of any sentimentalised archaism, but rather with regard to the music's electric and innovative _replenishment_ and _development_ of ancient archetypes of feeling and form.

In June 1922, together with the composer Manuel de Falla (1876-1946), Lorca arranged an evening's music and discussion at the Alhambra, Granada. This was to be an evening dedicated to questioning the increasing commercialism which they both felt was having a deleterious effect on the development of contemporary flamenco.[10] Lorca (1896-1936) gave a lecture in which that development was seen in contrasting relation to the original, unpolluted sources of the music: he spoke about the relation of flamenco (which Lorca suggests did not attain its definitive form until the eighteenth century) to the roots of the music in ancient Andalusian Gypsy figures and phrases. The origins of these figures and phrases were traced by Lorca back to India.

Imbued with "the mysterious colour of primordial ages", deep song was for Lorca "akin to the trilling of birds, the song of the rooster, and the natural music of forest and mountain [...] It comes from remote places and crosses the graveyard of the years and the fronds of parched winds. It comes from the first sob and the first kiss."[11] As such, deep song – *cante jondo* – was intimately related to Lorca's understanding of what, elsewhere, he called the *duende*. By this Lorca meant something that was neither angel nor muse, but rather "the spirit of the earth", something "roused in the very cells of the blood." An unstranslatable term, the *duende* conjures the intensity of "dark sounds", emissaries of both death and an expansive, transformative sense of wonder. In "tender intimacy", our *duende*-driven souls discover "volcanoes, ants, gentle breezes and the Milky Way clasping the great night to her waist." The *duende* draws one to "the edge of things, the wound" – the place where forms fuse themselves "in a longing greater than their visible expression."[12]

It is natural – and logical – to associate Lorca's last words with the art of his fellow-countrymen, Pablo Picasso (1881-1973) and Joan Miró (1893-1983). Regarding the former, think of the almost alchemical transformation of perception which took place in both Analytical and Synthetic Cubism; of the archetypal agony and ecstatic energy of such a work as *The Three Dancers* of 1925, the combination of socio-historical protest and Mediterannean mythologising in the 1937 *Guernica*, or the mysterious, practically Jungian potency of an image like *The Shadow* from 1953. As for Miró: from the magical realism of *The Farm* (1921-2) through the Taoist-like "void" paintings of the 1920s to the variegated, serpentine metamorphoses of *The Constellations* (1940-41) and the summarising simplicity of the cosmic signs in such a work as *The Gold Of The Azure* (1967), the spirit of the *duende* is unmistakeable.[13]

What, one might ask, has any of this got to do with either the spirit of jazz or the music of Jan Garbarek? In both cases, the answer is, a lot. One should remember Lorca's belief that, "Every art and in fact every country is capable of *duende*, angel, and muse."[14] "I have heard", wrote Lorca, "an old maestro of the guitar say, 'The *duende* is not in the throat; the duende climbs up inside you, from the soles of the feet.' Meaning this: it is not a question of ability, but of true, living style, of blood, of the most ancient culture, of spontaneous creation."[15]

What else is the history of jazz at its improvised, emotional heart but the spontaneous *making-new* of ancient figures, phrases and feelings – that creative dialectic of the old and the new which perhaps transmutes one's very sense of such temporal categories?[16] Opening up – and opened up by – the mystery dimension of what Lorca would have called the *duende*, and what jazz musicians call "soul", the music that is jazz is one of the greatest manifestations of both deep song and the *duende* this century. If, in terms of the mainstream of the music, the work of bassist, band-leader and composer Charles Mingus (1922-1979) is exemplary here, in terms of the spread of that art form around the world the work of Jan Garbarek is surely no less so. One could hardly have a finer contemporary manifestation of the spirit of deep song and the *duende* than **Madar**, the beautifully flowing trio recording which Garbarek made in August 1992 with the Tunisian oud master Anouar Brahem and the (late) Pakistani tabla virtuoso Ustad Shaukat Hussain.[17]

In the most immediate cultural and geographical sense, the marriage of the spirit of deep song and the *duende* with modern jazz has long been evident in the work of such notable Spanish improvisers as the saxophonist Pedro Iturralde (born 1929) and pianists Tete Montoliu (1933-1997) and Chano Dominguez (born 1960). In his sleeve-note to Dominguez's early 1990s album **Chano**, Adolfo Montejo rightly wrote of the *duende* – the magic – in the music.[18] And it is exactly such magic that distinguishes the spiritual quest in much modern and contemporary jazz around the world, from Miles Davis's **Sketches of Spain** and Coltrane's **Olé** onwards.

It was not for nothing that the critics Nat Hentoff and Kenneth Tynan found it appropriate to apply the concept of the *duende* to the art of Davis – the trumpeter who, late in life, became a painter, and who, because of both the restless variety and formal and emotional breadth and depth of his work, was sometimes called the Picasso of jazz.[19] The effect of jazz early in the century upon Picasso has been documented, as has the similar, later impact of the music upon Miró. A beautiful photograph, taken in the summer of 1966 at the sculpture labyrinth which he had created recently for the Foundation Maeght in southern France, shows Miró in smiling appreciation of the open air pianism of Duke Ellington, with John Lamb and Sam Woodyard in support.[20]

From Léger, Mondrian and Matisse to Picasso, Miró and Pollock; and from Max Beckmann and Romare Bearden, Daniel Larue Johnson and Ed Love to Stuart Davis and Larry Rivers, Karel Appel and Jean Dubuffet, Alan Davie and Harvey Daniels, Douglas Vogel and Jean-Michel Basquiat, painters have been fascinated by jazz. A similar list of examples could be supplied in the fields of literature, sculpture and film, from Jean Cocteau and Jean Arp to Michel Leiris and Jean-Paul Sartre, Jack Kerouac and Geoff Dyer, Ted Joans, Spike Lee and beyond.[21] Why should this be so? Why should jazz and these other arts have experienced such a symbiosis this century – a symbiosis epitomised by the tribute which Coleman Hawkins paid to Picasso in the legendary 1948 solo tenor saxophone recording which he dedicated to the artist?[22]

One has only to recall how advanced aspects of jazz and other art forms were intolerable to the Nazi and Soviet authorities to sense at least part of the answer to the question. (And, in terms of the "deep song" of jazz, one should also remember that, together with the millions of Jews who were exterminated by the Nazis, something like six-hundred thousand Gypsies perished in the Holocaust.) While the Nazis brought together many avant-garde works of painting and sculpture in their infamous 1937 *Degenerate Art* show – and had less than complimentary things to say about what they called "nigger music" – the Soviets twice banned jazz officially.[23] They might just as well have tried to drain the oceans. For jazz has spread around the world, speaking to people of all colours and creeds.

Few art forms have done so much this century to celebrate the courage of the human spirit: to inspire (and document) its cross-cultural journeys to the deeper aspects of life, its *duende*-like quest for that moment when "forms fuse themselves in a longing greater than their audible expression" – to adapt Lorca slightly. The development of jazz epitomises the human search for both sensuously grounded and spiritually open, trans-national meaning and affirmation, in a world which would often seem to have been stripped of precisely such qualities. Born from the misery of a people who had been torn from their original culture and turned into human chattel, jazz – grounded in the spirit of gospel and blues – was the means by which that people asserted its collective body and soul, its worthiness, its dignity. And in giving the world jazz, Afro-American culture did far more than encourage a foot to tap here or a finger to click there, in careless abandon.

When Jan Garbarek heard Coltrane for the first time, in a 1961 radio broadcast of *Countdown* – a fast-moving piece which compresses an enormous amount into its near two-and-a-half minutes, including the fiery opening solo drum figures of Art Taylor – he was introduced not just to the particular magic of the sound of Coltrane on tenor saxophone, but to that particular combination of primal directness and technical authority which has characterised so much of jazz. The balance of these two elements has always been a crucial factor in the development of the music.

Like any art form, jazz can present its practitioners – and listeners – with some seductive options, or temptations. In jazz, one of the chief – and pervasive – temptations has been to assume that the art of the music attains Olympian heights in terms of the equation: the more and faster the notes played, the greater the excitement – and aesthetic satisfaction. Musicians as diverse as John Coltrane and Oscar Peterson have shown that, interpreted by the right sort of musical intelligence, such an equation can indeed ring true and produce great art. However, many examples – think of early Armstrong and Bix Beiderbecke, Lester Young and Miles Davis, Bill and Gil Evans, as well as aspects of the art of Peterson and Coltrane themselves – could be cited in order to show how successfully the best of jazz has been able to resist the temptation to decline into a mere display of aural gymnastics.[24] In Garbarek, resistance to such temptation has long taken on an extraordinary rigour.

Together with drummer Jack DeJohnette, in August 1981 the Polish trumpet player Tomasz Stanko joined Garbarek on bassist Gary Peacock's recording session **Voice from the Past – Paradigm**. An exceptional trumpeter, who has recorded some of the most beautiful, lyrically and rhythmically compelling records of the past four decades, Stanko (b.1942) heard Garbarek when he visited Warsaw in 1966 with Karin Krog, and was impressed. In the early 1970s Stanko was invited to sit in with the Triptykon Trio of Garbarek, Arild Andersen and Edward Vesala at Frankfurt's Jazz Keller.[25]

Several years later, the trumpeter participated in a superb concert by Vesala in Helsinki, with one set by a quartet (including Garbarek) and the other featuring a sort of "mini-big band" which besides Stanko and Vesala included Garbarek, Charlie Mariano, Juhani Aaltonen, J-F. Jenny-Clarke and Vesala's wife, Haarla, on harp.[26] So by the time Stanko came to record with Garbarek on the **Paradigm** session, he was fairly familiar with the Norwegian's sound and ability. Nevertheless, the distilled range of Garbarek's work on this recording astonished Stanko.

The trumpeter's comments on Garbarek's contributions to the date, which follow in his characterful English, are fascinating: "This was a longer date, so I had an opportunity to get closer with Jan. I was shocked down that this cat, while having his very own, sophisticated, definitely stable sound and style, had developed such a gigantic technical ability that allowed him to imitate – although this was not any pastiche trip whatsoever – Coleman Hawkins, to use the Shepp sound, the Coltrane sound and many other jazz saxophone teqhniques. He was in full control of all this stuff, and I didn't know if it was just natural talent or if he had worked to develop such facility. I even wondered why he had not used these skills more. We musicians, if only having such abilities, quite automatically tend to display what we can do, what is sort of difficult and rare, while Jan – quite to the contrary."[27]

Garbarek himself has said that, perhaps what distinguishes him from other musicians is what he *doesn't* play.[28] One might think of Garbarek as a sculptor of sound, working, like the great Romanian Brancusi, to carve out of the initial block of his material only those forms that speak of the essence of things. This aspect of Garbarek's art was underlined recently by the Oslo-domiciled, Moldavian pianist Misha Alperin, when I asked him what it was that he regarded as central to Garbarek's many achievements over the years.

"Of course", Alperin wrote in reply to my question, "Jan Garbarek changed attitudes to the saxophone in contemporary jazz [...] Year by year, the technical potential of jazz performance grows, but the philosophical, individual potential declines. This is why Garbarek is so unusual. We awaited him, probably intuitively, and with him we expected poetry in improvised music."

"This", continued Alperin, "is his greatest quality: he managed to subordinate the instrument to its vocal origin. His vocalism affected all of us. He showed himself to be a musician with the intense attitude towards sound found in 'academic' or 'classical' music (of course, in jazz sound was always the ultimate thing). His concern for sound, tone, his work on timbres and colours and with dynamics – it was as if what was always deemed the hallmark of quality in chamber music finally surfaced in jazz. When the boundaries between the genres disappear (if this ever happens) and the circle is closed, the Garbarek phenomenon could be much more significant in the future than it is today."[29]

As Alperin says, in jazz, sound has always been "the ultimate thing." No matter what the instrument, the essential goal in the music has always been to achieve a personal sound, as far away from the factory line as possible. At the same time, that sound will have a good deal to do with a musician's sense of jazz history, in terms of factors of both tradition and innovation. Herein, once again, lies the beauty of jazz: the constant, creative dialectic between past, present and future.[30]

In terms of the saxophone, jazz history offers the beginning musician two great and utterly distinctive initiatory examples. One is the big, rich sound and 'vertical', or harmonically-oriented improvisatory passion of Coleman Hawkins (1901-69) – the first real jazz tenor saxophonist and a musician who, from his initial recordings of the late 1920s to the bebop years of the 1940s and beyond, never stopped listening – and contributing – to creative developments in jazz. The other is the cooler, more 'horizontal' or melodically-oriented approach, full of floating, oblique delights, developed by Lester "Pres" Young (1909-59). Famous for the flowing beauty of his collaborations with vocalist Billie Holiday in the late 1930s – it was Holiday who decided to call Young "The President" of the saxophone, hence "Pres" – Young had the courage to develop an entirely different sound from that of Hawkins: a sound which is sometimes described as almost feminine in comparison with Hawkins' weighty masculinity of approach. And it was Lester Young who came up with the classic remark which, together with Lorca's idea of deep song, supplies the governing idea of much of this book.

Stan Getz liked to tell the story of a particular Jazz At The Philharmonic tour, when Young was being bothered by a fellow-musician anxious to advertise the extent of his techical prowess: "We were all tired, and everybody was sort of asleep on the bus. Pres was sitting in an aisle seat, dozing, when a well-known saxophonist took out his ax and began walking up and down the aisle playing licks. Nobody paid any attention to him, so finally he went over to Lester and said, 'Hey, Pres, whaddya think of that?' Pres, his eyes half-closed, said, 'Yes Lady [expletive deleted], but can you sing me a song?"[31]

Following his early infatuation with the music of John Coltrane, and subsequent interest in such other members of the 1960s avant garde as Archie Shepp, Pharoah Sanders and Albert Ayler, Garbarek was always drawn to the big sound of the Hawkins vintage, to musicians like Ben Webster, Chu Berry and Gene Ammons. One of Garbarek's all-time favourite recordings is Ammons' 1952 recording of *Travellin' Light*, currently available on the **Red Top Savoy Sessions**.[32] However, over the years, his appreciation of the melodic intelligence and song-like sensitivity of Lester Young has grown and grown.[33] As we shall see later, a good deal of Garbarek's mature sound can be related to other impulses than those of jazz, and in particular, music from the East. However, in terms of the jazz tradition, it is interesting to ponder the extent to which, like Dexter Gordon – one of his chief elective affinities for many years – Garbarek has been able to synthesise the essentially "hot" approach of Hawkins with the "cooler" approach of Young. Certainly, Garbarek is a musician whose sensitivity to the inter-relation of sound and phrasing has led to a remarkable range of fresh inflections and development of the saxophone's potential as an expressive instrument.[34]

In particular, Garbarek is a musician who has been able to exploit what one might call both the sophisticated and primitivistic potential of that curious hybrid of an instrument – a conically bored brass body brought to life by a reed – which was invented by the Belgian, Adolphe Sax, as recently as 1841. Initially, Sax's new intrument received both criticism (even today, certain temperaments find the saxophone a difficult instrument to take) and admiration. One of the admirers was no less a person than Berlioz, who went into print to express his positive feelings for Sax's invention: " The tone colour of the saxophone bridges the gap between the tone colours of the brass and woodwind instruments. But it also brings to mind, however, more remotely, the sound of the strings. I find its principal advantage to be the richly changeable beauty of its various expressive capacities. At one time low and calm, then passionate, dreamy and melancholy; occasionally tender, like the breath of an echo, like the uncanny, fading vibrations of a bell, long after it has been struck. I know up to now of no other instrument that possesses this particular sound, which seems to lie at the limits of that which is audible."[35]

Berlioz's reflections may bring to mind the unique and beautiful range of sound and emotional projection which the late Stan Getz brought to the tenor saxophone.[36] However, the words of this Romantic composer are surely no less applicable to the tenor work of Garbarek. One thinks, for example, of the range of inflections brought to bear in the theme and solo of the 1971 *Sart* (which can be translated from the Norwegian as 'soft, tender'); the cello-like sound in the title track of **Dansere** (Dancers) and the various dynamics and overtones conjured in the comparatively brief tenor and organ duets of *Linje* and *Enigma*, from **Aftenland**; or the rolling range of phrase lengths and emotional qualities exploited throughout the 12-minute, solo tenor *5th Piece*, from **All Those Born With Wings**. In all such examples, one is made aware of the extreme sophistication of Garbarek's approach to his instrument.

In the majority of those examples, however, one is also made aware of how much that sophistication is set in the service of what art historians would call a primitivistic vision: i.e. the (essentially Romantic, and, as I shall shortly argue, quintessentially shamanic) attempt to conjure the power of beginnings: to return the imagination to the plenitude and power of origins. Apart from the obvious question of tone, it is this sense of a quest for something primal that differentiates Garbarek's music from the more historically inflected work of Getz, for example, and which – for all the differences in their respective sounds – aligns the approach of Garbarek much more with that of Coltrane.[37]

In a 1998 *Desert Island Discs* programme on BBC radio, the English saxophonist and composer John Harle expressed some interesting thoughts about the origins of the saxophone. His remarks may be seen to have a particular bearing on the way in which Garbarek has developed aspects of that primitivistic vision sketched out above: "Adolphe Sax was responsible for bringing into the public eye the modern family of saxophones. But the *idea* of a conically bored metal instrument blown by a reed is as ancient as Egypt or Greece. And one of the areas that I've always felt the sax was equally at home in, as well as modern music, is ancient music. And the idea of it as almost like a primitive reed pipe, with a lot of folk influences and a lot of early music influences, is very dear to me."[38] As it surely is to

Garbarek, whose long, deep tones and sudden skirling flights into the extreme upper register can create a disconcertingly naked effect, redolent of nothing so much as an ancient shaman's simultaneously ecstatic and imploring calls to the spirit world.

This ostensible paradox in Garbarek's art – extreme sophistication and technical command set in the service of a primal poetics – places his work very much within the Romantic/Expressionistic line of much late-nineteenth and twentieth-century creativity (the backbone of which, as we shall shortly see, is constituted by aspects of ancient shamanic consciousness and practice). From Van Gogh and Gauguin to Brancusi and Beuys, Hepworth and Moore; and from Kandinsky and Klee to Miró and Pollock, Davie and McKeever, Tàpies and Widerberg, for example, painters and sculptors have witnessed – and helped shape – the emergence of elements of a primal poetics in their art. The words of Constantin Brancusi may be taken as typical here: "Simplicity is not an end in art but we arrive at simplicity in spite of ourselves, in approaching the real sense of things. Simplicity is complexity itself, and one has to be nourished by its essence in order to understand its value."[39]

The question of the relation of simplicity and complexity in art goes to the heart of the question of jazz's status as an art form. For just as a musician such as Garbarek (or Miles Davis, another key elective affinity for the saxophonist) is able to turn the paradox of simple complexity – or complex simplicity – into a matter of outstanding expression, so does jazz place paradox at the (shape-shifting) centre of its evolving poetics. In one of the most penetrating essays to have been written about the music, the late American critic Martin Williams observed that jazz handles paradoxes of both life and music in ways that no music has done before.[40] It brings the old and the new, the linear and the cyclical into as fruitful and mutual a variety of relations as individual and group, composition and improvisation, offering intellectual stimulation at the same time as it gets the heart and body *moving* . Think of the trios of Oscar Peterson and Bill Evans, or the combinations of structural interest and propulsive swing in such equally distinctive figures as Jelly Roll Morton and Charles Mingus, Duke Ellington and George Russell, Count Basie and Woody Herman.

The blues, backbone of jazz, and the so-called blue or flatted notes of the blues scale, handle emotional complexities and contradictions in ways which may serve to release us from the tyranny of false dualisms. Most important of all, jazz's various approaches to and shaping of time (from early two- and four-beat syncopation to the smoother 4/4 of the Swing era, the dynamic drive of 1940s Bebop, Afro-Cuban and Latin polyrhythms, the rolling and tumbling power of Elvin Jones, crisp, multi-layered cross-accents of Tony Williams and much post-1960s "energy/pulse" playing, for example) may serve to unite heart and mind, body and soul, and perhaps release us from the strait-jacket of Judaeo-Christian historical (i.e. linear) time.

Jazz can intensify our sensitivity to sound, and the interplay of melody and mode, harmony and rhythm, to the extent that we may begin to experience the replenishing, mythical and magical circles of time that we carry deep within us. Think again of the power of Elvin Jones, mixing 4/4 and 6/8 time as he stoked the ascensional, gospel- and blues-charged quest of John Coltrane on the 1964 **A Love Supreme** suite – or of the blend of poetry and power in the brooding percussive episodes with which Jack DeJohnette framed the compulsive ostinato development of *Parallel Realities*, the title track of the trio album which he recorded with Herbie Hancock and Pat Metheny in 1990. Or consider the subtly turned, yet potent shuffle rhythms which Manu Katché supplies across the ostinato pulse which propels Garbarek's keening tenor sky high on the 1990 *Saga*. At such moments we may indeed wonder if in jazz – as Williams suggests, in his Jung-like way – the ancient gods, so long banished from consciousness, do not in some way prepare for their metamorphosis.[41]

To a so-called critical thinker like Adorno, such a proposition would merely be further evidence of both the irrationalism and nostalgia which he claimed to detect in so much mass culture of the modern world. But to anyone with some sympathy for and interest in the world of archetypes – the world of what students of mythology call "the eternal return", where time is conceived of as circular rather than linear, and where the ostensible illogicality of dreams may embody a far deeper logic than that of either the Stock Market or Marxist critical theory – Williams' proposition may strike a chord. And that chord may settle with particular consequence in the mind of anyone who believes – as I do – that the deepest logic of both dreams and creativity is best understood in the light of shamanism, the ancient practice of what today would be called altered or expanded states of consciousness.

Song (1975, stonecut on paper 45.8 x 61.3 cms. Collection of the Winnipeg
Art Gallery, G-84-73 c. the artist, Holman Eskimo Co-operative.
Photograph Ernest Mayer, Winnipeg Art Gallery) Agnes Nanogak, Holman

Anne Trueblood Brodzsky has called shamanism "that *ur* religion,
that vibrantly interconnected life-way."[42] To sense a shamanic note in
life is to begin to intuit the ultimate totality, or wholeness of existence
– the interdependence of self and world, body, soul and spirit. In his
The Shaman: Patterns of Religious Healing Among the Ojibway
Indians, John A. Grim suggests that it is shamanism which, over the
years, has preserved the human capacity for evocation and wonder,
rather than domination, in life.[43] Shamans are not priests, bound to
the book: they are ecstatic animists, sensitive to the life-force in
everything – a life force which they apprehend through both
experiential and reflective channels. One of their prime tasks is to
recover and heal the souls of those members of their tribe who may be
suffering from "soul-sickness", or what we today would call clinical
or reactive depression, or even suicidal tendencies.[44]

Shamans are able to effect such healing because of their
command of certain artistic forms of expression – forms of expression
which help take them back to the paradisal time of origins, when
human and animal, world and Universe were as one. Masters of the
magic of mask and metaphor, drum and dance, shamans are able to
descend deep into the underworld or fly high into the celestial realms,

in search of the synoptic, paradisal vision which will bring healing energy back to the sick individual or tribe. Great inner strength is need to undertake such journeys – a strength which shamans traditionally acquire through an initiatory crisis. Here, they "die" to their old selves, wandering in the wilderness of their (a-social) unconscious before being "reborn" to a new perspective on social life, a perspective of fresh (yet archetypal) wisdom.

This wisdom concerns such matters as the central role of the paradisal Tree of Life in any existence that would have lasting value: whether a real tree or symbolic notched stick, the shaman's actual backbone or pointing staff, the Cosmic Tree functions as the fundamental bridge between the three worlds of everyday existence, the underworld and the celestial realm. Shamans acquire (lived) knowledge of such symbols of the depth dimension in life from various sources: from the elder shamans who have helped them through their initiatory ordeals; from the realm of the ancestors, a crucial realm which they will continue to visit throughout life; and – of particular importance – from their "power animals" or bird spirits. These last come to the shaman during his or her initiatory ordeals. Energising the animal within, they help the shamans to sing the "deep song" of themselves: the song which propels them on their journeys to the most fundamental, archetypal aspects of themselves. Here, what later generations would call angel, muse and *duende* meet, as the shaman comes to "inhabit" Existence, for a short while at least, in its most intense form.[45]

It does not take a great deal of reflection to sense how closely the variously grounded phenomena of shamanism – whether approached in the spirit of anthropological science or the poetics of metaphor – suggest parallels with both the Jungian view of the psyche and the creative process, as it has unfolded itself (over both continents and millenia) in what we today would call the Romantic or Expressionistic vein. And it takes little more reflection to realise how much such an archetype of both psychic and spiritual orientation may help us to rethink aspects of our current dilemmas regarding matters of religion and politics, spirituality and creativity.[46] As a shamanically-oriented thinker and poet like Kenneth White has argued, this has nothing to do with rushing to put on bear-skins, but everything to do with rediscovering and making new "an earth-sense, a ground-sense, and a freshness of the world [...]" such as fired the shamans of old.[47]

Over a century ago, the philosopher Eduard von Hartmann wrote: "We stand directly before the time when the Jewish-Christian cosmic theory has only the chance of *dying out entirely or becoming pantheistic.*"[48] Whatever one's response to the baldness of such a statement, it is a fact that the last one hundred years or so have seen an unprecedented revival of interest in pantheistic consciousness, in the idea of *the return of Divinity (or divinities) to the world.*

Mircea Eliade, perhaps the finest scholar of comparative religion this century, and author of a classic work on shamanism, said that "It was the [Judaeo-Christian] prophets, the apostles, and their successors the missionaries who convinced the Western world that a rock (which certain people had considered sacred) was only a rock, that the planets and the stars were only cosmic *objects* – that is to say, that they were not (and could not be) either gods or angels or demons. It is as a result of this long process of the desacralisation of Nature that the Westerner has managed to *see* a natural object where his ancestors saw hierophanies, sacred presences."[49] What the prophets started, the Inquisition and Newtonian science continued. And the leap of faith of Newtonian science into the belief that the ordered mechanism of the universe must have been the responsibility of an Ultimate Watchmaker, so to speak, hardly served to diminish the enervating (social and psychological, poetic and political) consequences of its mechanistic view of life. The world we live in today might be described, with due acknowledgement to William Blake and Laurie Anderson, as the ironically diminished product of the single vision of Big Religion, Big Science, and Big Business.[50]

Not only has Nature been thus desacralised: humanity has been no less profaned. For all the talk of affluence in the modern world, alienation and anomie predominate. Apart from the immediately apparent (and pressing) socio-economic dimensions of this condition, consider how many of us today live what the American Henry David Thoreau (1817-62) called lives of "quiet desperation."[51] The solution to such a predicament was offered, at least in part, by Thoreau himself, in words which recall both the perception of Novalis that every illness is ultimately a musical problem, and the importance to the ancient shamans of the power of such ecstasy-inducing factors as repetitive (but subtly shifting) patterns of drumming and archetypal song. Thoreau suggested that, "Every man is the builder of a temple, called his body, to the god he worships [...] We are all sculptors and painters, and our material is our own flesh and blood and bones."[52]

To which I would add: and our unconscious, both personal and collective (and hence, our shamanic inheritance). I would also point to the fact that, as much as – if not more than – within the disciplines of sculpture or painting, it is within the realm of music that the temples of which Thoreau wrote have since been either dreamed or created.[53]

One of the most resonant of all such temples is the music which Jan Garbarek has come to create in the "deep song" that is his oeuvre: an oeuvre which, like that of an ancient shaman – and like that of a twentieth-century Lorca or Hesse, Picasso or Miró – can take us from earth to sky, from the intimate to the infinite – and *back again*. And the building blocks of this temple come, not from any theological school or dogma, but rather through the pure practice (and practise) of music. In an extensive interview of the early 1990s with the jazz writer and broadcaster Jürg Solothurnmann, Garbarek made plain his feelings here: "I'm not related to any congregation, I'm not an actively religious person in any sense myself. But I remember I was on an album [**Making Music**] with Zakir Hussain, where I had the opportunity to play with the wonderful Indian flute player Hariprasad Chaurasia. He's regarded as a master of Indian music ... a master of any music, as far as I'm concerned. He was always being asked about meditation because everyone thought he was very much into this. And he said plainly that the music was the greatest meditation of all, and he was just staying with the music, practising every day, presenting the music to the best of his ability. And this, he said, was as close as he could ever get to any spiritual source. I feel very much the same way."[54]

So, one might add, have a considerable number of key artists of the avant garde this century, in all fields of creativity. For such artists, questions of the transcendent dimension in life have been approached through the *embodied* practise of their art. As Lorca's compatriot Miró once observed, if you wish to leap high, you must first have your feet planted firmly on the ground. Over the past hundred years and more, a large part of the struggle of painters and sculptors, musicians and poets – and many other artists and thinkers – has been precisely this: to find the (post-Christian, post-Darwinian, post-Marxist) ground upon which they can stand firmly, and from which, engaging the *duende*, they may take poetic – shamanic – flight into song.

In August 1914, at the beginning of the First World War, Jean Sibelius wrote (perhaps with the music of Scriabin in mind) to his friend Axel Carpelan: "How great is the pathos and anguish of our times! We approach the long-prophesised religious age. But it's a religion impossible to define – least of all in words, but perhaps music is a manifestation of it."[55] Over half a century and another world war later, the British composer Michael Tippett published a revised and expanded edition of his *Moving Into Aquarius* – Aquarius, the mythical, longed-for age of poetic and psychic replenishment, of human synthesis and spiritual harmony.

Much of the first (1959) edition of the book had been devoted to a defence of the imaginal realm – what Tippett called the dreams and the beauty of spiritual treasure – in a world which was coming to place more and more of its faith in the efficiency of machines, rather than whatever spiritual treasure might lie in a composer's dreams. In the new edition, Tippett published the text which he had written for a recent BBC television programme, entitled *Poets In A Barren Age*. As Tippett made plain, both the title and the content of this text, which debated the role of the arts – and specifically music – in a world seemingly unleashed from the constraints of any commanding symbolic order, owed an obvious debt to the great Romantic poet, Hölderlin.[56]

As evinced by a good deal of his gospel-inflected 1944 oratorio *A Child Of Our Time*, Tippett was nothing if not sensitive to the unspeakable suffering that has been the lot of all too many this century. To the end of his life, however, Tippett retained his faith in the potentially healing and inspirational powers of art, of music. These are powers of similar, central importance to the beliefs of ECM producer Manfred Eicher.

"Music", Eicher has said, "can be part of a long-lasting healing process. In the darkness of life it might caress your soul."[57] In a November 1994 Swiss interview, Eicher spoke more polemically of the capacity of the arts to precipitate such a process: "When I look at this world, dominated by ignorance and brutality, I often think that this is the end of homo sapiens. One of the things we need to remember, more than ever, is the capacity of human beings to create. Art, literature, cinema, music: all are of utmost importance for our culture. In these times of financial crisis and depression the first thing that government administrators do is cut funding for the arts. It's absurd.

Art, which can deeply touch and motivate people, is the only real cure for society's ills. It's also the only thing that survives all the crises."[58]

For Hölderlin, the potentiality of such a healing process – expressed in his case through the Orphic heightening of speech into the poetry that might be song – was already problematic. "Where", asks the magnificent elegy *Bread and Wine*, "are the temples, the vessels,/Where, to delight the gods, brim-full with nectar, the songs?"[59] A substantial influence on such subsequent, major figures of our century as Nietzsche and Rilke, Heidegger and Celan – and the subject of two particularly beautiful ECM productions – Hölderlin asked himself and future generations two simple, but crucial questions: is it possible for human beings to "dwell poetically" on earth – and, what are poets for, in a destitute, or barren, time?[60]

Hölderlin's questions were taken up in a key essay by Martin Heidegger, titled after the German poet's reflections. Linking aspects of *Bread and Wine* to Rilke's two extraordinary sequences of poetic-philosophical meditation, the <u>*Duino Elegies*</u> and the <u>*Sonnets to Orpheus*</u>, Heidegger summarised the extent of our century's destitution thus: "The earth and its atmosphere become raw material. Man becomes human material, which is disposed of with a view to proposed goals [...] At bottom, the essence of life is supposed to yield itself to technical production [...] Self-willing man everywhere reckons with things and men as with objects. What is so reckoned becomes merchandise."[61]

By the "essence of life" Heidegger meant, not the so-called rationality of will-full technocracy, but rather the potentially healing poetics of our relation to the world apprehended in terms of what Heidegger called its primal, unconcealing Presence or Being. (Zen would convey this abstractly phrased point in a sensuous, seventeen syllable haiku.) To see, feel and perhaps even become part of this Being is, of course, especially difficult in a society which measures meaning in terms of "sayable" (graspable) efficiency: hence the enormity of the poet's task today. For it is the poet whom Heidegger charges with the task of recalling us to the true plenitude of existence. "The hard thing", wrote Heidegger, " consists not only in the difficulty of going over from the saying work of language, but in the difficulty of going over from the saying work of the still covetous vision of things, from the work of the eyes, to the 'work of the heart'." Great poets today, suggests Heidegger, are those able to sing the essential song: the song of "the healing whole in the midst of the unholy."[62]

As Tippett once pondered, such a task must surely seem stupendously difficult, if not unthinkable, today. For as Hesse's Steppenwolf had already reflected: "Our whole civilization was a cemetry where Jesus Christ and Socrates, Mozart and Haydn, Dante and Goethe were but the indecipherable names on mouldering stones; and the mourners who stood round affecting a pretence of sorrow would give much to believe in these inscriptions which once were holy [..]".[63] Worse: ours has been the century of absolute unholy will-fulness, the century which has had to contemplate the consequences of what the late Leonard Bernstein called "global death, total death, the extinction of the whole race."[64]

Bernstein summarised his theme thus: "The twentieth century has been a badly written drama from the beginning. Act 1: Greed and hypocrisy leading to a genocidal World War; post-war injustice and hysteria; a boom; a crash; totalitarianism. Act 11: Greed and hypocrisy leading to a genocidal World War; postwar injustice and hysteria; boom; crash; totalitarianism. Act 111: Greed and hypocrisy – I don't dare continue. And what have been the antidotes? Logical positivism, existentialism, galloping technology, the flight into outer space, the doubting of reality, and overall a well-bred paranoia [...] And our *personal* antidotes: Making it, dope, sub-cultures and counter-cultures, turning on, turning off. Marking time and making money. A rash of new religious movements from Guruism to Billy Grahamism. And a rash of new art movements, from concrete poetry to the silences of John Cage. A thaw here, a purge there. And all under the same aegis, the angel of planetary death."[65]

All of which led Bernstein, writing in the mid-1970s, to one overwhelming question: "is great art still possible in our century of death?"[66] There may be some who will ask: and if it is, what of it? Here, the simple but profound faith of Martin Williams, as expressed in the opening essay to his _The Jazz Tradition_, cannot be improved upon. "Art", says Williams, " does not reflect society and environment and consciousness so much as it tells us what environment and society and consciousness do not know. It compensates for conscious attitudes; it reveals to us that there are other, perhaps opposite but still tenable ways of looking at things or feeling about things. Art tells us what we do not know or do not realize. And it prepares the way for change."[67] In the valley of death, (shamanic) art can shape a path of life.

Having considered aspects of an earth-oriented (and thus, for Bernstein, tonally rooted) greatness in the music of Mahler and Stravinsky, Bernstein concluded his ruminations by reflecting that, from the musical point of view at least, the future looked much less bleak than he might have imagined some years previously. Why? Because Bernstein – a life-long supporter of tonality in music – believed that, after decades of ideologically driven attacks upon tonality (or music relating to a fundamental key centre, or harmonically mensurable overtone series) young composers were now able to explore what Bernstein called "their innate and long-denied sense of tonality."[68]

Avant-garde compositional techniques and attitudes had now matured to the point where, what had once seemed extraordinary in Alban Berg – i.e. the marriage of a serial tone row with aspects of tonality (as, most famously, in the quoting of parts of a Carinthian folk tune and the chorale from Bach's *Cantata* no. 60 in Berg's *Violin Concerto*, its tone row already open to the implications of traditional triadic harmony) – might now become part of the mainstream of contemporary composition. And after what he saw as some years of crisis, jazz, said Bernstein, was now alive and well. "So", he concluded, " all in all things don't look so bad. We are in a position where one style can feed the other, where one technique enriches the other, thus enriching all music. We have reached that supra-level of musical semantics [..] where those apparently mismatched components can unite – tonal, non-tonal, electronic, serial, aleatory – all united in a magnificent new eclecticism."[69]

George Russell does not feature once in Humphrey Burton's recent and well-researched study of Bernstein's life and work.[70] Nevertheless, there is an extraordinary correspondence between Bernstein's words and such music of Russell's as the 1969 recording of **Electronic Sonata For Souls Loved by Nature**. With its collaged blends of propulsive ostinato and abstracted rubato rhythm, Russell's chunky, funky pianistics (a touch reminiscent of Monk), shape-shifting electronic tape, African speech and music samples, free jazz trumpet, rock guitar – and the spiralling, piping, reflective and (above all) jazz-rich tenor lines of Jan Garbarek – the sonata embraces exactly that "supra-level" of musical semantics so prized by Bernstein.[71]

Not only that: many of Bernstein's thoughts echo those uttered almost a decade before the **Electronic Sonata** recording by the ex-Dizzy

Gillespie drummer turned pianist, composer and author of the much-praised _Lydian Chromatic Concept of Tonal Organisation_. Published in 1953, Russell's magnificent volume has been an inspiration to questing jazz musicians ever since, suggesting ways in which the creative jazz musician can combine harmonically 'local' ideas and tonally rooted 'gravities' of expression with more 'outer-directed' impulses of scale-inflected ideas and chromatic transformations.[72]

In the interview which accompanied his superb 1960 recording **Jazz In The Space Age** Russell was asked how he saw the future of jazz. His reply, which builds upon the ideas of "rooted" and "outer-directed" forms of expression, merits quoting more or less in full: "Jazz is changing; the '60s could well be a crucial decade. One thing is certain. A variety of sounds and rhythms, many of which are alien to what audiences are used to, will find their way into jazz [...] Progress is inevitable. Today's musical palette is just not adequate. ALL feelings relative to life and beauty cannot be validly expressed with techniques now in vogue. What is more, jazz is an evolving art; it is not meant to be restricted. The very nature of the music and its history indicate this.

The jazz music of the future? What will it be like? Well, the techniques are going to get more complex, and it will be a challenge to the composer to master the techniques and yet preserve his intuitive approach. And it will be a challenge for the improviser to master these techniques and also preserve the intuitive, earthy dignity of jazz.

Specifically, it's going to be a pan-rhythmic, pan-tonal age. I think that jazz will by-pass atonality, because jazz actually has roots in folk music, and folk music is scale-based music; and atonality negates the scale. I think jazz will be intensely chromatic; but you can be chromatic and not be atonal.

The answer seems to lie in pan-tonality. The basic folk nature of the scales is preserved, and yet, because you can be in any number of tonalities at once and/or sequentially, it also creates a very chromatic kind of feeling, so that it's sort of like being atonal with a Big Bill Broonzy sound. YOU CAN RETAIN THE FUNK."[73]

Russell concluded: " Every artistic evolution has been spirited by people of direction and purpose. It is people of this stripe that have moved jazz upwards and outwards, and given it real meaning. The innovators of today's generation, some discovered, some to be found, will do what has to be done. However, their row won't be easy to hoe. Has it ever been for the Parkers, the Ellingtons, the Youngs, etc.? Breaking new ground is one thing, but convincing the world that it is the thing to do is quite another. The artist must believe in himself and what he has to give ..."[74]

I have quoted Russell at such length for several reasons. Firstly, as will already be apparent, I regard him as a key figure in the music of our century, whose thoughts on the art which he has done so much to develop merit the closest attention. Secondly, these reflections of 1960 predate by only a year or so the emergence of the Beatles on the pop scene, thus serving to remind one what an enormous gulf had developed between the intellectual, musical and spiritual resources available to the creative jazz musician and that world of blues-oriented atavism which groups like the Beatles, the Rolling Stones and Cream were to "re-import" to America later in the decade.[75]

During the late 1950s and 1960s, musicians such as George Russell and John Coltrane, Ornette Coleman and Don Cherry, Cecil Taylor and Archie Shepp, Bill Dixon and Paul Bley, Albert Ayler and Eric Dolphy, Sun Ra and the Art Ensemble of Chicago – musicians of the so-called and often reviled 'New Thing' – produced some of the finest music in jazz. As evinced by such a swinging, blues-soaked piece as Coleman's *Ramblin'* (1959) much of this music had more in common with so-called 'old things' than many a suspicious and dismissive critic (or musician) of the time, defensive of supposedly mainstream values in the music, might have suspected.[76]

Such 'old things' concerned not simply such formal elements as the polyphony of New Orleans music, often recast in the fierce heterophony of the new jazz; not just the blue note of Armstrong or Bechet, transformed into both questing prayer and hymnal affirmation by the likes of Coltrane and Ayler, Shepp and Dolphy – but rather the shamanic backbone of jazz, the transformative dialectic of suffering and affirmation, emotion and intellect, body and soul which has always lain deep in the history of the music.[77] And like Coltrane, albeit in a different register, George Russell is one of the great shamans of jazz, shaping a world wherein player and listener alike are free to move in a richly orchestrated, immensely stimulating and energising world of both vertical and horizontal mystery, of shape-shifting musical and spiritual potentiality: the world of "deep song".

Unfortunately for Russell and other members of the 1960s avant garde, their multi-faceted replenishing of the deepest roots of not just jazz, but all music making, coincided with the rise in popularity of soul music among black audiences – a rise in popularity which took place at the considerable expense of American blues music – as well as with the transformation of the pleasantries of pop into the pretensions (in several senses of the word) of rock music. Whether consciously so or not, the latter harnessed (some might say, colonised) certain aspects of shamanic power in music, presenting such power in relatively simplistic but extremely popular forms. Think of the extensive 'jams' of Cream upon material like Willy Dixon's *Spoonful*, the Aldous-Huxley-inspired lyrics of The Doors or the related psychedelic aura which came to surround the Jimi Hendrix Experience.[78]

The consequences for jazz are well known. At a time when many of its leading practitioners were bringing factors of structure and improvisation, emotion and intellect into freshly conceived domains of shamanic intensity, as inspiring as they were challenging – one thinks of the echoes of shaman/bird song in Dolphy's fascination with the quarter tones of bird calls, or the overwhelming intensity of so much of what Coltrane produced at the time – the music came to experience what Leonard Bernstein referred to as "some years of crisis".[79] A good many of the musicians of the American avant garde either had to continue their already considerable efforts of self-support (for example, the AACM – the Association for the Advancement of Creative Musicians – in Chicago or the JCOA – the Jazz Composers Orchestra Association – in New York) or leave America in search of work. Russell himself came to Scandinavia in 1964, and stayed for several highly productive years, while the Art Ensemble of Chicago left for Paris in 1969, with little certainty about when they might return.[80]

"The innovators of today's generation", Russell had said, "some discovered, others yet to be found, will do what has to be done." By the end of the 1960s, one of the great innovators of the years to come was poised to make his mark in improvised music. By an extraordinary and happy coincidence, so too was one of the great innovators in the production of such music. The musician, whose early talent had been nurtured in the small groups and big bands which George Russell led in Scandinavia during the latter half of the 1960s, was, of course, Jan Garbarek, and the producer, Manfred Eicher.

Over the past thirty years, Garbarek and Eicher have together done an enormous amount to help replenish and develop the archetypal creative impulse – the "deep song" of life – of which Lorca spoke in the 1920s. Avoiding any hint of that rosy-tinged nostalgia which some have wished to read into Lorca's ideas, they have made the energy of deep song *new*. The electric impulse of life has been shown to be capable of synthesising elements of jazz and (so-called) "serious" music with aspects of folk music and other means of expression from all over the world: the assertive shamanic power of the 1960s American avant garde has been blended with the poetics of a no less shamanic, but essentially lyrical European and Nordic sensibility. "Music", Manfred Eicher has said, "is my Utopia."[81]

Fashioned as they are from out of a pure devotion to the poetics of music, the many contributions which Garbarek has made to that Utopia – contributions both intuitive and cerebral, earthy and celestial – may serve to precipitate reflection upon the acuity of Mircea Eliade's belief that "The 'sacred' is an element in the structure of consciousness, not the history of consciousness."[82] For here is music redolent of nothing so much as the Jungian (and shamanic) idea of the development of individuation, or the emergence of the Great or Cosmic Self within one.[83]

Garbarek's hard-won sensitivity to the texture, weight and emotional resonance of a single note can conjure *cantabile* melody of both transcendent spaciousness and pan-tonal rootedness, in music energised by a cross-cultural rhythmic sensibility as unforced as it is selectively varied. From the shamanic point of view, what is so remarkable about this music is the *duende*-like courage which Garbarek has had to explore worlds of solitude and suffering (most notably on the 1979 **Aftenland** album) – worlds which have eventually granted him access to a broadly conceived, spiritually affirmative language.

This is, for example, the language revealed in the insistent, driving phrases and rhythms (in staggered divisions of duple time) of *Aichuri, The Song Man* (from **Legend Of The Seven Dreams**) or the keening lyricism of *The Creek*, from the *Mangas Colorados Suite* on the 1995 **Visible World** (music concerning aspects of the legacy of the Chiricahua Apache Chief after whom the suite is named); the piquant, yet hymnal ascension of *Star*, from the 1991 album of that name, or the thematically integrated – and individuated – totality explored and affirmed in the 1990 *Molde Canticle*.[84]

As Rilke emphasised, when he paid homage to the most legendary of all the ancient shaman-musicians: "Once and for all, if there is song/Orpheus is there."[85] In a world driven by the partial and the political, the profane and the profitable, it is hard to imagine where else deep song might be found today, if not in the pan-tonal, pan-rhythmic and – ultimately – pantheistic song of a musician such as Garbarek. "If Pan had a church today", wrote Chris Doering in his June/July 1980 _Musician_ review of the **Magico** album which Garbarek recorded with Charlie Haden and Egberto Gismonti, "this is what they would play there."[86]

Doering's image is a fine one – provided one remembers that it is precisely that: a particular image, or metaphor. The music that Jan Garbarek has created has flowed out into the lives of thousands upon thousands of listeners: and each of these will have heard the "deep song" of that music in his or her own way. Beyond the boundaries of any particular religion, here is the spirituality of song which suggests that, yes, it _is_ still possible for us to dwell poetically on earth; it _is_ still possible for us to look up into the lovely blue, and sense the ineffable wonder of existence.[87] Here is the open-ended song which, sensitive to the mysterious totality of life as it is, might yet sing us back into awareness of that domain of existence which so concerned Hesse, Bernstein and Tippett, no less than it did Hölderlin, Heidegger and Rilke: "the healing whole in the midst of the unholy".

Jan Garbarek with Egberto Gismonti: during rehearsal,
the Roundhouse 1981
Christian Him

Notes to Chapter Two

1. See respectively e.g. *Lokk* (Cattle Call) from **Dansere** (Dancers); *He Comes From The North* from **Legend Of The Seven Dreams**; *One Day In March I Go Down To The Sea And Listen* from **It's OK to listen to the gray voice**; the title track of **Dansere; Ragas and Sagas**; *Red Roof* from the 1978 **Photo With ..** , Part 5 of *Molde Canticle* from the 1990 **I Took Up The Runes** and Garbarek's collaborations with Charlie Haden and Egberto Gismonti on the 1979 **Magico** and **Folk Songs**; *Ligne* from **Aftenland; Madar** and **Officium**. The material on **Officium** includes a 12th century and an anonymous Gregorian piece, besides polyphonic music from later centuries, including pieces from the *Officium defunctorum* (Offices for the Dead) of Christobal Morales (c. 1500-53). In the concerts which they have given since this 1993 recording, Garbarek and the Hilliard Ensemble have at times featured music from both much older and more recent, twentieth-century sources. See Chapter Five below.
2. See e.g. Soluthurnmann, J. 'An interview with Jan Garbarek', in *Jan Garbarek: Edition of Contemporary Music* ECM, Munich 1995 (reprinted in *Avant magazine* no. 1, London Spring 1997 pp. 4-6). Denying that he has ever said that the music which he plays now cannot be called jazz ("I've never said this, it must be a misquotation") Garbarek continues: "[W]hat I'm playing today - whatever it is - I'm playing because I once learned the language of jazz. What I'm playing I could not play without this fundament."
3. Hadler, M. 'Jazz And The Visual Arts' *Arts Magazine* June 1983 p. 100.
4. *Steppenwolf* (trans. B. Creighton, rev. W. Sorell) Penguin Books, Harmondsworth 1972. See e.g. pp. 154-8 & 252-3.
5. Adorno 1967 op. cit. p. 130.
6. Palmer, R. *Sonny Rollins: The Cutting Edge* Eastnote/Hull Studies In Jazz, Hull University Press, Hull 1998 p. 26.
7. See the discussion of Rilke's ideas in Heidegger, M. 'What Are Poets For', in his *Poetry, Language, Thought* (trans. A. Hofstadter) Harper Colophon Books/Harper and Row, New York 1975 pp. 91-142. See also 'Poetically Man Dwells', ibid. pp. 213-29.
8. *cante chico* - young lad's songs. See Mitchell, T. *Flamenco Deep Song* Yale University Press, New Haven and London 1994 pp. 172 & 164.
9. Ibid. pp. 134-7.
10. One of the many composers who supported the idea was the Catalan Frederico Mompou, whose beautiful **Musica Callada** (Silent Music), played by Herbert Henck, is available on ECM New Series 1523. See Mitchell op. cit. p.165.
11. Lorca 1980 op.cit. (*Deep Song*) p. 25.
12. 'Theory and Function of the Duende' in *Lorca* (trans. J. L. Gili) Penguin Books, Harmondsworth 1967 pp. 127-39.
13. See Tucker 1992 op. cit. (*Dreaming*) pp. 114-19 & 308-16. Miró inspired two jazz recordings: Dave Brubeck's 1961 **Time Further Out: Miró Reflections** (Sony Columbia CK 64668) and Tommy Smith's 1995 **Azure** (Linn AKD 059).
14. 'Play and Theory of the Duende' in Lorca 1980 op. cit. p. 47.

15. Ibid p. 43.
16. By this I do not mean to reinforce the inadequate view that jazz is best seen as "the sound of surprise", in Whitney Balliett's famous phrase. As Richard Palmer has argued most cogently, factors of composition, structure and form are central to jazz - and such factors are hard-earned. This is a view with which Garbarek would readily concur - although he also respects a literate musician like Derek Bailey, whose goal would often seem to be to eschew familiar factors of composition, structure and form precisely in pursuit of "the sound of surprise". See Palmer 1998 op. cit. (_Sonny Rollins_) pp. 157-8 and, for a stimulating overview of various "idiomatic" and "non-idiomatic" approaches to improvisation, Bailey, D. _Improvisation: Its Nature and Practice in Music_ Moorland Publishing/Incus Records, Ashbourne 1980.
17. On Mingus, see the excellent study by Priestley, B. _Mingus: A Critical Biography_ Quartet Books, London 1982. **Madar** is discussed in Chapter Five below.
18. **Chano** (Nuba Records 7756). See contextual discography.
19. Sleeve-note to **Sketches of Spain** (CBS 460604 2). On Davis's painting, see Davis, M. & Gutterman, S. _The Art Of Miles Davis_ Byron Preiss/Prentice Hall Press, New York 1991. The late critic Kenneth Tynan applied the concept of the _duende_ to Davis in his sleeve-note to the 1972 Prestige double-album reissue of some of Davis's 1950s material for the label, **Tallest Trees** (PR 24012).
20. The photo is reproduced in _à proximité des poètes et des peintres: quarante ans d'édition maeght_ Adrian Maeght, Paris 1986 p. 91.
21. See Hadler op.cit. & Goldson, E. (ed.) _Seeing Jazz: Artists and Writers On Jazz_ Chronicle Books/Smithsonian Institute 1997.
22. Available e.g. on **The Essential Coleman Hawkins** (Verve 2304 537). For analysis of this thoroughly prepared, harmonically and rhythmically extraordinary recording see Chilton, J. _The Song Of The Hawk: The Life and Recordings of Coleman Hawkins_ Quartet Books, London 1990 pp. 260-61. For development of the present argument, see Tucker, M., sleeve-note to **Azure** (Linn AKD 059).
23. See Zwerin, M. _La Tristesse de Saint Louis: Swing Under The Nazis_ Quartet Books, London 1985; Kater, M. H. _Different Drummers: Jazz In The Culture Of Nazi Germany_ Oxford University Press, New York & Oxford 1992, and Starr, F. S. _Jazz Red and Hot: The Fate of Jazz in the Soviet Union_ Oxford University Press, New York & London 1983.
24. Peterson, in particular, has sometimes been unfairly maligned for allegedly showcasing technique at the expense of musical penetration. For a thoroughly argued appreciation of the range of Peterson's pianism, see Palmer, R. _Oscar Peterson_ Spellmount Ltd, Tunbridge Wells, 1984. Of course, Peterson has terrific technique: but hear, for example, how such technique is manifest in the finely varied touch and sense of space evident in his 1959 reading of **Porgy and Bess** (Verve 519 807-2) or the delicacy of his contribution to _Tranquillity in the Woods_ on Niels-Henning Ørsted Pedersen's 1998 **This Is All I Ask**.
25. Stanko recalls Garbarek "sitting on a bench in this storage area behind the bar, which was used as a musicians' room, where musicians would sit to smoke a joint and have a drink between numbers. Jan - as usual,

with this Giaconda smile of his - was as cool and even-tempered as usual, with a glass in his hand, full of - as I had noticed - apple juice, exclusively. We'd known already that Jan is quite an untypical jazz musician, being so cool and balanced and - contrary to ourselves - living very straight and clean. So it was kind of a contrast. I liked him very much then, this cool of his." Personal communication, February 1998.

26. I am extremely grateful to Edward Vesala for making a tape of this concert available to me. Garbarek's playing exhibits both the forcefulness that he would show on Gary Peacock's 1981 **Voice From The Past - Paradigm** recording and a wonderful, yearning rubato quality (in a long free-ballad section).

27. Personal communication, February 1998.

28. And also, one might say, what he chooses not to release on record. Peter Erskine, the exceptional, dynamically (and historically) sensitive drummer who played in the trio with Garbarek and Miróslav Vitous that recorded **Star** (and who appeared with Garbarek and Palle Mikkelborg on Gary Peacock's 1987 **Guamba**) recalls that, during the **Star** date, the trio created a lengthy, really burning collective improvisation, with Garbarek on tenor. This was so strong that Erskine and Vitous felt it might even "headline" the album. However, after listening to the playback, Garbarek felt that the way he had played on this piece was too similar to how he had played in the past. At his request, the piece was dropped from the finished album. Personal communication, July 1998. Garbarek has appeared on only two "live" sessions on ECM, both with Keith Jarrett and the Belonging quartet. If the May 1979 **Nude Ants**, from the Village Vanguard, is slightly disappointing, with Garbarek sounding a touch "off-mike" at times, the April 1979 **Personal Mountains** from Tokyo is a stunning document of one of the finest quartets of the decade. Such are its many qualities that one wonders why Garbarek has not made more "live" records (as Jarrett certainly has). Over the years, I think I must have seen Garbarek in concert some sixty to seventy times, with a variety of groups: more than a few of these occasions would, in my opinion, have made excellent recordings. (Given ECM's championing of so much excellent European music over the years, it is somewhat ironic that one of the very best of the comparatively few "live" recordings on the label is the May 1980 **Urban Bushmen** by the Art Ensemble of Chicago.)

29. Personal communication May 1998. I am grateful to Alison Minns, of the University of Brighton, for her translation of Alperin's Russian. A fine pianist and composer, whose work in the Moscow Art Trio often exhibits a welcome, leavenous sense of humour, Alperin has recorded some especially interesting projects in recent years. These have included collaborations with Bulgarian and Tuvan vocalists and choirs and a poetic tribute to the spirit of contemporary Nordic jazz, **North**. See the contextual discography.

30. See the thoughtful essay by Geoff Dyer 'Afterword: Tradition, Influence and Innovation' in his _But Beautiful: A Book about Jazz_ Jonathan Cape, London 1991 pp. 165-204.

31. Quoted and referenced (in the original American) in Palmer 1998 op. cit. p. 142.

32. Savoy SV 0242.

33. In an August 1998 Oslo interview, Garbarek was asked what sort of music he listened to now. He replied: "When it comes to jazz, it's quite a while now since I listened to Coltrane. It's more likely to be Gene Ammons, Lester Young or Stan Getz." Helgheim, R. 'Jan Garbareks ritar', _Dag Og Tid_ 27/8/98. I am grateful to Jan Horne for bringing this interview to my attention. On the importance of Lester Young from the spiritual point of view, see Daniels, D. H. 'Goodbye Pork Pie Hat: Lester Young As A Spiritual Figure' in Morgenstern, D., Nanry, C., & Cayer, D. A. (eds.) _Annual Review of Jazz Studies no. 4_ Transaction Books, New Brunswick (USA) and Oxford (UK) 1988 pp.161-177. Although Daniels does not mention shamanism, there are clear shamanic implications in much of this fascinating text.

34. Garbarek has long been conscious of the key relation between tone and phrasing: "The tone is tremendously important, it determines the quality of phrasing and everything else. There are many things you can't play if you have _this_ tone, but which work well if you have _that_ tone, and so on. You have to find out what is right for you.' Økland, E. 'Intervju Med Jan Garbarek', in Angell, A., Vold, J. E., Økland, E. (eds.) _Jazz I Norge_ Gylendal Norsk Forlag, Oslo 1975 p.120. On Dexter Gordon, see Britt, S. _Long Tall Dexter: A Critical Musical Biography of Dexter Gordon_ Quartet Books, London 1989 and Don McGlynn's excellent 1996 video _Dexter Gordon: More Than You Know_ (Academy Video/BFI films CAV 058). Here Niels-Henning Ørsted Pedersen underlines how responsible Gordon was, during his lengthy stay in Denmark in the 1960s, for improving the quality of Danish modern jazz. (Gordon played in Oslo and also at the Molde Jazz Festival in the 1960s; see Chapter Three below for his impact on Garbarek and Jon Christensen.) At one point in the video, Gordon echoes Louis Armstrong – with whom he played in the 1940s, as well as Lionel Hampton and the Billy Eckstine Band – when he says, "You've got to have heart to play this music, to stay in this business."

35. Excerpt from Berlioz's article in the _Journal des Debats_, 21st October 1849. Quoted from Gwozdz, L. _The Saxophone_ (an English translation of Jaap Kools' work) Egon Publishers Ltd. 1987, p. 199 in Williams, J. A. H. _The Golden Mine Of A Million Marvellous Sounds: The Development of the Saxophone as a Symbol_ unpublished BA (Hons.) final year dissertation, Brighton Polytechnic 1990. The saxophone was first heard in public at a demonstration concert for chamber wind instruments in 1854, for which Berlioz had transcribed some of his own music – and at which Adolphe Sax (1814-94) was a soloist. See Lindemeyer, P. _Celebrating The Saxophone_ Hearst Books, New York 1996 p.20.

36. See Palmer, R. _Stan Getz_ Apollo, London 1988.

37. See Chapter Four below. Of course, the range of expression developed by Getz - who recorded a Scandinavian folk tune (the beautiful Swedish melody _Ack, Värmeland, du Sköna_) as early as 1951 - was both deep and wide: witness only such albums as **West Coast Jazz, For Musicians Only, The Steamer, Focus, Jazz Samba, Captain Marvel, Sweet Rain, Change of Scenes, Voyage** and **People Time.**

38. Desert Island Discs, BBC Radio 4, 29/5/98.
39. There are various sources for this now-famous quotation, which occasionally varies slightly in phrasing - but not in meaning. See e.g. Lipsey, R. _An Art Of Our Own: The Spiritual In Twentieth-Century Art_ Shambhala, Boston & Shaftesbury 1988 pp. 242-6.
40. 'Introduction', _The Jazz Tradition_ Oxford University Press, New York 1970 pp. 3-15. Over the years, I have returned to this essay again and again.
41. Ibid. p.15.
42. Brodzsky, A. T., Danesewich, R., Johnson. N. (eds.) _Stones, bones and skin: Ritual and Shamanic Art_ Artscanada/The Society for Art Publications, Toronto 1977 p. ix.
43. Grim, J. A. _The Shaman: Patterns of Religious Healing Among the Ojibway Indians_ University of Oklahoma Press, Norman & London 1987 pp. 207-8.
44. See Tucker 1992 op.cit. (_Dreaming_) pp. 76-89.
45. For a thorough, cross-cultural survey of shamanism see Eliade, M. _Shamanism: Archaic Techniques of Ecstasy_ (trans. W. R. Trask) Bollingen Series 76, Princeton University Press, Princeton 1974.
46. See Flaherty, G. _Shamanism and the Eighteenth Century_ Princeton University Press, Princeton 1992 for an innovative study of the various ways in which an increasing awareness of shamanic consciousness altered the poetics of European artistic creativity in the eighteenth century, and for a twentieth-century perspective, Tucker 1992 op.cit. (_Dreaming_) Chapters 4 & 5 and passim.
47. 'A Shaman Dancing on the Glacier', in _On Scottish Ground: Selected Essays_ Polygon, Edinburgh 1998 p. 48. This excellent essay shares and elaborates upon the fundamental insight of the polymath sculptor Joseph Beuys (1921-86) that to speak of shamanism is _not_ to speak of a nostalgic turning to the past, but rather of an awareness of the potentiality of transformation which is still very much alive within the idea of shamanic consciousness, and which has great relevance to life today. For an introduction to Beuys and White, see Tucker op. cit. pp. 286-293 & 198-202.
48. Quoted in McFarlane, J. _Ibsen And The Temper of Norwegian Literature_ Octagon Books, New York 1979 p.143.
49. 'The Sacred and the Modern Artist' in Apostolos-Cappadona, D. (ed.) 1996 op. cit. (_Art, Creativity and the Sacred_) p.182.
50. Blake prayed to be kept from "single vision and Newton's sleep." Laurie Anderson's **Big Science** recording, with its critique of the 'golden cities, golden towns' of modernist techno-progressive ideology, was released in 1982 on Warner Brothers WB K 57 002.
51. Thoreau, H. D. _Walden, or, Life in the Woods_ Signet/New American Library, New York 1960 p. 15.
52. Ibid.
53. See e.g. Berendt, J.-E. _Nada Brahma: The World Is Sound_ East West Publications, London and The Hague 1987 and Tucker, M. 'The Body Electric: The Shamanic Spirit in Twentieth-Century Music' in Steer, M. (ed.) _Music and Mysticism_ Contemporary Music Review, Harwood Academic Publishers 1996, volume 14 parts 1-2; part 1 pp. 67-97.

54. Soluthurmann 1995/97 op. cit. p. 4.
55. Tawaststjerna, E. *Sibelius Volume 111: 1914-57* (trans. R. Layton) Faber & Faber, London 1997 p. 3.
56. Tippett 1974 op. cit. pp. 148-56.
57. Zwerin, M. 'Manfred Eicher's Ever-Widening Circles of Jazz' *International Herald Tribune* 20/10/94.
58. Borgeaud, Y-P. 'Manfred Eicher et le label ECM: Le plus beau son après le silence' *L'Hebdomadaire*, Switzerland November 1994.
59. *Hölderlin: Poems and Fragments* (trans. M. Hamburger) Cambridge University Press, Cambridge 1980 p. 247.
60. Ibid. pp. 251 & 601. See also *Hymns & Fragments* (trans. R. Sieburth) Princeton University Press, Princeton 1984 p. 249. The two ECM productions are the 1984 **Hölderlin: Gedichte** (ECM New Series 1285) and the 1993 **Scardanelli-Zyklus** (ECM New Series 1472/73). Hölderlin's thoughts about our capacity to "dwell poetically on earth" come from one of his very last prose-poem reflections, 'In Lovely Blue'. See Sieburth pp. 248-53.
61. Heidegger 1975 op. cit. pp.111- 135.
62. Ibid. pp.138-40.
63. Hesse 1972 op. cit. pp. 92-3.
64. *The Unanswered Question: Six Lectures at Harvard* Harvard University Press, Cambridge 1976 p. 314. Taking their title from that which Charles Ives gave to his 1906 (rev. 1930s) meditation on musical meaning, a five-minute piece scored for trumpet, flute quartet and strings, these Charles Eliot Norton Lectures were delivered in 1973. For the Ives piece, see e.g. Deutsche Grammophon 439 869-2.
65. Ibid. (Bernstein) pp.314-15.
66. Ibid. p. 380.
67. Williams 1970 op. cit. p. 12.
68. Bernstein op. cit. p. 421.
69. Ibid. p. 421-2. Bernstein's last chapter is devoted to a celebration of the multivalent qualities in Igor Stravinky's music (qualities which Adorno had criticised during his own championing of Schoenberg: see Adorno 1973 op. cit. passim). Some suggestive parallels can be drawn between what Bernstein observes about Stravinsky (in terms of polytonality and polyrhythm, for example) and the later, independent development of the work of Russell - whose 1949 *A Bird In Igor's Yard* paid joint homage to the worlds of Charlie Parker and Stravinsky. See **Crosscurrents** (Capitol EMI M 11060). It is this breadth - and depth - of approach in Russell which has always made his work so rewarding. See Chapter Three below.
70. *Leonard Bernstein* Faber & Faber, London 1994. Given the range of Bernstein's interests, it is unfortunate that jazz is not listed in the Index here.
71. Soul Note 121034-2. The recording is discussed in more detail in Chapter Three below. In 1980 Russell recorded the piece again, with different personnel: see **Electronic Sonata For Souls Loved By Nature-1980** (Soul Note 121009-2).
72. See Russell's 'The "River Trip" Explanation Of Jazz Improvisational Styles' in his *The Lydian Chromatic Concept of Tonal Organisation*

Concept Publishing, New York 1959 pp. xviii-xix and Chapter Three below.

73. Sleeve-note to **Jazz In The Space Age** Chessmates/GRP 18262. Also available in expanded form as 'Where Do We Go From Here' in Cerulli, D., Korall, B., Nasatir, M. (eds.) *The Jazz Word* The Jazz Book Club/Dennis Dobson, London 1963 pp. 185-92.

74. Ibid.

75. Such a comparison is not intended to be dismissive of either the resources or possible effects of rock: see Tucker 1992 op. cit. (*Dreaming*) pp. 210-14 for a brief exploration of shamanic qualities in rock music and Whiteley, S. *The Space Between The Notes: Rock and the counter-culture* Routledge, London 1992.

76. *Ramblin'* was the first track on Coleman's **Change Of The Century** release (Atlantic/London Series SAH-K 6099). In the accompanying sleeve-note, Coleman describes the piece as "basically a blues, but it has a modern, more independent melodic line than older blues have, of course." At the same time, aspects of the piece - particularly Charlie Haden's magical strummed bass solo (which, much later, was to inspire the melodic hook in Ian Drury's pop hit *Sex and Drugs and Rock'n'Roll (Is All My Body Needs)* - take one way back down the alley. For a classic dismissal (and misunderstanding) of 'Modernism' in both post-bebop jazz and twentieth-century culture in general, see Larkin, P. 'Introduction To All What Jazz' in *Required Writing: Miscellaneous Pieces 1955-1982* Faber & Faber, London 1983 pp. 285-98.

77. See Tucker 1992 op. cit. (*Dreaming*) Chapter Eight and Tucker 1992 op. cit. (*Alan Davie*) pp. 71-92.

78. Ibid. (*Dreaming*) pp. 210-14 & 222-24; Whiteley 1992 op. cit. passim and Haralambos, M. *Right On: From Blues To Soul In Black America* Eddison Press Ltd., London 1974.

79. On shamanic elements in Dolphy and Coltrane see Tucker op. cit. (*Dreaming*) pp. 226-7 & 229-232.

80. For musical aspects of the changes in jazz in the 1960s, see e.g. Budds, M. *Jazz In The Sixties: The Expansion of Musical Resources and Techniques* University of Iowa Press, Iowa City 1978. See also Litweiler, J. *The Freedom Principle: Jazz After 1958* William Morrow & Company Inc., New York 1984 passim. On some levels, this is a useful and wide-ranging book. Unfortunately, Litweiler's commitment to a particular concept of freedom in jazz leads him to make some unnecessarily dismissive remarks about musicians whose work does not always accord with that concept e.g. Keith Jarrett. See pp. 233-35 and the discussion of Litweiler's critique of Jarrett in Carr, I. *Keith Jarrett: The Man and His Music* Grafton Books, London 1991 pp. 188-91.

81. Heidkamp, K. 'Portrait: Manfred Eicher' *Lufthansa Bordbuch* no. 6, 1995 (concluding words of portrait).

82. Preface (unpaginated) to *The Quest: History and Meaning in Religion* University of Chicago Press, Chicago & London 1975.

83. See Tucker 1996 op. cit. (*The Body Electric*) passim.

84. Ibid. pp. 67-8 & 90-4. *Molde Canticle* is examined in detail in Chapter Four.

85. 'Ein für alle Male/ist's Orpheus, wenn es singt': *Sonnets to Orpheus* Part

1 no. 5. See <u>*Sonnets to Orpheus*</u> (trans. C. F. MacIntyre)
University of California Press, Berkeley & Los Angeles 1960 p.
11 and Bly, R. <u>*Selected Poems of Rainer Maria Rilke*</u> Harper &
Row, New York 1981 p. 203 for slightly different translations.
86. <u>*Musician*</u> June/July 1980.
87. See note 60 above ('In Lovely Blue').

Edward Vesala (Queen Elisabeth Hall, London November 1993)
Christian Him

Jan Garbarek Quartet c. 1962 (Jan Garbarek, Torgrim Sollid, Hans Marius Stormoen, Morten Lassem) Collection Jan Horne, Oslo

Jan Garbarek & Jon Christensen (Kongsberg Jazz Festival 1965)
Artur Sand
Collection Jon Christensen

Traneflight

As jazz has evolved, so have a variety of questions concerning its status. For this is music which, rooted in the folk forms of gospel and blues as it is, became first a popular and then a commercial art. Then – in some of its aspects at least, as developed by musicians as distinct as Art Tatum and Bud Powell, Dizzy Gillespie and Charlie Parker, Miles Davis and John Coltrane, Keith Jarrett and Jan Garbarek – that music evolved into something which has come closer and closer to what is called "serious" or "art" music. Where is such music – whatever it be called – best presented? In a smoky and (allegedly) atmospheric club or prestigious (but possibly antiseptic) concert hall? How should it be played? With the concerns of the musicians themselves or those of the paying customers most in mind? Should such music be subsidised, or should its fortunes remain dependent on the forces of the market place? How should it be recorded – 'live', or with the creative aid of studio overdubs, etc.? And, last but not necessarily least, how – and by whom – should such music be promoted, analysed and written about?[1]

Any jazz musician – or committed jazz fan – will have his or her own responses to such questions. In his 1976 _All You Need Is Love_, subtitled 'The Story Of Popular Music', the writer and film-maker Tony Palmer addressed several of such points, with respect to the overall history of jazz and its contribution to the development of popular music. Unfortunately, his treatment of the current state and potential of what was then contemporary jazz served only to reveal the ignorance – if not prejudice – which can often come to the surface when this subject is addressed.

Allowing jazz its "right of development" away from what he called "its limited origins", Palmer chose nevertheless to sum up his thoughts by informing his readers that, "Once a mainspring of popular music, jazz has become an esoteric sideshow: fascinating, often stimulating, but ultimately redundant. Saxophonist John Coltrane, for example, occasionally seemed happiest when working in one chord for forty-five minutes."[2] While writing his book, Palmer had interviewed Dizzy Gillespie. The doyen of Bebop trumpet players had been playing at a Playboy Club, before a mostly white audience – of twelve people. "Perhaps", Palmer concluded, "the Playboy Club is the inevitable, and sadly appropriate, dead end for jazz."[3]

These are the sort of remarks that can have the committed enthusiast – never mind musician! – choking with rage. Think of the way in which the modally-oriented Coltrane brought a fervent, ritualistic intensity to a popular song like *My Favourite Things* – and of how influential and popular his various versions of that song were in the 1960s. Or remember the efforts of the New York and Chicago-based avant garde of the 1960s, touched on in the previous chapter, to present the challenges and rewards of their music to the public in new and appropriate ways. Consider also the importance of venues like the Little Theatre Club in London in the late 1960s – and the way in which some of the musicians who helped develop the venue, and/or played at it, like John Stevens, Paul Rutherford and Trevor Watts, had been made aware of new developments in jazz partly through the strong exposure given to contemporary jazz by the radio in Germany, which they had experienced while on RAF duty there.[4] As we shall shortly see, in the 1960s, Scandinavia – and, in particular, Norway – did as much as, if not more than, any other region in the world to provide a more nurturing environment for the development of contemporary jazz than that suggested by Palmer's would-be "dead end" example of the Playboy Club.

Regrettably, in both musical and socio-cultural terms, Palmer's attitude to the development of jazz is not an isolated example of the lack of informed empathy which can attend discussion of this art form, within the wider contexts of both popular and "serious" music, and the contemporary plastic and literary arts. Three recent publications serve to illustrate this point.

The first is the Helsinki-based, Nordic Arts Centre's large catalogue – <u>The Nordic '60s</u> – of the major touring exhibition of that name which the centre organised in 1990. The exhibition was devoted to avant-garde developments in the plastic arts and culture in general in Scandinavia, during the decade which saw both Western material affluence and youthful political protest and intellectual revolt attain previously unimaginable levels. This was also the decade which saw some of the most important American mainstream, post-Bebop and avant-garde players, such as Ben Webster, Kenny Drew, Dexter

Gordon and Stan Getz (the last of whom had moved to Denmark in 1958), Archie Shepp and Cecil Taylor, George Russell, Don Cherry and Albert Ayler either moving to Scandinavia for some fruitful years or making important recordings there. One recalls the words of Albert Ayler, as spoken in his introduction to the January 1963 recording which he made in Denmark with, among others, the 16 year-old double-bassist Niels-Henning Ørsted Pedersen: "I had always wanted to come to the Scandinavian countries. I'd heard a lot about the Scandinavian people [...] When I come here, I feel quite free, really free I feel, free when here ... One day, everything will be as it should be."[5]

What do you suppose we learn in the 300-plus pages of _The Nordic '60s_ about the fructifying presence in Scandinavia of such exceptional figures of the 1960s avant garde as Ayler and Shepp, Taylor, Cherry and Russell? The answer is – precisely nothing. In the catalogue, occasional lip-service is paid to jazz as an element in the development of a rebellious youth consciousness in the 1950s beat era, but no detailed discussion of the impact of jazz in either that decade or the 1960s is offered at all. The various contributors to the exhibition and catalogue prefer to tell us of a 1965 Rolling Stones concert in Oslo, for example, rather than the concert which the John Coltrane quartet gave in that city two years previously. And they prefer to recall a 1969 performance in Oslo of the music of Karlheinz Stockhausen, at the recently opened Henie-Onstad Art Centre, situated at Høvikodden on the Oslo fjord (some few miles west of the capital) rather than a concert of the music of George Russell which took place at the same venue in April that year.[6]

The second publication is Norman Lebrecht's _The Companion To 20th-Century Music_, published by Simon and Schuster in 1992. Hailed as something of a breakthrough for its unstuffy, genre-inclusive and revisionist overview of the development of music this century, the book has more than a few good aspects to it. Lebrecht is not afraid to challenge reputations, and offers some fresh, listener-friendly insights. He even includes jazz in his allegedly all-over focus (Boulez and the Beatles, Ellington and Eno, Arvo Pärt and Charlie Parker, Ravi Shankar and Shostakovich, Takemitsu and Tavener, for example). Unfortunately, this is precisely where the problem lies. What, for example, do we learn of Keith Jarrett?

Unmentioned in _All You Need Is Love_, Jarrett is an artist who, by the time Palmer had decided to dismiss jazz as a music with but little future, had long taken the improvisational spirit of that music far beyond the confines of the Playboy Club, inspiring and delighting a variety of large and enthusiastic audiences world-wide. Lebrecht tells us only that Jarrett "drifted through Miles Davis' 'free jazz' phase to a spaced-out New Age minimalism that provided excellent aural wallpaper."[7] Perhaps it is just as well that we can read in *The Companion To 20th-Century Music* about Charles Aznavour, but not Albert Ayler; and that we learn nothing at all about Anthony Braxton or George Russell, Bill, Gil or Herschel Evans, Archie Shepp or Pharoah Sanders, Lennie Tristano or Oscar Peterson, McCoy Tyner or Cecil Taylor – not to mention Jan Garbarek, or a host of other artists who have recorded critically acclaimed and commercially successful albums for ECM.

The third and final publication is the more recent, 800-plus pages *Documenta X-The Book: Politics Poetics*. Published to accompany and comment upon the multi-media events at the 1997 version of Kassell's regular and now-famous *Documenta* art exhibition, here is culture in all its official glory, complete with imposing graphics and lengthy interviews with such noted, would-be guardians of cultural consciousness as Benjamin Buchloh. The overall purpose of exhibition and book was to examine questions of cultural identity since the Second World War, in the light of the growing globalisation of capitalist-dominated economic infrastructures and related frameworks of ideology and theory, resistance, reflection and creativity. Evoking a "vast narrative" of post-war history, and exploring "the complex relations between singular art works and socio-political situations which are inextricably 'local' and 'global'", the collage technique of the book included one chapter on music: the punk music of London and Los Angeles.

Yes, that's right: within this "vast narrative" of post-war history, a narrative which often concentrated on questions of Euro-American relations, on the tensions between centres and margins of socio-political discourse and the poetics of creativity, there was not one single mention of jazz – the music which, more than any other this century, has embraced precisely such questions of centres and margins, of cultural dominance and independent, regionally-based development, of politics and poetics.[8]

This is particularly the case since the Second World War. In an interview of the late 1980s, the Austrian-born but American-domiciled keyboards artist Joe Zawinul commented that, in jazz, "you'll always see that very rare individual come up. I don't care if there are millions and millions who play, those one or two guys will always be there, a little further along. They're the ones who make it sing, who are telling the story the right way."[9] Since the death of Django Reinhardt in 1953, at the all-too-early age of 42, one of the chief distinguishing features of jazz has been the way in which a good many of the ones "who make it sing" have – like Zawinul himself – come from Europe. Unlike Zawinul, however, most of these musicians have felt no need to emigrate to America.

Furthermore: Europe has not just produced some of the finest musicians of recent jazz history. Many of these musicians (and visiting Americans) have had their music recorded and produced by European producers, producers who have made a variety of exemplary contributions to the documentation of contemporary jazz. Think here of Joachim-Ernst Berendt and Hans Georg Brunner-Schwer, Gunnar Lindqvist and Lars Westin, Denis Preston and Nils Winther, Mathias Winckelmann and Jost Gebers, Michel Orier, Leo Feigin and Sigurd Loch – and, of course, Manfred Eicher.[10] Over the past thirty years, Eicher in particular has shown a continual, remarkable capacity to nurture the development of a poetic, essentially European aesthetic in jazz, as well as a sensitivity to the world-wide possibilities latent within a variety of fresh, genre-dissolving combinations of both musicians and instrumentation. Each aspect of Eicher's achievement is epitomised (and often synthesised) by the work which Garbarek has recorded for ECM. Together with engineers Martin Wieland – an important figure particularly in the early days of ECM – and Jan Erik Kongshaug, the internationally respected – and sought after – engineer and owner of Rainbow Studio, Oslo, Eicher has brought the art of improvised music, and the recording of that music, to new levels of aural clarity and poetic suggestion.

In the sleeve-note to the 1965 **Zo Ko So**, a fine album of linear, essentially "cool school" music from Hungarian guitarist Attila Zoller, Austrian saxophonist Hans Koller and French/Algerian pianist Martial Solal, producer and jazz writer Joachim-Ernst Berendt observed that these three musicians – whom he had just recorded for the German Saba label at a studio in Villingen in the Black Forest, Germany – had had "the courage to be what they were born to in life – Europeans [sic]."[11] Since then, a steady, ever-enlarging stream of players and composers has put Europe – and Scandinavia – more and more firmly on the jazz map.

One thinks, for example, of Hans Koller (with whom Joe Zawinul worked in the early 1950s, and whose work, like that of Garbarek, exhibits many painterly qualities of form and texture); Swedish baritone saxophonist Lars Gullin (a lyrical, deeply poetic musician whose more overtly jazz – or swinging – compositions offer fascinating complement to those of Garbarek); German trombonist Albert Mangelsdorff (an improviser of quicksilver intelligence and conviction, whose work ranges from the completely free to the Ellington-inflected, and who was one of the first European musicians to make creative jazz use of folk sources from Asia); West Indian, British-domiciled alto saxophonist Joe Harriott (his incisive, blues-soaked abstractions not that far removed from Garbarek in spirit) and Polish multi-intrumentalist Zbigniew Namyslowski (like Gullin, a musician whose strongly folk-influenced work offers intriguing complement to that of Garbarek).[12]

Outstanding figure that Garbarek is, he is also part of the continuum of courage indicated by such names. In interview, Garbarek has often spoken of both the high quality of the musicians with whom he has been fortunate enough to have played and recorded, and the commensurate level of a great deal of other European and Scandinavian activity in jazz and improvised music. Exemplary here are such creative spirits of the past thirty and more years as the Swedes Nils Lindberg and Bernt Rosengren, Georg Riedel and Jan Johansson, Palle Danielsson and Bobo Stenson; the Finns Juhani Aaltonen and Edward Vesala, Heikki Sarmanto and Otto Donner; the Germans Alexander von Schlippenbach and Manfred Schoof, Wolfgang Dauner and Eberhard Weber; the Austrians Mathias Ruegg and Wolfgang Puschnig and the Swiss Daniel Humair, Irene Schweitzer and Pierre Favre; the Poles Krzysztof Komeda and Tomasz Stanko, Michal Urbaniak and Urszula Dudziak, and the Czechoslovakians George Mraz and Miroslav Vitous; the British Tubby Hayes and John Surman, Evan Parker and Tony Oxley, John Taylor and Norma Winstone; the Belgians René Thomas and Philip Catherine and the French Barney Wilen, Francois Jeanneau, Michel Portal and Louis Sclavis; the Italians Aldo Romano and Enrico Rava, Paolo Fresu and Furio Di Castri; the Danes Niels-Henning Ørsted Pedersen and Palle Mikkelborg, Kenneth Knudsen and Pierre Dørge; and – last, but by no means least – the Norwegians Egil "Bop" Johansen and Bjarne Nerem, Karin Krog and Arild Andersen, Svein Finnerud and Espen Rud, Terje Rypdal and Jon Christensen.[13]

Not one of these fifty-plus names is featured in Palmer's _All You Need Is Love_ – although, to be fairer than Palmer deserves, Ian Carr gets quoted at the very end of the book.[14] Neither is any one of these names mentioned in Lebrecht's _Companion To 20th Century Music_ (where no less than twelve column inches, for example, are devoted to the Beatles and the Rolling Stones). To appreciate why this should matter to anyone interested in either music or life – or both – one can do no better than turn to an article written by jazz critic David C. Hunt at the end of the 1960s: the decade that for many, like Tony Palmer, was the golden era of "progressive pop". In his 'Today's Jazz Artist: His Communication and Our Technological Age' Hunt suggests that, in a world which more and more reveals the dominance of technology – and technocratic modes of thought – today's jazz artist remains a valuable spokesman. Why? Because, says Hunt, "Philosophically, he has the beautiful capacity, through a musical instrument, to dramatize the human condition. His artistic talking, shouting, singing, moaning, and crying serve to awaken us to the artificial living patterns of our society – the slightness of understanding, the easy acceptance – all that reeks of sterility."[15]

Hunt chose one musician in particular to illustrate his point: John Coltrane (1926-67). Working his way through and beyond the complexities of post-1945 Bebop, tenor and soprano saxophonist John Coltrane recorded with some of the greatest names of modern jazz – including Sonny Rollins and Cecil Taylor, Tommy Flanagan and Art Taylor, Paul Chambers and Cannonball Adderley, Miles Davis and Bill Evans. He then developed one of the most striking bodies of contemporary music, with his classic quartet of the 1960s featuring pianist McCoy Tyner, bassist Jimmy Garrison and drummer Elvin Jones (and various appearances by Eric Dolphy). In the last years of his life, the shamanic intensity of Coltrane's search for meaning in (and through) music led him to encourage – and be encouraged by – such other avant gardists as Ornette Coleman and Marion Brown, Albert Ayler and Archie Shepp. As musicians like drummer Rashied Ali, saxophonist Pharoah Sanders and pianist Alice Coltrane came into his group, Coltrane embraced ever more intense and wide-ranging levels of polyrhythm, sound and meditation in music.

Whatever the period of his music, the work of Coltrane speaks of what Sufi philosophy would call the purity of the heart's quest for transformational, devotional rhythm and song. And that quest aroused echoes around the world. As Hunt says: "The late John Coltrane is the perfect example of a jazz artist who has achieved worldwide prominence through a deep spiritual communication. Truth in the arts demands an intense involvement in life to find aesthetic choices in line with the individual kind of depth in the artist's work. Coltrane's life took on special significance as he [...] immersed himself in the most defined depths of human activity. His resulting acts of creation became focal points of truth in the lives of other human beings."[16]

One of those human beings was – and remains – Jan Garbarek. One day in 1961, as a teenager with virtually no interest in jazz, Garbarek happened to hear Coltrane's 1959 *Countdown* played on Norwegian radio. The teenager's sense of what life might hold in store was to be changed forever. More than intrigued – mesmerised – by the sound of the music, the title of which he had not managed to catch, Garbarek hurried out to a record shop to ask, with touching naivety, for a jazz record. Returning home with a Gene Krupa recording, he quickly realised that, good as this music was, it was not the magic which had just transfixed him. Fortunately, it did not take many more enquiries to ascertain that the record which he should have bought was Coltrane's Atlantic recording **Giant Steps**. This the young Garbarek duly did: and the rest, as they say, is history.[17]

The Norway of the 1950s that Garbarek had grown up in was very different from the Norway that would develop in the 1960s. In their *History Of Norway: From The Ice Age To The Age of Petroleum*, authors Ivar Libæk and Øivind Stenersen offer an illuminating quotation from a representative Norwegian adult who, born in 1946, grew up in Sarpsborg, in the south of the country and near the Swedish border : "Even though chocolate, sugar, meat and coffee were no longer rationed in the early 1950s, there were still lots of products we couldn't find in the shops. So we squeezed ourselves into one of the neighbourhood's few private cars and headed for Strømstad in Sweden [which, unlike occupied Norway, had been neutral during World War Two]. The car belonged to an army officer who had brought it home after attending courses in the USA. We felt like royals as we swept into the backyard with the Studebaker's boot filled with tins of pineapple."

"It was easy to see who people were in the '50s. White-collar jobs still had a lot of prestige, and those who had taken their A-levels usually wore their student caps on 17th May, Constitution Day. Workers wore overalls to work and farm children smelt of cowsheds. Everyone dreamed of buying a new car, but most had to do with a moped, a motor cycle or an old used car [...] The USA was our great idol. We admired and copied Americans, never worrying about being influenced [...] We chewed American chewing gum, drank Cokes and played rock'n'roll on the jukebox."[18]

In terms of jazz, America and Sweden exerted a joint magnetism on a good many of the leading Norwegian players of the late 1940s and 1950s. In their survey *Jazz Tenor Saxophone In Norway: 1917-1959* Johs Bergh and Jan Evensmo argue that in the fifties, Norway had a handful of tenor saxophonists more or less comparable to the leading players in any other part of Europe.[19] Three of these were Bjarne Nerem (1923 – 91), Kristian Bergheim (born 1926) and Mikkel Flagstad (born 1930). If the first and last of these were at times heavily indebted to Lester Young, Bergh and Evensmo consider that Bergheim, who always resisted cool school tendencies, had the potential to become a Norwegian Sonny Stitt.[20] Whatever their stylistic persuasion, each of these players gravitated to Sweden's Stockholm in the 1950s, with Nerem (who had first played in Sweden in 1947/48) not returning to Norway until 1973. They were joined across the border for various periods by such other Norwegian luminaries of the time as trumpeter Rowland Greenberg (1920 – 94) and a marvellous drummer who was to become fully domiciled in Sweden: Egil "Bop" Johansen (born 1934). In the 1950s, Sweden – which in the late 1940s and 1950s had already played host to Bebop innovators Dizzy Gillespie and Charlie Parker – offered both affluence and a jazz scene seemingly beyond the contemporary reach of Norway.[21]

All this was to change, initially towards the end of the decade, and with increasing speed during the 1960s. While Sweden retained both its affluence and an important jazz scene, with Stockholm's Gyllene Cirkeln (Golden Circle) club assuming the legendary status that the Nalen venue, for example, had enjoyed previously, Norway – together with her jazz musicians – now joined her neighbour in experiencing to the full both the possibilities and the problems of an affluent, increasingly high-tech and youth-oriented world.

Jazz in Norway can be traced back to the dance-band craze of the 1920s. Subsequently, the music evolved to embrace the various American innovations and schools. Rowland Greenberg, for example, created a considerable reputation for himself as both an outstanding soloist and leader of various groups rooted in the swing style of the later 1930s, while multi-instrumentalist Arvid Grahm Paulsen (1922-63) became something of a Norwegian equivalent to Benny Carter. With a healthy mixture of traditional, swing and predominantly cool school post-bop elements, the period 1955-65 is generally considered to be the first "golden age" of Norwegian jazz. In 1960, there were some thirty jazz clubs in the country, and the Norwegian Jazz Federation began printing its periodical *JazzNytt* – an excellent publication which has survived and developed to this day.[22]

In that same year – not long before Garbarek, as yet completely unaware of Norwegian jazz history, heard Coltrane on the radio – television was officially introduced to the Norwegian public. During the 1960s, some 900,000 sets were bought by Norwegians. After October 1960 permits were no longer necessary in order to purchase cars, and by 1967, an election broadcast could contain the following technologistic rhetoric: "New inventions, new production methods, new raw materials open up un-thought-of possibilities for increasing our prosperity [...] We must adopt policies enabling our country to utilize these technical advances [...] Then we can meet the future with confidence and optimism."[23]

While the youth or pop culture of America continued to exert its spell, for many the material wealth of the American Dream came to seem less a promise than a prison. The assassinations of John and Robert Kennedy and Martin Luther King; the century's biggest-ever riots, in racially-torn Detroit in 1967; the massive protests against the continuation of the Vietnam War: all such factors helped turn dream into nightmare. In common with other countries in the West, Norway experienced both the alienation of (largely) affluent youth from an essentially paternalistic, materialistically and technologically oriented rhetoric (alienation epitomised by the May 1968 student riots in Paris) and a parallel expansion of the means by which such alienation might be expressed (new or increased access to higher education, records, cinema, video, multi-media arts centres, etc.). Having taken the Latin line at school, Garbarek studied at Oslo University in the late 1960s, where he took some preparatory courses in Polish, philosophy and psychology – and hoped to go on to study Arabic and Sanskrit, eventually – before the commitment to becoming a professional musician made him curtail his studies. However, Garbarek is far indeed from being a typical example of what Norwegians now call the generation of "sixty-eighters".

In interview, Garbarek has at times emphasised the indirect (and deeper) realms of the politics that might lie within music, as opposed to the simplistic, surface messages that mark much of the music of the rock groups dear to many of the aforementioned "sixty-eighters".[24] During the 1960s, the Coltrane-fired Garbarek would meet and work with such major figures of Afro-American music as George Russell and Don Cherry, as well as such exceptional, burgeoning Norwegian talents as singer Karin Krog (whose first LP was recorded in 1964) and the sometimes Zen-inspired poet Jan Erik Vold (whose debut collection _mellom speil og speil_ – [between mirror and mirror] – was published the following year, winning the prestigious Tarjei Vesaas debut prize). Garbarek thus had the chance to develop his creativity in musical contexts which were simultaneously more challenging and subtle than those explored by rock groups like the Beatles or the Rolling Stones, Jefferson Airplane or Cream, for example. These are all groups whose music Garbarek remains scarcely aware of today, just as he was largely unaware of it (and them) in the 1960s.[25]

There is, nevertheless, a good deal in Garbarek's early work which speaks strongly of the 1960s. In particular, there is much which speaks of that decade's increasingly world-oriented quest for a sense of meaning beyond that offered by the promises of either materialism or such previously separated spheres as "high" and "low" culture, East and West, "jazz" and "rock'n'roll". If Garbarek knew very little about the world of rock, guitarist Terje Rypdal certainly did, with musicians like Hank Marvin and Jimi Hendrix crucial to his early concepts of sound, phrasing and form. When Garbarek and Rypdal got together in the late 1960s, with bassist Arild Andersen and Jon Christensen, they were able to create music which moved organically between worlds of jazz and rock, structure and improvisation, dense sound textures and lucid linear development. This is evident throughout their two well-known albums, the 1969 **The Esoteric Circle** and the 1970 **Afric Pepperbird**, as well as in a good deal of the (internationally) less heard but equally fine 1969 **Briskeby Blues** and 1970 **Hav** (Ocean) which they recorded with Jan Erik Vold for Norwegian Philips in Oslo (with Bobo Stenson also present, on electric piano, on **Hav**).

Such genre-crossing (and redefining) activity is no less evident in the work which these four musicians created with George Russell in the late 1960s and early 1970s, as documented, for example, in the high-energy **Trip To Prillarguri** which was recorded by the George Russell Sextet (with Stanton Davis on trumpet) "live" in Sweden in March 1970. And it is just as much present in one of the most unusual albums to which Garbarek, Rypdal, Andersen and Christensen can ever have contributed: the 1969-71 **Popofoni** double album. Like Russell's 1969 version of his *Electronic Sonata For Souls Loved by Nature* this was recorded at the Henie-Onstad multi-media arts centre at Høvikodden, which had opened in August 1968.[26] Garbarek and his colleagues are joined by Karin Krog and Bobo Stenson, as they collectively interpret works by the contemporary Norwegian composers Arne Nordheim and Alfred Janson, Gunnar Sønstevold (once a jazz pianist in Norway's legendary Funny Boys quintet of the 1930s) and Kåre Kolberg, and Rypdal himself. These are works in which the exploratory, cross-cultural, cross-genre spirit of the 1960s receives some of its most potent and provocative documentation, as political as it is poetic in import.

Jan Garbarek was born in Mysen, some miles east of Oslo, Norway's capital city, on the fourth of March 1947. His Polish father, Czeslaw Garbarek, had been deported by the Nazis to Norway in the Second World War, where he was part of the forced labour which the Nazis exploited on the infamous 'Blood Road' in the north of the country. After the end of the war, during his slow, stop-and-start journey south to liberation, Czeslaw met a Norwegian girl, from a farming background, in the Trøndelag area in the Western lower middle part of the country (the administrative centre of which is the city of Trondheim, with its pictureque wooden houses, lively culture and splendid Nidaros Cathedral). The couple married, thought of returning to Poland, but decided to stay in Norway. Here they lived for a short while in Mysen, in a camp for displaced persons after the war, before moving to Oslo.

Initially, the family lived in a student home in Bjørn Farmannsgate in the centre of the city. When Garbarek (an only child) was six the family moved to Årvoll, an Eastern suburb of the city. Here Garbarek lived until he was twenty one, when he married his childhood sweetheart, Vigdis, and moved to Gamlebyen, the old city centre. A couple of years or so later, the (young) Garbareks moved east again, a little beyond Årvoll to a block of flats at Romsås – a typical 1960s medium-rise development on the edge of Lillomarka, a beautiful, rugged area of thickly forested hills and lakes. Here Jan, Vigdis and daughter Anja remained until the early-to-mid-1980s, when the family moved back to Oslo, this time to the western side of the city, not far from one of the city's major tourist attractions, the Gustav Vigeland park. Today, Anja – who is carving out a singing career in progressive pop music – is married to an Englishman and lives in London, while her father and mother divide their time between their place in Oslo and a home in the mountains, some four to five hours drive north-east of Oslo, beyond the Winter Olympics town of Lillehammer.

The meeting of different cultures; the impulse of both city and countryside, and the transmutation of suffering into joy: such key features of the mature Garbarek's work were thus woven into his life long before he ever picked up a saxophone. Neither of Garbarek's immediate family had any special interest in music – there was no musical instrument at home – and he had no early introduction to music at school. In interviews, Garbarek has always pointed out how, as a youngster, he must have heard – and liked – some of the usual pop things on the radio, whether Louis Prima or Elvis Presley, for example. Curiously, it was not until he was nearly fifty that he recalled (to Norwegian writer Roald Helgheim) the excitement which he had felt as a child at the sound of the horns and drums of the street parades which take place in Norway every first and seventeenth of May (the latter date being the anniversary of Norway's attainment of independence from neighbouring Sweden in 1905). A good deal of such excitment might be inferred from the pageant-like, pipe and drum atmosphere of the stirring *2nd Piece*, from Garbarek's 1986 solo album **All Those Born With Wings**.[27]

In every respect, it would seem that, before he heard Coltrane, Garbarek was a boy with the normal interests and ambitions in life: he has said that he might have just taken off his ice-skates before happening, quite by chance, to hear *Countdown* on Norway's *Jazz Half-Hour* radio programme that fateful day in 1961.[28] In <u>Stone Fences</u>, a finely worked collection of lyric reflections about the transition from childhood to adolescence in the Norway of the 1950s, Norwegian poet Paal-Helge Haugen (who was born two years before Garbarek and who supplies one of the texts on the 1969/71 **Popofoni** album) writes of the distant worlds that the "glowing dial – green Magic Eye" of the radio at that time could tune into dream-like proximity: "sound from unknown places/dance music from a hotel flooded with light/metallic voices addressing the masses/weepy Hawaiian guitars on a white beach/a melancholy forest of violins/and one blue saxophone".[29]

The impact of that "one blue saxophone" on Garbarek was such that, abandoning earlier dreams he had had of learning the drums, he began to beg his parents for a saxophone. After some months, his pleas proved successful. Having already taught himself various fingering positions on the tenor, Garbarek took himself and his newly acquired instrument to the Music Conservatory in Oslo for some instruction. However, the half an hour a week which he put in, cycling down to town with his precious instrument on his back, was to prove less than inspiring, and he quit after two terms. He did not bother to look for another teacher, but concentrated instead on listening to his **Giant Steps** record morning, noon and night. He also began to play with other young, would-be musicians.

One of the most important of these early fellow-enthusiasts was the pianist Morten Lassem. He and Garbarek had grown up together in Årvoll, playing football and the like. Lassem, who was from a musical home, had taken his piano playing more and more seriously, and he and Garbarek now began to play music together in earnest. At the same time, they began to search out the jazz scene in Oslo. Around the end of 1961 or beginning of 1962, they discovered Gamlebyen Jazz Club, in the basement of one of the buildings of Gamlebyen school, a little east of what is now the centre of Oslo. Garbarek recalls it as being "down in a narrow basement, with red lights, fishing nets in the roof, and so on."[30] Striking as such atmospheric details of the time were to the two impressionable youngsters, it was the presence of pianist Arild Wikstrøm at the club which was to have the more lasting impact: not just on them, but on many a searching young musician of the time, such as Jon Christensen – who first came into contact with Garbarek at Gamlebyen.

Wikstrøm (1941-87) has become something of a legend in Norwegian jazz. Always a central figure at the Gamlebyen club, where he performed with such notable, emerging modernists as trombonist Frode Thingnæs (born 1940) and tenorists Bjørn Johansen (born 1940) and Knut Riisnæs (born 1945), he would also make a strong contribution to the atmosphere which was later to develop at Club 7. (Opening in 1963, and operating in a variety of venues over the years, this club became famous in the 1960s and 1970s for the extent to which it profiled contemporary developments across the arts.) A man blessed with an open mind – Jon Christensen remembers Wikstrøm deep in conversation with Cecil Taylor when the avant-garde pianist visited Oslo in the early 1960s – Wikstrøm focused very much on a modally-inclined interdependence of rhythm and melody as the ground of musical expression, rather than the challenges of Bebop chord changes, for example. In the school dances of the time, the funkiness of hard bop material like *Moanin'* and *Blues March* was proving especially popular, and apart from his contemporary jazz inclinations, the percussively-oriented (and Coltrane-inspired) Wikstrøm was always interested in rhythm 'n' blues and soul material.[31]

Early on, Garbarek and Christensen sensed a strong musical affinity. They began to build on their mutual desire to develop expressive possibilities from the (often modal) music which Coltrane was recording at the time, rather than from the harmonic complexities evident earlier in Bebop. Fuelled by the odd hot dog or Coca-Cola, their Friday evenings at Gamlebyen soon took on initiatory, rite-of-passage proportions.

The saxophonist and drummer have both spoken of the Wikstrøm of the early and mid-1960s as somewhat of a guru for young musicians such as themselves, and of something almost like a jazz "clan" or "school" developing around the pianist. And, according to Norwegian jazz writer Tor Dybo, it was with the Arild Wikstrøm group, one evening at Gamlebyen, that Garbarek's debut as a paid musician took place.[32] As Garbarek has recalled, the debut occurred in the most remarkable of circumstances: "I was ill the first time I played with Wikstrøm. I had a very high fever, flu I guess. I was in bed, hadn't been to school. It was Friday evening and there was to be a session at Gamlebyen. Then at 7.00 the phone rang. The call was from the club: they asked if I could play with Wikstrøm because Bjørn Johansen [the regular tenorist] had been taken ill. This was a big thing, you know – so big I could hardly take it in. My mother must have seen some sort of crazy light in my eyes, because she let me go, and paid for the taxi so I could get down there and play. It was a tremendous experience, of course. I can't remember if it was fifteen or twenty five kroner I got paid that night ..."[33]

The other great initiatory or transformational experience of Garbarek's earliest jazz years took place in 1962, when the quartet which he led won the non-traditional section of the Norwegian Amateur Jazz Championship which took place that year in the Sentrum cinema in Oslo. The championship had been held every year since 1954: and in 1960 pianist Finn Melbye's winning quintet had included drummer Jon Christensen – soon to play a major role in the development of both Norwegian jazz in general, and the music of Jan Garbarek in particular. However, the drummer in the quartet that won the championship in 1962 was Torgrim Sollid, who, together with bassist Hans Marius Stormoen, joined Morten Lassem and Garbarek in playing the winning programme of mostly Coltrane-inspired originals, plus one number by Wikstrøm.[34]

Not only did the quartet (which had got together specially for the occasion) win the championship: Garbarek won first prize as soloist. Underneath a photograph of the jubilant fourteen-year old being hosted aloft, one of the Oslo papers ran a prescient review. One Septim declared that "Jan Garbarek plays tenor saxophone in a robust style and has the potential to be a soloist of distinction. His own composition 'Trouble For Hans' was clearly influenced by Bossa Nova, which suited an authoritative tenor saxophonist with a full and passionate sound." [35]

That sound quickly came to the attention of some of Oslo's leading names in the contemporary jazz world. The singer Karin Krog met Garbarek at Gamlebyen, liked both him and his sound and began to feature him in her groups, with Jon Christensen often on drums. The young Garbarek could not have come into contact with a better musician.

One of the most musical and wide-ranging singers of the past decades, Karin Krog (born 1937) has always had what the jazz world calls "big ears." Her elective affinities include Billie Holiday and Peggy Lee, Sarah Vaughan and Anita O'Day, Betty Carter and Betty Roche, Ray Charles and Nat King Cole. She has always been inspired by instrumentalists, from Lester Young and Dexter Gordon (with whom she recorded a fine LP in 1970) to Don Byas and Don Ellis, Stan Getz, Ben Webster and Illinois Jacquet. Above all, she has said, it was Coltrane who inspired her to see the potentiality of music in a fresh light – a light confirmed by pianist Cecil Taylor when he visited the Metropol Jazz House in Oslo in the late autumn of 1962, with Jimmy

Lyons and Sunny Murray. When Krog asked him what, if he were a singer, he would sing today, Taylor said: "I would sing sounds."[36]

A year later, Krog sang on the first LP ever recorded of Norwegian jazz. Long a collector's item, **Metropol Jazz** took its name from the Metropol Jazz House which had opened at Akersgata 8 (just two minutes from the Stortinget, or Parliament, in central Oslo) in Autumn 1959 – and which, until its demise in the summer of 1965, provided the most important venue for a mixture of avant-garde, traditional and modern mainstream jazz in Norway (with the latter two genres also receiving important and related exposure at the Big Chief Club, across town in Majorstua). Between 1961 and 1965, playing visitors to the Metropol included J. C. Higginbotham, the Dutch Swing College Band, Rowland Greenberg, Bjørn Johansen, Bengt Hallberg, Stuff Smith, Coleman Hawkins, Ben Webster, Bud Powell, Leo Wright, Kenny Dorham, Idrees and Jamila Sulieman, Mark Murphy, Don Byas, Johnny Griffin, Art Taylor, Kenny Drew, Dexter Gordon, Bernt Rosengren, Dollar Brand (as Abdullah Ibrahim was then known), Ted Curson, Don Ellis, Cecil Taylor – and Jan Garbarek. In an interview of 1987, Garbarek would recall how, at a time when he was too young to be allowed to enter the club, he had once stood pressed outside Metropol in order to catch at least a faint hint of the tenor power of the visiting Dexter Gordon.[37]

Along with Ole Jacob Hanssen, Jon Christensen was house drummer at Metropol. Today, whether using sticks, brushes or his bare hands, Christensen – who has appeared on innumerable ECM albums – is rightly regarded as one of the most sensitive and creative drummers, or "shaper of sounds", in contemporary jazz. I cannot remember a single live performance by this musician where I have not marvelled at his ability to combine a polyrhythmic, crisply articulated yet bar-slipping groove with a poetic, shape-shifting variety of energising, diversely weighted dynamics and pulse. Unique as it is, such a distinctive drum conception had to begin somewhere.

Together with bassist Per Løberg (born 1942), the self-taught Christensen (born 1943) began playing in rock'n'roll and skiffle bands in the fifties, graduating to swing and bop material and playing with alto saxophonist and drummer Gunnar Brostigen's big band (which featured emerging modernists such as Frode Thingnæs and Bjørn Johansen) towards the end of the decade.[38] Christensen remembers the early to mid-1960s – years which included his first trip abroad, when the Karin Krog Quartet, also featuring Per Løberg and the very fine, Bill Evans-ish pianist Egil Kapstad, made a successful appearance at the 1964 Antibes Jazz Festival – as a challenging, yet immensely rewarding period of initiation and apprenticeship: "At this time there was a sort of circuit in Scandinavia, with the Jazzhus Montmartre in Copenhagen, Gulleyne Cirkeln in Stockholm and the Metropol in Oslo. So the visiting American stars would work this circuit, playing with the local rhythm sections: Alex Riel and Niels-Henning [Ørsted Pedersen] in Copenhagen, Leif Wennerström or Rune Carlsson, Roman Dylag or Torbjörn Hultcrantz in Stockholm, Ole Jacob Hanssen or myself and either Erik Amundsen, Bjørn Pedersen or Per Løberg on bass here. The club – which was also a restaurant – was very nice, with maybe two hundred people if full, and three sets a night. All kinds of people came there, from all sorts of backgrounds – and there were many jam sessions. For me, it was a kind of constant learning process."

"On my first gig, with Bud Powell in '62, for example, I went out a week before and bought every Bud Powell record I could find, listening to the arrangements again and again, hearing how Max Roach might change from brushes to sticks here, and sticks to brushes there. I just absorbed the dynamics of the whole thing. I'd heard stories about how difficult Bud could be, but the gig seemed to go OK. And then there were guys like Dexter [Gordon] – who was so kind to me, so supportive, always encouraging me to become more myself."[39]

Recorded in November 1963 – the month that the classic John Coltrane Quartet made its one and only appearance in Norway, at Oslo's Njärdhallen sports hall in the western suburbs of the city, and an event that left its mark on both Garbarek and Christensen – the **Metropol Jazz** recording documents a swing/mainstream/modern orientation among its participants.[40] Sixteen-year old Garbarek is not present as, together with Egil Kapstad, Erik Amundsen and Jon Christensen, Karin Krog offers a nicely sprung, Coltrane-inflected version of *My Favourite Things*. Elegant, clean-lined piano from Kapstad and some fine brushwork from Christensen underpin Karin's modal tribute to such diverse personal favourites of the singer as Cecil Taylor and Don Ellis, Steve Swallow and Gene Ammons, Dexter Gordon and Charlie Parker, Charles Mingus and Eric Dolphy and – of course – the members of that classic Coltrane Quartet: Coltrane himself, McCoy Tyner, Jimmy Garrison and Elvin Jones. A good deal of the track features Karin's widely conceived vocalese: at times contemplative in an almost Asian manner, at times classic, post-Betty Carter scat, and finally playing abstractly with the pure concrete potentiality of vowels, the performance suggests how closely she had paid attention to Cecil Taylor's words a year earlier.[41]

Although Garbarek is not present on this version of *My Favourite Things*, Karin Krog and he were to feature the tune – which became one of their several Coltrane numbers – during the time they played together. It is unfortunate that Garbarek was not to record commercially with Krog until November 1966, when he contributed to two numbers – *All Of You* and *Dearly Beloved* – on the singer's second solo LP **Jazz Moments**. (Recorded shortly after her appearance with Garbarek at the Warsaw Jazz Festival in October, this recording features the excellent rhythm section of Kenny Drew, Niels-Henning Ørsted Pedersen and Jon Christensen.) Unfortunate because, striking as Garbarek's work on **Jazz Moments** is, with some soon-to-be characteristic melodic distillation and meditative "drifting" within his solos, a touch reminiscent of Sonny Rollins on the *Beloved* cut, it does not indicate anything like the full range of either tone or rhythmic expression which he explored during the early years that he spent with Krog.[42]

For this, one must turn to the various radio and T.V. concert broadcasts which Krog and he made with Jon Christensen and others between March 1965 and July 1968. Fortunately, these can be enjoyed, with good sound, at the Norwegian Jazz Archives in Oslo. And to understand how a young Norwegian could embrace and develop such a range of expression, which we shall shortly consider in a little detail, one must appreciate the extent to which Garbarek simply drank and drank in a variety of influences at the time, largely American, but also Scandinavian, and both live and on record.

One of the highlights of Garbarek's recorded oeuvre is *Molde Canticle*, a five-part work specially commissioned for the Molde Jazz Festival of July 1990 and recorded on ECM in August of the same year. Over the years, the festival at Molde – which began in 1961 and has long been one of the finest festivals in the world – has meant a great deal to Garbarek. It was at Molde, for example, that he first came into contact with George Russell, in 1965; and it was at Molde, in 1968, that he and Christensen first heard a reading by the Norwegian poet Jan Erik Vold.This was to lead to three excellent L P recordings and one single together, as well as some extremely popular tours in Norway (sometimes taking in schools) and the USSR.[43]

In an interview with Norwegian jazz writer and photographer Terje Mosnes, published in Mosnes' 1980 _Jazz I Molde: Festivaler Gjennom 20 År_ , the saxophonist recalled the excitement of his first trip to the festival, undertaken by train, bus and ferry in 1962. From the musical point of view, the chief excitement for Garbarek that year was supplied by Swedish tenorist Bernt Rosengren, who appeared at the festival in a quartet with Kjell Karlsen (piano), Erik Amundsen (bass) and Ole Jacob Hansen (drums). As Garbarek recollected: "What I remember most of all from that year at Molde was Bernt Rosengren. I'd begun to play saxophone because I'd heard Coltrane, and Bernt Rosengren was almost Coltrane. An outstanding saxophonist."[44]

Born the same year as Karin Krog (1937) Rosengren had been a member of the Newport International Youth Band in 1958. His big, strong sound, very much out of the post-war approach of such a Chicago tenor school player as Gene Ammons, was a feature of the influential Swedish quintet Jazz Club-57, the first band in Sweden to embrace American hard bop in the late 1950s. **Bombastica! 1959-60** – a recent CD reissue headlined by Rosengren and pianist Lasse Werner (1934-92) – gives a good picture of Rosengren's meaty sound and solid phrasing. Now and then, these take on a touch or two of Coltrane's flinty purposiveness and harmonic colouring, as in the second, up-tempo take of the title track (an Afro-Cuban 16 bar piece dedicated to Dizzy Gillespie and distinguished by some minor seventh/flatted fifth elements typical of the dedicatee).[45]

As 'Bernta Rosengrena' the tenorist would soon feature in the opening screen credits to Roman Polanski's 1962 _Knife in the Water_, a film which brought pianist and composer Krzysztof Komeda's music and Rosengren's huge yet reflective sound to an international audience. Rosengren's playing here has long been some of Garbarek's favourite from the Swede. Certainly, few film openings can have integrated so successfully the images of an implicit narrative with soulful jazz saxophone: Rosengren's interpretation of Komeda's lovely _Ballad for Bernt_ flows beautifully through the somewhat Bergmanesque opening sequence, as a tense couple drive along a quiet road at dawn, the morning sunshine playing upon the passing reflections of tree and sky in car windscreen.[46]

Later, Rosengren's 1965 **Stockholm Dues** (which included a tribute to Don Cherry, soon to exert a particularly fruitful influence on Garbarek) was to find a special place in Garbarek's record collection, and it would not be long before the two saxophonists were working together in the George Russell Big Band in Stockholm. The impact of Rosengren upon Garbarek at this time was surpassed only by the enormous impression which seeing Coltrane in Oslo in 1963 made upon him, and matched only by the experience of witnessing Dexter Gordon and Sonny Stitt jamming at Molde earlier that year, in a quintet driven by Jon Christensen.[47] Other key Molde moments for the neophyte saxophonist included Benny Golson's rendering of his *I Remember Clifford* in 1964 and meeting Booker Ervin, who was very helpful to Garbarek in a conversation about reeds and mouthpieces, in 1965. This was a year that saw both Dexter Gordon and Lars Gullin appear at the festival, as well as the Kenny Drew Trio (with Niels-Henning Ørsted Pederen and Alex Riel). Garbarek only heard Gullin the once, but the impact of the Swede's ballad playing, in particular, has stayed with him all his life.

It was in this richly programmed year that what must be seen as the single most important event in the early development of both Garbarek and Christensen took place. For this was the year when George Russell sat in with Garbarek's group at a jam session late one evening at the Alexandra Hotel in Molde, and immediately raised the energy level of the music several notches or more. This, combined with the two Norwegians being able to hear the way in which Russell's own sextet could create, not just steaming passages of multi-layered, swinging excitement, but also the rubato tone-poem moods of a piece like *A Lonely Place*, really opened up their ears.[48]

It is this quality of openness which so distinguishes the work which Garbarek and Christensen were to create, not only with Karin Krog over the next three years or so, but also – at practically the same time – with George Russell himself, before eventually coming to form the quartet with guitarist Terje Rypdal and bassist Arild Andersen which would record **The Esoteric Circle** and **Afric Pepperbird**. Essential as the generative impact of Coltrane upon Garbarek had been, and would always be, throughout the latter half of the 1960s the saxophonist's openness of mind and questing musical imagination continued to be stimulated by a variety of other players.

Apart from classic modal albums like the 1959 **Kind of Blue**, Garbarek was particularly struck by the sense of space and quartet interplay in such Miles Davis albums as the 1964 **My Funny Valentine** concert with George Coleman, Herbie Hancock, Ron Carter and Tony Williams (later, he would admire the late-1960s **Bitches Brew** session, and in particular, the organisation of all its elements). If Albert Ayler, Archie Shepp and Pharoah Sanders were the avant-garde players who, along with Coltrane, most affected Garbarek's developing concept of the variable, "gliding" qualities conceivable within the increasingly dramatic dynamics of saxophone sound at this time, he also came to admire (and play) a good many Ornette Coleman compositions, while also absorbing the oblique and characterful logic of many of Wayne Shorter's 1960s Blue Note albums.[49]

At the same time, Garbarek listened hard to the work of such earlier saxophonists as Coleman Hawkins, Ben Webster and Chu Berry, Illinois Jacquet, Earl Bostic and Johnny Hodges, featuring compositions like *Daydream* and *Lush Life* in concert programmes of the time. Early on, his lyrical sensibilities were especially touched by Bill Evans, to whom he would eventually dedicate a valedictory piece, played in duet with guitarist Bill Frisell, on the 1981 **Paths, Prints**.[50] And one night in 1966 in Stockholm, after a concert he had played with George Russell, Garbarek happened to hear Keith Jarrett live. He felt an immediate empathy with the pianist's lyricism, and it became a kind of ambition of the young Norwegian to play one day with the pianist (which he was to do, so memorably, in the mid-to-late 1970s). Another pianist whose lyrical sensibility and sense of space also came to mean a good deal to Garbarek was Paul Bley.

As for Christensen: he continued to listen to such initial favourites as Gene Krupa and Buddy Rich, Art Blakey, Max Roach and Philly Joe Jones, Elvin Jones and Tony Williams, while also beginning to dig back into the richness of the legacy left by such earlier masters as Sonny Greer, Baby Dodds and Jo Jones. Christensen has never been impressed by advances of drum technique in themselves, always listening for the poetry – the magic – of a drummer, from whatever era in the history of the music. Throughout the later 1960s, he would listen with much interest to a good deal of the magic in the "New Wave" drumming from both America and Europe, exemplified by such names as Sunny Murray and Don Moye, Andrew Cyrille and Jack DeJohnette, Stu Martin and Gunther "Baby" Sommer, and acquire albums by the Sun Ra Arkestra.

Christensen remembers that, in the mid-1960s, Johs Bergh – husband of Karin Krog at the time, and an important and highly respected figure in Norwegian jazz circles to this day – would invite Garbarek and himself over to their house now and then, in order to help widen their knowledge of jazz history through an enjoyable – and stimulating – variety of 'blindfold tests'. Bergh himself remembers how keen Garbarek was to expand his knowledge, especially of pre-Bebop players: "I made a tape for Jan – I think he might have asked if I could do this for him – of all the greats: Hawkins, Chu Berry, Ben Webster, Lester, Herschel Evans, Hodges, Don Byas and so on. He listened *very* carefully to all those guys."[51]

By this time, the Karin Krog Quintet featured Karin herself, Jan Garbarek (tenor saxophone), Terje Bjørklund (piano), Per Løberg (bass) and Jon Christensen (drums). Pianist Terje Bjørklund (born 1945) had moved from his native Narvik in the north of Norway to study music at the University of Oslo in the early-to-mid-1960s. Compared to the harmonic refinement of Egil Kapstad, Bjørklund brought a more propulsively sprung rhythmic quality to the music, part out of Wynton Kelly, part out of McCoy Tyner, together with something of the more "open" harmonic feeling which pianists like Tyner and Herbie Hancock were currently developing in their music.[52] However, on the various radio broadcasts and concert recordings of the Karin Krog Quintet which have survived from the mid-1960s, there is no hint of pushing avant-garde principles at the expense of other, older qualities of feelings and form: on the contrary.

In a fascinating Oslo radio broadcast from Spring 1965, the group – announced as "the Terje Bjørklund quartet, with Karin Krog" – play a programme of *In a Mellotone*, *Corcovado*, *Miles' Mode*, *Baby Won't You Please Come Home* and *Señor Blues*. Garbarek is absent on *Baby* but elsewhere reveals a sensitively selected variety of tone and phrasing. Digging into the meat'n'gravy of hard bop over the strong ostinato pulse of Horace Silver's *Señor Blues*, he sips selectively from the mainstream – with some pleasing moments of double time – on *Mellotone* and floats some Latin warmth out into the Oslo spring night on *Corcovado*. Only on *Miles' Mode* do his Coltranish inclinations become (appropriately) apparent, the sound and phrasing more compressed and intensely projected than elsewhere. The historical awareness, variously conceived qualities of phrasing and range of saxophone sound on this date are remarkable, coming as they do from a teenager who had only picked up a saxophone for the first time some three or four years previously.[53]

Later in the year – a year which saw the Metropol Jazz House close, as jazz clubs all over Norway suffered from the rise in popularity of post-Elvis and Beatles-type pop – the same group, but now billed as the Karin Krog Quintet, played at the first Kongsberg Jazz Festival. The repertoire featured *Baby* and *Señor Blues* again, but also *My Favourite Things*, *Out Of This World* and *Mr. P.C.* (named by Coltrane after bassist Paul Chambers, and recorded in 1959 on the **Giant Steps** album). On these three latter and very Coltrane-oriented numbers, a modal and somewhat ritualistic feeling is evident: the inclusion of Ornette Coleman's *Lonely Woman* in the programme served to underline the (meditatively) avant-garde nature of a good deal of the set.[54]

Following the crisis of the jazz club scene in Norway in 1965 – and the example of the musician-run Emanon association in Sweden – the Norwegian Jazz Forum was established, on the initiative of Karin Krog, Johs Bergh and others, with the aim of promoting and caring for the music in as professional a way as possible. (Karin Krog was the Forum's first Chair; the final incumbent, when the Forum came to an end in 1970, was Vigdis Garbarek.) One of the most interesting of the venues which the Forum used initially was the auditorium in the Munch Museum which had opened in 1963 to house all the many works which the painter Edvard Munch (1863-1944) had left to the City of Oslo. Situated in the district of Tøyen, some ten to fifteen minutes walk north-east of the city centre, the venue was immediately successful. Later, the Forum would promote concerts with equal success at the Henie-Onstad Art Centre at Høvikodden, some kilometres to the west of Oslo.

In May 1965 the Jan Garbarek Quartet (with Bjørklund and Christensen joined by bassist Sture Jansson) opened their programme at the Munch Museum with Coltrane's *Naima* (again, from **Giant Steps**) and concluded the well-received proceedings with *Mr. P.C.* In the autumn of that year the NJF arranged further concerts at the museum, together with two weeks of no less than twenty jazz concerts for schools in the Oslo area. In March 1966 the Karin Krog Quintet (with Per Løberg back on bass) played the Munch Museum again, with a programme which included *Señor Blues* once more, but also the Miles Davis modal classic *All Blues* and Carla Bley's characterful *Sing Me Softly Of The Blues* (which Karin would record ten years later with Archie Shepp). The radio broadcast of the concert reveals Krog to be in great form on all three tracks, as are Garbarek and Christensen. Just as the saxophonist shows a sure sense of pitch and a well-modulated richness of tone and rhythmic conception in his thoughtfully cast lines, so does Christensen evince the fast-growing conviction of his bar-slipping, crisply articulated and melodic/textural concept of rhythm.

The mid-1960s was the period when Krog, Christensen and Garbarek all made their initial international breakthroughs. Following her success at Antibes in 1964, Krog was invited to perform at Prague and Warsaw in 1966, which she did in the company of Swedish bassist Kurt Lindgren – and nineteen-year old Jan Garbarek. The initiative and invitation for the trip East came from Polish pianist and composer Krzysztof Komeda, who had heard the Karin Krog Quintet at the 1965 Kongsberg Festival (where Komeda had appeared in a quartet with Tomasz Stanko). Again, surviving radio broadcasts give a fascinating glimpse of the historical breadth of sensibility which informed Garbarek's burgeoning talent at the time.

The programme at the Warsaw Jazz Festival, for example, embraced Juan Tizol's *Caravan*, as well as the standard *Dearly Beloved* and Davis's *All Blues*. On the last-named, the medium-reflective tempo is perfect, with Garbarek inclining a touch more towards Shepp than Coltrane in his sound, while on *Beloved*, he features a brief, repeated introductory descending figure reminiscent of that with which Charlie Parker began his lovely October 1947 quintet recording (with Miles Davis and Duke Jordan) of *Bird of Paradise*. Garbarek then phrases both obbligati and solo with a combination of thematic directness and pithy paraphrase reminiscent of Rollins. *Caravan* is particularly striking, opening with what sounds like Garbarek blowing eerily through his mouthpiece alone, over Lindgren's arco bass. After Krog's subsequent atmospheric invocations, Garbarek drifts across Lindgren's strong ostinato figures before fashioning the sort of riff-sparked, ascensional – yet sensual – solo that would later distinguish such a track as the 1973 *Hasta Siempre*, from the first Jan Garbarek/Bobo Stenson quartet release on ECM. [55]

During the Warsaw festival, Garbarek recorded for the first time. With Kurt Lindgren, he offered a "live" duo reading of *Walkin'*, the hard bop blues that Miles Davis had recorded so memorably – and extensively – in April 1954 with Lucky Thompson and J. J. Johnson, and a rhythm section of Horace Silver, Percy Heath and Kenny Clarke.[56] Lindgren had been one of the two bassists (Björn Alke, another fine Swedish player, being the other) on Lars Gullin's beautiful **Portrait Of My Pals** recording of June 1964. Together, Garbarek and he explore the theme and improvisation of *Walkin'* over some eight minutes, the placing of the hard-grained and somewhat dry, overtly measured saxophone phrases across the strong, if slightly stiff pizzicato beat generating no little tension, with the traditional, earth-rooted feeling of the blues altered at times by judicious moments of abstracted, Dolphy-like chromatic dis-placement from Garbarek.[57]

In retrospect, the brief, freely cast coda, with its powerful drone-like figures in arco bass, is especially interesting, hinting at what was to come shortly in such a key early composition as the 1967 *Til Vigdis* – as well as in the extensive, freely conceived rubato passages of the live *Mr. J.C.* from the same year. And, chance as it may have been, the fact that Garbarek's first recording should have featured bass so prominently is no less interesting, given the later recorded fruits of his collaborations with Arild Andersen and Palle Danielsson, Gary Peacock and Charlie Haden, Niels-Henning Ørsted Pedersen and Miroslav Vitous, and – in particular – Eberhard Weber.

While Krog and Garbarek were busy in Eastern Europe, Jon Christensen had been building up his musical experience with George Russell in Sweden, Denmark and Norway. In the latter half of 1965, Russell had asked both Norwegian instrumentalists to join him in Stockholm, but, Garbarek being still at school, only Christensen had been able to take up the offer. Norwegian newspapers of the time rightly made much of the story, as the young drummer was thrown into the deep end of Russell's unique world of avant-garde exploration and down-home roots; the full-blooded affirmation of swing and bop and the rubato reflections of an exceptionally acute, searching mind; vertical, beautifully structured yet also freed-up harmonic and polyrhythmic density, and linear, melodically arresting airiness. Christensen responded to the challenge with alacrity, absorbing the drum arrangements of such Russell classics as *Ezz-thetic*, *All About Rosie*, *Stratusphunk* and *Waltz From Outer Space* before going on to create the richly diversified parts for such extended works of the late-1960s as *Now And Then*, the *Othello Ballet Suite* and *Electronic Sonata For Souls Loved by Nature*.

Jazz enthusiasts sometimes like to fantasize about where, in the jazz history they have not experienced at first hand, they would like to have been present. Hearing Armstrong or Morton in the late 1920s,

Coleman Hawkins around the mid-1930s, Billie Holiday and Lester Young in the late 1930s, Ellington in the early 1940s, Parker towards the end of that decade, Davis, Adderley and Coltrane in 1959, Ornette Coleman and Don Cherry in 1960, or Sonny Rollins and Sun Ra, Oscar Peterson and Bill Evans in the mid-1960s all have a strong place in my own fantasy league. However, top spot – or thereabouts – has to go to the period that George Russell spent in Scandinavia from late-1964 to 1969. For the music that Russell created then has practically everything about jazz (and music in general) that I love.

I find it hard to think of any other instrumentalist or composer this century whose work manifests such a combination of the logical and the ostensibly "irruptive", the joys of swing and the rewards of a penetrating, deeply thought through sense of structure – as well as a sheer abundance of physical and emotional, intellectual and spiritual energy – to the extent that the music of George Russell does. Russell (born 1923) once offered the following Zen-like advice: "Follow your essence and don't let anything or anybody talk you out of it. You'll embark on a trip where you'll come into contact with *it*, and it will take over."[58] Following his own advice led Russell, at one time (in the early 1940s) the drummer with the Dizzy Gillespie Band, to create *The Lydian Chromatic Concept Of Tonal Organisation*. This is the theoretical treatise on the relations between "inner" (tonally grounded) and "outer" (related, yet melodically and chromatically freer) frameworks for creative improvisation which, legend has it, the young Garbarek absorbed in a night.[59]

In a fine essay on Russell, written to accompany the 1967 premiere recording of *Othello Ballet Suite*, the Norwegian writer (and later, Green activist) Sigmund Kvaløy observed that Russell had become "a sensitive registrator of his own times – a world that has been brought together communicationally, and is becoming one tremendous crossroads of cultural clash and harmonization – of agony and enrichment."[60] For Kvaløy, the musician who had absorbed the implications of Russell's ideas (which are never prescriptive, rather enabling in nature) was the kind of person who had "the ability to transcend local bondages and bounds – without 'losing style' – one who can tear off the blinkers of time and place, but who – at the same time – can take note of 'local tonal gravity', and see what kind of local action the 'outer view' implies – one who has integrated the freedom and the desire to choose consciously and vary his position of view, to shift between the magnifying glass and the telescope."[61]

The musician who has absorbed Russell's ideas can be both "inside" and "outside" the harmonic (and rhythmic) framework of any given piece of music, using a scalar-based sensitivity to enlarge and intensify the possibilities open to the creative improviser. The same point applies to history. For all its exploratory, on-the-edge brilliance, a brilliance which can take his pieces both intellectually and sonically into the world of contemporary "art" music, Russell's music (which, incidentally, is often leavened by a rich sense of humour) is deeply rooted in the values of the past, particularly those of gospel and blues. Long before intellectuals thought up the term Post-modernism, Russell was mixing notions of historical epoch and the flow of deep time, structure and (ostensible) chaos, the serious and the humorous, symmetry and asymmetry, creating a vibrant new musical alchemy of individual and group, the intimate and the immense, the political and the poetic.[62]

One of Christensen's special memories of his early days with Russell is of a December 1965 concert in Copenhagen, arranged by Danish Radio at the Tivoli Concert Hall, and featuring the music of Russell and Stockhausen – both of whom were present at the event.[63] There were also important concerts at Stockholm's Golden Circle, tours to various schools and two special concerts arranged by the Norwegian Ny Musikk [New Music] association at the Aula Hall at the University of Oslo, one in March 1966 and the other in August 1967. By the time of the second of these concerts, which was organised in co-operation with NRK, the Norwegian Broadcasting Authority – and some of which is preserved on video at the Norwegian Jazz Archives – Garbarek had not only joined Christensen, but also begun to play a major role in both Russell's small group and big band. Sitting next to his earlier idol Bernt Rosengren in the sax section at the 1967 concert, he is in commanding form in either section or solo role (or both) on such numbers as *Ezz-thetic*, *Stratusphunk* and *Oh jazz, po jazz,* ripping through several particularly enjoyable, heavily swing-inflected and smile-inducing choruses of *Honeysuckle Rose* on the last piece.[64]

On *Othello Ballet Suite* (1967) and the two versions of *Electronic Sonata For Souls Loved By Nature* from this period (the first, recorded for big band, from 1967 and the second, for sextet, from 1969) Garbarek is the chief featured soloist. Russell's own description of the latter version of *Electronic Sonata* is indication enough of the character of the music: "The music features an on-stage live 'jazz' sextet playing (painting would be a more descriptive term) a pan-stylistic tapestry of serial music, jazz, folk, rock and raga melodies upon the electronic music canvas supplied by the tape which is itself composed of all the aforementioned styles of music re-composed electronically into a world of tonal and non-tonal sound. The end result seems to be music that is reaching out to embrace the whole world of music."[65]

Like Christensen, Garbarek responds superbly to the challenges and opportunities of Russell's magical, shape-shifting charts, his tone now much fuller and more expressive – generally in a somewhat Archie Shepp-like manner, but with a distinctive personality already present – than on the 1966 *Walkin'* . He also provides several musical themes, one of which would resurface as *Vips* on the 1969 **Esoteric Circle** recording, a session organised by Russell. Together with the earlier, autumn 1966 Russell piece *Now And Then* – a work that makes radical play with notions of dynamics, of structure and seeming dissolution, the vertical and the horizontal – all of this immensely vital, widely conceived and intelligently layered music repays the most careful and repeated listening. (It is particularly interesting to compare the two versions of *Electronic Sonata*, both of which are spun off and around an hypnotic ostinato double-bass riff, as spacious as it is funky, and both of which feature creatively integrated use of the specially prepared electronic tape: the later sextet recording contains considerably more passages of reflective abstraction than the earlier big band version).[66]

On the big band session from 1967, recorded in Stockholm, Garbarek and Christensen – together with Terje Rypdal and Arild Andersen – were in the company of some of Sweden's finest post-bop and contemporary players. These included trumpeters Jan Allan and Bertil Lövgren, saxophonists Claes Rosendahl, Lennart Åberg and Arne Domnérus, guitarist Rune Gustafsson, vibraphonist (and pianist and organist) Berndt Egerbladh, pianist Bengt Hallberg and bassist Georg Riedel, with the Swedish-domiciled Norwegian Egil "Bop" Johansen joining Christensen on drums. Early in the year, a good many of these musicians, together with Bernt Rosengren, Garbarek and Christensen, had played a two week engagement at Stockholm's Gyllene Cirkeln – which newspapers at the time reported as the final jazz concerts at the club. The seventeen-piece band was joined by a special guest: trumpeter Don Cherry, who like George Russell had moved from America in the mid-to-late 1960s, first to Paris and then, eventually, to Scandinavia – and who had recorded an invigorating, shape-shifting album with Russell's (chiefly American) sextet at the Beethoven Hall in Stuttgart in August 1965.[67]

Along with George Russell, Don Cherry (1936-95) was to have a crucial impact upon Garbarek at this time. One of the originators of 1960s Free Jazz, Cherry's effervescent and wide-ranging melodic work in the Ornette Coleman quartet of 1959-61 had already acquired legendary status. A founder member of one of the key groups of the early 1960s, the New York Contemporary Five (which included Archie Shepp and John Tchicai), Cherry played and recorded with John Coltrane and Sonny Rollins, later coming to Denmark and playing (at the Jazzhus Montmartre in Copenhagen) and recording there with Albert Ayler in 1964. He then formed a wide-ranging group, initially with Argentinian saxophonist Gato Barbieri, German vibraphonist Karl Berger, French bassist J. F. Jenny-Clarke and Italian drummer Aldo Romano, which, in various incarnations, lasted until the autumn of 1966.

Cherry was always open to new musical experiences – and always keen to synthesise aspects of those experiences, in the light of his belief that the "capacity for unity" is one of the prime elements that jazz music has always had. On such vital albums of the mid-1960s as **Togetherness, Complete Communion** and **Symphony For Improvisers** (the latter two recorded for Blue Note) he brought North and South America and Europe together, as surely as he did characterful themes and free-flowing improvisation.[68]

From the mid-1960s onwards, Cherry – who was part Choctaw Native American, part Afro-American – became increasingly interested in and involved with ethnic music. Travelling the world, he integrated aspects of Indian, African, Native American, Far Eastern and European instrumentation, scales and rhythm into a suite-like approach to the magic of sound, rhythm and song. One could say that he sought the healing vibrations of music in a manner reminiscent of the Jungian concept of individuation, or the emergence of the Great or Cosmic Self within one. To young Norwegians of the 1960s like Garbarek, Christensen and Andersen (the last of whom Cherry featured in his **Eternal Rhythm** recording at the November 1968 Berlin Jazz Festival) Cherry was a revelation.

In 1998 Garbarek would record the late trumpeter's beautiful composition *Malinye*, in tribute to a musician whose prolific inspiration he has long acknowledged.[69] As Garbarek recalls: "It was Don who first got us interested in our own folk music, who made us realise how much there was to check out in our own backyard. We were to make a radio broadcast once, and Don asked us if we couldn't perhaps play a Norwegian folk tune. That wasn't exactly what we young Norwegian 'jazzers' were into at the time! But, we came to change [..] He was an enormous influence: a very fine person, and the first world musician, really. For example, he dressed in Indian clothes, read Tibetan philosophy and played Turkish folk music. He himself was a mixture of black, white and Indian – and lived in Skåne [in southern Sweden]. So everything about Don spoke of a world-wide attitude to life."[70]

Cherry often spoke of children as exemplifying the quality of open-mindedness which he looked for in music – and life. One recalls Paul Klee's story about the time he asked a young child what he was drawing: "I don't know", replied the child, "I haven't finished yet." It is this quality of open-mindedness – and open form – which is so evident in the tape which the Norwegian Jazz Archives in Oslo have of a radio broadcast of a concert by Cherry and Garbarek, Jon Christensen and Per Løberg which took place in May 1967 at the recently opened Sogn Jazz Club. In the summer of 1968, Cherry would play at the Molde Festival, but his debut in Norway took place in this small but highly atmospheric club – its walls graced with original works of art by Edvard Munch – in the University of Oslo student community of Sogn, a few kilometres north-west of the city centre.[71]

Very much in the bright, bouncy spirit of Cherry's Blue Note recordings of the mid-1960s, with Cherry playing functional, feeding piano now and then, the music of that May evening finds the thirty year-old trumpeter and twenty-year old saxophonist exchanging and developing ideas like a couple of kittens with a ball of string, moving now in, now out of the strong, mobile – and melodic – cross-rhythms of Løberg and Christensen. At this stage in his development, Garbarek's tonal and dynamic debt to Shepp is again obvious, and the spirit of Ornette Coleman is never far away. However, there are also clear signs of Garbarek's growing maturity, particularly in his dynamic sensitivity and related ability to employ discrete, well-honed phrases within an ambitiously long and well-sprung sense of line.[72]

For Garbarek, the summer of 1967 – the summer of love, in pop mythology – was a busy time. Two days before the date at Sogn with Don Cherry, he had performed in pianist Egil Kapstad's *Syner* (Visions) for Choir and (eight piece) Jazz Orchestra at the Munch Museum. Presented – and recorded – by Norsk Jazz Forum, with financial assistance from Norsk Kulturråd, this Oscar Wilde-inspired work embraced both contemplative and up-tempo, wide-interval chromatic writing for solo instruments and ensemble, the whole now and then reminiscent of Mingus's way with a rolling church rhythm and a dissonant chord or two. Unfolding in twelve discrete sections, the work features much fine, atmospheric flute from Helge Hurum. Bjørklund and Christensen are impressive throughout, and the six vocalists (who include Laila Dalseth, the noted Norwegian jazz singer who has usually tended to work in more mainstream contexts that Karin Krog) no less so. Revealing an occasional Dolphy-esque volatility, especially in section six of the piece, Garbarek shares tenor duties with the now seemingly more modern mainstream-oriented Bjørn Johansen, who takes a couple of satisfying, deep toned solos.

The next month, Garbarek was involved in a recording project of similar ambition to that essayed in *Syner*, only this time in Sweden. Here he participated in the recording of bassist and composer Georg Riedel's ballet music **Riedaiglia** – the title of the piece an acronym of the names of Riedel and leading Afro-American choreographer Alvin Ailey, whose ballet – originally titled *The Seven Deadly Sins* – this was. Musician and choreographer worked hard to bring the two disciplines together. The ballet (which was broadcast on Swedish television) features much improvisation and the variegated, sometimes primitivistic music – coloured by both Mingus-like blues and post-Schoenberg chromatic abstraction – is certainly redolent of the sensual, liminal spirit of dance.

Riedel is one of this century's most interesting, provocative composers for voices, and the choir do full justice to the sometimes savage, wildly leaping and sliding intervallic quality in the (ur-phonetic) vocalese here.[73] The twenty-piece Swedish Radio Jazz Group contained some of Sweden's choicest improvisers, including pianist Jan Johansson (already a cherished figure, both for his work with Stan Getz and such distinctive, folk-inflected records as **Jazz på Svenska**, recorded with Riedel in 1962-64), trumpeters Bosse Broberg and Bertil Lövgren, alto saxophonist Arne Domnérus (whose creamy-toned soloing on the date can only have helped confirm Garbarek's growing admiration for Johnny Hodges) and a young bassist named Palle Danielsson. Norwegian Egil "Bop" Johansen was on drums, with Trinidadian conga player Rupert Clemendore adding the sort of energy and excitement that he also brought to George Russell's Big Band at this time.

Although Garbarek solos on tenor – and does so well, the spiralling, gliding upper register figures and forceful, yet reflective tone immediately recognisable as his alone – the record sleeve lists him as also playing soprano. While there are one or two brief touches of gurgling colour from that instrument in the work, Garbarek was not to take up the soprano seriously for some years yet, never really relishing the possibilities of the instrument until he acquired the small, curved Italian model on which he has played ever since.[74]

Back in Oslo, in late September Garbarek recorded two pieces "live" at Sogn Jazz Club – Eddie Harris's *Freedom Jazz Dance* and his own composition *Til Vigdis* (To Vigdis). Apart from Garbarek himself on tenor, the music featured visiting American Frank Phipps on valve trombone, Arild Andersen on bass and Jon Christensen on drums. Earlier that year, in April, an extensive "live" version of Coltrane's *Mr P. C.* had been recorded with Per Løberg and Jon Christensen, in the somewhat primitive conditions afforded by a workers' hut in Asker. Retitled *Mr J. C.* in honour of Coltrane, who had died on July 17th that summer, this side-long track now joined the two "live" September pieces to constitute **Til Vigdis**, the first L P recording by Jan Garbarek.

Issued in a stereo-sound edition of five hundred, with a front cover black and white photographic portrait of its dedicatee, Vigdis Garbarek, this record of "Jan Garbarek trio & quartet" was financed by the Norwegian Student Society, with assistance from the Norwegian Jazz Forum. Hallvard Kvåle did the recording and Karin Krog supplied a touching sleevenote. Written in English, it was addressed directly to Garbarek. Part of it is as follows: "Dear Jan [...] My first impression of you is from the Gamlebyen Jazzclub, when your group used to drop in and jam. This was 4-6 years ago, your quartet had won our yearly Amateur Contest and although, if I may say so, you tried very hard to play like Coltrane, you did this with an authority which I feel is very unusual for a 15 year old saxophone player [...] From our many travels together I especially remember two occasions. Once, travelling through that part of Norway where your mother comes from (Trøndelag) and where you had spent many summer holidays, and another time, touring Poland where your father was born and raised. On both occasions you stated the strong roots you felt you had in both these places, which led to very exciting conversations about roots, heritage, temperament and music, jazz and races, and how the roots we have can be combined with expressions within a form of music which originated in very different surroundings."[75]

From the perspective of the late 1990s, Krog's words would seem to offer prescient anticipation of much of what Garbarek was to develop on ECM from the 1970 **Afric Pepperbird** onwards. However, the singer's observations are no less applicable to a good deal of **Til Vigdis**. If the fourteen-minute treatment of *Freedom Jazz Dance* (including a typically strong, characterful and variegated solo from Christensen) is chiefly remarkable – and enjoyable – for the clear evidence it provides of these young Norwegians' ability to groove hard within an harmonically open framework, both *Mr J.C.* and *Til Vigdis* offer a fascinating foretaste of that lyrical feeling for space and reverie that would soon come to distinguish so much of Garbarek's art.

The eighteen and a half minutes of *Mr J. C.* open at a fast, clipped tempo, immediately recalling the energy and conviction of Coltrane's original, May 1959 version of *Mr P. C.* with Tommy Flanagan (piano), Paul Chambers (bass) and Art Taylor (drums). However, Jon Christensen's crisp, multi-directional figures and overall textural sensitivity soon begin to bring to mind not so much Art Taylor's hard-bop drive as a combination of the melodic colour and clarity of Ed Blackwell and the more spread accents of Sunny Murray – that key drummer of the 1960s avant garde who had visited Oslo in 1962 with Cecil Taylor. Similarly, an increasingly pliant quality in Garbarek's sound – and sense of line – quickly takes the music away from the somewhat brittle-toned pastiche of the opening bars, to conjure eventually a rubato fantasy in shifting tempi, initially for solo sax and then with bass and drums re-entering. In the solo sax section a minor-keyed pentatonic quality supplies poetic counterpoint to some "down home" blues phrasing, long-held "bell" notes alternating with passages of fast-executed, yet (once again) gliding ascensional figures. As pizzicato bass and drums re-enter, converting Garbarek's abstracted ruminations into a lovely three-way field of energy, Latinesque accents intimate an almost Ellingtonian atmosphere. Finally, more full-throated, long-held notes from Garbarek precipitate the recapitulation of the original clipped tempo, sound and theme of the piece.

A feeling that the musician is absolutely in love with – and attuned to – the expressive possibilities of his instrument; the presence of what one might call narrative structure in music, realised through an acute sensitivity to matters of melody, musical dynamics and psychological drama; the ability to move away from the parent, governing framework of a piece to ostensibly distant, yet related aspects of essentially poetic expression; the desire (and ability) to bridge worlds: such central aspects of the mature Garbarek are already in evidence here. Nothing could be further from the relentless, historicising "power play" aesthetic which contemporary musicians like the Germans Peter Brötzmann or Rüdiger Carl were beginning to develop from (or in dialectical relation to) the provocative achievements of the contemporary Afro-American avant garde.[76]

When story-telling – such as we hear in much of *Mr J. C.* – achieves compelling status, it approaches the realm of myth. It is exactly such a realm which is in nascent evidence in *Til Vigdis*, the title piece of the album. To observe that the piece lasts six and a half minutes, for example, would be to miss the point of the music somewhat. Over a deep, more or less static drone from trombonist Phipps, enhanced by Andersen's arco bass and Christensen's dark-toned, ritually-phrased accents, Garbarek floats the sort of considered, yet dynamically dramatic, tonally varied and arching figures which speak of that existential engagement with the mythic, or timeless, which would come to mark such structurally comparable pieces as the 1976 *Vandrere* (Wanderers) and the 1986 *Third Piece*.[77]

Although neither Karin Krog nor Terje Bjørklund was present on **Til Vigdis**, in 1967-68 Garbarek, Andersen and Christensen continued to work in the Karin Krog Quintet, to mounting acclaim, while Karin also began to work in a quartet with Bjørklund, Andersen and drummer Svein Christiansen. There were also special, one-off events for various members of the quintet, such as the December 1967 T.V. showing of the programme *Interludium* – a profile of the music of the Norwegian Arild Boman, where Garbarek, Andersen and Christensen were joined by alto saxophonist Calle Neumann and (jazz) organist Boman. Initially a classically trained pianist, Boman was one of the first to take up jazz organ in Norway (George Russell featured him on *Stratusphunk* in his August 1967 Aula concert) and, in the spirit of the time, became quite involved with the idea of working from graphic scores, rather than conventional music notation.[78]

The music in *Interludium* is fascinating: part unpretentious, grooving jam session, redolent of the deepest roots of jazz, and part rubato tone poem, intimating something of the atmospheric finesse of a good deal of what would later be created by Garbarek on ECM. Early on, Garbarek and Neumann dig happily into their unison riffs (there is a lovely moment when the camera catches the twenty-year old Garbarek smiling briefly, but fully, to Neumann) while Boman spices his Jimmy Smith-like grooves with some freely splashed touches of chromaticism. Andersen and Christensen already exhibit a maturity of conception beyond their years, the bassist's lines fleet and fine and the drummer at one point conjuring some soon-to-be typical cymbal textures with stick and hand.

After an exploratory arco feature from Andersen (with a sensitive, shifting T.V. montage of images of the other musicians, a Cubist-inflected idea that continues, with foci-shifting discrimination, throughout the session) the music moves into its most striking phase. Garbarek's very deliberate, Aylerish vibrato colours a lovely, liquid rubato theme, uncannily close in shape and mood to Kenny Wheeler's *Baba*, as recorded some eleven years later on George Adams' ECM release **Sound Suggestions**. The musicians play with this motif for some minutes, shifting tempi (as they do throughout the session). Finally, at the end of the broadcast, Boman's static, swelling organ chords strike what in retrospect seems another somewhat anticipatory note, intimating aspects of modality and mood which would be developed in such subsequent music by Garbarek as that on **Places**, recorded a decade later in Oslo with John Taylor (organ), Bill Connors (guitar) and Jack DeJohnette (drums).

The Pollock-like linear energy of *Interludium*'s introductory, superimposed graphics, and the range of poetically conceived camera angles and montage, epitomise the imaginative quality of the best of (black and white) Norwegian television at this time. *Interludium* was produced by Svein Erik Børja, a creative and much respected man in media and music circles in Norway, who played a considerable, initiatory role in the development and production of the early records which Jan Erik Vold made with the Garbarek Quartet. A quarter of a century later, Garbarek would play solo saxophone in honour of Børja, at his funeral service in Oslo's East Crematorium.[79]

Another special occasion for the young Norwegians was the visit which Marion Brown made to Norway in May 1968, and which resulted in a memorable evening of freely conceived, organic music making with Garbarek, Andersen and Christensen at Sogn Jazz Club.[80] But this can hardly have matched the experience these three young lions were soon to have. With Karin Krog and Terje Bjørklund, they travelled to the Second Montreux Jazz Festival in Switzerland. Here, the Karin Krog Quintet won Second Prize in the festival's competition for European groups, with Garbarek winning Second Prize as soloist. (First Prize in the group category was won by the Alex Riel/Palle Mikkelborg Quintet, featuring Bernt Rosengren, while John Surman took First Prize as soloist, appearing with the Mike Westbrook Orchestra.) Norwegian newspapers reported a set of "very up-to-date" music by Krog and her companions, with plenty of percussion effects from tambourine and cow bells.

This is the first time that Garbarek was reported as having played a "blockfløyte" live. The literal translation of this is "recorder". However, Arild Andersen has told me that he cannot remember Garbarek ever playing such an instrument, and suggests that Garbarek must have been playing several wooden flutes by this time, one of them perhaps a gift from Don Cherry.[81] Whatever it is he plays, Garbarek certainly gets the sound of a wooden flute on the second of the three numbers of the T. V. concert which was given by the quintet after their return from Montreux (which the Norwegian Jazz Archives have on video).

The concert is particularly interesting in that it presents the first concrete evidence of that interest in Norwegian (and other) folk music which would come to play such a major role in Garbarek's later work: the music in the session is listed as being *Lazy Afternoon*, *Norsk Folketone* and *Karin's Mode*. The material is played, often rubato, without break: there is a strong, meditative atmosphere throughout the performance, with the combination in the second piece of Garbarek's "blockfløyte" and Krog's percussion (bells attached to the fingers of her hands) conjuring a mood in parts as Asian as it is Norwegian.[82]

In November 1968, the final jazz concert of the year at the Hennie-Onstad Art Centre at Høvikodden underlined the fast-increasing breadth of conception in contemporary, jazz-oriented Norwegian music circles, offering an evening of "Jazz And Electronics" with the Arild Boman Octet. Featuring Boman himself, Lisbeth Sønstevold (harpsichordist, and daughter of the jazz pianist-turned-composer Gunnar Sønstevold), Jan Garbarek, Helge Hurum, Calle Neumann, Frode Thingnæs, Arild Andersen and Jon Christensen, this unusual octet shared a boundary-breaking evening with a performance of Stockhausen's electronically generated masterpiece of the 1950s, *Gesang Der Jünglinge* (Song of the Youths).[83]

Around this time, Christensen had begun to get all kinds of job offers: and so it was Norwegians Espen Rud and Svein Christiansen, with whom Krog had been working of late, who shared the drum chair on Krog's third LP, the October 1968 **Joy**. Released under the name of Karin Krog & Friends, the record gives a good overview of the contemporary programme featured by the quintet.[84] The music embraces Garbarek's meditative, somewhat Eastern *Karin's Mode*, featuring pitch-sliding vocalese from Krog and a keening solo from Garbarek, Herbie Hancock's *Maiden Voyage*, Monk's *'Round About Midnight* (a "live" cut from the Kongsberg Festival, with the singer accompanied by Arild Andersen and Palle Danielsson) and two engaging and highly sensuous rubato performances from Krog – the opening *Mr. Joy* and concluding *Lazy Afternoon*, the latter flowing out of *Maiden Voyage*. Recorded with private funding in some two hours, the record drew the praise of George Russell, who was then living in Oslo, enjoying (and contributing to) the various artistic and musical discussions occurring at places like Kunstnernes Hus (The Artists' House) in the centre of town. Russell's sleeve-note concluded: "The thing that gives the record cohesion is that all the participants are of their time, they all reach for the same goal, a tremendously broad range of music."[85]

Apart from the Karin Krog Quintet itself, two other special – and very different – groups of the time indicate what a range of jazz-inflected music was in the air in the Oslo of the late 1960s. One is the Svein Finnerud Trio, the improvising modern jazz group which began in 1967 and featured Finnerud (piano), Bjørnar Andresen (bass) and Espen Rud (drums). The other is the "psychedelic" pop group Dream, featuring Terje Rypdal.

Recorded in March and October 1968, the first Svein Finnerud Trio recording – released as the second Norwegian Jazz Forum album – quickly acquired something of a cult status in Norway. Oslo-based painter and multi-media artist Per Kleiva, who was intensely involved in the various debates about the nature (and responsibilities) of contemporary art which took place in Norway at this time, remembers the excitement generated in the late 1960s and early 1970s by the trio's combination of Cecil Taylor-lish three-way freedom, Paul Bley-like lyricism and Dada-esque theatricality and (occasional) back-beat accents, particularly at the concerts which they gave at Høvikodden: "They were a tremendous group, very inventive – very special. Bjørnar, the bassist, was also involved with electronics, and worked with George Russell in that capacity. And he did the engineering on the Jan Garbarek Quartet's first record, which they recorded at Høvikodden in late 1969. This was an extraordinary time, really, with a lot of fresh ideas in the air – new jazz, poetry readings, multi-media happenings and so forth. And some really good music came out of it all."[86]

The Henie-Onstad Centre at Høvikodden was host to a good many dance performances at this time. However, in 1969 it was the Bergen Festival which premiered *Mot Solen* (Towards the Sun) – Edith Roger's and Barthold Halle's contemporary ballet, or "theatrical poem" – about the life of Edvard Munch. Here, Garbarek joined Harald Bergersen in playing the saxophone parts in the music which Alfred Janson (born 1937) supplied for the project (which after its Bergen premiere went to the National Opera, Oslo). Janson is one of the key figures in Norwegian music of this period, and is no less an important figure today. An accomplished pianist, with a background in jazz, Janson was one of the first in the 1960s to proclaim the necessity of seeing serial, post-Schoenberg Modernism not in terms of its being an absolute imperative for the contemporary composer, but rather as one option among others. Cultivating a wide-ranging, yet penetrating variety of musical means, Janson has always been sharply, creatively aware of the politics in poetics.[87]

Distinguished by a discriminating yet dramatic breadth of resource, both acoustic and electronic, "romantic" and contemporary in aura, with organ, harpsichord and shimmering strings offset by some striking moments of silence and saxophone meditations, the music for *Mot Solen* offered pointed complement to the ballet's emphasis upon Munch's spiritual integrity. This was an integrity placed in sharp contrast to the hypocrisy of the bourgeois classes who had once dismissed Munch, before later changing their minds as they came to realise how much investement value the lonely Expressionist's pictures had accumulated.[88]

Newspaper pictures of the time give tantalising glimpses of such politically oriented, poetically manifested aspects of the period: one photograph from Høvikodden shows Finnerud and Rud together with Garbarek and Rypdal, Andersen and Christensen – and all of the musicians either attired or masked in a manner reminiscent of Zurich or Berlin Dada.[89] Stage settings at Høvikodden sometimes featured what look like colourful yet potentially ironic references to the pop "flower power" of the time. However, from the musical point of view, the most interesting indication of the contemporary creative temper lies in the details of the various personnel of the groups of this period. Although Garbarek enjoyed played with Svein Finnerud on more than one occasion, including what the local press saw as a challenging, controversial concert at Molde's town hall, the (contemporary) guitar playing of Terje Rypdal was to have a more lasting impact upon him.[90] And, little as Garbarek knew of that world, Rypdal came from the world of pop.

Born in 1947, Rypdal had begun studying piano at the age of five. Three years later he changed to trumpet, and picked up his first guitar at twelve. As a teenager he played in a band called the Vanguards, loosely based on the intrumental singles format developed by the Ventures in America and the Shadows in England. Eric Clapton, Pete Townshend and (especially) Jimi Hendrix quickly expanded Rypdal's sense of how a guitar might sound, and in Spring 1967, together with Christian Reim (organ), Hans Marius Stormoen (bass) and Tom Karlsen (drums) he began the progressive pop band Dream. "At first", Rypdal has recalled to _Down Beat_'s Bill Milkowski, "we were doing instrumental things that were similar to the Jimmy Smith/Wes Montgomery stuff. But later, we became very influenced by the whole psychedelic era. We were just trying to make a collage of everything that we were hearing and enjoying – everything from Wes Montgomery to Charles Mingus to Jimi Hendrix."[91]

In the spring of 1968 Stormoen (who had been part of the young Garbarek's quartet in 1962) left Dream, soon to be followed by Karlsen. In October of that year, the papers made much of the news: Garbarek and Christensen were to join Dream. The formation of such a Norwegian "super group" might lead one to think of parallels with the Cream trio in England – particularly when one learns that part of the new Dream's repertoire was the pop-blues hit _Black Magic Woman_, on which Garbarek and Christensen sang part-harmonies! However, the record which Rypdal made in the same month that the new Dream was formed reveals that, however much the guitarist and his companions may have absorbed some of the atmosphere of the blues-loving psychedelic sixties, their playing at this time exhibited many a jazz virtue of phrasing and sound.

Recorded with, among others, Garbarek and Christensen, Reim and Karlsen, Calle Neumann, Knut Riisnæs and Frode Thingnæs, trumpeters Ditlef Eckhoff and Jarl Johansen and bassist Terje Venaas, the 1968 **Bleak House** is – like **Metropol Jazz, Jazz Moments** and **Til Vigdis** – a real collector's item. It documents the burgeoning breadth of imagination that over the past decades has steadily and increasingly come to characterise the work of a truly unclassifiable guitarist and composer – who during his ostensibly "pop" years had been studying composition at the University of Oslo, and who was soon to learn much from George Russell. Not only that: on two of the four tracks on which Garbarek appears – the big band, boppish *Wes* and the blues-burning, shouting title track (where Rypdal's scorching solo comes very near in sound quality to Clapton's contemporary "violin note") – the saxophonist's rapidly increasing breadth and power of both tone and rhythmic conception are strikingly evident. And on the three-part *Winter Serenade* – described on the sleeve as "a free form composition based on an idea by Terje Rypdal" – one is given an early and affecting example of how, for this generation of dynamically sensitive Norwegians, heterophonic freedom and solo lyricism could go hand in hand.

Only several months were to pass before the new Dream experienced a further change in personnel. With the departure of Christian Reim, Arild Andersen came into the band – and in March 1969 the Jan Garbarek Quartet was born. An advertisement in English for the quartet's appearance in Gothenburg a year later carried the already deliciously dated lines: "Mr. Pop and Mrs. Jazz found out a now art of loving: Exciting – Jan Garbarek (tenor sax)/ Terje Rypdal (el. guitar)/ Arild Andersen (bass)/ Jon Christensen (drums)."[92] Exciting the music certainly was – but with precious little of such period fluff to it.

Arild Andersen (born 1945) was the perfect complement to the other three members of the quartet. With a distinctive rich tone and a rhythmic conception as strong as it was flexible, he supplied both scurrying root figures and clear-cut melody, energising textures and lucid transitional ideas. Like the other members of the quartet, Andersen was also (and remains) a sensitive listener. At the beginning of the 1960s, he had started his musical life as a guitarist in the (Dixieland) Riverside Jazzband from Strømmen, just outside Oslo. Hearing Erik Amundsen at the Metropol inspired Andersen to think of playing double-bass: jamming on that instrument later at Penguin, another of Oslo's clubs of the time, he met Terje Bjørklund, who taught the young bassist a good many tunes. At Club 7 Andersen then began playing with people like Knut Riisnæs, Christian Reim and Torgrim Sollid, before an enthusiasm for Gary Peacock and Richard Davis led him to contemplate more avant-garde possibilities for his instrument. At the same time, he played some dates now and then in the boppish trio led by one of Norway's most respected modernists, pianist Roy Hellvin, accompanying the occasional visiting American – and appeared on one side of the 1967 **Til Vigdis**. By 1968, the year he became a professional musician, Andersen's lovely singing tone, excellent intonation and increasing speed of ideas had caught the ear of Don Cherry, who first encountered Andersen at the Molde festival in 1968.

In the sleeve-note to his November 1968 **Eternal Rhythm**, which featured the as yet relatively unknown bassist from Oslo, Cherry observed of Andersen: "His sound is so beautiful. You will keep hearing from him."[93] George Russell – with whom Andersen was to study – was no less impressed, and the Jan Garbarek Quartet, with Andersen, quickly became the core of a good deal of Russell's concert activity, as documented on the March 1970 **Trip To Prillarguri** "live" session from Estrad, Södertalje in Sweden (with Stanton Davis on trumpet and Russell himself on piano).

The music's many pleasures include the trilling, suspenseful lines floated over the ostinato, riffing modality of Garbarek's opening *Theme*; a deeply grooved, rocking version of George Russell's *Souls* and a poised, potent reading of his classic *Stratusphunk*. The record also offers the only opportunity commercially available, so far, to hear Garbarek playing an Ornette Coleman composition. The bluesy, almost jump-band theme of *Man On The Moon* leads into freely phrased rubato passages of blistering, cross-rhythmic power from all participants. Rypdal's keening rock textures behind Stanton Davis's solo are particularly arresting, while Garbarek's subsequent solo evinces the fast-developing, ferocious power of his sound at this time: he moves from piping, surreal abstractions in the extreme upper areas of the tenor to full throated, practically bestial blues-soaked phrases in the middle and lower registers of the horn. Above all, the record demonstrates the considerable empathy – and speed of thought – these genre-crossing musicians were able to draw upon.

Produced by George Russell, with technical supervision by Bjørnar Andresen, the October 1969 **The Esoteric Circle** gives a good picture of the Jan Garbarek Quartet's repertoire at the time. From the opening, hymnal-and blues-inflected sound and phrasing of the beautiful, rubato ballad *Traneflight* (with Garbarek, as gospel-like as he has ever sounded, both literally and metaphorically singing through his horn) to the light, bright, calypso-oriented *Breeze Ending*, the indebtedness of the music to such Afro-American masters as Coltrane and Rollins, Pharoah Sanders, Archie Shepp and Albert Ayler is clear. However, a striking quality of originality is no less evident.

Whether one considers the combination of textural abstraction and eventual near r'n'b power which informs Jon Christensen's opening solo (and subsequent work) on *Rabalder*, or the way in which soloists Garbarek and Rypdal float across and around the tonal stations of *Esoteric Circle* (its title, given by Russell, implying psychological and spiritual rather than musical qualities); the distilled, upper-register lyricism of *Nefertite* or the almost Webern-like details of the one minute and ten second "sound arch" that is *Gee*, it is obvious that this is music of new and singularly energising dimensions. Rypdal, especially, is in remarkable form throughout. His hyper-expressive, near-whiplash qualities of abrasive (Rickenbacker) guitar surreality mesh perfectly with Garbarek's chromatic displacements on the scurrying *SAS 644*, while, in very different vein, his pianissimo glisses and chimes add just the right amount of silvered hue to the otherwise tenebrous mood of the title track.

The same month, the quartet contributed to one side of Jan Erik Vold's recording **Briskeby Blues**, on the Norwegian Philips label. The politically committed, yet Taoist-like Vold (born 1939) is unique in Norwegian literature, his images (and spoken delivery) holding lightness of touch and gravity of content in stimulating, often humorous balance. Garbarek and Christensen were initially drawn to the poet because of the rhythmic quality in his reading, and, from **Briskeby Blues** through the 1970 **Hav** and the 1973 single **Trikeskinner/Tre Små Ting** (Tramlines/Three Little Things), to the 1977 Zen-inflected, double album masterpiece **Ingentings Bjeller** (Nothing's Bells), the work which they were to create together rates as some of the finest jazz-meets-poetry ever recorded.[94]

131

On **Briskeby Blues,** seven of the thirteen tracks on which the quartet appears are under a minute long and a further four under two, with none lasting longer than three minutes. Such compressed frameworks elicit a maximum of dynamic sensitivity, inventive "soundscapes" and – above all – lyrical creativity from all participants. Garbarek contributes a touch of atmospheric flute – uncredited on the sleeve – to *Min nye blå dyne* (My new blue duvet cover) but it is his tenor that really compels attention, the acutely focused lyricism and dynamic range of his lines presaging a good deal of what would soon emerge on ECM.

A radio broadcast from a 1969 concert at Sogn Jazz Club gives further, fascinating evidence of the breadth of conception the quartet brought to its music, in a performance which shifts theme and tempi, mood and manner with practically theatrical assurance. (By this time, the quartet were well aware of Sun Ra, and a good deal of the 1970 **Afric Pepperbird** would attest to their parallel familiarity with the Art Ensemble of Chicago.) The 1969 programme was as follows: *Karin's Mode, Daydream*; *Upper and Lower Egypt*; *Capricorn Rising*; *Smått*, and *SK 644* (aka *SAS 644*). Apart from tenor, Garbarek plays a little piano and clarinet in a set which has practically everything. From wild, rocking modal grooves to soaring, Hodges-like lyricism, four-way, criss-crossing freedom and more than a touch of rock'n'roll; abstracted, pointillist textures and old-time trad and swing grooves – the shape-shifting and highly humorous *Smått* – the music is as alive and exploratory, as fresh and affirmative as music ever gets. As announcer Knut Høyland says, here, indeed, are some "experiments with sound".[95]

The same year, the quartet became involved in one of the most provocative, genre-crossing projects of the decade, released in 1972 as the double album **Popofoni**. Throughout the decade, a variety of debates in Norway had kept cultural activists and newpapers alike busy. For example, should Norway continue to develop the Munchian, Expressionistic strain within its figurative and landscape tradition in painting – as represented by a contemporary artist like Frans Widerberg; or should it build upon the achievements of post-1945 International Modernism, such as one could find transmuted in the painterly abstractions which another contemporary artist, Jakob Weidemann, had introduced into Norwegian art early in the decade?[96] Should Norwegian music cut the umbilical chord which had bound so much of that music to the legacy of Grieg (1843-1907), and embrace wholeheartedly not just the multi-faceted, Modernist-inflected achievements of Harald Sæverud (1897-1992) or the lonely musings of such a pioneer of full-blooded serial Modernism as Fartein Valen (1887 -1952) – but also the whole post-Cage world of aleatory composition, unpremeditated improvisation and multi-media happenings? And, most pressingly, should Norway join the EEC – or not?[97]

From today's perspective, one might question the need to see matters in such dualistic terms. Why not, for example, celebrate and build upon the achievements of Weidemann *and* Widerberg, Sæverud, Valen and Grieg *and* (the best of) the post-Cage world? As one might infer from its title, part of the point of the **Popofoni** recording was precisely this: to question dualistic thinking and suggest at least the possibility of different worlds coming together.

Commissioned by the contemporary Ny Musikk association, with support from Norsk Kulturråd, the various compositions on the 1969-71 double album find the musicians playing with both eruptive power and filigree delicacy.At times, the music is marked by strongly Eastern elements of drone and texture. The record also embraces serialism and pure jazz improvisation, waltz time, swing and rock accents, with moments of biting social critique contrasting well with some engaging passages of popular dance band parody. In terms of Garbarek's playing, **Popofoni** offers the most extreme examples of his contemporary interest in splitting notes, investigating both the fundament and the extreme upper partials of the harmonics of his sound. However, there are also many lovely passages of unaffected lyricism – and not just from Garbarek. Karin Krog, in particular, is in tremendous form throughout.

The recording brought together some of Norway's most distinguished contemporary composers and jazz, or improvising, musicians. In retrospect, such an admirable attempt to bridge worlds – to see life through both magnifying glass and telescope, as it were – can serve to recapitulate, or summarise, a good many of the themes of this chapter. Far from the "dead end" which Tony Palmer was shortly to see for jazz in a Playboy Club in America, **Popofoni** was recorded in what was at the time one of the world's most dynamic and popular multi-media art centres. And rather than concerning themselves about whether or not the music they played would remain popular, jazz musicians Krog and Garbarek, Rypdal and Stenson, Andersen and

Christensen played music which, subsidised as it was, had the courage to challenge certain contemporary notions of "internationalism" and "nationalism", "high" and "popular" culture.

The record contains six pieces, beginning with Gunnar Sønstevold's *Arnold* (the title inspired, not by Arnold Schoenberg, but rather the contemporary Norwegian sculptor Arnold Haukeland, renowned for his skyward-oriented abstract works in steel and aluminium), Arne Nordheim's *Morgen Raga* (Morning Raga, partly inspired by the beauty of the voice of Yma Sumak) and *Solar Plexus* (along with Alfred Janson's following *Valse Triste* the most politically overt piece on the record, initially concerned to comment on the banality of events like European Pop Song Contests, but mixing that theme with some caustic passages of freedom-crying social comment and political critique).

Alfred Janson's side-long *Valse Triste* then followed: this was an extraordinary collage of elements, including a Glenn Gould-like taping and orchestration of speaking voices, voices and music alike questioning aspects of folk and popular culture, Pop and Modernism, regionalism and nationalism. These were years in which the issue of Norway's membership in the EEC was coming to a head, and Janson, although fervently anti-EEC, drew upon a sophisticated awareness of international cultural developments. With its sensuous lyric by Paal-Helge Haugen and some hyper-expressive, upper-register ballad lines from Garbarek, Kåre Kolberg's *Blow Up Your Dreams* was potentially the record's most overtly "Romantic" or "mind-expanding" piece, in the sixties sense of the phrase. However, the expressivity of the piece was kept in sharp focus by the intelligently pared-down, two-part framework supplied by a composer of wide-ranging sensibilities (who had contributed an excellent sleeve-note to George Russell's big band version of *Electronic Sonata*). Finally, Terje Rypdal's relatively brief, post-Second Viennese School *Episode* (the volatility of its seemingly rootless, searching chromatic theme conveyed by Rypdal himself on flute and Garbarek on bass saxophone) offered a suitably open-ended coda to the quite extra-ordinary recording.

With its reverie-rich front cover abstract/concrete enamelled image by artist Sidsel Paaske – redolent of sky and water, butterfly and stone, the intimate and the infinite – and incisive sleeve-notes by Sønstevold and Nordheim, Janson and Kolberg, **Popofoni** remains an essential, inspiring document of the best of that otherwise often simply indulgent Utopianism that characterised so much of the latter half of the 1960s. For the first – and so far only – time in his life, Garbarek contributed a short, intellectually-oriented essay to the record.[98] Here, he underlined the importance of the improvisational spirit in jazz, and the interest of many contemporary jazz musicians in extending conceptions of their music, perhaps breaking down the boundaries between genres.[99]

The various world-bridging qualities of **Popofoni** combine to suggest an appropriate coda to this overview of the saga that was the journey, in the 1960s, of Garbarek, Christensen and colleagues to the initial depths of their creative jazz selves. This was a journey fuelled in large part by the transformative mysteries of that "Traneflight" which so touched Garbarek early in the decade, and which he continues to cherish and build upon today. For what was it, after all, that the young Garbarek had heard in the music of Coltrane, if not the impulse and the inspiration to journey into other worlds? To throw caution to the wind, moving beyond the frontiers of the familiar, and to begin perhaps to come into contact with the nourishing, truly creative forces of life, relishing what Carlos Castaneda, in his _Don Juan_ series of books, would later call "the cracks between worlds"... but to attempt to do this with discipline and (unfashionable idea that this may have been to some in the 1960s) extremely hard work. During the 1960s, few musicians can have worked as hard – and successfully – at mastering the fundaments of a potentially deep and transformative language as did Jan Garbarek.

Karin Krog Quintet (Kongsberg Jazz Festival 1965)
Artur Sand
Collection Jon Christensen

Bernt Rosengren Stockholm Dues (1965 Swedish recording, photo
Bo Trenter) Reproduced with kind permission of Bernt Rosengren

Notes to Chapter Three

1. See Hentoff, N. 'Whose Art From? Jazz At Mid-Century', in Hentoff, N. & McCarthy, A. J. (eds.) _Jazz_ (with an Introduction by Graham Collier) Quartet Books, London 1977 pp. 325-42.
2. Palmer, T. _All You Need Is Love: The Story Of Popular Music_ (ed. P. Medlicott) Futura Publications Ltd., London 1977 (first published 1976) p. 64.
3. Ibid. p. 65.
4. See Carr, I. _Music Outside: Contemporary Jazz In Britain_ Latimer New Dimensions, London 1973 pp. 41-43 & passim.
5. The concluding sentences of Albert Ayler's spoken introduction to his **My Name Is Albert Ayler** (Debut DEB 140/Fontana 688 603), recorded in Copenhagen on January 14th 1963. On November 23rd 1962, Cecil Taylor, Jimmy Lyons and Arthur (Sunny) Murray had recorded in Copenhagen at what the sleeve called the Cafe Montmartre: **Cecil Taylor at the Cafe Montmartre** (Fontana SFJL 928/88 602 ZY). A year later, the New York Contemporary Five recorded two volumes of music at what the sleeve now called the Jazzhus Montmartre, on November 15th 1963 : **Archie Shepp & The New York Contemporary Five Volume 1** (Polydor 623 235) and **Volume 2** Storyville SLP 1009). On the 14th September 1964 Albert Ayler, Don Cherry, Gary Peacock and Sunny Murray were in Copenhagen to record **Vibrations** (Freedom 28 461-2U). Each of these releases features informative sleevenotes from Erik Wiedemann.
6. _Nordiskt 60-Tal/The Nordic '60s_ Nordic Arts Centre, Helsinki 1991 pp. 67 & 71. The organisers do alert us to the opera by Terje Rypdal and Kaj Nissen - _Orfeus vender seg och ser på Euryfike_ (Orpheus turns around and looks at Eurydice) - which took place at the Henie-Onstad Art Centre in 1972.
7. Lebrecht, N. _The Companion To 20th-Century Music_ Simon & Schuster Ltd., London 1992 p.172.
8. _Documenta X- The Book: Politics Poetics_ Cantz Verlag, Ostfildern-Ruit 1997 passim. Perhaps it is in the nature of jazz's vitality to remain beyond the consciousnesss of the self-appointed guardians of whatever it is that such people see as being of cultural significance.
9. Woodard J. 'Joe Zawinul: The Dialects of Jazz', _Down Beat_ vo. 55 no. 4, April 1988 p. 19. For Zawinul's early years in Europe and America, see Silvert, C. 'Joe Zawinul: Wayfaring Genius' _Down Beat_ vol. 45 no. 11, June 1 1978 pp. 13-15. Weather Report was at times one of the favourite groups of both Jan Garbarek and Eberhard Weber: while it would be both misleading and wrong to describe their music as a European version of Weather Report, an affinity is evident in at least some of their music e.g. the development of Garbarek's _There Were Swallows_ ... from the 1992 **Twelve Moons**. See Tucker 1987 op. cit. ('Eberhard Weber') for Weber's unease at the music of his band Colours being compared at times with Weather Report (p. 14).
10. The labels associated with each of these producers are: MPS (Berendt and Brunner-Schwer); Swedish Columbia/Odeon (Lindqvist); Dragon (Westin); EMI Lansdowne Series (Preston); Steeplechase (Winther);

ENJA(Winckelmann); FMP (Gebers); Label Bleu (Orier), Leo (Feigin), ACT (Loch) and ECM (Eicher). Together, the work of such producers represents an immense contribution to jazz and culture in general over the past decades. See the contextual discography.

11. **Zoller Koller Solal** (Saba SB 15061).
12. See the Nordic/European contextual discography, and bibliography.
13. Ibid.
14. Palmer 1977 op. cit. p. 281. Having dismissed the future of jazz earlier in his book, Palmer now concluded by suggesting that perhaps jazz offered an "escape route" from aspects of the ever-more predictable and "colossus" nature of the popular music industry. His examples were few, but diverse: Woody Herman, Earl Hines, Ian Carr and Chick Corea.
15. Rivelli, P. & Levin, R. (eds.) _Giants Of Black Music_ (with a Foreword by Nat Hentoff) Da Capo Press Ltd., New York 1979 p. 66. This is an essential volume of essays about the avant garde of the 1960s, including several telling interviews.
16. Ibid. Hunt concludes his article thus: "The alternative to degenerate man as a slave in a world of central control is a rebirth of man as a spiritual animal. Recognition of today's jazz artist and his continual focus on the human approach to universal truths will aid in that rebirth." (p. 67) Agreed: but I would substitute 'shamanic' for 'human'.
17. For the Coltrane/Krupa story see Bourne 1986 op. cit. p. 27 and Stendhal 1984 op. cit. Over the years, Garbarek has been asked countless times just what it was in Coltrane that struck him so forcefully that day in 1961. His replies have always emphasised spiritual, rather than musical aspects of the question - the mystery of whatever it was that lay within and even "underneath" the sound that Coltrane projected: "What captured me was exactly that which you can't pin down, or even talk about. It was something that lay deep within - something that could be sensed in the music, no matter what notes or style he [Coltrane] played." Ibid. In this interview with Bjørn Stendahl, Garbarek goes on to contrast the impact of a famous image of Charlie Parker on film, looking straight ahead, open-eyed, while playing, with the various images one sees on photograph and film of Coltrane playing, again looking (seemingly) straight ahead, but with his eyes closed. Garbarek reveals that he has never been especially "grabbed" by listening to Parker, and suggests that Coltrane was looking, not straight ahead, but deep _inwards_. For various estimates of Coltrane's importance, see _Down Beat_ special Coltrane edition, vol. 46 no. 13 July 2 1979.
18. Libæk, I. & Stenersen, Ø. _History Of Norway: From The Ice Age To The Age Of Petroleum_ (trans. J. Aase) Grøndahl Dreyer, Oslo 1995 (second, rev. ed.) p. 138.
19. Bergh, J. & Evensmo, J. _Jazz Tenor Saxophone In Norway: 1917-59_ Norwegian Jazz Archives, Oslo 1997 p. 17.
20. Ibid. p.18. Discussing Bergheim's playing on a private recording of a January 1959 session by vibraphonist Per Nyhaug's Rainbow Orchestra, Bergh and Evensmo comment on the unusual mixture of a pure dance programme combined with "some of the strongest jazz elements found

in Norwegian jazz music of the fifties". They suggest that Bergheim's playing here "points forward to that of Bjørn Johansen, Jan Garbarek and Knut Riisnæs." (p. 21.) I remember enjoying a fine evening of Bergheim's modern mainstream tenor at the 'Malla' (Amalienborg) Jazz House in central Oslo, just off Karl Johansgata, in the mid-to-late 1970s: see Kristian Bergheim's Quintet: **Live At Malla** (Norjazz LaM 7701). Among other things, this observation of Bergh and Evensmo alerts one to the issue of the changing nature of jazz programmes and audiences in Norway in the late 1950s and 1960s. Dybo, T. *Jan Garbarek: Det åpne roms estetikk* (Jan Garbarek: The aesthetic of open space) Pax, Oslo 1996 suggests that Metropol was the location where the contrast between the urge to dance and the desire to listen to jazz music became most evident, citing in particular the impact of visits by Cecil Taylor and Don Ellis (pp. 23-4). Garbarek, who has been involved with music specially written for modern dance, has never played his own music *for* dancers, although he has said that it can be fine when people dance to the music he and colleagues play. See Økland 1975 op. cit. p.119.

21. For Parker's time in Sweden, and the warm reception he and his music were given there, see Russell, R. *Bird Lives!* Quartet Books, London 1973 pp. 292-7.
22. Back issues of *Jazznytt* can be read (in Norwegian) at the Norwegian Jazz Archives, Oslo. They contain some particularly informative interviews with e.g. Garbarek, Christensen, singer Karin Krog and bassist Arild Andersen: see bibliography.
23. Libaek & Stenersen 1995 op. cit. p.146.
24. See Tucker, M. 'Jan Garbarek: Beyond The Nordic Ethos', *Jazz Journal International* vol. 30 no. 10 , October 1977 p. 8: "I think in some ways, indirectly, what we [the Garbarek/Stenson quartet] play is more political than a lot of self-proclaimed political music - if you think about the interaction in the quartet, for example, what it might imply. The school system is very important here, the way children could grow into - and through - music, but often don't." Garbarek has played a good many school concerts, but has rarely, if ever, spoken to such (or, indeed, any) audiences about the music which he has played, his reasoning being that a break from being talked to at school may be both welcome in itself, and fructifying to the listening (and whole) imagination.
25. "I never got into the Beatles in the '60s; people used to recommend the Rolling Stones to me, telling me they were 'really tough', or rough, but they sounded like a light dance band to me. Coltrane's **Live at the Village Vanguard** - now, that was really 'rough'!" Personal communication, December 1997. In an Oslo interview of 1970, Garbarek suggests that the recent fuss over the potential of the group Blood, Sweat and Tears had been somewhat exaggerated: for the jazz elements which the group brought into their rock music had long been used in jazz. *Jazznytt* no. 2, Oslo May 1970.
26. On this centre,which played an important role in Norwegian cultural life at the time, see Hovdenakk, P., Rajka, S. & Bjerke, Ø. S. *Henie-Onstad Art Centre 1968-1993* (with a contribution by Elisabeth Hartmann Krafft) Henie-Onstad Art Centre, Høvikodden 1994.

Classically trained pianist and art historian Ole Henrik Moe (born 1920) was the first director of the centre and played a key part in the development of avant-garde musical events at Høvikodden. See the CD **Arkivalia Volume 1** (Henie-Onstad Centre, no serial number) which contains a good introductory essay, and music by Moe himself (a light-hearted look at Chopin), Kagel, Cage, Scriabin, Xenakis, Stockhausen and the Norwegians Arne Nordheim, Finn Mortensen and Bjørn Fongaard.

27. Helgheim, R. 'Den Synlege musikken' (Visible Music) *Klassekampen*, Oslo 23/3/96.

28. Ibid.

29. Haugen, P-H. *Stone Fences* (trans. W. Mishler & R. Greenwald) University of Missouri Press, Columbia 1986 p. 73.

30. Økland, E. 'Jan Garbarek' in Angell, O., Vold, J. E. & Økland, E. 1975 op. cit. (*Jazz I Norge*) p. 119. This six-page interview is indispensable for Garbarek's early days, and I have drawn upon it accordingly here. I am grateful to Tom Bækkerud for his considerable help, some twenty or more years ago, in translating this text for me.

31. See Karlsten, T. 'Intervju Med Arild Wikstrøm', ibid. pp. 74-8 (which includes an atmospheric photograph from 1964 of Wikstrøm, Per Løberg and Jon Christensen with vocalist Jamalia Sulieman). Wikstrøm the pianist can be heard in the Bjørn Johansen quartet, with Erik Amundsen (bass) and Ole Jacob Hanssen (drums) on one number, *Th' Rubyiat*, from the 1963 **Metropol Jazz** (Norsk Grammofonkompani H 506; see note 40 below) and with Karin Krog, Bjørn Johansen, Jan Berger (guitar), Per Løberg and Jon Christensen, on *Moonshine Lullaby*, one side of a 1964 single re-released as the first track of the 1994 double CD **Karin Krog Jubilee: The Best of Thirty Years** (Verve 523 716-2). See also the August 1978 **Club 7 15 År, 1963-1978: Club 7's Jubileumsplater** (MAI 7812/13) where Wikstrøm sings the Tamla Motown classic *I'll Be Doggone* with an eight-piece band which includes bassist Hans Marius Stormoen. Stormoen (the bassist in the quartet with which Garbarek won the 1962 Norwegian Amateur Jazz Championship) is also present on a jam session with drummer Ole Jacob Hanssen, as well as in a performance by the Bryggerigangen Bluesband (with guitarists Tom Gjertsen and Bent Patey and drummer Jan Lie). Other musicians on this "live" double record, recorded at Club 7, include Bjørn Johansen, Vidar Johansen, Calle Neumann, Odd Riisnæs (brother of Knut), Jon Balke, Christian Reim, Sveinung Hovensjø, Espen Rud and Jon Christensen.

32. Dybo op. cit. p. 36. Dybo's information comes from his interview with Garbarek of 22/2/91: he suggests that Garbarek was only fourteen years old at the time of this debut. Much the same information about this appearance with Wikstrøm is given by Garbarek in Økland 1975 op. cit. but with neither details of his age at the time nor any clear sense that this paid debut with Wikstrøm was his actual debut as a musician, as Dybo states.

33. Økland 1975 op. cit. (*Jazz I Norge*) p.119.

34. For aspects of Hans Marius Stormoen's subsequent activity, see e.g. note 31 above and the discussion of the late-1960s group Dream below.

Garbarek and Sollid were to be reunited on the 1975 **Østerdalsmusikk** (MAI 7510), which also featured a. o. Knut Riisnæs and Ole Jacob Hanssen - and which is discussed further in Chapter Four below. Lassem and Sollid can be heard together on the 1977 **Søyr** (MAI 7705), including "live"material from the Kongsberg Festival of that year. A fine, characterful trumpeter as well as drummer, Sollid has done a considerable amount to bring aspects of Norwegian folk music and jazz together, to the extent that he is sometimes described in Norway as "the father of mountain jazz". See bassist Carl Morten Iversen's 'Torgrim Sollid: et møte med fjelljazzens far' (a meeting with the father of mountain jazz) *Jazznytt* 4.5, Oslo 1995 for Sollid's discussion of the problems some young musicians (including himself) had in the 1960s, because of the misguided belief that, if one wanted to become a jazz musician, one had to imitate the life of such a musician as (supposedly) lived in the Bebop years i.e. get involved with drugs of one sort or another. Such temptations were always eschewed by Garbarek, who is to this day a non-smoker and teetaller.

35. Quoted in Dybo op. cit. p. 38 ("full and passionate sound" is the nearest I could get to the original and more powerful "blodfull klang").

36. Angell, O. & Vold, J. E. 'Intervju Med Karin Krog', *Jazz I Norge* p. 82. See also Stendahl, B. 'Portrett: Intervju med Karin Krog' *Jazznytt* 5, Oslo 1981 pp. 4-8 for a good overview of Krog's early days and subsequent, richly diversified career, including her work with Don Ellis in America in 1967 and her participation in such Free Jazz sessions as those documented on the 1969 **Open Space: The Down Beat Poll Winners In Europe** (MPS 15006) - recorded the year she won the *Down Beat* Talent Deserving Wider Recognition Poll, with John Surman, Albert Mangelsdorff, Francy Boland, Niels-Henning Ørsted Pedersen and Daniel Humair - and **Gittin' To Know Y'All** (MPS 15038). This was recorded with a. o. Bernt Rosengren, Terje Rypdal, Eje Thelin, Willem Breuker and the Art Ensemble of Chicago. Krog was an early jazz pioneer in the field of "voice and electronics".

37. Andersen, S. 'Lyrisk urkraft'(Lyrical primal creativity) *Nordlys*, Tromso 27/6/87. Although Garbarek has never felt a special relation to Bebop music, feeling much more of an affinity with both the 1960s avant-garde and pre-Bebop, or Swing players, Dexter Gordon has long meant something special to him. As a young man, he even affected one or two Dexter stage mannerisms for a - very - short while. Niels-Henning Ørsted Pedersen has said (half-jokingly) that Kenny Drew, Alex Riel and he used to like to play with the young Garbarek so much because he "almost played better Dexter than Dexter!" Personal communication, August 1998. For Garbarek's interest in pre-Bebop musicians, especially from the point of view of saxophone sound and timing, see *Jazznytt* no. 3, Oslo 1984 p. 6.

38. Personal communication, December 1997. See Økland, E. 'Intervju med Jon Christensen', *Jazz I Norge* p. 114 for Christensen's memories of playing at the 1957 "Nordiske Rockeshow" in Oslo's Nordstrandshallen, in front of a "skrikende publikum" (schrieking public).

39. Personal communication, December 1997.

40. **Metropol Jazz: Jazz Sounds From Norway** (Norsk Grammofonkompani

H 506 LP). With an informative sleeve-note by Johs Bergh, the record also features performances by the Rowland Greenberg quartet, Laila Dalseth, Jan Berger and Erik Amundsen, the Bjørn Johansen quartet, the Frode Thingnæs quintet, Karl Otto and Hans Hoff, the Helge Hurum Orchestra, the Big Chief Jazzband, the Bjørn Stokstad Sextet and the Thor Dynna quintet. The record was made possible by the initiative of guitarist Dynna, who persuaded the record company for which he worked to take an interest in the project.

41. Krog also studied singing technique with classical singer Anne Brown, from 1961 onwards. In *Jazz I Norge* she recalls Taylor as playing in Oslo in 1963 (as does Tove Semb in his memories of Metropol: see *Jazz I Norge* op.cit. p.97, where the visit of the Taylor trio is described as being in the autumn of 1963.) However, given the November 1962 date of Taylor's **Live At The Cafe Montmartre** session in Denmark and the information which Taylor would later give to A. B. Spellmann that he "went to Europe in 1962", I wonder if the visit did not take place in autumn 1962. See Spellmann, A. B. *Four Lives In The Bebop Business* MacGibbon & Kee, London 1967 p. 75 and Carr, I. 1987 op. cit. p. 487: "[In] 1962 [Taylor] spent six months in Europe with Jimmy Lyons (alto sax) and Sunny Murray (drums), playing in Oslo and Stockholm and recording [..] at the Cafe Montmartre, Copenhagen." In August 1998 Karin Krog suggested to me that Taylor's visit had indeed taken place in 1962.

42. Dybo 1996 op. cit. p. 39 suggests that a T. V. recording of Garbarek with the Kenny Drew Trio at Molde in 1965 shows the young saxophonist to be more fluent improvising with material which is "horizontal" (melodic) rather than "vertical" (harmonic) in orientation and potentiality: the former represented, in this case, by the standard *It Could Happen To You* and the latter by a blues piece, *The Midgets*. By the time of Garbarek's extensive "live" recording of *Autumn Leaves* with Per Løberg and Jon Christensen at "Asker Jazz Club" (in reality a working men's hut) in April 1967, he certainly had the ability to move at ease within - and outside - the harmonic framework of such a "classic" standard. Nevertheless, it remains the case that Garbarek's melodically-oriented, modal- and scalar-inflected aesthetic has long steered a very different course from the roller-coaster harmonic trips beloved of Bebop - the jazz music which most thoroughly absorbed Western classical principles of harmonic structure. (I am grateful to Jon Christensen for the loan of his copy of the private recording of *Autumn Leaves*, coupled with *Mr. P. C.* : see note 75 below.)

43. For details of these collaborations, see below and Chapter Four.

44. Mosnes, T. *Jazz I Molde: Festivaler Gjennom 20 År* (Jazz In Molde: Festivals Throughout Twenty Years) Nordvest, Ålesund 1980 p. 30 .

45. **Bombastica! 1959-60** (Dragon DRCD 287). For other representative recordings by this excellent musician, see the contextual discography, including references to Don Cherry.

46. *Knife In The Water* is available on Connoisseur Video CR 080. The film music, which was once available on a Polish Muza L P, has been reissued on Krzysztof Komeda **Crazy Girl** (Power Bros PB 00145). In 1997 Rosengren took part in a tribute to Komeda (1931-69), with

leader Tomasz Stanko (trumpet), Joakim Milder (saxophone), Bobo Stenson (piano), Palle Danielsson (bass) and Jon Christensen (drums): **Litania: The Music Of Krzysztof Komeda** (ECM 1636). The music, which includes *Ballad For Bernt*, received outstanding reviews in the jazz press and was performed live at several festivals, including Jazz Baltica 1998.

47. Mosnes 1980 op. cit. pp. 31-2.
48. Ibid. p. 32. See also Tucker, M. 'Jan Garbarek: The Poetics of Space', *Wire Magazine* no. 7, Summer 1984 where Garbarek recalls that, "[George's] Lydian concept, together with manuscripts he had dealing with rhythmic ideas, really opened up my horizons. Ideas of different strata within music, the pan-tonal ideas, were all of enormous importance. Most generally - apart, obviously, from his other personal qualities - he has been a tremendous musical inspiration. He taught me not to avoid difficulties." (p.20.) As an ex-drummer, Russell was able to develop a similarly fructifying relation with Jon Christensen.
49. In his *Free Jazz* Universal Edition, Graz 1974, Ekkehard Jost discusses the high degree of dynamic differentiation, or "gliding dynamics", in the sound of Albert Ayler and other saxophonists of the 1960s avant garde. (See e.g. p. 127.) Much of what Jost says illuminates the development of Garbarek's sound at this time. Garbarek himself has commented thus on some of his key influences of the 1960s: "In Coltrane's case I would say that it's really the spirit of the man coming through every note he plays [...] For the other players I could give some very schematic characteristics. Archie Shepp had an ability to move in a split second from extreme roughness to the most refined lyricism. Even in the course of one note he could do that. For Albert Ayler it was just this tremendous outpouring, his 'horn of plenty', so generous. His melodies, his sounds, his breathing, just so flowing, open. Also hitting me very strongly. For Pharoah Sanders it was his earthiness, his feeling for folk music, the way I saw it at that time, for singing. Yes, they all had their very strong influence on me." Soluthurnmann 1995/97 op. cit. p. 4. It is often suggested that Gato Barbieri was an influence on Garbarek at this time, but Garbarek has said that he had the *idea* of his sound in his head before he had ever heard the Argentinian. See Tucker 1977 op. cit. p 19.
50. *To B. E. (+81)* . Garbarek was in the audience for one of the last concerts which Bill Evans gave, at the Molde Festival in July 1980. Unfortunately, the dating of Evans' death in Garbarek's dedication is wrong: the pianist died on September 15th 1980.
51. Personal communication, September 1998.
52. Bjørklund is an interesting, multi-faceted musician (and composer) who in 1983 received the Buddy Award for his contributions to Norwegian jazz, the highest honour awarded by the Norwegian Jazz Federation. (Krog, Christensen and Garbarek won this award in, respectively, 1965, 1967 and 1968.) Bjørklund can be heard playing fine modern mainstream piano on Asmund Bjørken's late-1970s **Jazz Accordion My Way** (Sonor Records SONCD 3002) and appears with Warne Marsh (and Torgrim Sollid) on the cool-school, 1983 **Sax Of A Kind: Warne Marsh In Norway** (Hot Club Records HCR 7). Marsh considered

Bjørklund one of the finest pianists and most intuitive accompanists he had ever played with: see Iversen 1995 op. cit. p. 9. Moving north to Trondheim, where he played an important pedagogical role in helping develop the region's jazz music scene, Bjørklund gradually moved away from jazz piano in the 1980s to concentrate on "serious" or "art" music composition: he was chosen as Festival Composer for the 1993 Festival of Northern Norway. The 1994 **Music For Strings** (Hemera HCD 2923) is a fine introduction to this side of his creativity, traversing sonorous terrain of Bjørklund's own somewhere between Grieg, Sibelius and Vaughan Williams, Rautavaara and Arvo Pärt. The record includes the pieces *Arctos* (Journey to the North) and *Sarek* (inspired by Sven Hornell's pictures from the national park in Sweden's Lappland, a huge wilderness area). See Chapter Four below.

53. The Norwegian Jazz Archive has issued some instructive and enjoyable rare recordings of Norwegian jazz from the 1920s to the mid-1950s (see the discography). It would be nice if some of these early, historic broadcasts featuring Krog, Garbarek and their colleagues could be made available to the public. Among other things, they would serve to demonstrate what a strong, convincing blues player the young Garbarek could be when he wanted.

54. There was a Norwegian "mini-festival" at Kongsberg in September 1964, with a. o. guitarist Leif Simensen, Karin Krog, Bjørn Johansen and Egil Kapstad. This set in motion the idea of the festival proper, which began in summer 1965. Other material featured in this period by the quintet included a tribute to Eric Dolphy, as played at Kongsberg in 1967 (see note 57).

55. Further evidence of the young Garbarek's openness of approach is supplied by Randi Hultin, in her *Born Under The Sign Of Jazz* (trans. T. Challman) Sanctuary, London 1998 pp. 303-7. Here we can see not only Hultin's picture of Garbarek with Karin Krog and Kurt Lindgren at the Warsaw Jazz Festival in 1966, but also her shot of Garbarek sitting in at a jam session with the Monty Sunshine Band at the same festival. According to Karin Krog, Garbarek found it an inspiring, enriching experience to work with Lindgren, a very well-schooled bassist whose musical knowledge Garbarek respected and admired. Sadly, like his compatriot, the pianist Jan Johansson (1931-68) Lindgren was to die in a car crash, in the early 1980s. Personal communication, August 1998.

56. In his sleeve-note to the original British release of **Walkin'** (Esquire 32-098) Ira Gitler pointed out the relation of the 12 bar *Walkin'* to *Gravy*, an almost identical blues theme recorded by Gene Ammons for Prestige in 1950.

57. A July 1967 broadcast of the Karin Krog group, from Kongsberg Cinema, features the composition *Remembrance of Eric Dolphy* , where Garbarek's solo makes effective dynamic use of that "screaming" quality so typical of avant-garde tenor in the 1960s, but which Garbarek also knew of as an expressive resource from the work of an earlier musician like Illinois Jacquet, for example. Garbarek's tone here already has something of that surreal, unearthly quality that would appear in parts of the title track of the 1970 **Afric Pepperbird**.

58. Wilson, P. 'George Russell's Constant Quest', *Down Beat* vol. 39. no. 8 April 27 1972 p. 29.

59. "I drank it down one evening" says Garbarek, in Økland 1975 op. cit. p. 121.

60. The essay is available on the CD reissue, Soul Note 121014-2. For Kvaløy's later development as a thinker and activist - he has been called Norway's leading environmentalist - see his essays 'Complexity and Time: Breaking the Pyramid's Reign' and 'Getting Our Feet Wet', in Reed, P. & Rothenberg, D. (eds.) _Wisdom In The Open Air: The Norwegian Roots Of Deep Ecology_ University of Minnesota Press, Minneapolis & London 1993 pp. 112-52.

61. Ibid. (Soul Note)

62. Russell offers an incisive introduction to his ideas in "The 'River Trip' Explanation of Jazz Improvisational Styles", in _The Lydian Chromatic Concept of Tonal Organisation_, Concept Publishing Co., New York 1959 pp. xviii -xix. See also Blumenthal, B. 'George Russell: Stratus Seeker', _Down Beat_ vol. 50. no. 10, October 1983 pp. 24-6. Here, Russell recalls the inspiration he received in the late-1940s and early 1950s from the "legendary scene" at Gil Evans' basement apartment on New York's 55th St., where people like Charlie Parker and Gerry Mulligan, John Lewis and Miles Davis used to drop in. "We had a very broad approach to everything.We'd go to Juillard and listen to Robert Craft prepare a concert for Stravinsky or Hindemith, or we'd listen to Dmitri Mitropolous prepare a concert. We listened to all kinds of music. I'd go to Miles' house, and we'd sit down for hours at the piano and trade chords." During this period Russell concentrated on "the ladder of fifths, which produced the Lydian scale. That's when I knew I was onto something, because the ladder of fifths is a piece of objective truth rather than subjective knowledge. The ladder of fifths has been around for centuries; the pentatonic scale, the primary scale of ancient musics, is basically five fifths [...] Some people hear the Lydian scale [which one can visualise or hear, e.g., as C major with an F sharp, i.e. a raised 4th] and say, 'It's not going anywhere.' Well, it isn't going anywhere but up; it's evolving to embrace the whole chromatic scale, which is simply two Lydian scales, on C and F sharp." Russell also reveals that, between 1960 and 1963, a time when his sextet featured such musicians as Don Ellis, Eric Dolphy and Sheila Jordan, six albums were recorded, but work in America was virtually non-existent. The latter situation was to change dramatically in Scandinavia. For further perspectives on Russell, see the articles and sleeve-notes in the bibliography by Harrison, Kolberg, Kvaloy, Riggins and Wilson.

63. Russell had long been aware of the music of Stockhausen. His 1961 arrangement of '_Round Midnight_, on **Ezz-thetics**, begins with an eerie acoustic equivalent of electronic sounds. In turn, Stockhausen came to be impressed by Russell's improvising abilities, requesting that Russell play piano at a social gathering which found them together, and writing a letter of support for Russell's (successful) application for the first of his two Guggenheim Fellowships (for which Russell wrote Stockhausen a note of gratitude). The two men discussed ideas together at the time of the 1965 Tivoli concert: it is regrettable that there is no mention of Russell in either Stockhausen's own _Towards A Cosmic Music_ (trans. & ed. T. Nevill) Element Books, Shaftesbury 1989 or Michael Kurtz's

Stockhausen: A Biography (trans. R. Toop) Faber & Faber, London 1992. During his time in Oslo in the later 1960s, when he lived off Majorstua, near the spacious Frogner Park, with its rows of figurative sculptures by Gustav Vigeland, Russell came into contact not only with the jazz community, but also leading "serious" or "art" music composers of the time, such as Kåre Kolberg - who wrote the instructive notes for the **Essence of George Russell** release.

64. Among other things, the concert was memorable for a guest appearance by Sweden's Bengt Hallberg, who conducted (and played piano on) his own widely recast, somewhat Free Jazz-inflected arrangement of *Dinah*. Hallberg was the first foreign musician to play Metropol (followed by Stan Getz and then Ernestine Anderson), and had an especially successful late summer engagement there in 1963, at a time when the organisers were increasingly conscious of the possible impact of television and the pop world upon young jazz audiences. See the front page feature in *Metropol News*, Oslo November 1963.

65. From a letter of the late 1960s by Russell, possibly addressed to the Norwegian broadcasting authorities. I am grateful to Jan Horne for making this document available to me.

66. The tape was composed in the Electronic Music Studios of Swedish Radio in Stockholm. In the sleeve-note to the sextet version of the Sonata, Russell credits engineer Gote Nilsson of that establishment for "invaluable assistance in both the areas of engineering and composition."

67. Recently reissued as **At Beethoven Hall: Complete Recordings** (MPS 539 084-2)

68. Cherry speaks about jazz's "capacity for unity" in the sleeve-note to **Complete Communion** (Blue Note BST 84226). For an excellent appraisal and analysis of his music at this time, see Jost 1974 op. cit. pp. 133 - 62.

69. The dedication of *Malinye* reads: "for Don, in loving memory and gratitude for his prolific inspiration".

70. Combination of personal communication, May 1984 and Scherwin, J. 'Det skenbart ENKLA', *Tonfallet* (Sweden) no. 7, 1993 p.13.

71. The Sogn Jazz Club, which when full could accomodate around 350 people, was started in March 1967 on the initiative of Steinar Kristiansen and lasted until May 1978, when singer Radka Toneff gave the last concert at the club. Concerts usually took place on a Sunday evening: musicians and singers who appeared over the years included Monica Zetterlund, Steve Kuhn, Dexter Gordon, Clifford Jordan, Art Farmer, Jimmy Heath, George Russell, Don Cherry, Albert Nicholas, Freddie Hubbard, Phil Woods, - and, of course, Jan Garbarek and Jon Christensen, who played often at the club, including some immensely popular sessions with the Garbarek-Stenson Quartet and Jan Erik Vold. I heard a fine performance by singer Radka Toneff at Sogn in 1976 - by which time, I seem to remember, the Munch paintings had been (officially) removed. In August 1998, after years of different use, the premises at Sogn became a jazz club again. (See Helgheim, R. 'Historisk jazzklub-opning', *Dag Og Tid*, Oslo 27/8/98.) Personal communication from Steinar Kristiansen, August 1998.

72. Norwegian newspapers reported the concert as an outstanding success, particularly in the light of the fact that there had been no rehearsal beforehand, but simply a "humming of a few themes while the view from Holmenkollen [the great hill behind Oslo, which leads into the beautiful, expansive Nordmarka area of rolling countryside] had been admired." (Jon Christensen's archives.) Christensen was soon to play with another musician very interested in folk forms, the Polish alto saxophonist Zbigniew Namyslowski. The quartet of Namyslowski and Christensen, Adam Makowicz (piano) and Roman Dylag (bass) played the Molde and Warsaw festivals in 1967.

73. Riedel was born in Czechoslovakia in 1934 and came to Sweden just before the war. He began composing in the 1950s: his first composition, *Stocks and Bonds*, was recorded by the Lars Gullin Quintet (including Reidel himself and drummer Alan Dawson) on November 5th 1953. A long-time member of the Arne Domnérus group, Reidel recorded with Jan Johansson on some of the pianist's most beautiful records e.g. the 1962-4 piano and bass **Jazz på Svenska** (Megafon). Recorded in the later 1960s, the two extended compositions (*Conversation Symphonette* and *Three Dancers*) of his **Jazz Ballet** (Philips PHS 600-140) remain some of the most rewarding, genre-crossing work of the decade, with some superb writing for voices. As sleeve-writer Don DeMichael comments: "There is a touch of the 'Sprechgesang' of Schoenberg's *Pierrot Lunaire* in Riedel's use of the voice in musical composition. But a touch is all it is, for Riedel, unlike Schoenberg, has utilized the voices for rhythmic more than melodic effects."

74. Keith Jarrett recollects Garbarek playing soprano saxophone in the late 1960s "in a free-jazz context at a jam session in Oslo ... Jan was playing soprano sitting down, Arild Andersen was playing bass and maybe Bobo Stenson was playing piano sometimes, and Jon [Christensen] was on drums. I've rarely heard better free playing than I heard that night." Carr, I. 1991 op cit (*Keith Jarrett*) p. 75. Garbarek himself recalls that he didn't introduce the soprano fully to his work "until '71, '72 maybe. Because I didn't really like the sound that most people got with the straight horn. But I'd heard this record with Johnny Hodges playing soprano and I sort of felt that he was using a curved one, because it sounded so different from all the other sopranos I'd heard. So I waited until I came across a curved one and found that, yes, I liked it." Lake, S. 'Jan Garbarek: Saga of Ice and Fire' *Down Beat* vol. 44 no.19 November 17, 1977 p. 16.

75. From sleeve-note to **Til Vigdis** (NJFLP-1). Side One of this recording is constituted by *Mr J. C.* (18.30) and Side Two by *Freedom Jazz Dance* (14.15) and *Til Vigdis* (6.30). A private vinyl recording exists of the April 1st live recording of *Mr J. C.* (here called *Mr. P. C.*) coupled with a side-long live version of *Autumn Leaves* from the same session, again with Per Løberg and Jon Christensen. *Autumn Leaves* is fascinating, with touches of Gordon and Rollins in the initial exposition (including a passing reference to *Softly, As In A Morning Sunrise*). Some Shepp-like dynamics then precipitate a lovely passage of old-time, swing/bounce rhythm; pedal point, rubato abstractions follow, with a rougher tone

eventually taking us back through old-time grooves to a pizzicato bass solo, (diminished tempo) reprise of the theme and brief, Latinesque coda. Throughout, Garbarek makes judicious play with contrasts between asymmetry and symmetry, the contemporary and the historical in his phrasing: the record is eloquent testimony to that nascent, increasing breadth of conception in his work, which would be developed to such extraordinary, cross-cultural degree on ECM.

76. A European aesthetic which Jost Gebers' FMP (Free Music Production) label would do much to document from 1969 onwards. See Jost, E. 'European Jazz Avantgarde - Where Will Emancipation Lead?' in Gebers, J. (ed.) **For Example: Workshop Freie Musik 1969-1978** FMP, Berlin 1978 (a special production of 3 LPs and booklet, with texts and numerous b & w photographs documenting the free music sessions of this period which took place at the Akademie Der Kunste in Berlin). Jost details the various stages of what he calls the "detachment" of European Free Jazz from American Free Jazz at this time, from the "kaputt play" of records like Brötzmann's **Machine Gun** and Manfred Schoof's **European Echoes** (both FMP) to the more variegated approach of the Globe Unity Orchestra, for example. Jost's concern is to document the plurality of approaches within European Free Jazz, and this he certainly does. However, the great range of music on ECM which had been recorded by 1978 is not mentioned at all by Jost, indicating a certain ideological bias at work. The Triptykon Trio of Garbarek, Arild Andersen and Edward Vesala played at the Berlin "Anti-Festival" in November 1972 (see _Jazznytt_ 1, Oslo 1973) and the Garbarek-Stenson Quartet played at the sixth Free Music Workshop at the Akademie der Kunste in 1974. The latter event is documented by a single photograph of the quartet in action, on page 45 of a booklet which otherwise devotes many pictures to the groups and artists represented.

77. Garbarek draws attention to the early use of a drone effect in _Til Vigdis_ in Dybo op. cit. p. 130. Following Dybo's earlier comparison between this number and _Third Piece_, Garbarek suggests a further parallel with musical characteristics of the Norwegian 'lokk' or cattle call.

78. Information from Jon Christensen, August 1997.

79. The television programme which Jan Horne made of the George Russell sextet's April 1968 performance of _Electronic Sonata_ at the Henie-Onstad Centre was of comparable quality to _Interludium_. Scandalously, Horne's programme would later be wiped by broadcasting authorities keen to "rationalise" budgets. One is reminded of what happened to some of the more avant-garde material taped at the BBC in the 1960s.

80. Brown also played with Garbarek, Andersen and Christensen in Trondheim, in a "mini-festival" which featured the popular Swedish singer Monica Zetterlund, with accompaniment from Steve Kuhn (piano), Palle Danielsson and Jon Christensen. Newspapers reported an extraordinary, extremely healthy audience figure of 2, 200. Critic Randi Hultin was instrumental in setting up this visit of Brown, to whom she had sent Garbarek's **Til Vigdis** recording. Brown was "very surprised" by its quality. Hultin, R. 'Jan Garbarek', _Jazz Forum_ no. 21, 1973 p. 50.

81. Personal communication, September 1998.
82. Dybo 1996 op. cit. p. 39 suggests that on Karin Krog's 1966 **Jazz Moments** there is a track entitled *Old Folk Song*, and that this indicates the growth of Garbarek's interest in folk material at this time. There is no such track on the **Jazz Moments** LP, but rather a version of *Old Folks* (the tune which Charlie Parker, among others, played). The 1968, post-Montreux Festival T. V. recording contains the first recorded evidence I have been able to find of the beginnings of Garbarek's interest in folk material. However, in a review of an autumn 1966 Munch Museum NJF concert by the Karin Krog quintet, journalist/critic Rolf E. Schade observes that Garbarek began *Caravan*, the concert's final number, by playing "a type of glissando-flute, in duet with Karin Krog's singing. Shifting to tenor sax Garbarek made something more and more 'Arabic'- sounding out of the number." ("en slags glissando-fløyte, i duett med Karin Krog's sang. Etter a ha skiftet til tenor-sax laget Garbarek mer og mer 'arabisk' lat ut av nummeret.") Schade noted that the concert also contained versions of Coltrane's *Chasin' The Trane* and *Spiritual* (played as a suite) and Charles Lloyd's *Sombrero Sam*. Jon Christensen's archives. (In August 1998 Karin Krog suggested to me that Garbarek may have been playing a slide whistle on *Caravan*.)

Dybo op. cit. (p.156, note 21) paraphrases Garbarek as suggesting that, around 1964/65, he made a radio broadcast for NRK with Don Cherry, on which the (now late) artist Sidsel Paaske sang some folk verses. Jon Christensen, who played on the broadcast, has confirmed the story, but agrees it is difficult to date the event precisely. Cherry was certainly in Stockholm, if not Oslo, in December 1964, when he subbed for Lars Gullin (who was caught in a snowstorm) in a pre-Christmas radio broadcast of the music of Gullin's recently recorded **Portrait Of My Pals**. This, Cherry said, was his first time in Stockholm. See Knox, K. (with Lindqvist, G.) *Jazz Amour Affair: En bok om Lars Gullin* Svensk Musik, Stockholm 1986 p. 105. The fact that Cherry's appearance at Sogn Jazz Club in Oslo in May 1967 was described by the Norwegian jazz press as Cherry's Norwegian debut reinforces the difficulty of dating this first encounter of Garbarek with the trumpeter as being in 1964/5. Would Cherry have travelled the five to six hundred kilometres or so from Stockholm to Oslo in 1964/65 solely for a radio broadcast, and without any public performance being arranged for him at the same time? A 1969 newspaper report by Randi Hultin speaks of Cherry and the Jan Garbarek quartet of that time appearing at Bikubben and Sogn together, and then making a special broadcast for NRK. Hultin here reiterates that the trumpeter's appearance at Sogn in May 1967 was Cherry's first visit to Norway ("første besøk i Norge"). Jon Christensen's archives. Steinar Kristiansen has said to me that Cherry's first visit to Oslo definitely took place in 1967. Personal communication, August 1998.

This may seem an undue amount of time to spend on such an issue, but the idea that Cherry visited Oslo and met and played with Garbarek in 1964 has taken some root: see e.g. Toop, D. *Ocean of Sound: aether talk, ambient sound and imaginary worlds* Serpent's Tail, London/New York 1995 p. 133: "When Don visited Oslo in 1964, Garbarek and his friends were influenced by Coltrane. The nomadic trumpet player from America made them aware of their own traditions." He did; but not in 1964, I would suggest.

83. I do not know if such programming was then unique in the world, but the Henie-Onstad Centre certainly offered some outstanding, genre-crossing evenings of music at this time. Randi Hultin has shown me a photo of Garbarek playing in a concert with singer Sheila Jordan at the Centre, for example, around the end of the 1960s.

84. **Joy** (Sonet SLPS 1405) was recorded at the Arne Bendiksen Studio, Oslo on October 2nd 1968. The personnel lists Krog as (voice, rhythm instruments) and Garbarek as (tenor, rhythm instruments). T. V. broadcasts from the time show Garbarek playing a tambourine occasionally, something he would also do with the Garbarek/Stenson and Belonging quartets, as well as during the time he spent touring with Shankar in the mid-1980s. By the time of the recording of the 1988-89 **Rosensfole** Garbarek's Asian-inflected percussive skills had developed considerably, and constitute a good part of the record's (multi-tracked) appeal.

85. Ibid (**Joy**).

86. Personal communication, August 1998. For an introduction to Per Kleiva's work, which is as poetic and technically innovative as it is (often) politically engaged, see Renberg, U., Flor, H. & Vold, J. E. *Per Kleiva* Labyrinth Press, Oslo 1986.

87. See Holbaek-Hanssen, H. 'Alfred Janson: The "friendly" modernist', *Listen to Norway* vol. 1 no. 1 Oslo 1993, p. 30-31 and Janson's 1987 recording (with a. o. Palle Mikkelborg, Tore Brunborg, Arild Andersen and Jon Christensen) **Interlude** (Norwegian Composers NCD 4918). This includes extensive notes in English.

88. The role of Munch was danced by Jens Graff. The intertwining saxophone parts of *Mot Solen* were completely written out by Janson, who recalls that Harald Bergersen played tenor saxophone and Garbarek alto saxophone. Personal communication, August 1998. Subsequently, Garbarek has worked quite often with modern or contemporary dance companies in Norway.

89. A similar quality was evident in the appearance of Garbarek, Andersen, Bjørklund, Kurt Lindgren, drummer Svein Christiansen and Ola B. Johannessen (bells) when they accompanied Karin Krog in the May 1969 Norwegian television broadcast of Arne Nordheim's anti-European Song Contest piece *Her og Nå*. This piece can be heard as part of Nordheim's *Solar Plexus*, on **Popofoni** (Sonet SLP 1421/22, issued in 1972). The Finnerud Trio re-appeared in the mid-1990s, but with drummer Svein Christiansen in place of Rud: see the 1994 **Travel Pillow** (Prisma FTCD 9401) and the review of their well-received performance at Oslo's Rebekka West, which I was fortunate enough to hear: Helgheim, R. 'Musikk som betyr noko' (Music that means something) *Klassekampen* 9/4/94 p 15.

90. In Jon Christensen's archives, two concerts by the quartet of Jan Garbarek (tenor), Svein Finnerud (piano), Arild Andersen (bass) and Jon Christensen (drums) are recorded as having taken place in Molde on 13/14 December 1969. A review headline of the time ran 'Jazz eller

Hva?' (Jazz or What?). After asking whether the concert, with its "non-stop bombardment of hard rhythmic means and sound effects", and various theatrical aspects of body language from the musicians, had been "jazz or new music", the reviewer (pih) suggested that the concert had been both these things - and wondered how many of the c. 500 audience in the town hall had been able to follow the intense, highly avant-garde music, which seemed so distant from the traditional roots of jazz. The review concluded that it was necessary to have musicians experimenting, seeking new paths: after all, jazz would always have its Dixieland, and the public was free to choose whether it preferred that or "Jan Garbarek *anno* 1969". Jon Christensen's archives.

91. Milkowski, B. 'Terje Rypdal: Sculptor In Sound', _Down Beat_ vol. 54 no. 10, October 1987 p. 20. Mingus gave what is now regarded as a legendary concert (with Clifford Jordan, Eric Dolphy, Johnny Coles, Jaki Byard and Dannie Richmond) at the Aula Hall, the University of Oslo, in 1964. (Garbarek - and Christensen - have listened to various Mingus recordings with much interest.) Rypdal's interests in the mid-to-late 1960s also included late Coltrane: he bought the 1965 **Meditations** soon after it came out. At first, he "didn't understand a thing", but later came to find the music fascinating. According to Rypdal, some of the music he has since recorded with Ketil Bjørnstad, David Darling and Jon Christensen on ECM came out of impulses still felt from **Meditations**. Personal communication, August 1998. Rypdal revisited some of his earliest days as a musician in his guest appearances on guitarist Knut Mikalsen and his Bop Quintet's 1997 **Road Song** (Villa Records AS VRCD 005). See also Rypdal's half-hour long *The Vanguardian*, dedicated to (and played by) Mikalsen, on the 1986/91 Sandvika Big Band **Contemporary Music For Big Band:The Music of Terje Rypdal and Kjell Samkopf** (SSCD 002).

92. From the archives of Jon Christensen.

93. For Andersen's early days and development, see Stendahl, B. 'Portrett: Intervju med Arild Andersen' *Jazznytt* 4, Oslo 1981 pp. 5-6. Andersen received the Buddy Award in 1968: named after the legendary Buddy Bolden, the award was once in the form of a statue, an unpretentious, naturalistic piece in black-painted plaster, created by (the late) Lise Fogg. In 1970 trombonist Frode Thingnæs was the first to receive the award in its new, more abstract incarnation, sculpted by Jo Vogt (see _Jazz I Norge_ p.164). Terje Rypdal received the Buddy Award in 1985.

94. Vold contributes some interesting perspectives on beat literature, jazz and poetry in Vold 1976 op. cit. (_Entusiastiske Essays: Klippbok 1960-75_) and also offers some reminiscences of and reflections upon his time with the Garbarek/Stenson quartet. See e.g. pp. 9-24 and 635-6.

95. It is the sheer breadth of ideas, and disciplined energy, which so distinguish the music of this quartet at the time - plus a good deal of humour. This last was something that would disappear (or rather, become transmuted, as in the bitter-sweet, wry quality in a such a track as the 1984 *I'm the knife-thrower's partner* or the near-ecstatic affirmation of the 1986 *Second Piece*) in both Garbarek's live and recorded performances of later years.

96. See Hellandsjø, K. _Jakob Weidemann Og Det Abstrakte Maleris_

Gjennombrud I Norge 1945-1965 (Jakob Weidemann and the Breakthrough of Abstract Art in Norway) Gylendal, Oslo 1978 passim and Tucker, M. 'Dreamer In A Landscape' in *Frans Widerberg: A Retrospective Exhibition* Newcastle Polytechnic/Brighton Polytechnic, Newcastle upon Tyne 1986 passim.

97. Norway has twice - in 1972 and 1994 - had a national referendum in which the idea of membership in the EEC has been rejected. See Libæk and Stenersen op. cit. (*History of Norway*) pp. 154-55 and 174-75. Conceptual artist Nam June Paik's visit to Oslo in 1961 is sometimes seen as the event which marked the final "loss of innocence" *vis à vis* Norwegian culture and its awareness of and relation to avant-garde events abroad. Dybo (1996 op. cit. p. 42) asks Garbarek if the name (and ideas of) John Cage meant much to him and his playing companions in the 1960s. Garbarek replies by saying that, while Cage's name was not known to them, his ideas may well have been in the air anyway, given that there were so many "happenings" in Oslo at that time. Besides, adds Garbarek, Don Cherry had been in Oslo a few times - and he was "certainly a very 'happening' person." For an impression of Cherry late in life, his vitality undimmed, see the 57-minute VHS video **Don Cherry's "Multikulti"** (VIEW 1348), with Peter Apflebaum, (saxes/keyboards), Bo Freeman (bass) and Joshua Jones (drums).

98. The 1998 **Rites** album contains a sleeve-note by Garbarek explaining the inclusion of a piece which is not composed by him, and on which he does not play - Jansug Kakhidze's *The moon over Mtatsminda*.

99. See *Jazznytt* no. 2 May 1970 where Garbarek emphasises that on **Popofoni**, there had never been any question of "blending" forms, as in contemporary, emergent jazz-rock, for example: the musicians had played "pure contemporary music". The Popofoni project is hard to date exactly: following initial recordings in 1969, a good deal of the material was subject to later electronic treatment in the studio at Høvikodden.

Garbarek's text for the eventual 1972 release concludes: "[M]any jazz musicians today are interested in extending the conceptions, breaking down the barriers between the different musical traditions, and the same thing happens among the performers of other forms of music.They are drawing closer together: it is getting more and more difficult to classify them. The means of expression overlap each other. Personally I think the element of improvisation will manifest itself more strongly in all music and also in other art forms (ballet, theatre, film, for example). A project like Popofoni is a natural part of this process." Earlier in the essay Garbarek had considered how much improvisation is, of course, not necessarily a matter of absolutely spontaneous or unpremeditated activity. Recently, he has responded to the suggestion that he does not improvise as much today as he did some years ago by pointing out how much improvisation can be involved in bringing a single note to full, resonant life within a melody which he might choose to play night after night. See Kristiansen, S. 'Jan Garbarek:Intervju', *Jazznytt* 1, Oslo 1996 pp. 6.

According to composer and lecturer Olav Anton Thommessen (born 1946 and currently Professor of Music at the Norwegian State

Academy of Music in Oslo) the cross-genre spirit of the late 1960s has not continued to flower in Norway, and the "jazz" and "serious" people are now back in their respective camps, as it were. There was recently talk of reviving and developing the spirit of Popofoni in a Teknofoni project, but nothing has materialised so far. Personal communication, June 1998. (For a representative example of the combination of historical sensitivity and contemporary breadth in Thommessen's own work, see his **Nordic Council Music Prize 1990** release on Caprice CAP 21403.)

Electric Connection: George Russell and Jan Garbarek
(Oslo 1969) Collection Jan Horne, Oslo

Jan Garbarek, Jon Christensen, Arild Andersen, Frank Phipps
(Sogn Jazz Club 1967) National Jazz Archives, Oslo

Don Cherry, Jon Christensen, Jan Garbarek, Per Løberg
(Sogn Jazz Club 1967) Arne Johan Johansen
Collection Steinar Kristiansen, Oslo

North

In autumn 1997 the Vienna Art Orchestra celebrated their twentieth anniversary with an extensive European tour, including several dates in Britain. Led by Mathias Rüegg, the Orchestra had long been renowned for an ability to bring Afro-American and European elements of jazz expression into a variety of syntheses as enjoyable as they are provocative – as evinced by such classic albums as **Suite For The Green Eighties, The Minimalism of Erik Satie, Blues for Brahms** and **For Jean Cocteau**. On their celebratory tour, the Orchestra chose to pay tribute to a number of outstanding European creative spirits in jazz, in the extensive suite *An Echo from Europe: from Django (Reinhardt) to Django (Bates)*.

It seemed only natural that, together with the work of its dedicatees and, for example, Hans Koller, Albert Mangelsdorff and the contemporary French clarinettists and saxophonists Michel Portal and Louis Sclavis, the suite should feature music by Jan Garbarek. This Rüegg and the Orchestra did through an imaginatively recast version of one of Garbarek's most atmospheric compositions, the contemplative, hymnal *Star*. Featuring Robert Riegler on electric bass, the Vienna Art Orchestra played the piece in an engaging combination of strong shuffle rhythms and legato accents, a touch reminiscent of Pat Metheny's *Last Train Home* from the 1987 Geffen album **Still Life (Talking)**. Recorded in 1991 with Czechoslovakian double-bassist Miroslav Vitous and American drummer Peter Erskine, and subsequently featured on Garbarek's tours with this trio, as well as in duet with Miroslav Vitous, the original, far more rubato treatment of *Star* features Garbarek's judicious use of a pedal harmoniser device with his soprano saxophone, underlining the expansive, cosmic aura of the piece's tender yet questing theme.

In his programme notes for the tour, Rüegg spoke of how, "With Jan Garbarek, Europe has gained a real star, a magnet for audiences that can sometimes number in the thousands, yet who manages to retain a style of his own that remains true to the vast and cool quality of his Nordic origins."[1] As Rilke remarked, fame may well be but the sum of the various misunderstandings which gather about a name.[2] Nonetheless, these words of Rüegg point to the heart of a very large part of what pianist Misha Alperin has called "the Garbarek phenomenon". For, rooted in the Afro-American avant garde of the 1960s as so much of Garbarek's early work was, over subsequent decades he has developed a body of work which, as Rüegg suggests, speaks of something very different from both the urban tensions and the rhythmic impulses of so much American (and American-inspired) jazz.

What might Rüegg have meant by the phrase "the vast and cool quality" of Garbarek's Nordic origins? The beautiful words which the English producer and writer Keith Knox penned in memory of Swedish baritone saxophonist and composer Lars Gullin (1928-76) may furnish a clue. Gullin's compositions, wrote Knox, "recall much that is common to Swedish folk music, but the similarities have a great deal more to do with feelings than materials. Nordic contrasts of winter and summer, night and day, combine with the landscape to work a special alchemy that brings a certain awareness of the closeness of man and nature; and the music of the soul is sad music. Lars' music and the folk music of Sweden have this melancholy of endlessness in common."[3]

From Grieg and Alfvén, Rangström and Nielsen to Nils Lindberg and Lars Gullin, Jan Johansson and Bengt-Arne Wallin, Niels-Henning Ørsted Pedersen and Jan Garbarek (and beyond), Nordic musicians and composers have been inspired by the tones and textures, as well as the melodic potential, of their countries' folk music.[4] The Swede Wallin, whose **Old Folkore In Swedish Modern** from June 1962 remains, with fellow Swede Jan Johansson's 1962-4 **Jazz på Svenska**, an early classic of the jazz-meets-folk school of music, once observed that, "folk-lore might be called a kind of definitive music, not as notes on paper but as a living phenomenon, created by the right people, inherited and made perfect through the generations – and still full of life today."[5] In the notes to his 1976 **Samse Tak!** (Pull Together!) – a fascinating album based upon a variety of cable layers' songs and folk melodies, and featuring Bertil Lövgren (trumpet), Knut Riisnæs (tenor saxophone), Terje Rypdal (electric guitar), and Georg Riedel (bass) – Norwegian drummer Egil "Bop" Johansen put the recording in historical perspective: "At the beginning of the 1960s musicians such as altoist Arne Domnérus, pianist Jan Johansson, trumpeter Bengt-Arne Wallin, bassist Georg

Riedel, guitarist Rune Gustafsson and myself began to search for other vehicles for improvisation than the familiar Afro-American elements of Swing, Bebop, Cool, Free-Form, etc. [..] We had come to realise that we should be able to add a dimension of our own to our improvisations."[6]

The differences between the folk music of the various Nordic countries can be appreciable – as can the ways in which composers and musicians come to that music. For Niels-Henning Ørsted Pedersen (born 1946) – who, along with Garbarek, is the outstanding Nordic jazz musician of his generation – the folk songs of Denmark were part and parcel of the Danish Folk High School environment in which he grew up. Pedersen remembers that, in his youth, every morning at around quarter to eight there would be a song to sing, with seasonal relevance.[7] This legacy is strikingly apparent in the many superbly interpreted folk melodies which so distinguish this virtuoso bass player's oeuvre, from the 1973 *I skovens dybe stille ro* (In the deep peace of the woods) which opened his first **Duo** album with (the late) Kenny Drew, to the many beautiful melodies of the 1984 **The Eternal Traveller** and the 1994 **Scandinavian Wood**, for example. On the 1998 **This Is All I Ask**, the importance of folk tradition to the bassist was further underlined by a haunting new version of *I skovens dybe stille ro*, played in memory of Drew by NHØP and Oscar Peterson.[8]

The contrast with Garbarek – with whom NHØP played at the 1965 Molde festival, in a quartet also featuring Kenny Drew and Alex Riel – could hardly be greater. Garbarek's path to the treasure-house of folk melody did not begin until an Afro-American musician, Don Cherry, pointed out the way there to him.[9] And just as there is a big difference in the way in which each of these two technically outstanding musicians came to appreciate (and express) the beauty of simplicity in folk music, so is there an appreciable difference in the nature of the folk music which each has come to feature in his work.

To my ears, there seems to be what I would call a more consonant or North European sound in a good deal of the material which NHØP has adopted from his own tradition, especially in comparison with the (at times) more cutting, almost Balkan feeling of some of the Norwegian folk music which Garbarek has dealt with in a comparable fashion. Garbarek himself has said that he found the most "exotic" material, so to speak, in his own backyard – material which has led him to sense and explore intriguing, border-crossing connections between Norwegian folk music and that of India, *via* various currents in Asia Minor.[10]

Despite such differences, it remains true to say that a communality of feeling does run through a considerable amount of Nordic, folk-inflected music: feeling which has a great deal to do with the sort of considerations that Keith Knox brought to bear in his 1977 tribute to Lars Gullin. Factors of musical difference and emotional communality were in equal evidence on NHØP's 1991-92 recording **Uncharted Land**. For here, Jan Garbarek appeared on four tracks, including an eighteen-minute arrangement by Garbarek of a Norwegian traditional melody, *Nordavind* (Northern Wind). The music features keening, ascensional vocals from the Ars Nova choir, shape-shifting, "wind-in-the-forest" percussive textures from Marilyn Mazur and superbly structured, urgently explorative solos from guitarist Mehmet Ozan, Garbarek and NHØP himself. Placed immediately after the transcendental, poised peace of NHØP's reading with pianist Ole Kock Hansen of the Danish melody *Natten Er Så Still* (The Night Is So Still) the driving, "on-the-edge" power of *Nordavind* serves to emphasise the differences in the two men's folk sources, while also underlining the reciprocal nobility of their Nordic sensitivity towards the grandeur of Nature.[11]

Late in life, Jean Sibelius – in whose work the immediate impact of folk elements is rarely apparent, yet whose music speaks deeply of the North, in the manner that Knox observed of Gullin – received a letter from the young Danish composer Per Nørgård. Recent experience of Sibelius's music, said Nørgård, had changed his view of the whole history of music over the past two hundred years, giving him a touchstone by which he might assess the extent of human universality attained by composers, especially of our century. For Nørgård (born 1932), Sibelius's music was associated with "the elementary, inmost and quite timeless forces of existence, with nature in the widest sense."[12] This was why, said Nørgård, each time "the open human mind" came to Sibelius's music, it would feel "a new surge of the primal sources of life which always, and each time stronger, stimulate it to lead a simpler, prouder and ineffably richer life."[13] For Nørgård, it was the principle of metamorphosis which lay at the heart of Sibelius's formal and spiritual achievement – an achievement which stimulated the young Danish composer to speak of how, through the music of Sibelius (and also Vagn Holmboe's *Sinfonia Boreale*) he had come to feel a "mystical connection with existence at the same time as

I recognised my nature as something indefinably northern." "[T]he pure northern air, the powerful darkness and the crystal-clear undimmed light", Nørgård continued, "this Nordic feeling of nature, is today for me one of the most precious things of my life."[14]

Nørgård's words are in large part reminiscent of what the Swedish composer and conductor Wilhelm Stenhammar wrote to Carl Nielsen in 1910, shortly after conducting the Dane's *Symphony no. 1 in G minor*: "Your symphony does not try to ingratiate itself with the audience, nor is it, thank God, either blandly smooth or sensational. For me its greatest value is its very Nordic chastity and formal simplicity, which I find so bracing in these sensually voluptuous times."[15] Following his early admiration for Wagner, Bruckner and Brahms, Stenhammer (1871-1927) determined to put melody at the centre of his creative world and compose a symphony that was somehow 'Nordic' in character. Having completed his *Symphony no. 2* he was pleased to hear a friend tell him that he could hear "the rustle of tall pines in the first movement" and that he had found the overall air of the work "bracing".[16]

Formal considerations aside, it is hard not to sense the force of both Stenhammer's and Nørgård's ideas when listening to such contemporary Nordic music as that of the Finn Einojuhani Rautavaara (born 1928) or the Norwegian Terje Bjørklund (born 1945), for example. Exemplary here are the hovering, liquid melodies of Rautavaara's 1972 *Cantus Arcticus*, featuring both Sibelius-like writing for strings and choruses of wild bird song, and the grave beauty of the intensely melodic string writing in Bjørklund's recently recorded *Arctos* (Journey to the North) and *Sarek* (inspired by the Nordic wilderness national park of that name in Swedish Lappland). When one remembers how a Danish "loner" like Rued Langgaard (1893-1952) could produce such a mystical, completely unfashionable work as the 1916-19 *Music Of The Spheres* – or when one hears such a lucid, sonorous work of practically picturable images for chamber orchestra as the four-part, Taoist-inflected *Landscapes* by the contemporary Danish composer Ole Buck (born 1945) – it becomes more and more evident that what Nørgård called "something indefinably northern" in music very often has a melodically strong, mystical, nature-sensitive quality to it.[17]

There is something "indefinably northern" about the music of Jan Garbarek, something of that "Nordic chastity and formal simplicity" of which Stenhammer spoke to Nielsen. When Garbarek recorded a piece by Grieg, on the 1992 **Twelve Moons,** it was noticeable that he chose one of Grieg's simplest pieces, the *Arietta* from Book 1, *op. 12* of the *Lyric Pieces*.[18] And if one considers the most structurally ambitious work which Garbarek has composed and recorded to date, the 1990, five-part *Molde Canticle*, it is striking how much Garbarek avoids the chromatic touches and textures of some of his earlier work, replacing them with a folk-like modality, unfolding in crystal-clear space.

The lovely C minor processional opening theme, in the Aeolian mode, is harmonised in a strictly modal fashion: the simplicity of parallel harmonies (often moving in contrary motion to the melody) is preferred to the chromatic washes which such earlier lovers of Norwegian folk melody as Grieg and the Englishmen Percy Grainger and Frederick Delius often spread across their scores. Lucid pentatonic improvisation – as in the magically dancing, often Eastern-sounding touches of Part Two – keeps thematic melody very much in focus, which it continues to be throughout the respective key changes (F minor and B flat minor) of the Latinesque Part Three and blues-charged, funky Part Four: this last ending with a fine example of Garbarek's extraordinary ability, perhaps enhanced here by a pedal harmoniser, to make the tenor sound like some mythical instrument from Asia Minor.

The triple meter variation of the concluding Part Five is a particularly beautiful example of Garbarek's ability to combine the simple and the complex: some spaciously phrased cross-rhythms from Nana Vasconcelos set the noble theme floating high and wide, before the final moments of thematic – and triumphant – recapitulation present, once more, the plangent, yearning simplicity of the opening melody.[19]

In interview, Garbarek has at times spoken of his strong feelings for the melodic aspect of Polish music: for that side of his heritage which came through his father. Chopin and Szymanowski, Lutoslawski and Penderecki have each meant something special to Garbarek, but especially the first two. And he has always admired Polish jazz musicians, such as Krzysztof Komeda and Tomasz Stanko, Zbigniew Namyslowski and Adam Makowicz, Michal Urbaniak and Urszula Dudziak, recording with Stanko in the early 1980s, under the leadership of Gary Peacock.[20] It is thus only natural to suggest that a good deal of Garbarek's capacity for (and sensitivity to) melodic invention may well have something to do with that part of his Polish background which inclines to the Slavic. And this, indeed, is partly why Miroslav Vitous wrote the sort of music for Garbarek and himself which they recorded together on the 1992 **Atmos**.[21] Nevertheless, I would suggest that the compelling emotional aura which has come to surround so much of Garbarek's work is essentially Nordic, as opposed to Polish, in import.

As attested by records as diverse as **Luminessence** and **Aftenland, Dansere** and **Dis, It's OK to listen to the gray voice** and **All Those Born With Wings, Legend Of The Seven Dreams** and **Rosensfole, I Took Up The Runes** and **Twelve Moons**, Garbarek has produced a body of work which speaks of nothing so much as the melodies and the moods, the sounds and the soulfulness – the spirituality – of the North. For nearly thirty years now, such work has been developed by Garbarek on a record label, ECM, whose producer, Manfred Eicher, has spoken of what has been practically a crusade on his part to help develop (and achieve recognition for) the poetics of an essentially European sensibility in improvised music. And much of the energy of that crusade has come from Eicher's sensitivity to, and love of, a particular part of the world: the (Nordic) North. As Eicher has said, "There's a different energy, a purity and intensity that is evident there."[22]

In this chapter we shall investigate how several strands of what one might call a mythology of the North have played a key role in the evolving oeuvre of Garbarek. And since the presence of a Nordic dimension in Garbarek's work has precipitated, not just the admiration that one finds in Mathias Rüegg, for example, but also some of the most dismissive responses which have been made by critics of Garbarek's work, this will present an appropriate opportunity to examine some of the critical debate that has evolved about that work. Necessarily, this will also involve examining aspects of Manfred Eicher's particular commitment(s) to the poetics of music, as well as aspects of what some critics have seen as the overly atmospheric "ECM aesthetic" which they claim Eicher has been responsible for developing.

Manfred Eicher
ECM

There are moments in life when a chance sequence of events can acquire the seeming inevitability of destiny. If the eighteen-year old Jan Garbarek and twenty-three-year old Jon Christensen had not met George Russell at the Molde Festival in 1965, they would not have been playing in Russell's sextet, with Terje Rypdal and Arild Andersen, at a festival in Bologna in the summer of 1969. And had Garbarek not appeared at that festival, the sound of his tenor saxophone might not have caught the ear of Manfred Eicher – a classically trained double-bass player with an enthusiasm for modern and avant-garde jazz, who happened to be in Bologna at the time. Eicher was thinking of starting his own record company, while Garbarek had been thinking of ways to distribute the music he was currently making with fellow Norwegians Rypdal, Andersen and Christensen.

Eicher remembers hearing "this incredible, dense saxophone sound, which seemed to be hymning something *real*: from the first there was this quality of singing in Jan, which I found very moving."[23] The saxophonist and producer-to-be met: Garbarek offered Eicher a tape of his current quartet, but Eicher said he would prefer to work on a fresh production of his own with the group. For a while, Garbarek wondered if this had been a polite version of the "don't call me, I'll call you" syndrome, but a few months later, he responded to Eicher's written request to find and book a studio in Oslo. Eicher then made the first of what would become at least half a lifetime's journeys to Oslo (travelling by train, this first journey took the Munich-based Eicher over forty-eight hours). Recorded on the 22nd and 23rd of September 1970, late at night at the Arne Bendiksen studio, Oslo, **Afric Pepperbird** was released in January 1971, with an understated but nonetheless striking sleeve-design by B. and B. Wojirch. Issued without any sleeve-notes, it was the seventh album on Eicher's new, independent label: ECM – Edition of Contemporary Music.[24]

Born in 1943 in Lindau, a beautiful southern German medieval town on the shores of Lake Constance, near the Austrian and Swiss borders, Manfred Eicher began to study the violin at the age of six. Changing to contrabass when he was fourteen, Eicher graduated from Berlin's Musikhochschule in 1967. In his teens he had begun to appreciate the cool jazz of musicians and arrangers like Lee Konitz and Gil Evans: and in the 1960s, Eicher travelled, not to rock, but jazz festivals. He hitch-hiked to Munich to catch a concert by the classic Coltrane Quartet, for example, and listened with equal enthusiasm to Ornette Coleman and Paul Bley (the latter with Gary Peacock), the Miles Davis Quintet (with Chick Corea) and the Charles Lloyd Quartet (with Keith Jarrett). As Eicher put it in an interview of 1994, jazz was something that guided both him and friends of the time "to feel strength and hope for something to change."[25]

Eicher has often reflected on aspects of the qualities that he felt in a variety of avant-garde jazz of the 1960s. This was a time, he has said, when "there was still something called magic. A work of art was not a sign of something, it was the sign itself."[26] The modal moods of Miles Davis's **Kind of Blue** led the young Eicher to the three-way interplay of Bill Evans with Scott Lafaro and Paul Motian; a little later, he became interested in the range of music being released on Bernard Stollman's avant-garde ESP label, which had started in 1964 with the recording of the (now classic) **Spiritual Unity** album by Albert Ayler, Gary Peacock and Sunny Murray.

Much as Eicher appreciated the music on both ESP and other avant-garde labels of the time, his sensitivity to the pure presence of music began to make him feel that something was missing from the recordings he was hearing: "There was this interactive feel in improvised music all the time, but very often it didn't come through on record. It's very difficult to record jazz – to get all this intensity on tape in a transparent way. Since I am a musician myself, I thought that – using my skills and ability to *listen* to music, to become an active, involved listener – I would be able to transfer it to another aesthetic."[27]

Eicher was no slouch as a musician. Very much in the post-LaFaro spirit of the late-1960s avant-garde, his free-ranging, lyrical double-bass improvisations can be heard on the May 1968 trio release **Celebrations**, recorded for Calig under pianist Bob Degen's name and also featuring the fine Afro-American drummer Fred Braceful. A year later, however, Eicher – who by now had had considerable experience as a production assistant with Deutsche Grammophon – signalled the direction his creativity would henceforth take. Laying his double-bass aside, he produced the extraordinary quartet recording **Wolfgang Dauner – Eberhard Weber – Jürgen Karl – Fred Braceful**. Bearing the legend 'Produced by Manfred Eicher + Jazz By Post' this is a record which (like all the early ECM records) should be heard by anyone mistaken enough to think that Manfred Eicher began his involvement in independent production by recording string quartets.

Like Eicher, pianist Dauner and (at the time, double-bassist) Weber had long been stimulated by Bill Evans' legendary trio of 1960-61, with LaFaro and Motian. Here, Dauner's *Pamukalle* and *Tape Two* furnish vibrant evidence of the extreme rhythmic differentiation they brought to the classic format by the end of the decade, with Braceful avoiding straight time for all but a few isolated bars and Weber running the fleetest of leaping lines across Dauner's often staccato accents. The remainder of the record is truly – as the jazz world used to say – "something else". The altered tape speeds of *Blues*, outrageously crude vocal parodies of *Beat* and strangled phonetic querying of musical parameters in *Über Musik* and *Bemerkung* join the neo-classical pastiches of *Op 5* and desiccated concluding fragments of *Über Musik* to underline the complexity of the record's neo-Dadaist response to the contemporary development of both mass culture and free jazz in Germany.

Together with Eicher, neither Dauner nor Weber ever felt very happy with the so-called "kaputt play" side of European free jazz as it developed in the late 1960s.[28] They preferred, as Weber has put it, to have "some light and shade, some delicacy as well as energy in the music."[29] Weber recalls a recording of a Free Jazz meeting in Baden-Baden around that time, supervised by Joachim-Ernst Berendt, with some amusement: "Dauner, Pierre Favre and I discussed a little before recording and decided to start very freely before bringing in some contrasting harmonies. After a few minutes the red light went off in the studio, as Berendt reminded us that this was a Free Jazz Meeting: we were not to play harmonies! So Dauner played with his elbows and the tape rolled again."[30]

Eicher's idea of production has always been a strong one. Ralph Towner, for example, has recalled what a considerable input Eicher made to the first **Solstice** record of December 1974, when he advised Towner to forget about playing piano, for most of the session at least, and concentrate instead on what made him really special – his 12 string and classical guitar playing.[31] However, no matter how strong his input may be – parallels with the *auteur* theory of film direction are appropriate, provided one remembers how much this producer's synoptic sensibility is set at the service of the musicians he works with – Eicher's concept of production has never had anything in common with the ideological reductiveness of approach which Weber remembers from that late-1960s Free Jazz Meeting.

A 16,000 Deutschmark loan from record shop owner Karl Egger led to the first ECM recording by Eicher: **Free At Last,** by the Mal Waldron Trio, was recorded on November 24th 1969. In retrospect, the fact that it was such a wide-ranging musician as Waldron who recorded the first ECM album is especially interesting. Born in 1926, the Bud Powell- and Thelonious Monk-inspired pianist had played for appreciable periods with both Charles Mingus and Billie Holiday, accompanied Coltrane on his first post-Davis gigs and worked and recorded with Eric Dolphy before settling in Europe after some film work there in the mid-1960s. Waldron also wrote the jazz standard *Soul Eyes* – and would record one of the most haunting of all jazz compositions inspired by the North, the 1977 *The Seagulls of Kristiansund*, where long-time playing partner Steve Lacy's pellucid soprano solo is outstanding in its evocation of a keening, wing-turned Northern mood.[32]

Free At Last came with a brief sleeve-note from Waldron, in which he stated that the album represented his meeting with free jazz. "Free jazz for me", he wrote, " does not mean complete anarchy or disorganised sound. In my vocabulary, disorganised sound still means noise. And don't forget that the definition of music is organised sound. Therefore, on this record you will hear me playing rhythmically, instead of soloing on chord changes."[33] Good as the record is, with Waldron's wide-ranging, rhythmically forceful and often deeply-grooved pianism complemented by bassist Isla Eckinger and drummer Clarence Becton, it pales a touch in comparison with the next piano recording on ECM: the 1970 **Paul Bley With Gary Peacock** (the third ECM release, following the late-1969 album **Just Music** from Europeans Alfred Harth, Dieter Herrmann, Johannes Kramer, Franz Volhard, Thomas Stowsand, Peter Stock and Thomas Cremer).[34]

In retrospect, the Bley/Peacock album assumes especial significance. Firstly, the music was refreshingly varied. The programme ranged from two funky Ornette Coleman blues and the Jerome Kern standard *Long Ago And Far Away* to up-tempo and rubato ballad originals by Bley himself, Annette Peacock and Gary Peacock (the bassist would later record *Moor*, his characterful contribution here, with Garbarek, on the 1981 **Voice From The Past** album). Secondly, while ECM recordings were shortly to feature a much better piano than the one heard here, the recording already reveals aspects of that startling clarity and spatial depth – or "travelling" resonance – of sound for which Eicher's productions would soon be remarked. (This is particularly the case with the brush-work of Paul Motian, as heard on four of the five tracks on which he appears: Billy Elgart plays on the remainder of the album.) Lastly, the record sleeve, designed by B. and B. Wojirch, introduces that restrained yet expansive note for which ECM would shortly become so well known. The tonal and textured nuances of its black and white, radically abstracted front cover image are (in part) as redolent of the paintings of Klee as of the photographs of Brassai. They struck an unusual, unclichéd note for jazz record sleeves of the time, offering poetic intimation of the spaces within (or towards) which the engaged listener might travel, through creative participation in the aural/visual imaginal field offered by the album.[35]

Following this Bley recording, Eicher produced and released albums by Marion Brown, The Music Improvisation Company and Wolfgang Dauner (with Eberhard Weber and Fred Braceful). Each of this distinctive albums is rewarding in its own way. There is no doubt, however, that it was with the 1970 **Afric Pepperbird**, by the Jan Garbarek Quartet, that Eicher really came into his own as a producer.

It was this record that he sent to Keith Jarrett, in order to show the pianist the kind of work that could happen at ECM – an inititative which was to lead not just to the first of what would become Jarrett's many releases on ECM, the November 1971 **Facing You**, but also to the six records (including one double album) which Jarrett and Garbarek would make together in the 1970s.[36]

As Poul Henrik Poulsson noted in his *Jazznytt*, Oslo review of the album in October 1971, **Afric Pepperbird** was a breakthrough record on several counts.[37] The sound was terrific: fresh, fully spread and transparent, revealing every detail of the music in sonorous depth. No less striking was the rhythmic conception in the music: pleasingly diversified, this ranged from burning passages of criss-crossing energy to more rubato passages manifesting what were practically tone poem conceptions. If the use of "little instruments" like bugle or thumb piano brought aspects of the Art Ensemble of Chicago to mind, a good deal of the music projected a distinctly European atmosphere.

With Jon Christensen's vocalising on *Blupp* offering a brief and humorous coda to the proceedings, the programme embraced both poetic, almost Webern-like miniatures – Arild Andersen's *Mah-Jong*, *MYB* (or, *My B*) and *Concentus* – and the twelve steaming minutes of Garbarek's *Beast of Kommodo*. If the title of the saxophonist's *Blow Away Zone* gave accurate indication of the pleasures on offer within the eight and a half minutes of this fiery, very Aylerish outpouring over an implicit tonal centre, the beautifully graduated tone and finessed, "false" upper-register meditations of *Scarabée* gave notice of that essentially meditative, lyrical sensibility that was soon to become more and more evident in Garbarek's recordings (as did the spacey flute coda of *Kommodo*).

The record received a good deal of favourable international attention. Remembering how impressed he had been by a recent performance of Andersen and Christensen with Stan Getz at Antibes, France's Gerard Noel drew particular attention to the rhythmic qualities of **Afric Pepperbird**. He also alerted his *Jazz Hot* readers to the beauty and power of Garbarek's sound: now of an almost transparent, diaphonous quality, now full and "crying" in the best Paroah Sanders manner.[38] In January 1971 West Germany's *Jazz Podium* made **Afric Pepperbird** its Record of the Month. Writing in September 1971, *Jazz Journal* contributor and critic Barry McRae found the record "surprisingly good [..] a worthy album from

Norway."[39] Whether consciously so or not, _Down Beat_ reviewer Joe H. Klee echoed George Russell as he ended his January 1972 combined review of **The Esoteric Circle** and **Afric Pepperbird**. Klee advised his readers that, "Garbarek should be heard. Wary as I am of generalisations, I would venture that not since Django Reinhardt has there been a European jazz musician so original and forward-looking as this young Norwegian."[40]

In the course of his _Jazznytt_ review, Poul Poulsson made reference to an interview which Garbarek had given in the magazine in May 1970, when he spoke critically of the temptation to think of developing a solo chiefly in terms of the creation of expressive sounds of one sort or another, at the expense of melody.[41] Recorded on April 14th and 15th 1971, **Sart** (Soft, Tender) found the quartet of **Circle** and **Pepperbird** augmented by pianist Bobo Stenson, with all of the musicians aiming to strike a creative balance between an aesthetic of "expressive sounds" and melody. Surprisingly, Ian Carr's review of the 1990 CD reissue of **Sart** found the resultant music disappointing. Carr claimed, for example, that "This is not the music for which Garbarek is known and loved [today]; it is rooted in the free (abstract) jazz idiom of the Sixties, and on all six tracks there is not one half-decent rhythm or groove [..] The approach [on the fourteen minute title track] is minimalist, and it's full of space [..] The lasting impression is of fine musicians merely toying with music."[42] All of which makes strong and curious contrast to the plaudits the record (justly) received at the time of its initial release.

Under the headline 'Song of Norway' _Melody Maker_'s Richard Williams reviewed **Afric Pepperbird, Sart** and the August 1971 **Terje Rypdal,** where the quintet of **Sart** was augmented by vocalese from Inger Lise Rypdal (Rypdal's wife at the time) and atmospheric oboe and cor anglais from Eckehard Fintl (with Tom Halversen replacing Bobo Stenson on one track and Bjørnar Andresen replacing Arild Andersen on another). Enthused about all three releases, Williams felt that the title track of **Sart** was "probably the biggest evidence of the power of these men. Garbarek's tenor is utterly convincing, moving from a blatting scream to a more open, relaxed sound, working inside the group to create a deeply moving statement. Rypdal lays out as the three rhythm men use space with the utmost intelligence (if there's one thing these guys know how to do, it's keep their music uncluttered and free of useless 'filling')."[43]

Klee's January 1972 _Down Beat_ review of **The Esoteric Circle** and **Afric Pepperbird** had begun by suggesting that "Jan Garbarek [..] reminds one of the craggy mountain fjords of his native Norway. His playing is full of jagged edges and beautiful surprises, Coltrane-influenced but all his own."[44] It was not so much the music of Garbarek as that of Rypdal which encouraged Williams to essay such a geographical parallel in his own review. Considering the unfolding beauty of the textural colours in much of the guitarist's eponymous release (as well as the similar qualities in Rypdal's _Ved Soerevatn_, recorded on the 1969 Baden-Baden Free Jazz Meeting **Getting To Know Y'All**) Williams remarked, "Obviously, it's easy to say that these cool, spacey sounds are reminiscent of the snowy mountains and plunging fjords of Norway – and for all I know, they probably are."[45]

Klee and Williams were not alone in such early attempts to convey something of the special quality in the music of these Norwegians by reference, however simplistic, to the _genius loci_ (or spirit of place) of the country in which that music had been created. In Germany's _HiFi Stereophonie_ of May 1972 an anonymous review of the **Sart** and **Terje Rypdal** releases suggested that the magical, dramatic quality of the music in the former record – and the deep sense of space out of which that music emerged – could lead one to think of the Norwegian fjords.[46] With the release in 1973 of the November 1972 **Triptykon**, featuring Garbarek, Andersen and Finnish drummer Edward Vesala, the inclination to think of the music in terms of its relation to a Nordic spirit of place can only have increased. If the tenor-drums duet of _Etu Hei!_ essayed a few brief minutes of somewhat familiar Free Jazz energy playing, the rest of **Triptykon** not only built on the rubato achievements of **Sart** (the opening, reflective and very beautiful _Rim_, for example, where Garbarek phrases with a spacious lyricism worthy of Johnny Hodges) but also introduced elements that were unmistakably Norwegian in both structure and feeling. This is particularly evident in the"fairy tale" wooden flute melodies of _Selje_, projected across Andersen's spare yet resonant bass and Vesala's tinkling, forest chimes percussion, and the keening tenor melody, occasional ragged tempi and "out of tune" arco lines of the concluding _Bruremarsj_ (Wedding March). Here, Garbarek's earlier love of Ayler's folk-like melodies was transmuted into a Nordic folk context all his own – albeit realised, at this time, with what would seem a touch or two (or three) of good-natured irony.[47]

After **Triptykon**, the opportunities for critics to essay a "Nordic" interpretation of Garbarek's work were to increase exponentially. On the second Jan Garbarek/BoboStenson album, the 1975 **Dansere** (Dancers), Garbarek recorded *Lokk*, a stunning, cavernous-toned version of a traditional Norwegian cattle call, ascribed to one Thorvald Tronsgård on the record sleeve. The spirit of folk music was present in several parts of the forty-five minute suite *Låter* (Songs/Sounds), commissioned from Garbarek by the 1977 Kongsberg Jazz Festival and interpreted by Garbarek himself, on tenor throughout, with Bobo Stenson, Palle Danielsson and Jon Christensen, and a string, brass and woodwind orchestra conducted by Helge Hurum. (One composition from the suite, the folkish ballad *Weaving A Garland*, would later be recorded, on soprano, on the 1980 **Eventyr**.) In 1979, on the world-ranging album **Folk Songs** which he recorded with Charlie Haden and Egberto Gismonti, Garbarek contributed the lovely, limpid *Folk Song*, based on a Norwegian traditional melody which, in its original form, would have been in neither major nor minor key, but which here acquires a distinctly minor flavour. This was followed by Garbarek's own **Eventyr**, an album dedicated entirely to fresh interpretations of a diversity of Norwegian folk melody – the spirit of which could also be sensed in the haunting flute and soprano meditations of *Footprints*, from the 1981 **Paths, Prints**.

By 1983, it seemed only natural that jazz critic Howard Mandel should title the piece on Garbarek which he wrote for *Musician* magazine, 'Jan Garbarek: Sax Solitude and Northern Light'.[48] The titles of Garbarek's 1984 **It's OK to listen to the gray voice** were all derived from the Swede Tomas Tranströmer, a poet whose work reveals a very close relationship to the Nordic landscape, while the cover of Garbarek's 1986 solo album **All Those Born With Wings** featured two extraordinary colour photographs of the Aurora Borealis, or Northern Lights, taken by Steinar Berger. Little wonder, then, that in his review of the album, *Time Out*'s film critic Geoff Andrew should say that the music's combination of restrained yet romantic lyricism and eruptive, rhythmically startling accents suggested nothing so much as the vast, desolate yet inspiring panorama of the Northern lights. "Jazz it is", concluded Andrew, "but also much, much more."[49]

Almost a decade and a half previously, the unabashed, yet exquisitely focused lyricism of **Red Lanta**, the album of intimate duets which Garbarek (playing soprano, bass saxophone and flutes) recorded with American pianist Art Lande in November 1973, had led critic Manfred Sack, writing in *Die Zeit* , to begin his review with the question, 'Jazzbesuch bei Grieg?'[50] The record ended with a composition of Lande's called *Cherifen Dream of Renate*. Lande's composition as this was, the combination of Garbarek's flute, Lande's gentle pianism and the simple, yet plaintively inflected steps of the folk-like theme – the whole seemingly set in a vast panorama of nurturing silence – was inescapably reminiscent of Nordic folk music: perhaps more Swedish than Norwegian, but Nordic nonetheless.[51] On the two albums which Garbarek made with Keith Jarrett in April 1974 – **Belonging** and **Luminessence** – a good many of the titles (such as *Numinor, Windsong* and *Solstice*) – were sufficient to incline many listeners' minds, including my own, towards the North. By the time of Garbarek's appearance on the December 1974 **Solstice** quartet album, recorded under guitarist Ralph Towner's name and with electric bassist Eberhard Weber joining Jon Christensen in one of the most liberated and melodic "rhythm sections" ever heard, a *Down Beat* review could speak of the presence of "mysticism and musical alchemy" in a session which showed Garbarek to be possessed of "a lyricism dripping with hoar frost."[52]

Following the intensely contemplative, near-Munchian mood of much of the 1975 **Dansere**, Garbarek recorded the album that, more than any other from this period, marked him as a musician of the North. Recorded with Ralph Towner – and, on several tracks, the pre-recorded drones of a wind harp, with a brass sextet also appearing on one title – the 1976 **Dis** (Haze/Mist) contained six pieces. Their titles were *Vandrere* (Wanderers), *Krusning* (Water Ripples), *Videnne* (Mountain Plateaus), *Skygger* (Shadows), *Yr* (signifying, as a noun, drizzle or mist, but as an adjective, intoxicated, full of the creative forces of life) and *Dis* (Haze, Mist – although also the male God of the Underworld in Roman religion, the equivalent of the Greek Pluto).

Individually, the pieces were both striking and varied, with the wind harp employed selectively and Towner contributing many a beautiful nuance of texture and tone. In contrast to the lovely, lilting soprano mood of *Krusning* – where Ralph Towner's classical guitar is outstanding, from the point of view of both tone and touch – the A flat minor, C minor and E minor structure of *Skygger* , for example, provokes a tenor solo of granite-like protestation from Garbarek. Taken together, the six pieces conjured a primal, shape-shifting world strongly redolent of both Nordic landscape and myth. As much spiritual as sensuous in appeal, this was a world which served to take the sympathetic psyche deep into the archetypal realm. However, it was also a world which precipitated the first really serious, or rhetorical, divisions in critical opinion, not just about Garbarek, but about ECM as a whole.[53]

The vast majority of reviews of **Dis** were (rightly, in my view) very favourable. Larry Friske's review for the _Madison Isthmus_ was typical in its emphasis on the Nordic dimension in the music, suggesting that **Dis** sounded "as chilly and barren as the emptiness of the frozen tundra on the cover. The approach and total texture strike one as uniquely Scandinavian."[54] (It would seem that Friske got carried away by his imagination here: Franco Fontana's cover photo, simply reversed on the back of the sleeve, captures not any frozen tundra, but rather the meeting of low, lapping wave and sand at distant shoreline.) Comparing the record to aspects of the West Coast "cool school" in the 1950s, Friske commented that "Garbarek and his associates extend the concept to the extreme. His broad tonal colours seek out the listener's intellectual curiosity."[55]

Not every listener's intellectual curiosity was stirred, however. As we have seen, _Melody Maker_'s Richard Williams was one of the earliest and strongest supporters of Garbarek, his April 1972 'Song of Norway' review of the **Terje Rypdal**, **Afric Pepperbird** and **Sart** albums going so far as to suggest that Miles Davis should consider hiring immediately the musicians featured throughout these ground-breaking releases. And as we have also remarked, Williams was not at all insensitive to the idea that the particular aura of some of this music might be seen in relation to aspects of the spectacular scenery of Norway. It is somewhat curious, then, that it should have been Williams who produced perhaps the definitive example of all the reviews that have subsequently come to question the cultivation of such a deliberate musical atmosphere, or ambience, by Garbarek as that which is to be found on **Dis**.

Under the headline 'Jan's blue mood' Williams suggested that, "Those who accuse ECM's Manfed Eicher of an unhealthy concentration on what might be termed 'avant-garde mood jazz' will have a field day with Garbarek's latest album. To an even greater degree than the bulk of the label's output, **Dis** attempts to create a tastefully exotic ambience; and, in so doing, could easily be accused of putting manner before matter."[56] After an attempt to draw a (far-fetched) parallel between **Dis** and Mike Oldfield's **Tubular Bells**, Williams went on to suggest that, "The problem with 'ECM Music' is this: all great jazz musicians make mistakes sometimes, through attempting something beyond their known capacity. But there's rarely any hint of that kind of danger or even adventure on an ECM record." Williams concluded, "Now that, of course, is a judgement by jazz standards, and Eicher's answer would probably be that this music needn't be considered as jazz. So be it."[57]

Williams' review – to which we shall return – is typical of the dismissive criticism of the Nordic dimension in Garbarek's work which was shortly to enjoy a certain vogue. John Fordham has usually written very positively about Garbarek, from the early 1970s to now. However, even Fordham's faith was tested by the saxophone and flute duets with classical organist Kjell Johnsen that comprised the December 1979 **Aftenland** (Evening Land). "One of the most dolorous and God-forsaken sounds on the planet", suggested Fordham, " is that of the Norwegian saxophonist Jan Garbarek, the Ingmar Bergman of the European jazz scene."[58] Ingmar Bergman of the saxophone or not, there was something about the playing of Garbarek at this time that sat ill with such an otherwise open-minded critic as Barry McRae, long-time _Jazz Journal International_ contributor and critic.

Once, McRae had been able to appreciate some of the many qualities in **Dis**, stating that what he called this "strangely atmospheric record" was "a far cry from the fire of the black avant-garde, but [..] none the worse for that. Its gentility is not weakness and there is a quality in Garbarek's compositions that will appeal to many [..]."[59] However, by the time of the December 1981 **Paths, Prints** – with titles like _The Path_, _Footprints_, _Arc_, _Kite Dance_, _Considering The Snail_ and _Still_ all composed by Garbarek, and recorded together with guitarist Bill Frisell, Eberhard Weber and Jon Christensen – McRae had had enough of the Nordic in both the saxophonist's compositions and improvisations. Hungry for more of what he saw as the "committed playing" that Garbarek had recently produced on Gary Peacock's August 1981 **Voice From The Past – Paradigm** album, recorded with a quintet which also featured Tomasz Stanko and Jack DeJohnette, McRae opined that on **Paths, Prints**, "we are subjected to a slice of Nordic atmospheric nonsense to top all such ECM items in the past. The content is minimal, the feeling of projection and commitment slight, and most _Jazz Journal International_ readers will question the need for its generous playing time and high quality recording."[60]

Obviously, something about **Dis** and **Paths, Prints** got stuck in the respective throats of Williams and McRae. Both are unusually intelligent and almost invariably perceptive writers. McRae has written some of the most stimulating criticism of recent years, including _The Jazz Cataclysm_, his now-classic text on the development of avant-garde jazz from post-Bebop innovations to the Free Jazz of the 1960s. And Williams, author of _The Man In The Green Shirt_ – a refreshingly conceived book on Miles Davis – has written many a passionate and rewarding article in praise of central jazz virtues, besides a good many reviews warmly supportive of ECM releases, from the earliest days of the label through to such recent triumphs as Tomasz Stanko's **Litania: The Music of Krzysztof Komeda**. The key to this issue seems to me to be that McRae and Williams were simply listening to these two records – **Dis** and **Paths, Prints** – with the wrong ears, as it were, applying inappropriate criteria to the music.

In his study of the great Danish film director Carl Th. Dreyer, _Speaking The Language Of Desire_, Raymond Carney suggest that, in order to appreciate the qualities in Dreyer's rigorously disciplined oeuvre, one may have to "unlearn certain viewing habits."[61] A standard criticism of Dreyer from those unsympathetic to his radically simplified yet spiritually rich world is that "nothing happens" in his films. The same point is often made about Ingmar Bergman or Andrei Tarkovsky, by those who have but little if any empathy with these directors' very particular ability to _let time live in the image_, as Tarkovsky once said, rather than subjecting time to the increasingly crass demands of the pseudo-myths and so-called "realistic" narrative constructions of mass-culture cinema.[62] As Carney makes plain, it is pointless to go to a showing of a Dreyer film, where most of the "action" will be concentrated on the inner dimension of soul or spirit, and complain that one has been unable to enjoy the far more "eventful" and ostensibly "unmediated" film aesthetic of a director like Jean Renoir, for example.[63]

Much the same applies to the music of Jan Garbarek. Building upon the immense spiritual charge already present in the music of John Coltrane, Garbarek has been able to inflect that spiritual energy and drive with increasingly distinctive and transmutative elements of both musical detail and spiritual substance from his own culture. It is true that Garbarek has said that, in terms of his musical identity, one might say that he lives in a spiritual neighbourhood which is scattered geographically all around the world: and the next chapter will be devoted to investigating some of the most striking evidence of such a world-ranging aesthetic in his work. However, Garbarek has also said that he would like to be considered part of his own tradition, implying aspects of a musical, cultural and spiritual tradition located in the North. In the same article in which he spoke of his sense of belonging to a world-wide "spiritual neighbourhood", Garbarek remarked of Norway that, "The country is very special. There are very dramatic changes of the seasons, and the landscape is also dramatic. I can't say to what extent growing up in Norway would influence you, but I imagine deep down it must have some influence."[64]

The last point acquires added resonance when one reflects upon Garbarek's answer to the question which writer Mark Prendergast put to him in 1989, regarding how much Garbarek's upbringing had affected his subsequent musical life. Garbarek replied: "Probably a great deal. I was raised in Oslo and I wasn't involved in music – or particularly interested in music – until I was fourteen. I can't say much about musical influences in my childhood in that sense. A very normal average Oslo boy's life, that was my situation. It might not be too different from an average British boy's life. I used to spend a lot of time in the countryside where my grandparents lived – further North. They were mountain farmers and I would spend a couple of months every year there. In fact when I was very small I even lived there for a couple of years and I find that I very frequently come back to this period in my life."[65]

It is not for nothing then, that Garbarek has composed and improvised music for performances of Ibsen's *Brand* and *Peer Gynt*, participated in a ballet devoted to the life and work of Edvard Munch, and arranged and recorded a Grieg piece; shared three albums with Jan Erik Vold, one of Norway's finest poets, and set Norwegian folk songs in a contemporary setting; built epic melodies upon the seemingly modest (yet potent) foundations of a Sami *joik*, or created music in the urgent, drum-driven spirit of the shamans of the Far North. To appreciate how much musical and spiritual substance there is within the so-called "Nordic atmospheric nonsense" that some critics have claimed to discern in Garbarek's work, one has to cease seeing that work through the filter of a sensibility attuned solely to the finger-clicking and (often, but not exclusively) risk-taking imperatives of jazz. This is, of course, a music which has long been distinguished by its own various "atmospheres", from New Orleans onwards: "atmospheres" which both demand and repay properly tuned attention and respect.[66] If the music of John Coltrane can – and should – be related to aspects of a spiritual tradition going back to African polytheism, as authors Bill Cole and Norman Weinstein, for example, have been concerned to demonstrate, why should the music of Jan Garbarek not be seen in the light of aspects of the light and the landscape, the culture and the spirituality of the North?[67]

This is particularly the case in so far as Garbarek's long-time producer (and friend) Manfred Eicher has long spoken of his own strong feelings for the light and landscape of the North. These are feelings which we shall shortly set within a broad consideration of aspects of that "mythology of the North" which can be detected in the work of Garbarek. Before we do so, however, it is necessary to return to Richard Williams' review of **Dis**, in order to refute a particular critical canard about ECM that, for one reason or another, has tended to resurface over the years. This is contained in the idea that there is something which Williams called 'ECM Music' – the implication of the capital 'M' being that a single identity runs throughout the music which is recorded on the label. Note also Williams' expression, 'the bulk of the label's output'. What might this mean?

By 1977, the year of Williams' review, ECM had recorded around a hundred albums. The music on these albums ranged from the freely improvised music of The Music Improvisation Company, the Just Music group, Dave Holland and Derek Bailey, to the increasingly song-like work of Garbarek and Eberhard Weber; from the compositions and improvisations of Mal Waldron and Paul Bley to those of Keith Jarrett and Chick Corea, Wolfgang Dauner and Robin Kenyatta, Bobo Stenson and Arild Andersen, Jon Christensen and Jack DeJohnette; Barre Phillips and Ralph Towner, Sam Rivers and Anthony Braxton, Gary Burton and Paul Motian; Terje Rypdal and John Abercrombie, Benny Maupin and Dave Liebman; Steve Kuhn and Michael Naura, Bill Connors and Enrico Rava, Don Cherry and Collin Walcott; Azimuth and Kenny Wheeler, Tomasz Stanko and Edward Vesala, John Surman and Julian Priester, Pat Metheny and Jaco Pastorius. It would be nice to know exactly how one might extrapolate any supposed 'bulk of the label's output' from such a range of music.

Of course, no matter how diverse the music on ECM, it has always been superbly recorded, in a clear, well spread and 'transparent' sound picture – an aesthetic of sound which is very different from the more 'compressed' or heated dynamics previously evident in much of the recording of jazz. Throughout the years, Eicher and recording engineers Martin Wieland and Jan Erik Kongshaug (the latter of whom is also a practising musician) have never, as is sometimes claimed, subordinated questions of musical quality or identity to any fetishisation of sound *per se*. On the contrary: they have brought to their many recordings an attention to both individual detail and overall "sound picture" which – *no matter how diverse the music may be* – has shown a uniform conceptual and technical thoroughness. To infer (uniform) musical content from such a (uniform) excellence of recording quality would be simply foolish.

What Williams' review reveals is, not any truth about ECM in the 1970s, but rather a particular facet of his own listening experience and expectations at that time. The same point applies to a good many of the points which the writer and critic Stuart Nicholson made more recently about both ECM in general and Garbarek in particular. Like Williams and McRae, Nicholson can be an unusually stimulating and rewarding writer: his books on Ella Fitzgerald and Billie Holiday, for example, have been justly praised by many. However, in his 1990 *Jazz: The Modern Resurgence* Nicholson supplied both a new version of Williams' canard about 'ECM Music' and a clear, albeit unintentional demonstration of precisely why it is important to set a good deal of the work of Garbarek (and Eicher) within a properly conceived Northern context – *without implying that that is all there is to be either said or understood about the nature of that work.*

Nicholson observes, retrospectively, that what he calls Manfred Eicher's "stance" as a producer "was in many ways the antithesis of the American jazz tradition. His concept was of a minimalist jazz, a European hybrid that emphasised quality of sound as much as content [...] Garbarek exemplified what Eicher was trying to achieve [...] Working within a self-limited harmonic and rhythmic palette he created an evocative tranquillity strongly rooted in European folk-forms that gave prominence to his saxophone *tone* as the main expressive force."[68] Nicholson is neither insensitive to nor unappreciative of what he takes to be the results of such self-limitation on the part of Garbarek. He observes, for example, that Garbarek "created music that projected the stark imagery of nature near the

Northern Lights. His work represented an ordered calm in the often frantic world of jazz; rigorous and highly disciplined, he had the ability to transport the subconscious to areas of thought that were mystically, even aesthetically beckoning."[69] However, despite such a seemingly positive appraisal, Nicholson is forced to conclude that, "Taken together, Garbarek's albums were inescapably monotonous, dwelling in a condition of evocative tranquillity."[70]

Nicholson's analysis is a classic example of the problem of half- (or rather, quarter-) truths obscuring the whole picture. Take, for example, his comment about Eicher's "stance" being in many ways "the antithesis of the American jazz tradition." Is this the tradition documented – and shaped – by a producer like Milt Gabler, or Alfred Lion? Hugues Panassié or John Hammond? Norman Granz, or Teo Macero? Creed Taylor, or Bob Thiele? Orrin Keepnews, or Giovanni Bonandrini? Within the Modernist and Post-modernist parameters of Nicholson's book, one presumes this tradition might include a good many of the musicians detailed above, as recorded in the first decade of ECM's activities. Subsequently, ECM has released further records by many of these artists. The company has also recorded music featuring, for example, the Americans Leo Smith and Lester Bowie, George Adams and Dewey Redman; Old and New Dreams, The Art Ensemble of Chicago, Don Cherry and Ed Blackwell, Codona and Oregon; Charlie Haden and Michael Brecker, Charles Lloyd and Billy Hart, Bill Frisell and David Torn; Marc Johnson and John Scofield, James Newton and Linda Sharrock, Peter Erskine and Lee Konitz, Hal Russell and Joe Maneri. If such figures do not constitute a considerable part of "the American jazz tradition" today, one wonders who does.[71]

The supposedly anti-traditional implications of something called Eicher's "stance" (whatever that might be) thus disappear, when one takes the simple trouble to examine (and listen to) a good deal of the ECM catalogue in detail. Of course, Eicher *is* a special producer. For my money, he is easily the most creative producer jazz has ever seen: a man blessed with extraordinary ears and a considerable, discriminating intelligence. Not only that: he has considerable visual sensitivity. Having long been deeply interested in European, Scandinavian and Russian art cinema (Bresson and Dreyer, Godard and Antonioni, Bergman and Tarkovsky, for example) Eicher turned to film himself in the 1990s, directing Erland Josephson (the Swedish actor renowned for his work with Bergman and Tarkovsky) in the award-winning *Holozän*.[72]

Eicher is thus a person with a near-synaesthetic poetic sensibility, hyper-sensitive to the potentialities of music. There can be no doubt that he has done an enormous amount to develop a fresh, European perpective upon the poetics of music – a perspective which has often had a distinctly Northern, or Nordic aura to it (and which the ECM New Series, begun in 1984, has done much to develop in the field of so-called "serious" or "art" music). The point to underline is that, contrary to the critical clichés that would imprison ECM in one or another ideological distortion of the reality of the label's richness – and contrary to the jibes that are sometimes made about 'Excessively Cerebral Music' – Eicher has produced not just an extraordinarily broad range of music, but a range of music which has brought body and soul, heart and mind together, in all manner of fresh, inspiring ways.

In his important book, _Towards Deep Subjectivity_, the philosopher Roger Poole once wrote about how crucial it is to create for oneself the kind of philosophical space in which the terms in which one thinks, or makes ethical choices, are not pre-determined by the ideological pressures (including false dualisms) of others' perception of the world. In a genuinely free philosophical space, argued Poole, "a space where one was free to think and be oneself in thinking, one chooses which problems one will deal with, _and in which terms_. So many ways of asking the question foreclose the issue and leave the individual with nothing but a rubber-stamping job to do."[73] If one were to substitute 'musical' for 'philosophical' and 'possibilities' for 'problems', one would have a very good indication of the kind of space(s) that Eicher has been able to help musicians to create.

The music that Eicher has produced has done much to revise both musicians' and listeners' awareness of the multiplicity of relations that can obtain between improvisation and composition, assertiveness and reflection – as well as the many ways that the concept of swing, so crucial to jazz history, might be newly inflected and developed – or even abandoned.[74] Early on, ECM associated itself with the phrase, "The most beautiful sound next to silence". For silence, one could also read space. A vital factor in many ECM productions, its diverse presence has radically affected the shaping and experience of time in the work. This is nowhere more so than in those productions devoted to the work of Garbarek. In the early days of their collaborations, especially, Eicher – who would stay at the Garbareks' flat in the eastern suburbs of Oslo, on the edge of the

Lillomarka forest – and Garbarek would spend hour upon hour together, walking and talking, sharing and developing both musical and poetic ideas of how the relations of space and time, tone and texture might be revisioned.

A sensitivity to space (or lack thereof) and its consequent relation to time thus lies at the core of the issue of how one responds to much of the Nordic-inflected music which has been recorded on ECM – whether that be the work developed over the years by the members of the original Jan Garbarek Quartet, or the music of Bobo Stenson or Edward Vesala; Nils Petter Molvær, Sidsel Endresen, Misha Alperin, Ketil Bjørnstad, Lena Willemark and Ale Möller; Karin Krog and John Surman, or the Christian Wallumrød Trio.[75] Just as Richard Williams' review of **Dis** said less about ECM than it did about certain listening expectations, or habits, in jazz, so does Nicholson's summary of Garbarek's ECM albums as being "inescapably monotonous" reveal very little about the music of Garbarek.

Nicholson argues that the commercial success of what he chooses to describe as Garbarek's "minimalistic" work in the 1980s (in such albums as **Wayfarer** and **It's OK to listen to the gray voice,** for example) might be understood in the light of the high status accorded to minimalist art in general during this period. He instances the contemporary success of the work of British and American artists David Mach, Carl Andre, Lisa Milroy and Richard Long in support of his point.[76] Such an attempt to look beyond the immediate context of jazz history in order to provide a cultural context for the work of Garbarek is, in principle, to be welcomed. However, if one is not prepared to accept the description of Garbarek's work at this time as "minimalistic" – which I am not – then the point of this comparison of Garbarek's music with these particular artists is largely lost. Rather than the artists Nicholson cites, there may well be others whose work provides more appropriate and resonant cultural context for that of Garbarek. As we shall shortly see, a good many of such artists come from the North. A sensitivity to their work, and its relation to that of Garbarek, may encourage a more appropriate response to the rich variety of ways in which Garbarek has been able to bring space alive than is evident in Nicholson's summary description of his work as "inescapably monotonous".

Like appeals to "the spirit of the age", suggestions that the spirit of place in a country might provide an explanation, or generative context, for aspects of that country's creativity are notoriously difficult to substantiate, certainly to everyone's satisfaction. For this whole area of thought is shot through with both the positive and negative connotations of the word "myth". In today's world of digitalised "hyper-reality", the spiritual import of the spirit of place can quickly turn into the sugared blandishment of the tourist cliché. It is understandable that, even as his music and album covers have come to embody a distinctly poetic relation to aspects of Norwegian landscape, music and mood, Garbarek has always been wary of potential picture postcard travesties of his work.[77] From the socio-historical perspective, the issue of the spirit of place of the North today is necessarily bound up with aspects of the development of nineteenth and twentieth-century nationalism, tourism and media. However, from the psychological, or poetic perspective, the appeal of the *genius loci* – or spirit of place – has much more to do with the continuing relevance of what both poets and phenomenologists would call the fundamental, or existential conditions of creativity.[78] And Garbarek is a musician whose work has long revealed the desire to strip away the superfluous, in quest of something existentially compelling, something fundamental – something *real*.

Two things are immediately apparent about the music of Jan Garbarek. The first is that, whether one likes that music or not, one has to agree that it is utterly distinctive. The second is that that music is played with a maximum of economy: there is absolutely no technical grandstanding for its own sake. (Of course, from the technical point of view, Garbarek is an outstanding musician. As we have already noted, he is also a most conscientious one, often practising for anything up to six or seven hours a day.) Is it too far-fetched to make the point here that the Viking culture of Scandinavia (circa 780 to 1070 A.D.) valued individuality extremely highly? Or that the greatest oral literature which has come down to us from after the end of that era – such as the spiritual advice known as *The Words of the High One* which was written down in Old Norse sometime in the thirteenth century – is conveyed with a lapidary power of utterance?[79] One presumes that it is not for nothing that Oscar Peterson – a man of formidable intelligence – calls Niels-Henning Ørsted Pedersen, his bass player for over a quarter of a century now, "the Viking": nor, indeed, that NHØP himself has written such a strong, individually phrased and dynamically refreshing piece of music as his *Viking's Blues*, from the second **Duo** album which he recorded with Kenny Drew in 1974.[80]

Whatever one may think of such long-range, putative parallels, it is fact that a good deal of contemporary Nordic culture carries the force of ancient visionary insight. In a short introduction to a 1977 volume of selected work by the Finnish poet Anselm Hollo, the American poet Robert Creeley made a point which can be applied not just to his contemporary Hollo, but to much of Nordic poetics in general. Hollo, said Creeley, "is not only 'European' but a Finn, which is to say he has both the solid human realness of the Nordic and the intensive visionary mind of those specific people."[81] One recalls Manfred Eicher's first memory of Garbarek in Bologna, his already extraordinary saxophone sound and song-like phrasing hymning what Eicher called something *real*. In a 1984 interview with *Jazz Forum*'s Pawel Brodowski, Eicher observed that, apart from musical matters, what had brought him close to Garbarek over the years was "my background and education. Actually, I consider myself a person much more of the North than the South. 'The idea of North'..."[82]

When he was young, family holidays had taken Eicher to the North German coast, where the clear, sharp light – long beloved of painters as distinct as Caspar David Friedrich (1774-1840) and Emil Nolde (1867-1956) – was very different from that which played across the expanses of Lake Constance. A little later, the young Eicher discovered Denmark and Dreyer, and the writing of such Scandinavians as the Swedes, Stig Dagerman and Gunnar Ekelöf. A flame had been lit: in interview after interview, Eicher has spoken of his love of Northern light, and of how the mood of the paintings of Edvard Munch, for example, may well have had an influence on the development of the music which ECM has produced in Oslo (where the vast majority of its recordings have taken place: initially at the Arne Bendiksen studio, to the north-east of the city centre; later at Talent Studio, very near the Munch Museum in Tøyen, and finally at Rainbow Studio, a little closer to the city centre).[83]

What Manfred Eicher (following the late pianist Glenn Gould) calls 'the idea of North' is a concept which, for at least two centuries now, has played a key role in the development of European poetics: in art and literature, music, architecture and interior design, no less than – in our century – film and fashion design.[84] In politics, as Francis G.

Garmo Stave Church (detail, Maihaugen Folk Museum, Norway)
George Ware

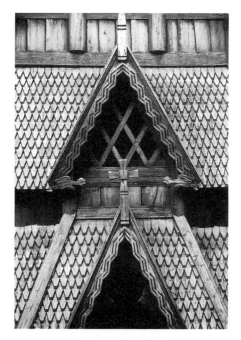

Gol Stave Church (detail, Bygdøy Folk Museum, Oslo)
George Ware

Nordic Myths: Contemporary Music Network Tour (Britain 1987)
designer: Bob Linney
Reproduced with kind permission of the Arts Council, London

Castles has detailed in his 1978 study _The Social Democratic Image of Society_, 'the idea of North' has been equally potent, with Scandinavian values of citizenship and social democracy playing a fructifying role in the evolution of left-wing politics in the post-Second World War, democratic West.[85]

Throughout the nineteenth century, the majestic fjords and mountain passes of Norway and the vast, uninhabited interior of Iceland had attracted an increasing amount of attention from British and European artists, thinkers and travellers. Disturbed by the alienating pace and scale of industrialisation in their own countries, such lovers of the North sought a sublime, healing experience of landscape in countries where the great god Pan still seemed to hold sway over the imagination. By the beginning of the twentieth century, the idea of the North as a key to the renewal of inner life had acquired a magnetic aura – partly through the landscape itself, and partly through the (Nordic) art and literature, music, architecture and design which that landscape had helped to inspire.[86]

To travel North today can be to feel a sea wind freshening in one's face, as the landscape changes from the agricultural, gently undulating plains of southern Sweden to first the heathlands and sandy beaches of Denmark and then the rolling hills of the Oslo fjord. Beyond those hills, hundreds of miles of forest and river, mountain and lake stretch westwards to the icy fjords of Norway, or continue North, beyond the Arctic Circle, to the mountains and plateaux of the Sami people – ancient guardians of the shamanic drum. To travel North can thus be to travel towards the (sensuously grounded) idea of something powerful and primal: something archetypal.[87]

The Danish artist Asger Jorn (1914-73) – a key figure in the post-Second World War COBRA art movement – once called the North "the dream centre" of Europe: the place where one might defeat the thousand and one distractions of everyday existence and feel life stirring once more in the depths of both oneself and the world. Jorn also remarked that there was something about the visionary element in Nordic art which people outside the region sometimes found hard to take, and suggested that "In today's cosmopolitan art world it doesn't figure at all [...] Nordic art is dangerous. It compresses all its power _inside_ ourselves [...] it works on the _mood_ more than on the senses or understanding."[88]

The *character of wholeness* which the word 'mood' suggests introduces the synthesising potentialities of the unconscious – which is exactly where much Nordic art draws its energy from. Garbarek himself has spoken of wanting to take people into different 'rooms' during a concert, believing that, "If music *could* suggest moods, like painting or poetry, and maybe move from mood to mood organically, that would be a good thing ... And, it's not as easy as people might think. I'm not talking about *illustrating* a mood, or an idea – pictures should come from music, not before it. There is mood, and there is mood! – just as there are some types of simplicity which may contain a lot, and some that may have very little to them."[89]

Here one approaches the diversely-faceted key to the question of the Nordic element(s) in Garbarek's work. For when one follows Garbarek into the various moods of his Northern-inflected work, three distinct aspects to those various moods, or soundscapes, are apparent. Each aspect speaks of that intensive visionary quality, typical of Nordic poetics, which was noted by Asger Jorn and Robert Creeley: but they each manifest and inflect such a quality very differently.

The first aspect is that which can be related to the striking quality of existentially open, sometimes angst-ridden quest which is apparent in much of the most notable Scandinavian culture of the past century and a half, epitomised by such figures as Henrik Ibsen, Edvard Munch and Knut Hamsun; August Strindberg and Edith Södergran, Karin Boye and Dag Hammarskjöld, Asger Jorn and Frans Widerberg. The ideas of Nietzsche played a crucial role in the development of some of these (particularly Munch, Hamsun and Södergran), but overall, the key, generative person here is the Dane, Søren Kierkegaard (1813-55). Written in a rich and provocative variety of ways, with much emphasis upon irony and indirect communication, Kierkegaard's books are all directed towards an existentially engaged, potentially transformative relationship with his reader – a reader whose unique individuality Kierkegaard wished to save from what he (rightly) saw as the post-Hegelian, post-Marxist threat of individuality being absorbed into the ever-growing abstractions of philosophical and political theory, or the spiritually enervating distractions of mass culture.[90]

The tenor of Kierkegaard (whom Garbarek read a little as a teenager, together with some of the reflections of Pascal, one of

Kierkegaard's elective affinities) is apparent in one of the most moving spiritual documents of our century: the diary of diplomat Dag Hammarskjöld which, after his tragic and untimely death in the early 1960s, was published as <u>Markings</u>. Here one can find much pointed, existentially-inflected self-criticism and telling irony, together with such pure, unaffected statements of spiritual reflection and longing as the following: "Landscape: only your immediate experience of the detail can provide the soil in your soul where the beauty of the whole can grow [...] The light died in the low clouds. Falling snow drank in the dusk. Shrouded in silence, the branches wrapped me in their peace. When the boundaries were erased, once again the wonder: that *I* exist [...] To have humility is to experience reality, not in relation to ourselves, but in its sacred independence [...] In the point of rest at the centre of our being, we encounter a world where all things are at rest in the same way. Then a tree becomes a mystery, a cloud, a revelation, each man a cosmos of whose riches we can only catch glimpses. The life of simplicity is simple, but it opens to us a book in which we never get beyond the first syllable."[91] There is much of the music of Jan Garbarek here.

The second aspect is intimately related to the first: it concerns what one might call the problematic legacy of Protestantism in Northern Europe, as examined in a variety of ways in the arts this century by such painters and poets, thinkers and film makers as Edvard Munch and Carl Dreyer, Pär Lagerkvist and Gunnar Ekelöf, Tomas Tranströmer and – most famously – Ingmar Bergman. Films of Bergman's such as *The Seventh Seal* (1956), *Wild Strawberries* (1957) and *The Virgin Spring* (1959), and, in particular, the trilogy *Through A Glass Darkly* (1961), *Winter Light* (1962) and *The Silence* (1963) all examined questions of religious faith and doubt in the light of what many this century have experienced as the paralysing absence – or silence – of the Protestant God in their lives.[92]

The third aspect is that which takes its character and colour from the fact that it was only a thousand years ago that Christianity "conquered" what Brian Bates, the British specialist scholar of the psychology of shamanism, has called the wisdom of the wyrd: the ancient, mystery-loving and animistic wisdom of the pagan and polytheistic Nordic world of Yggdrasil, Odin and Sleipnir; the ravens Thought and Memory; Thor, Freya and Balder.[93] And, no matter how hard the Christian missionaries tried to exterminate it, the pagan, polytheistic spirit of the Sami world, in particular, has survived into our century, to flourish recently in a wide range of art and literature, music and film – including projects where Sami musicians, like singer Mari Boine, have collaborated with Garbarek.[94] The shamanic spirit of such a world is also present in a good deal of recent art and music, literature and film in the wider Nordic world: for example, in such latter-day films of Ingmar Bergman as *Fanny and Alexander*, the dream-rich metaphors of Tomas Tranströmer, and the energising images of painters Asger Jorn and Frans Widerberg – the latter of whom is one of Garbarek's favourite artists.[95]

The first aspect of Nordic mood is, of course, present throughout a great deal of Garbarek's work. It is the Nordic, "on the edge" quality in both his intense, questing sound and "speaking" or "singing" phrasing which marks Garbarek as one of the most distinctive saxophonists of our time. *Vandrere* (Wanderers), the lengthy opening track of **Dis**, epitomises this quality, with its magnificent "breathing " tenor (and Ralph Towner's superb 12 string guitar) hovering – wandering – above and across the E major/flattened 6th, G major/flattened 6th and D flat minor stepping stones of a composition which, in another medium, might have been written by Knut Hamsun, one of the earliest explorers of the unconscious in modern literature.[96] The resonance of Garbarek's tenor lines on the title track of the 1975 **Dansere** also comes to mind here. Although the melody of the composition is based on a Balinese pentatonic scale, the music sounds like the perfect accompaniment to the undulating rhythms, dream-like colours and emotional tensions which run through Edvard Munch's great *Frieze of Life* paintings and graphic works of the 1890s, with their various telling blends of symbolism and abstraction.[97] Consider also the irruptive accents of *Skrik & Hyl* (Cries and Confusion), the keening soprano flights of *Svevende* (Hovering), or the heart-on-sleeve compassion that marks the concluding melody of the album, *Til Vennene* (To the Friends).

The Nordic edge to Garbarek's work is no less present in his contributions to Keith Jarrett's (jazz quartet) **Belonging** and (orchestral) **Luminessence** albums of April 1974. This is particularly the case on *Solstice*, the thirteen-minute concluding track of the former album, and *Luminessence*, the fifteen-minute title track of the latter collaboration. If I had to choose only one ECM album of Garbarek's to take to that proverbial desert island, it would be **Luminessence**. Here, magnificently hewn tenor and soprano saxophone improvisations cut into and across the now kinetic, now rhythmically "suspended" frameworks of the three compositions – *Numinor, Windsong* and *Luminessence* – which Jarrett wrote specifically for Garbarek, and which are played with both great gusto and measured gravity by a string section drawn from the Südfunk Symphony Orchestra, conducted by Mladen Gutesha.

There had been successful marriages of saxophone and strings in jazz before. Stan Getz's and Eddie Sauter's superb **Focus**, from 1961, comes immediately to mind, as do the 1958 and 1961 albums **An Image** and **Free Forms** by Lee Konitz and Ralph Burns, recently reissued on the compilation CD **Lee Konitz Meets Jimmy Giuffre**.[98] However, the **Luminessence** album carries not just fresh musical conviction, with Jarrett's flowing, organic – asymmetrical – writing for strings perfectly suited to Garbarek's uniquely charged tone and poetically diversified rhythmic conception: the album also embodies exactly that world of existentially "wounded" or open-hearted spiritual quest which has long been characteristic of (post-Kierkegaardian) Nordic culture.

In his five star *Down Beat* review of the album, Chuck Berg answered his rhetorical question about what it was that lay at the centre of what he called the Jarrett-Garbarek vision thus: "One guess is that Jarrett's icy strings and Garbarek's frozen tones are the musical equivalent of the existential revolution of Sartre, Camus and Beckett. The image evoked is of a stilled, empty landscape. It's as if Garbarek's saxophone was [sic] a solitary searcher seeking out significance or meaning in a devastated and silent terrain."[99] To an extent, Berg has a point. Garbarek himself has said that, while he was playing the music, he certainly felt a little like the character Berg describes, especially during the fifteen-minute title track: only twenty four bars of this piece were written out for Garbarek, the rest being improvised over the (previously recorded) strings.[100]

However, instead of Sartre, Camus and Beckett, one could instance Kierkegaard, Hamsun and Ekelöf. And instead of "frozen tones", one might remark a tremendous amount of warmth – or "heart" – in Garbarek's playing. Such warmth flows through a thematically appropriate amount of tonal and rhythmic diversity, especially in the title track. Here, passages of even-tempered modality contrast with some rich, neo-Romantic chromatic writing for strings, sprung, driving cross-rhythms, and piquant, quartal harmonies, with Garbarek's astonishingly expressive, yet exquisitely controlled high

189

register improvisations often informed by the melismatic spirit (if not the form) of the blues. The idea that this music is somehow one-dimensional and monotonous, as suggested by Richard Cook and Brian Morton in their _Penguin Guide To Jazz On CD_, I find simply incomprehensible.[101]

The same year that he recorded **Luminessence**, Garbarek also participated in another existentially charged session, this time with Ralph Towner and the Solstice Quartet. This was the first occasion that Garbarek had recorded with Eberhard Weber, whose haunting composition _Sand_ supplies the album's final moments. Weber's texturally indeterminate "soundscape" of arco washes and pizzicato reflection elicits a stunning, melodically – and modally – sculpted line from Garbarek: the stepped, yet gliding, uniquely "crying" notes of his opening and concluding thematic phrases sound as if they have emerged, echo-like, from the most distant _ur_-ground of primal longing.

Musician and lecturer Rod Paton, with whom I have had the pleasure of many hours' discussion about music in general (and Jan Garbarek in particular) has commented to me about what he rightly sees as the liminal (or "on-the-threshold") quality in a good deal of the **Solstice** album. Rod has noted, with typical insight, the following features of the mythically oriented (and opening) _Oceanus_ – a favourite piece of Garbarek's, where the musical and spiritual odyssey unfolds over a lovely, loose "doubled four" rhythmic pulse: "Ralph Towner places his chords against the freely evolving rhythmic/harmonic wash with a remarkable sense of timing. In fact, this feels more like painting than music – the modal harmony, spiced up with ninths and sevenths, is daubed onto the canvas of rhythm. The relation of harmony and rhythm in the music is fascinating: a very slow pulse of harmonic, or chordal change offset by the crisp business of Christensen. For all that business, there is so much space in the music. Although Christensen keeps up the rhythmic drive on the cymbal, Weber, instead of underpinning this in the traditional manner, sidesteps Christensen's accents and creates a melodic, shifting bass line. This, in turn, sets the harmonic progression further on edge, so that the whole sound becomes liminal. Garbarek is then able to create organic, rolling waves of melody, improvising to mini-climaxes but still leaving acres of space."[102]

Similar comments could be made about the group combination of poetic contemplation and rhythmic vitality which precipitates the reflective, searching nobility of the sculpted accents and tonal variety which Garbarek brings to his (comparable) tenor solo on *Melting*, from Bill Connors' 1977 **Of Mist And Melting** (with Gary Peacock on double-bass and Jack DeJohnette on drums). In the same year, Garbarek recorded his own album **Places**, with Connors (guitar), John Taylor (piano, organ) and Jack DeJohnette (drums). The very titles of the album – *Reflections, Entering, Going Places* and *Passing* – speak of the elemental in life: of the mysteries (both terrifying and nourishing) of what it can mean to stand on the earth and look at the sky, aware of how, as that "cloud visionary" Gunnar Ekelöf once put it, "all things are in all things, at once end and beginning."[103]

In his December 1978 *Down Beat* review of the album, Douglas Clark spoke of "an eerie, desolate, bleak quality" in the music, which Clark judged as its single most important aspect: "Never mind the melodies, the meters, the modes; they are like parts in a mobile, balancing one another, changing the effect in subtle ways as they turn. If this music moves you, it does so through the mood it projects. Not to say that this is mood music in the usual sense of that term – it isn't. The moods here are deeper and more unsettling."[104]

The *ad libitum* moods of **Places** flow in and out of each other with a paradoxical sense of suspended motion: as Clark observes, the absence of a bass in the instrumentation brings a floating, indeterminate quality to the music. This is a quality equally evident in the very cool, laid-back phrasing of Bill Connors, John Taylor's sustained, legato organ chords (which, as Clark again observes, have more in common with Lutheran church music than they do with Jimmy Smith) and Jack DeJohnette's dynamically dramatic cross-rhythms and shimmering cymbal textures. On top of all this, Garbarek charts his quest.

Embracing a sombre, practically Balkan modality on *Reflections*, he manages to blend the aura of a Bach-like chorale with some (tempered) Rollinsesque affirmation on the devotional *Entering*. *Going Places* (long one of my favourite Garbarek pieces) floats its now poised, now swirling soprano meditations, rhythmic asymmetries and eerily shifting, distant – and dissonant – organ harmonies over a magical, medium-tempo pulse in 7/4 time, while *Passing* anchors rhythm to a spacious groove almost reminiscent of (laid-back) rock music. Its repeated patterns stimulate both group and solo voices to conjure a mood of swelling, plangent regret and rumination. This is indeed music which, from both the technical and poetic point of view, takes one to the edge of things.[105]

In his October 1987 _Edmonton Journal_ review of Garbarek's solo album **All Those Born With Wings**, James Adams observed that, " [The record] of course, is long on mood and textures. Garbarek is no facile riff player or over-reaching virtuoso; what matters to this ascetic Scandinavian is the feeling behind each tone. His is a Bergmanesque brand of jazz – aural movie music framed by vast pools of reverberating silence, pervaded with a kind of existential religiosity."[106] The fact that one of the tracks on the album was dedicated to the memory of Russian film director Andrei Tarkovsky – who had died of cancer in Paris, four months after the recording session which produced **Wings** – serves to reinforce the appositeness of Adams' observations. Here, we approach the second aspect of Nordic mood in Garbarek's work: its relation to the theme of the seemingly "silent" or "absent" Protestant God, and the consequent struggle to revision the question of existential (i.e. lived) "religiosity" – or, as I would prefer to describe this condition, "spirituality".[107]

In this context, individual pieces from various albums, such as _Spor_ (Tracks) from the 1983 **Wayfarer**, are certainly relevant. Garbarek can rarely have played with such a piquant breadth and depth of tone as he does here, the ascending whole step/half step idea within the G major/A diminished/B flat major/octave G and release into E minor structure eliciting a peformance where the existential polarities of sorrow and gladness, leave-taking and presence are mediated, even transmuted, as movingly as they are in Rainer Maria Rilke's (non-Christian) _Duino Elegies_.[108] However, it is the overall mood of three albums in particular which it is important to consider here. The first, **Aftenland** (Evening Land) was recorded in December 1979; the second, **Paths, Prints** in December 1981 and the third, **It's OK to listen to the gray voice**, in December 1984.

Aftenland, an album of duets with classical Norwegian organist Kjell Johnsen, precipitated some of the most dismissive criticism which Garbarek has ever received. For Matthew Bateson, writing in _Jazz Journal International_, the album revealed Garbarek to be in danger of "mining his chosen territory to complete aridity."[109] The _Oakland Tribune_ advised that the album should be avoided by anyone already in a depressed state, while _Playboy_'s three-line review thought it "a perfect soundtrack for your next nervous breakdown."[110] This view was taken somewhat further by one Peter-M. Zettler: writing in the German *Audio* magazine of December 1980, he suggested that the album's Bergman-like "tristesse" was the stuff of which suicides are made, and gave the album a generous one star (out of a possible ten).[111]

In *Jazz Hot*, Jerome Reese claimed that, even more than **Hymns, Spheres** – Keith Jarrett's earlier album of organ improvisations – such an album did not merit release, since it was but "a pale imitation of the immense repertoire for organ this century, notably that of Messiaen, whose influence is evident enough [in **Aftenland**]."[112] And even critics partial to Garbarek, such as Richard Cook and Brian Morton, came up with some less than glowing words about this album: "On a check list of ECM and Garbarek clichés, this scores quite highly. Nordic? Unmistakably. Moody? Certainly. Atmospheric? Definitely. But funky and swinging it sure isn't."[113]

Like their dismissal of **Luminessence** (which is not even listed in the most recent edition of their *Penguin Guide to Jazz on CD*) the views of Cook and Morton here strike me as simply extraordinary. The only clichés evident in their assessment of **Aftenland** are their own: if any musician and record label deserved to be spared the application of those razor-sharp criteria "funky and swinging" by the end of the 1970s, it was surely Garbarek and ECM.

How is one to explain the considerable resistance which **Aftenland** provoked among certain sections of the critical fraternity in jazz? Certainly, the record does not "swing" in any conventional sense of the term: but neither did a track like *Saeta*, from Miles Davis's classic **Sketches of Spain** album. On the other hand, where else but in jazz would you find the stop-start playfulness of *Spill* (Play), or the subtle, nudging accents and melismatic call and response of *Tegn* (Sign) – the last track on the album, the stirring drone of its Dorian modality precipitating some wonderful passages of rapt, Middle Eastern-inflected supplication from Garbarek?

It is true that **Aftenland** projects a strong overall mood throughout its forty-plus minutes. One wonders, nevertheless, how critics familiar with the dynamic variety of jazz were not able to appreciate the extraordinary range of dynamics, timbre and emotional "hue" explored on *Enigma*, which moves from thunderous opening passages to some of the most haunting, fragile pianissimo reflections Garbarek has ever recorded. To accuse a recording which embraces both the drifting, rootless chromaticism of the title track and the intensely focused meditation of *Linje* (as near to serialism as it is to plainchant) – or the torrential improvising of *Kilden* (The Spring) and measured modality of *Tegn* – of being somehow one-dimensional, or arid, strikes me simply as evidence of closed ears and minds.And to suggest that the album is but a pale copy of Messiaen is surely nothing more than the worst kind of musical snobbery. Why stop at Messiaen? Isn't **Aftenland** also reminiscent, at times, of some of Darius Milhaud's works for organ?[114] But did you ever hear a piece for organ and saxophone by either of these two composers – or a recording for organ by them – which embraces as much formal variety as **Aftenland**? Like a good deal of ECM music, **Aftenland** – which brought together one of the most innovative jazz musicians of his time and a highly respected interpreter of church organ music – explored a new kind of musical space, between genres and beyond categories.[115]

In a review of the 1984 **Gray Voice** album, Kris Larsen suggested that "Jan Garbarek may pass from this world with just a handful of listeners. Why? Few people like seeing themselves in a mirror that reveals the root loneliness of their souls."[116] Garbarek has long had more than a handful of listeners, but Larsen's point is a good one. It applies with particular force to much of the critical reaction to **Aftenland**. In a review of the album in the *Manchester Evening News*, Chris Lee suggested that the music "could almost be described as a musical equivalent of Strindberg or Ibsen."[117] Here, surely, is a good deal of the reason why **Aftenland** aroused so much negative reaction: it explored depths of feeling and form which were simply too strong – too existentially naked – for a certain type of listener to take. Much of the music on **Aftenland** began life as a sequence of improvisations which Garbarek supplied for Edith Roger's production of Ibsen's *Brand* at the Oslo National Theatre in 1978. If the moods of **Aftenland** are in close accord with Ibsen's seminal study of the human consequences of an over-zealous (and essentially uncompassionate) spiritual commitment by the play's chief character, the titles for a good deal of the album were inspired by the 1953 collection of poetry *Aftonland* (Evening Land) by Swedish writer Pär Lagerkvist (1891-1974).

A lucent expression of natural piety in the face of nature, *Aftonland* is also a poignant valediction to the "absent God" of post-

Darwinian Western thought. This collection of reflections upon the eternal themes of life and death was coloured by two factors in particular. One was the poet's life-long, intensely personal sense of the absence of (the Christian, or Protestant) God: one of the very last entries in Lagerkvist's diary reads (with a typical inversion of Biblical text) "God, my God, why have I abandoned you?"[118] The second factor was Lagerkvist's sensitivity to ambiguity, to the layers of meaning that might be conjured, for example, by such a simple linking device as the expression "as though".

The effect of Lagerkvist's writing is sometimes compared to looking down into very still, clear and deep water. The metaphor is a good one, providing one remembers how much the refraction of light can deceive the eye. All his life, Lagerkvist remembered the lessons of Cubism which he had learned in Paris as a young man, and *Aftenland* – which is written in five distinct sections, each with a slightly different persona, or voice – conveys perfectly the interlaced complexities of the spiritual quest of a soul desperately wanting to believe in traditional values, but unable to do so.[119] The volume has inspired at least two vocal works in the world of Nordic "serious" or "art" music: Per Nørgård dedicated his 1954, *op. 10* choral setting of four poems from the collection to Sibelius, while Arne Nordheim's *Aftonland*, which scored four other poems for soprano and orchestra in 1957, was this Norwegian modernist composer's breakthrough work.[120] Excellent as both settings are, they capture neither the emotional extremes nor the mysterious, multi-planed totality that is Lagerkvist's work to anything like the extent that the Garbarek/Johnsen recording does.

Aftenland was recorded one snowy December day in 1979 in Stockholm's Engelbrekts Church, a lofty, brick and stone building designed early this century in Jugendstil fashion by L. I. Wahlman.[121] A year later, the more functional ambience of Oslo's Talent Studio saw the recording of **Paths, Prints** – an album of similar intensity to **Aftenland**, albeit an intensity realised with very different musical content and instrumentation. Electric guitarist Bill Frisell joined Garbarek's long-time colleagues Eberhard Weber and Jon Christensen to interpret an album of Garbarek compositions that ranged from the Messiaen-inflected scalar mystery of the opening, tenor-led *The Path* to the tender, elegaic soprano and bass melodies of the concluding *Still*. At times the music combines the modal and chromatic abstraction of much of **Aftenland** with an earthier, more rooted and tonal feeling, sometimes inclining to the rhythms of dance – as in the lovely, playful melodies and rhythmic variety of *Kite Dance*.The lengthy, medium-slow *Footprints* (not Wayne Shorter's 6/8 blues) is perhaps the outstanding piece on the record: it epitomises that combination of the earthy and the celestial, the rooted and the abstract, which distinguishes Garbarek's art at its plangent, searching best.

One of the many marvels of the piece is the way in which the simple and the complex condition and support each other, as in the opening, ethereal moments when Garbarek's elemental, folkish wooden flute melody emerges from Jon Christensen's simple, yet multi-toned percussive touches (with perhaps some overdubbed, Asiatic-sounding percussion from Garbarek also in the mix). Later in the piece, after some passages of exquisitely balanced motivic variation on soprano, the ostensibly simple theme is given added piquancy by some searing chromatic passing tones, realised with appropriate dynamic variation: gradually, the keening theme dissolves back into the infinity out of which it first emerged. (In the concluding minutes, the occasional closeness of Garbarek's tone to that which he employed at the beginning of Eberhard Weber's composition *Sand*, on Ralph Towner's 1974 **Solstice**, is remarkable.)

In his January 1983 <u>*New Musical Express*</u> review, Richard Cook rightly saw *Footprints* as central to the success of **Paths, Prints**, suggesting that the many features of the album blossomed "with sublime eloquence in the unfolding of *Footprints*, a trail beginning in wood flutes and tablas which crosses east-west into reeds and electricity – the soprano's bursting entry is an enchanted arrow – with the root rapture of melody never forsaken."[122] Cook here put his finger on something important in the development of Garbarek's music at this time.

The album had enough of the saxophonist's familiar qualities to make French critic Alain Gerber speak of his "allergie proverbiale à la sonorite et à la poetique de Garbarek [..]."[123] However, to anyone who, like Cook, had followed Garbarek's music with more sympathy than Gerber, **Paths, Prints** embodied the potentiality of a fresh synthesis of such familiar emotional polarities as joy and sadness, angst and ecstasy. There is still a good deal of Lagerkvist-like angst in **Paths, Prints**: a feeling that the music unfolds, for the most part, within the shadowed depths of a consciousness only too aware of the transience of all things. And it does this with a sense of deliberation which reminds one, not of the time sense in American jazz, but rather the filmic rhythms of Ingmar Bergman – as evident, for example, in the beautiful, long-held shot of water and reflected cloud which opens *Through A Glass Darkly*, or in the slowly unfolding interior scenes of *The Silence*.

Nevertheless, Cook is quite right to speak of the "rapture" of melody within the ululation that is in large part *Footprints*. Emerging from the loneliness – and the courage – of the confrontation with transience that marked **Aftenland** (a confrontation that many critics were either unable or unwilling to stomach) **Paths, Prints** leavens its elegiac introspection now and then with various flights of that "enchanted arrow" of melody to which Cook drew his readers' attention. On the December 1984 **It's OK to listen to the gray voice**, a strong feeling of confronting the transience of life remains: however, the elegiac and the enchanted (or ecstatic) now emerge – or merge, transmuted – in an increasingly vibrant range of musical frameworks.

The album, which besides Garbarek and Eberhard Weber featured guitarist David Torn and drummer Michael DiPasqua, drew the majority of its titles from a particular collection by Tranströmer: the 1978 *Truth Barriers*, which Garbarek had read in a dual language edition with English translations by the American poet Robert Bly.[124] A psychologist as well as a poet, Tomas Tranströmer (born 1931) is a poet of time, in several senses of that immense word. Often, his work – which is formally highly focused, but emotionally extremely open – will bury underneath the "big" time of history, searching out instead the ostensibly "little" time of the potentially transformative moment. This is the moment which may contain the sort of dream-like power which can open up our sense of time, perhaps to dimensions ungraspable within the overly familiar and restrictive patterns of everyday life. Thoroughly aware of the pressures of contemporary politics and technology, Tranströmer often builds elements of the latter into his largely nature-oriented imagery. There is nothing escapist or sentimental about this poet's sensitivity to landscape: it is landscape which offers him the essential breathing space where he can feel life perhaps grow stronger at what he calls the "open frontiers" of experience.[125]

Driving to work early one morning, the poet sees children on their way to school: the children, he observes, for whom no-one prays.[126] Aware of the spiritual vacuum at the heart of many lives, Tranströmer does not advocate rushing back into the arms of either the Christian or any other Church. Instead, he seeks to sharpen our awareness of the spiritual dimensions in life which lie somewhere deep within us, dimensions which flow beyond the confines of any particular creed or country: what Tranströmer has called "The innermost paradox, the garage flower, the ventilator to the good darkness. A drink that bubbles in empty glasses. A loudspeaker that sends out silence. A pathway that grows over again behind each step. A book that can only be read in the dark."[127]

What Robert Bly once wrote about Tranströmer applies equally to much of the work of Garbarek. In a memorable image, Bly drew attention to "poems [which] are a sort of railway station where trains that have come enormous distances stand briefly in the same building. One train may have some Russian snow still lying on the undercarriage, and another may have Mediterranean flowers still fresh in the compartments, and Ruhr soot on the roofs."[128] Bly went on to draw a distinction between the "otherworldly" pursuit of mystery in the Symbolist Stephane Mallarmé, and the fact that in Tranströmer, mystery is manifest in poetry which maintains a stubborn link with its occasion (or precipitation) in the "real" world. Or as Tranströmer himself puts it, in *The Journey's Formulae*: "[..] there/ he travels, at once eagle and mole."[129] Much the same point obtains in the music of Garbarek, which, no matter how far "out" it may go (as in the title track of **Aftenland**) is ultimately linked to the world through one or another variety of tonality and (bodily-based) rhythm (as in *Footprints*, for example).

Tranströmer has said that truth only appears at the borders, and the <u>Truth Barriers</u> collection weaves its way from dream to (possible, and ecumenical) epiphany with a variegated sense of the regenerative powers of the unconscious. It is fitting, therefore, that the **Gray Voice** album opens and closes on a note of dream-like suspension, achieved with means as simple as they are subtle.

The spacious, gently falling A minor melody of the opening *White noise of forgetfulness* is presented with the minumum of elaboration. There is no solo over rhythm support, in the traditional jazz sense, but rather, exquisitely attuned group playing, with everyone contributing equally to the overall mood signalled by David Torn's chilled guitar obbligato. The concluding *I'm the knife-thrower's partner* sets a solo soprano, folkish melody against a related, but slightly displaced, overdubbed scale: an understated waltz rhythm enhances the bitonal effect of eerie abstraction. Elsewhere on the album, as in Tranströmer's poetry, the dreaming is very much both of the earth and open to the sky.

The expansive, hymnal *Mission: to be where I am* is rooted firmly in E major, with David Torn's electric guitar fills and solo adding a sonorous (and appropriate) touch of American gospel. In *One day in March I go down to the sea and listen*, the blues-like structure acquires a Slavic edge through the use of a scale of pan-modal potential, mixing elements of F major with minor sevenths. With its floating theme in 12/8 time and trenchant soprano solo, the track is a particularly vibrant example of the synthesising powers of Garbarek's imagination: it also contains one of the most rhythmically exciting, texturally eruptive and sound-sculpting solos David Torn has ever recorded.

The crossing place explores the dualities implicit in its title, as it moves from the rubato, chromatic abstraction of Eberhard Weber's brooding, pizzicato bass figures to up-tempo, piping passages of joyous polyrhythms in 10/4 time. (Elements of this piece would re-surface, re-named as *Once I Wished A Tree Upside Down*, as part of Garbarek's contributions to Trilok Gurtu's 1990-91 **Living Magic** recording.) In the central and linked meditations of *It's OK to phone the island that is a mirage* and *It's OK to listen to the gray voice*, where Torn's shimmering, etched simplicity and Weber's lyrically sprung meditations are crucial to the overall mood, we are given aural glimpses of that mysterious, spiritually replenishing realm which drifts in and out of focus in Tranströmer's poetry. Be it the "snail trace and steel wire" of Schubert's music, an icy shoreline in March, or an unexpected clearing in the summer forest, it is the place where dualities no longer hold sway. *Island*'s pellucid soprano reveries hover above A minor and E flat minor: fittingly, it is impossible to locate precisely the three keys through which the majestic, major third tenor ascensions of *Gray Voice* unfold. Here, we are at the heart of Tranströmer's "open frontier", and "suffering and happiness weigh exactly the same."[130]

Like **Aftenland** and a good deal of **Paths, Prints**, the **Gray Voice** album explores tonally abstract regions of sound and space. However, the space which Garbarek sings into being here is, for the most part, very different from the space of the previous two albums. Far from the estrangement of *Aftenland*, for example, it is the space of what the

Jungian psychologist Erich Neumann has called *participation mystique* – a space that bids us dream and dance ourselves into the state of wholeness conjured by pieces as distinct, yet linked, as the two central, reverie-rich meditations of the album and *The crossing place*.[131]

The title of the last-named piece serves as an appropriate introduction to a consideration of that final – and most important – aspect of Nordic mood which may be discerned in Garbarek's work: the polytheistic, or shamanic, aspect. In art historical terms, the North has often been seen as that part of the world where feelings of terror-struck awe in the face of 'N'ature (what has been called the ante-room to God) are most likely to be experienced. Following Edmund Burke's discussion of a new aesthetic category, the sublime, in his 1757 *A Philosophical Enquiry into the Origins of our Ideas of the Sublime and the Beautiful* , for many artists and travellers Northern landscapes (at first British, and then Nordic) began first to rival, and then replace the Alps as the *locus classicus* for such an experience.[132] Underneath the new aesthetic category of the sublime, it is possible to trace the re-emergence in modern European consciousness of that most ancient of psycho-dynamic and creative responses to the presence of Nature: the shamanic.[133]

In his April 1987 *Wire Magazine* review of Garbarek's solo album **All Those Born With Wings**, Mark Sinker offered what in retrospect seems a remarkably prescient comment. "The first thing I'm reminded of," said Sinker, " is a tape a friend gave me of a Finnish *joik* concert – a strange semi-shamanic and fully ecstatic celebration of the infinite past in the present that survives with undiminished power into an age of electricity, microphones, synthesisers, and can still plunge deep into the heart of nomadic folk visions from a culture that spans Asia from Lappland to Ulan Bator and beyond."[134] Garbarek, Sinker concluded, "unearths living ghosts."[135]

In so doing, Jan Garbarek has come into contact with fundamental, archetypal aspects of what it can mean to live on Earth: aspects which predate the (relatively recent) dominance of life by such a category as the aesthetic and the (much older, but in world terms still relatively recent) historical mode of consciousness epitomised by both Judaeo-Christianity and Marxism. In such seminal works as *The Myth of The Eternal Return, or, Cosmos and History* (1954), *The Sacred and The Profane: The Nature of Religion* (1957) and *The Quest: History and Meaning in Religion* (1969) Mircea Eliade, the (late) distinguished scholar of shamanism, elaborated upon his fundamental intuition that, "The chief difference between the man of the archaic and traditional societies and the man of the modern societies with their strong imprint of Judaeo-Christianity lies in the fact that the former feels himself indissolubly connected with the Cosmos and the cosmic rhythms, whereas the latter insists that he is connected only with History."[136] Is it at all possible for the latter type of consciousness to become the former once again – for the historical to become reimmersed – and hence transformed – in the cosmic?

It is precisely the primitivistic quest for such a transition that has fired so much spiritually compelling avant-garde practice this century. For century after century, life in the West has been increasingly dominated by the idea that the content and the colour of that life arise, develop and disappear within the "progressive" (in at least two senses of the term) framework of time known as history. In Marxism, which inherits so much of its eschatological approach to life from Judaeo-Christianity, the two chief senses of that "progressive" combine: time and humanity are moving forward to a Paradisal Age of Plenty. Unfortunately, as we know from physics, things that move with great energy – whether objects or ideas – also create a similar amount of waste, or burnt energy. One of the chief problems of the twentieth century, in fact, has been exactly this: the possibility that all of life may be, both literally and symbolically, burnt up.

It is artists, above all, who have squared up to this problem. And they have done so, not – as with so many fanatical fundamentalists in recent years – with a crass, and often destructive wish to put the (historical) clock back, but rather with an heroic determination to penetrate the mysteries of life in a manner which may place us, once again, at the creative, cosmic core of life. In a little-known but important American T.V. interview of the mid-1960s, Ingmar Bergman (born 1918) revealed that, when he made *The Silence* (1963) he was "still bleeding" from his experience of the withdrawal of (the Protestant, and in Bergman's films, the hostile and authoritarian) God from his life, from his conviction that "God didn't exist anymore." Bergman continued:"[..] I'm now still convinced that there is no God anywhere in the world. That God is dead. But I am also convinced that in every man, you have – there is, there is a part of man who is – a human being in his mind – a room that is holy. That is, that is very special. Very high. Very secret room that is – that is a holy part of the human being."[137]

Commenting on this interview, the psychotherapist Ira Progoff has suggested that the creative power of Bergman's work represents "an excellent instance of how the dialectic of the psyche leads beyond itself in the life of a creative person to intimations of a spiritual dimension of reality. Inward for the imagery, outward for the artworks, unified in the waking dream that coheres each creative act, the continuity of experience brings forth a living myth."[138] As witnessed by such albums as **Legend Of The Seven Dreams**, **Rosensfole, I Took Up The Runes** and **Twelve Moons**, in the decade and more that has passed since **All Those Born With Wings** the Nordic dimension in Garbarek's work has been set more and more in the service of such a "waking dream", or "living myth". Herein lies a considerable part of the (psychic) importance of what both Garbarek and other Nordic musicians have done with folk material: the archetypal is made, not part of a museum, but fresh and generative. In Garbarek's work, such transmutative elements of what Progoff calls waking dream and living myth first blossomed in the 1980 **Eventyr** (Fairy-tales) – the album that, perhaps more than any other, reveals how much the psychic depths of Garbarek's work are rooted in Nordic soil.

In his penetrating 1980 study _Genius Loci: Towards A Phenomenology of Architecture_ the Norwegian architectural theorist Christian Norberg-Schulz examined the different ways in which the psyche is able to purchase a foothold on life, in three radically different types of place: desert, (classical) Italian and Nordic landscape. For Norberg-Schulz, Nordic (and in particular, Norwegian) landscape is characterised by "*an indefinite multitude of different places.*" While this is the kind of primal landscape where life's "original forces" are still to be felt, it is at the same time a landscape of diversity and freshness: "Behind every hillock and rock there is a new place, and only exceptionally is the landscape unified to form a simple, univocal space." In the Nordic landscape, continues Norberg-Schulz, people encounter "a host of 'natural forces', whereas a general unifying order is lacking. This becomes clearly manifest in the literature, art and music of the Nordic countries, where natural impressions and moods play a primary role. In legends and fairy-tales we encounter the mythical inhabitants of this world: gnomes, dwarfs and trolls. Still today Nordic man carries these beings within his psyche, and when he wants to 'live', he leaves the city to experience the mysteries of the Nordic landscape. In doing this he looks for the *genius loci*, which he has to understand in order to gain an existential foothold."[139]

Recorded with guitarist John Abercrombie and percussionist Nana Vasconcelos, **Eventyr** offers a richly conceived, shape-shifting suite of that folk-inflected world of the Nordic *genius loci* which Garbarek had already presented on such single tracks as *Bruremarsj* (1972), *Lokk* (1975) and *Folk Song* (1979), as well as in the fascinating, collective 1975 recording **Østerdalsmusikk** (Music of the Østerdal Valley, recorded on the Norwegian MAI label) and a good deal of *Ingentings Bjeller* (Nothing's Bells), which the Garbarek/Stenson Quartet recorded with Jan Erik Vold in 1977, on the Norwegian Philips label.

In an interview of October 1981, Garbarek explained that, while he had drawn inspiration for **Eventyr** from traditional melodies [and took the trouble to credit the original musicians associated with these melodies on the record's cover] he had interpreted the melodies in his own way: "I went down to the folk music collection in Chateau Neuf and asked if I could listen to their recordings: what I was really after were cattle calls and short, improvised verses. It wasn't difficult to find plenty of good material, but I had to feel that I could play it. For, really, I haven't got any special grounding in folk music; I play the old melodies in a quite untypical way. The purists may have their doubts, but it was absolutely necessary for me to play the music my own way. If I'd wanted to play the material in the traditional way, I would have had to practise for ever – without necessarily managing it, even after twenty years."[140] In a later interview, Garbarek elaborated upon the subject of his relationship with Norwegian folk material thus: "I haven't spent *that* much time researching the old Norwegian melodies – once when a big band commission specified something 'Norwegian' in the scoring and, of course, for the **Eventyr** recording. I will say, there is something special to them – they are not so Europeanised as Danish material, for example. There's a strong Balkan flavour, lots of scales with minor thirds; you find similarities to the Greek modes, particularly the Lydian. The funny thing was that when I did look through some sketches of the old cattle calls, I found that what I had been moving towards playing anyway – something direct, very 'loud' in a way, but with a floating, far-off feeling as well as the sense of closeness – was also in those old pieces."[141]

The opening track of **Eventyr**, the eleven-and-a-half minute *Soria Moria*, epitomises the process of the personalisation of archetypal material which one finds in Garbarek: over a near-static drone from Abercrombie and Vasconcelos, his soprano outlines a spacious melody which at times sounds as Middle Eastern in its piercing modality as it does Norwegian. Subsequently, the album features a psychologically – mythically – engaging, at times eerie (if not sublime) range of melody and rhythm, texture and mood. This is indeed music of the "living ghosts" – ghosts who cry out, laugh and sing in a haunting variety of voices.

The Aylerish breadth of line and upper register tenor piping of the rubato title track, its mood perfectly underscored by Vasconcelos's magical, "cathedral-in-the-forest" percussion, contrast beautifully with the sing-song, lilting melodies of *Lillekort* and *Snipp, Snapp, Snute*; while the lullaby-like tenderness of *Weaving A Garland* and darker meditations of *The Companion* (a duet with Vasconcleos on berimbau) are forcefully offset by the burning scalar improvisations of *Once Upon A Time*. (This was an entirely spontaneous piece, sparked by the fact that Abercrombie had brought a guitar to the studio with an unusual, intriguing tuning.) The final track, *East Of The Sun And West Of The Moon*, can only have disappointed Bebop enthusiasts misled by the title, and expecting to see how Garbarek might negotiate a classic song of modern jazz. A long way from the world of Sarah Vaughan, Dizzy Gillespie and Charlie Parker (and Stan Getz), the diversely-spun melodies of this ostensibly static piece supply a suitably twilight, evanescent coda to the session, with Abercromie's concluding mandolin glisses and Vasconcelos's vocalese dissolving into seemingly endless space.

The year that **Eventyr** was recorded, a piece called *Sameland* was the Norwegian entry for the Eurovision Song Contest. This was a time when conflicts between the Norwegian government and the (traditionally nomadic, reindeer-herding) Sami people reached crisis point, in what was an ongoing dispute over the projected damming of land (the Alta project) in a part of the north of the country used by the Sami and their reindeers. Composer S. Kjelsberg made reference to this political situation in the Eurovision Song Contest entry, which was heard and seen by some 600 million people. Unfortunately, just as the song came last in the contest, so were years of protest about the damming of the Alta eventually to prove fruitless: the project went ahead. However, both song and protest were significant indication of the growing determination of the Sami people to assert their identity and rights, after centuries of Christian missionary work intended to stamp out the shamanic heart of Sami culture, and many years of parallel repression from the political authorities.[142]

In the broad sense, elements of shamanic (or animistic, visionary) consciousness can be heard in Garbarek's work as early as 1967, when he recorded *Mr. J. C.*, his tribute to Coltrane – an artist of immense shamanic consequence – with Per Løberg and Jon Christensen. From a more specific perspective, the 1973 Garbarek/Stenson Quartet version of the late saxophonist Jim Pepper's peyote (and practically pentatonic) vision chant *Witchi-Tai-To* represents the beginning of a process that, from the mid-1980s onwards, has become more and more apparent in Garbarek's work.[143] This is that mixture of shaman-like incantation and rhythmic power which so distinguishes albums like **Legend Of The Seven Dreams** and **I Took Up The Runes**.

The very title of the latter album inducing images of one of the key moments of shamanic consciousness in Nordic mythology, when Odin hung from the World Tree Yggdrasil, undergoing the initiatory suffering necessary for the (eventual) acquiring of a broadened, deepened and enlightened – a shamanic – consciousness. And on the **Dreams** album, the swirling (synthesised) harmonium riffs and staggered ostinato drum patterns of *Aichuri, The Song Man* cannot help but recall the heart of archetypal shamanic consciousness: the shaman's world-bridging drum, fashioned, as the mythology has it, from the very wood of the Tree of Life, and alone able to propel the shaman on those world-bridging flights of the psyche that both create and gather in the healing energy of a synoptic vision.[144]

The recent renaissance of Sami culture is the most immediately visible evidence of contemporary shamanic consciousness in the North: and for nearly a decade now, Garbarek has made plain his empathy with aspects of that culture. His live appearances and recordings with singer Mari Boine, for example, or his continued fascination with the melodic and spiritual power and potentialities of the Sami *joik*, are testimony to a deep respect and regard for the reindeer-herder cultures of the Far North.[145] However, the re-emergence of shamanic consciousness in the modern world has been a feature of not just the recent Sami Renaissance, but Nordic avant-garde culture in general – and for a good many years now.

From Munch and Ibsen, Hamsun and Strindberg to Edith Södergran and Gunnar Ekelöf, Johannes S. Kjarval and Akseli Gallen-Kallela; and from Tomas Tranströmer and Ingmar Bergman, Tarjei Vesaas and Olavi Lanu to Asger Jorn and Frans Widerberg, Nordic artists have offered us a variety of courageous, exploratory ways to revision the relationships of body and soul, heart and mind. Underneath all such variety, often described as evidence of either a Romantic or an Expressionistic approach to life, the generative, archetypal pulse of animistic shamanic consciousness has continued to beat, offering us the possibility of *a bigger picture* of life.[146]

In an essay of 1935, published with the title *The Sunset: From A Romantic's Notes*, Gunnar Ekelöf spoke of how, as a young man, he had come to distrust what he called, "the I, the little daily will and life of the moment."[147] "I did not lose the feeling for the meaningful which otherwise occurs," continues Ekelöf, "I thought I knew that life's deepest streams always evaded the conscious-now-I, the near-sighted near. Our now is seldom more than a certain selfish absent-mindedness: it is only love sometimes and art sometimes that give us the possibility to gather life's, the past and coming, weight into a moment."[148] If we could only learn one hundred words of what Ekelöf called "the supra-earthly language", then everything we needed to say (and experience) might be said. We might even recover what Ekelöf hymned as "The whole longed for land of childhood ... Sunrise over the troll lake, the hot fragrant hill of wild strawberries in the midday sun, the bells in the forest and the clear, echoing voices around the lake in the evening ... And the simplicity and happiness of being – here and nowhere else."[149]

Ekelöf's words remind one of Henry Miller's belief that the Earth itself is Paradise: we simply have to make ourselves fit to inhabit it. And, as so much Nordic creativity demonstrates, it is art – such as that of Ekelöf himself, or the Norwegian painter Frans Widerberg – which can function, not simply in the realm of the aesthetic, but as one of the key vehicles to such a state of consciousness. In an important, extensive interview with journalist and photographer Terje Mosnes in January 1983, Garbarek was asked if he could think of any possible parallels between what he was trying to do in his music and other contemporary art forms.

Garbarek replied: "There is a painter I rate very highly, and for whom I feel a strong affinity ... I don't know if this will sound a little 'over the top' on my part... but I'm thinking of Frans Widerberg. In a way, all his pictures deal with the same themes, all the time. They are always interesting to me – a single, simple figure in a corresponding landscape, which has *so* much power."[150] Mosnes then asked

Garbarek if such an image could be seen as having a relation to some sort of cosmic power, to which Garbarek replied: "Exactly. And the titles of his pictures [for example, *Dreamer in a Landscape*, *Rider*, *Floater*, *Wanderer*, *Near The Fire*, *Towards the Moon*, *Liberators*] .. I think that, quite unconsciously, I've come to title pieces of mine in response to his. I could almost think of making an album just from the stimulus of the titles he has used for his pictures."[151]

The correspondence between the work of Garbarek and Widerberg – the most important Norwegian figurative artist after Munch – has long been apparent. In pieces like *Svevende* (Hovering) from the 1975 **Dansere**, or *Blue Sky*, from the 1978 **Photo With Blue Sky, White Cloud, Wires, Windows And A Red Roof**, the saxophonist floats spacious, reflective melodies across uncluttered arrangements, in a manner strongly reminiscent of Widerberg's control of both figure and ground and complementary contrasts of hot and cool colour. And just as space is crucial to Garbarek's music, so is it fundamental to Widerberg's imagery.

The painter is fond of placing his favoured motifs – horses and riders, naked, contemplative couples and ecstatic, hovering figures – at the far edge of both landscape and experience, the whole united in a rainbow-envelope of pure, energising colour. Born in 1934, Frans Widerberg is a man well aware of the violence which can so often erupt in life: the German occupation of Norway in the Second World War, Cold War crises and the atrocities of Vietnam have all left their mark on his personality. However, in Widerberg, a sensitivity to the ever-present factor of human suffering is balanced (if not transmuted) by an intense commitment to ideas of energy and metamorphosis, of spiritual "travel" and wonder. Here, space becomes energy, and light-drenched landscape a theatre for the soul. "Deep inside me", Widerberg has said, " I find a vision, I try to bring it out, make it shine and be recognised by others ... The inner landscape – that is what I am looking for."[152]

Like the shamans of old, Widerberg explores a world of archetypal import. And, just as Garbarek makes the folk material he plays *new* – one thinks of the range of arrangements, at times Indian- or even industrial-inflected, which he brought to Agnes Buen Garnås's beautiful interpretations of Norwegian folk melody on the 1988-9 **Rosensfole** – so does Widerberg bring the spirit of pre-history into a contemporary register, in a wide range of media.[153] These have included oil painting and watercolour, woodcut and lithography, etching and sculpture – and, especially in recent years, glass.

In the early 1990s Widerberg collaborated with the Danish glassmaster Per Hebsgaard (born 1948) in decorating the Volsdal Church at Ålesund, on Norway's west coast; in 1997-8 these two consummate artists worked together on an enormous, three-part glass frieze and horse and rider sculpture for a new transport corridor at Copenhagen's Kastrup Airport. The contemporary, the practical, is here reimmersed in the mythic, the poetic, as passengers are offered the opportunity to contemplate the deeper psychic dimensions of that phenomenon which, extraordinarily enough, is taken so much for granted today: flight.[154] It was particularly appropriate that, in the 1996 T.V. documentary which was made about the forty-year painting retrospective which Widerberg had that year at Oslo's Astrup Fearnley Museum for Modern Art, Norwegian director Bjørn Fredheim chose to use music by Jan Garbarek – and Niels-Henning Ørsted Pedersen – throughout.[155]

In the quintessentially Nordic, yet at the same time internationally-oriented work of Garbarek and Widerberg, we are offered a world where the sufferings of life are fully acknowledged, but where the suffering individual is also offered potentially transformative glimpses of that Paradisal realm that exists deep within every one of us – born as we are with the potentiality of wings. As Ekelöf wrote: " If you ask me where I am/Well I live here beyond the mountains/It is far but I am near/I live in another world/but you live in it too/It is everywhere, as rare as helium..."[156]

What else was Ekelöf writing about; what else is Widerberg painting; what else is Garbarek playing, but what Rilke once chose to call music: that "heart space" grown out of us?[157] In the heart space that is Garbarek's music, it is possible to sense the resonance of the whole modern shamanic tradition in Nordic culture. Remaining in creative touch with the *genius loci*, it is exactly such a tradition which may stimulate in us fresh awareness of that "very special, very high, very secret room" so valued by Bergman.

How might one begin to approach such a room – or perhaps learn to understand at least a little of that 'supra-earthly' language for which Ekelöf yearned? In the words of Tomas Tranströmer, from the collection which inspired most of the titles on Garbarek's **Gray Voice** album, one does so by having the courage to undertake a challenging, but potentially fructifying journey, far into oneself – the very journey evident in so much Nordic art and music. This, says Tranströmer, is a journey "upward into/the depths."[158] At such a crossing place, voices – no matter how grey they may at times appear to be – can speak in rainbows.

Night Light
Frans Widerberg
(1979, oil on canvas, 52 x 46 cms. private collection)

Palle Danielsson, Jon Christensen, Bobo Stenson, Jan Garbarek
c. 1976 ECM

Notes to Chapter Four

1. *Vienna Art Orchestra 20th Anniversary Tour*, unpaginated programme notes. Arranged by Rüegg, the suite featured *Chill Out Honey Pie* (W. & Chr. Muthspiel); *Contracts* (Jasper van't Hof); *Éspace no. 5* (Michel Portal); *Sketches* (Hans Koller); *You Must Believe In Spring* (Michel Legrand); *Ant Steps On An Elephant's Toe* (Albert Mangelsdorff); *Martin Finnucane* (Django Bates); *Star* (Jan Garbarek); *Introduction À La Marmalade* (Louis Sclavis) and *Liebestraum no. 3* (Django Reinhardt). The Orchestra alternated this programme with *Highlights 1977-97*, which included Uli Scherer's *Tango from Obango*, Fats Waller's *Jitterbug Waltz* and eight Ruegg compositions, including *Jell Roll, But Mingus Roll Even Better, Perpetuum Mobile* and the wonderfully titled *OK, But Who Is TOBER?*. A celebratory volume, with CD, was produced to mark the anniversary: *Vienna Art Orchestra 1977-97* Falter Verlag, Vienna 1997.

2. Rilke, R. M. 'The Rodin Book: First Part' (1903) in *Where Silence Reigns: Selected Prose* New Directions Books, New York 1978 p. 89: "Rodin was solitary before he became famous. And Fame, when it came, made him if anything still more solitary. For Fame, after all, is but the sum of misunderstandings which gather about a new name."

3. Knox, K. 'Lament For Lars', *Jazz Journal International* vol. 30 no. 10, October 1977 p. 15.

4. Discussing the work of the Swedish composer Wilhelm Stenhammar (1871-1927) John H. Yoell suggests that "Folklore as such held only a limited fascination for Stenhammar [...] he doubted the liberating effect of folk music at a time when these sources were fast drying up. Stenhammar clearly saw that the best urbanised society could do for folk music was keep it alive by artificial respiration." *The Nordic Sound* Crescendo Publishing Co., Boston 1974 p. 209. Such a comment glosses over an enormous area of enquiry: see, for example, the comments of George Russell in Chapter Two. Perhaps folk music (or folk sensibilities) could help urbanised society to begin to breathe in a healthier manner? Over the past century, one of the great achievements of Scandinavian culture is precisely the way in which the dualism implicit in Yoell's (or Stenhammar's) view has been transmuted, in a variety of artistic forms. The novelist Tarjei Vesaas, for example, in whose work folk-like traces and contemporary fictional devices combine, might be best described as a rooted cosmopolitan - as might Jan Garbarek. In 1979 I asked Garbarek if he felt that folk music had a future in an increasingly urbanised world. He replied that jazz had begun and developed as a folk music, and presumably still had plenty to say in an urbanised, industrialised world. He also commented that, as long as people are born and die, as long as they have children, or keep animals: then, no matter how urban the setting, the impulse to what one could call "folk expression" would continue. When Garbarek had a couple of students of the saxophone at one time, one of the most important parts of the advice which he gave to them was, try to play a melody as if you were playing it for someone close to you, a grandparent perhaps, whom you

might be seeing for the last time. Personal communication, January 1979. On folk and jazz, see the references in the Bibliography to Cotterell, R., Grottum, K., Kvifte, T., Mosnes, T. and Orvedal, I.

5. **Old Folklore In Swedish Modern** (DUX DRY 1700) Reissued (without this sleeve-note) as part of **The Birth and Rebirth of Swedish Folk Jazz** (ACT 9254-2).

6. **Samse Tak!** (Four Leaf Clover Records FLC 5013).

7. Personal communication, August 1998.

8. To be accurate, the piece was played because, as NHØP says in the notes, it reminded him so strongly of Kenny Drew. *Kenny*, the tender bass and piano duet dedicated to the pianist on the 1994 **Scandinavian Wood**, became the title track of NHØP's 1996 **Those Who Were**, with lyrics by Liza Freeman, sung by Lisa Nilsson.

9. And it was Stan Getz, with Bengt Hallberg (piano), Gunnar Johnson (bass) and Jack Noren (drums) who in the very early 1950s first made a jazz recording of the beautiful Swedish melody *Ack, Värmeland du Sköna* (which Grieg had already used) and which later became known as *Dear Old Stockholm* (recorded by Miles Davis and John Coltrane, among others).

10. See the sleeve-note to **Rosensfole** and Chapter Five.

11. Don Cherry believed that "There is something wonderful about the North. The birds fly there to have their young." Quoted in Knox 1986 op. cit.(*Jazz Amour Affair*) p. 105. Bringing together Danish and Norwegian perspectives on such wonder, **Uncharted Land** is a lovely, deeply human (and perhaps at times trans-human) recording. There is something rather moving about these two (very different) Scandinavian masters of contemporary jazz recording, nearly thirty years after they had played at Molde with Kenny Drew and recorded together on Karin Krog's 1966 **Jazz Moments**. The **Uncharted Land** recording came about after NHØP had won the substantial NOMUS music prize, which gave him the possibility of putting a special record date together. In his own words, the humanist NHØP chose for the date "people I feel close to my heart." Personal communication, August 1998.

12. Nørgård, P. 'Dear Mr. [Sibelius]' *Nordic Sounds* no. 3, 1997 p. 4.

13. Ibid.

14. Ibid. pp.4-5. On July 15th 1954 Sibelius replied briefly but warmly to Nørgård. His letter included the following lines: "[..] I was surprised to see how deeply you had penetrated into my music. Only rarely have I received a letter which showed such understanding. In reality the fact is that one can say extremely little in words about the essential nature of music." Ibid. p.6.

15. Quoted in P.G. Bergfors' sleeve-note to Royal Scottish National Orchestra/Peter Sundkvist **Stenhammar Symphony no. 2/Excelsior (Overture)** (NAXOS 8 55 3888). I am grateful to Julian Freeman for bringing this work to my attention.

16. Ibid.

17. For details of these recordings, see contextual discography.

18. One or two commentators in Norway expressed regret that Garbarek had not chosen to record a more substantial or exciting piece by Grieg.

However, the 'poco andante e sostenuto' *Arietta* obviously meant something special to Grieg. In *Remembrances*, in the last volume of his *Lyric Pieces op. 71*, he reworked *Arietta* - the very first of his *Lyric Pieces* - into a reflective waltz, the phrasing gently breathed over by the spirit of yesteryear. On Grieg and jazz, see Orvedal, I. 'Grieg and all that Jazz', *Listen to Norway* vol. 1 no. 1, Oslo 1992 pp. 44-9.

19. I am grateful to Dr. Rod Paton for his considerable help with matters of structural analysis here.

20. See Brodowski & Szprot op.cit. 1984 ('Jan Garbarek: Mysterious Wayfarer') p. 44.

21. See Shoemaker, B. 'Miroslav Vitous: Slavic Soul', *Jazztimes* no. 4 1993: "[..] all my melodies are Slavic, which is one reason why Jan Garbarek plays my music so well. He's Norwegian, but he has a Polish heritage, which is also Slavic - and so we have this Slavic melodic feeling that connects us. I try to communicate the soul of Slavic music - the sentiment, the lyricism - it's not quite sad, but sentimental. Those are my roots." I remember Garbarek enthusing about the fact that, when he played Keith Jarrett's *Luminessence* live at Oslo's Filharmonien in late-Spring 1982, his performance was part of a Slavic-oriented programme, conducted by Englishman Simon Streatfield. Besides *Luminessence* (which was broadcast on Norwegian radio, and showed Garbarek staying very faithful to the details of the 1974 recording) the programme featured music by Dvorak, Bartók and Enescu. Personal communication, Summer 1982.

22. Rosenbaum, J. 'A Cool Apostle of the Far North Does It His Way', *The New York Times* August 13, 1995. See also *Actuel*, France October 1989: "J'aime le Nord. Il y a une idée du Nord qui s'est introduite dans ma vie et ne m'a plus jamais quitté [...] Face aux plaines et aux glaciers du Nord, les tableaux d'Edvard Munch me sont revenus a l'ésprit. Une telle magie ne pouvait qu'influencer les musiciens comme elle m'influence moi, en tant que producteur." (No more precise dating available: ECM Archives, Munich.) Dybo 1996 op. cit (*Åpne roms estetikk*) pp.118-9 suggests that, for all the influence of Norwegian folk music on Garbarek, it remains difficult to speak of a specifically Norwegian sound in Garbarek ("en spesifkt *norsk* sound hos Garbarek"). Agreed: but the point I would emphasise is, rather, the *Nordic* quality of spiritual intensity in both Garbarek and his sound.

23. Eicher's remarks come from the film *ECM: The Most Beautiful Sound Next To Silence*, directed by Jan Horne for NRK television, Norway 1987; Mathieson, K. 'Editions of the Cool', *Wire Magazine* June 1993 p.18; Ullman, M. 'Starting From Zero: ECM at 25', *Schwann Spectrum*, USA Autumn 1994 p.7; and personal communication, October 1997.

24. **Afric Pepperbird** was originally scheduled to be recorded in the studio at the Henie-Onstad Art Centre, Høvikodden, where Bjørnar Andresen (of the Svein Finnerud Trio) was sound engineer. However, for some reason the session did not work out satisfactorily. Jon Christensen had been doing some work with Jan Erik Kongshaug, then sound engineer at the Arne Bendiksen Studio on the other (east) side of the city:

contacting Kongshaug, it transpired that the Arne Bendiksen studio was fully booked in the daytime. So **Afric Pepperbird** was recorded there at night, from around eleven o'clock in the evening to half-past three in the morning - when, understandably enough, guitarist Terje Rypdal fell asleep in his chair during a take. The studio was part of a bakery building, with a lift running right through it: the recording managed, nevertheless, to triumph over such somewhat surreal circumstances. The beginnings of the later, fabled ECM sound were founded on this accident of venue: it happened that there was a *circa* one metre square metal plate at the Arne Bendiksen Studio, which offered a simple but effective "reverb" effect - which was later to be developed with considerable (and sensitive) sophistication. Personal communication from Jon Christensen, December 1997, and Terje Rypdal, August 1998.

25. Quoted in Williams, R. 'Spontaneous combustion', _The Guardian_, 28/12/96.
26. Ullman 1994 op. cit. suggests that Eicher now misses the "protest" element of jazz, quoting Eicher as saying: "Now [1994] the music seems affirmative, nostalgic, neo-conservative." Ibid. p.10. Of course, the music recorded on ECM is affirmative, and, certainly in the case of Garbarek, can have connections with the deep past - but in an exploratory, fresh way. See below.
27. Ibid. p.7.
28. The musical and emotional impact of "kaputt play" is evident in a good deal of the all-out attack of Manfred Schoof's (still very exciting) June 1969 **European Echoes**, the first release on Jost Gebers' FMP label. One has only to compare this recording with the far more variegated and lucid dynamics of the second (and contemporary) ECM release, **Just Music**, to appreciate the differences in aesthetic approach between FMP and ECM.
29. Tucker 1987 op. cit. ('Eberhard Weber') p. 13.
30. Ibid.
31. Mitchell, C. 'Ralph Towner: A Chorus of Inner Voices' _Down Beat_ vol. 42 no.12, 19/6/75 pp. 40-41: " He [Manfred Eicher] is something else, I'll tell you that. He always reacts differently. Whenever I think I can predict what Manfred's going to do, he'll do something else [..] He's very subtle and quiet, really dedicated to the music [..] He's so experienced and has such a natural gift for sensing what to do as far as production goes. But he seldom gives orders on solo LPs - he's never told me to do this or do that. On the record I just did with Garbarek and Christensen [**Solstice**], he was much more aggressive. I intended to play much more piano on it, for example: he said that was ridiculous, that what I do that is so unusual is play the 12-string. He didn't want a regular piano-bass-sax-drums quartet, even if I did play wonderful piano. He was right." In the summer of 1978, Garbarek wrote to _Down Beat_ to protest about a review of the second Solstice record **Sound And Shadows** which had suggested that the musicians were very much under the control of Eicher: "[...] I resent your trying to make us sound like irresponsible amoebas, completely without personal direction, just timidly acting out the musical wishes of the unwanted,

powerful producer./ After all, the possibility exists that some musicians actually have this particular idea of how their music should sound, and if they choose to have it released on record, it might just be because it conceptually and feelingwise coincides with what the composer wants and also that each musician feels he can stand for what he plays within this context./ Whether the music succeeds or not is another question, but please leave us the right to take on the responsibility for what we play." _Down Beat_ vol. 45 no.13, 13/7/78 p. 9.

32. Recorded on Mal Waldron's **One-Upmanship**.

33. Sleeve-note to **Free At Last** (ECM 1001).

34. Produced by the musicians themselves, **Just Music** (ECM 1002) featured the Europeans Alfred Harth (tenor sax, clarinet, bass clarinet, trumpet) Dieter Herrmann (trombone), Johannes Kramer (guitar), Franz Volhard (cello), Thomas Stowsand (cello, flutes), Peter Stock (bass) and Thomas Cremer (percussion, clarinet). Harth would later record the 1983 **This Earth!** (ECM 1264) with Paul Bley, Maggie Nichols, Barre Phillips and Trilok Gurtu.

35. For a presentation of and commentary on the aesthetics of ECM music and design, see _ECM Sleeves of Desire: A Cover Story_ Lars Muller Publishers, Baden 1996. See also Shaughnessy, A. 'ECM', _EYE: The International Review of Graphic Design_ no. 16, Spring 1995 and my review of the Muller publication in _Contemporary Art_, issue 13, London 1997 pp. 92-3. Paul Bley has subsequently recorded six albums for ECM, either under his own name or sharing leadership, as well as participating in Alfred Harth's **This Earth!** and John Surman's **Adventure Playground** (ECM 1463). Often described as the ying to Cecil Taylor's yang in the evolution of jazz in the 1960s, the Canadian Bley has been quoted as saying "Music is a substitute for sunlight. That's why, the further North you go, the more intense the music becomes."

36. Carr 1991 op. cit. (_Keith Jarrett_) pp. 59-60. Carr suggests that, "When Eicher wrote to Jarrett, ECM had only one record on release, Jan Garbarek's **Afric Pepperbird**, but they had recorded an album of piano improvisation by Chick Corea and Eicher sent Jarrett a test pressing of that." In fact, six other ECM records had been recorded and released before **Afric Pepperbird**.

37. _Jazznytt_ no.3 October 1971.

38. _Jazz Hot_ May 1971.

39. _Jazz Journal International_ vol. no. 9, September 1971 p. 26.

40. _Down Beat_ 20/1/72.

41. _Jazznytt_ no. 2, Oslo May 1970. After outlining some of the many contemporary developments in and possibilities for "sound production", for moving away from "standard tenor tone", Garbarek says "But in all that one should not forget the melody line." ("Men i alt dette må man ikke glemme melodilinjen"). This would seem to have become practically an article of faith for Garbarek.

42. _New Hi-Fi Sound_ January 1990.

43. _Melody Maker_ 8/4/72.

44. Klee op. cit. (_Down Beat_ Jan. 1972).

45. Williams op. cit. (*Melody Maker*).
46. *HiFi Stereophonie* May 1972 .
47. See Johansson, A. 'Samtale med Jan Garbarek' (Conversation with Jan Garbarek) *Vår Musikk*, Oslo January 1974 where Garbarek expresses some reservations about what he sees as the possible commercialisation of folk-jazz, as in e.g. snippets of the music being used on Swedish T.V. every hour or so.
48. Mandel, H. 'Jan Garbarek: Sax Solitude and Northern Light', *Musician* February 1983.
49. *Time Out* 18-25th March 1987.
50. "Jazz goes Grieg?"
51. Garbarek told Lande at the time that his composition was harmonised like a Swedish folk tune. Personal communication, December 1980. See Johansson, A. 1974 op. cit. where Garbarek talks interestingly about Lande. A standard critical comment about the **Red Lanta** album was that Lande's playing was very reminiscent of Chick Corea. However, Garbarek reveals that Lande wrote most of the tunes on the album some years before the session, and certainly before Corea's two ground-breaking solo albums on ECM. In the very early 1970s, there was a possibility that Garbarek might join Corea's Return to Forever group, but in the end, nothing came to pass here.
52. *Down Beat* vol. 43 no. 7, 8/4/76 p. 21: " Jan Garbarek has developed from a talented post-Traner, retaining some of the master's tonal qualities but now constructing leaner solos, fervently blown, possessing a lyricism dripping with hoarfrost. If one thinks of Christensen as the subtle orchestrator of movement in this litany, and Weber as the doleful chorus, an elegaic counter-commentator, then Garbarek assumes the role of cantor, announcing the themes and working them over into his own interpretations."
53. Of course, there had been a diversity of critical opinion about some ECM music before this. For example, in *Jazz Journal International* of August 1974 critic (and pianist) Roger Dean found **Witchi-Tai-To**, the first Garbarek/Stenson album, "rather an unsatifactory record", while in *Down Beat* of 21/11/74 critic Charles Mitchell gave the record a glowing 5 star review.
54. *Madison Isthmus* 8/8/77.
55. Ibid.
56. *Melody Maker* 23/7/77. As I suggested in a letter to Richard Williams at the time, part of the beauty of **Dis** is the subtlety with which Garbarek exploits those two fundamental types of 'impressionistic' mood which Burnett James had explicated, with reference to Debussy, in his essay 'The Impressionism of Duke Ellington' in *Essays On Jazz* The Jazz Book Club/Sidgwick and Jackson, London 1962 pp.163-74 i.e. an impressionism stimulated by the world of natural appearances, and an impressionism of mood stimulated by the observer's response to those appearances. This latter may, of course, turn into the more agitated aesthetic of Expressionism. A large part of the beauty of **Dis** is the way in which Garbarek and Towner are able to inspire the listener's mind to move through such various moods - and *also hold them together*, in stimulating balance.

57. Ibid. (Williams)
58. Fordham, J *Shooting From The Hip: Changing tunes in Jazz* Kyle Cathie Ltd., London 1996 p.85. Over the years, Fordham has supplied some vivid characterisations of Garbarek and his music: see e.g. p. 67 for his (positive) review of the 1978 **Photo With ...** album, which concludes: " Garbarek's characteristic edge manages to overcome the frequently languid air of ECM sessions, though he is inclined to open one too many tunes by sidling quietly past the rhythm section's rather sepulchral introductions like a late-comer entering a church unnoticed."
59. *Jazz Journal International* vol. 30 no. 9, September 1977 p. 37.
60. *Jazz Journal International* vol.36 no.1, January 1983 p. 39.
61. Carney, R. *Speaking The Language Of Desire: The Films Of Carl Dreyer* Cambridge University Press, Cambridge 1989 p. 10.
62. Tarkovsky, A. *Sculpting In Time: Reflections on the Cinema* (trans. Kitty Hunter-Blair) The Bodley Head, London p. 63.
63. Carney op. cit. pp. 65-70.
64. Bourne 1986 op.cit. ('Jan Garbarek's Scandinavian Design') p. 25.
65. Prendergast, M. 'Northern Soundscapes', *Hi-Fi Review*, February 1989 p. 99.
66. If a reading of Leroi Jones' *Blues People* might provide a useful context for listening to or taking about the music of Coltrane, for example, why shouldn't jazz critics be prepared to read some poetry, or look at some reproductions of paintings, perhaps, in order to "tune themselves in" to music that does not fit an American prototype? Jazz is often (rightly) seen as music strongly connected to the post-Kierkegaardian, existential idea of authenticity: as a music which both takes one to and reveals aspects of one's deeper self. However, from time to time jazz has suffered from the revivalist or "re-tread" syndrome - especially in the decades since ECM was established. To my ears, there is considerably more of a "risk taking" and stimulating atmosphere on a good many ECM albums than there is in the vast majority of "neo"-this and "neo"-that jazz albums which have been released since the early 1980s.
67. See Cole, B. *John Coltrane* and Weinstein, N. C. 'John Coltrane: Sounding the African Cry for Paradise' *Naras Journal* Fall 1992 pp. 31-43 (reprinted from Weinstein's *Night In Tunisia: Imaginings of Africa in Jazz* Scarecrow Press Inc., 1992. Available from PO Box 4167 Metuchen, NJ 08840).
68. Nicholson, S. *Jazz: The Modern Resurgence* Simon & Schuster Ltd., London 1990 p. 280.
69. Ibid. pp. 281-2.
70. Ibid. p.282. One's confidence in Nicholson's judgements about both Garbarek and ECM in *Jazz: The Modern Resurgence* is not increased when one reads, for example, that the title track on the 1983 **Wayfarer** features "an agitated discourse with the leader's minimalistic soprano." (Ibid.) The three-part, richly diversified *Wayfarer* features tenor throughout.
71. Nicholson writes: "[..] whilst his [Eicher's] label certainly included artists whose work might be called 'rough and bombastic' - Sam

Rivers' **Conference Of The Birds**, the work of Jack DeJohnette's Special Edition, for example - these were always in considerable disproportion to the rest of the ECM catalogue." Ibid. p. 282. The 1972 **Conference Of The Birds** (ECM 1027) was recorded under the leadership of Dave Holland, and provided a rare (and rewarding) opportunity to hear Anthony Braxton and Sam Rivers in the same working context; Barry Altschul was on drums. None of these artists has produced work which I would describe as "rough and bombastic": neither has Jack DeJohnette. Since the publication of _Jazz: The Modern Resurgence_, Nicholson has written a good many reviews sensitive to - and in favour of - the diversity of music recorded on ECM. See e.g. his combined review of the Trevor Watts Moiré Music Drum Orchestra's **A Wider Embrace** (ECM 1449) and **Madar**. Of the latter, Nicholson states: "**Madar** [...] is one of Garbarek's most interesting albums to date [...] Credit must be given to Eicher for capturing his sound so accurately; seldom do producer and artist share the same vision so closely." _The Wire_ April 1994.

72. Eicher co-directed _Holozän_ in 1991. Shot in Iceland and based on the Max Fritsch novella _Man In The Holocene_, it was awarded the Special Jury Prize at the forty-fifth Locarno Film Festival. The cover of the 1992 David Darling album **Cello** (ECM 1464) features a Jean-Luc Godard image from the film _Passion_; correspondingly, Godard has used ECM music in his recent films. In 1997 ECM released the double CD soundtrack to Godard's **Nouvelle Vague** (ECM 1600/01). One of the most beautiful productions in the ECM catalogue is the 1991 Eleni Karaindrou album **Music For Films** (on which Garbarek appears).

73. Poole, R. _Towards Deep Subjectivity_ Allen Lane, The Penguin Press, London 1972 p. 147.

74. At the end of his three-and-a-half star _Down Beat_ review of **Dansere** in November 1976, Mikal Gilmore writes: "C'mon, guys: swing just a little." But how? And why, necessarily? See e.g. Pekar, H. 'Swing As An Element Of Jazz', _Coda_ August/September 1974 vol 11 no 11 pp. 10-12. For further, penetrating discussion of how difficult, if not impossible (and unwise) it is to legislate about whether or not a musician "swings" in any "approved" manner, see Hodeir, A. _The Worlds of Jazz_ (trans. N. Burch) Evergreen/ Grove Press Inc., New York 1972 pp.107 - 21. In these excellent pages, full of insight, Hodeir suggests that "A new kind of swing means, in one sense, a new kind of freedom and a new kind of order." Having considered the criticism that some new music may have "disrupted" traditional conceptions of jazz, Hodeir asks: "However, if this really is the age of disruptors, will the equation 'jazz = American music' hold true forever? Why shouldn't a disruptor come from the end of the earth?" (p.111). To American critics of the 1950s and 1960s, Oslo, Norway might have seemed just such a place: for in Scandinavia at that time, it was Danish musicians, in particular, who were absorbing mainstream and bop principles of rhythm to such a considerable degree, helped by the appreciable number of Americans who came to live in or around Copenhagen at the time - from Oscar Pettiford (who died in Copenhagen in 1960) and Sahib Shihab to Ben Webster and Kenny Drew, Dexter Gordon and

Stan Getz, for example. Palle Mikkelborg has suggested to me that it was the comparative immaturity of bebop-based Norwegian jazz at this time which, paradoxically enough, helped prepare the way for that extraordinary blossoming of fresh rhythmic conceptions in Norway which occurred from the late 1960s onwards. According to Mikkelborg - a highly intelligent, deeply poetic musician, who from his vantage point in Denmark is able to look both down into Europe and up into northern Scandinavia - Oslo was the perfect (if not the only) place for Manfred Eicher and Scandinavian musicians, in particular, to develop the free-ranging music which they have done on ECM. Personal communication, August 1998.

75. See Brembeck, R. H. 'Manfred Eicher: Seeker of Sound', _Inter Nations_, Germany Spring 1997, where, after talking about possible analogies between music and pictures, Eicher says: "You can also talk about sound in terms of the facets of light. Sound presents itself in the same way as light. There are prisms that come into existence according to the way you hear or want to hear it, how you understand space, how you understand time [...] But in the end, as far as I'm concerned, music is music and nothing else." ECM has done an exceptional amount both to develop and document what one might call a luminous quality of space in Nordic improvised music. However, one should also underline the quality of music created on other, Scandinavian labels such as the Danish Steeplechase, Swedish Caprice and Dragon, and a host of relatively recent Norwegian labels, including Kirkelig Kulturverksted, Odin and NOR: see the discography. The first Dragon release, the **Bengt Ernryd Quartet 1964-65** (Dragon LP 1) is of especial historical importance: it documents the impact of the Eastern-oriented ideas of American composer Alan Hovhaness on Swedish pianist Jan Wallgren, and the subsequent development of a modal basis for the improvisations of this quartet. Raga scales and near-Lydian modes inform the spacious and very beautiful music, which is played by Bengt Ernryd (trumpet), Jan Wallgren (piano, percussion), Gösta Walivaara (bass) and Jan Carlsson (drums). With a. o. Christer Boustedt (alto saxophone) and Lasse Werner (piano) Bengt Ernryd plays on the soundtrack of what is perhaps the best film ever made about jazz - the 1976 *Sven Klangs Kvintett* (Dragon LP 9). This is a delightfully paced study of a typical amateur group in a small Swedish town in the 1950s, and the impact upon the band of a newcomer with Bebop-style musical ambitions and commitment (as well as personal problems). Altoist Christer Boustedt (now, sadly, dead) played the lead role of the bebop-ish newcomer. Palle Danielsson has confirmed to me the accuracy of the film's atmosphere and historical details: Garbarek rates the film very highly. See **Sven Klangs Kvintett** (Dragon LP 9).

76. Nicholson op. cit. p. 282.

77. Terje Rypdal remembers that when the first Jan Garbarek Quartet toured in Germany in the early 1970s, there was much talk in the newspapers about "icy Nordic jazz". Since all the members of the quartet were then listening to music from all over the world, and responding to it, they found this characterisation somewhat curious, if not laughable. Later, a critic dismissed one of Rypdal's records because

of its allegedy "icy" Nordic qualities, which at the time confirmed Rypdal's sense that such clichés were not particularly illuminating with regard to what was actually happening in the music. However, as time has gone by - and with the guitarist moving to the rugged and beautiful west coast of Norway, near Molde - Rypdal has come to think that there really is something positive in the "Nordic" idea, after all. Certainly, a variety of superb records by this musician have done a great deal to confirm the positive consequences of such an idea: see contextual discography. The nature of much of the music that Rypdal's one-time colleagues in the Jan Garbarek Quartet have gone on to create would seem to suggest that Rypdal's change of heart about such a potential "Nordic cliché" is not unique to him. (See discography.) Personal communication, August 1998.

78. Fundamental is a word sometimes misused today, by people (rightly) wary of the fanatical. Picasso was inspired to produce perhaps the greatest single body of work in the arts this century by what he saw as the fundamental themes of life, love and death.

79. See 'The Words Of The High One' in Auden, W. H. & Taylor, P. B. _Norse Poems_ The Athlone Press Ltd., London 1981 e.g. the opening 'Young and alone on a long road,/ Once I lost my way:/ Rich I felt when I found another/Man rejoices in man." (p. 147.)

80. NHØP brought up the question of the Vikings and the value they placed upon individuality, when I asked him if there might be anything in the idea of the North which he would like to emphasise as being of especial importance to him. Personal communication, August 1998. The 1996 **Drømte Mig En Drøm** (SKALK CD 1) is a fascinating attempt by Mogens Friis, Knud Albert Jepsen and Erik Axel Wessberg to re-create the musical world of the Vikings. The ringing, clearly stepped signals and melodies (improvised with variations, as they would have been originally) are played on various lurs, horns, bone flutes, pipes and a lyre. Paul A. Harris's 12/6/87 _St Louis Press-Journal_ review of Garbarek's **All Those Born With Wings** spoke of "the feel of music for a primitive Viking ritual".

81. Hollo, A. _Sojourner Microcosms_ Blue Wind Press, Berkeley 1997 p. 15.

82. 'ECM: music with integrity. Manfred Eicher talks to Pawel Brodowski', _Jazz Forum_ no. 86, January 1984 p. 48.

83. See e.g. _Actuel_ 1989 op. cit. and _Lufthansa Borbuch_ 1995 op. cit.: "Here, in the northern city of Oslo, Manfred Eicher also perceives the 'sound of light' that he is constantly searching for. 'When I go out into the countryside,' he explains, 'and I see the silver light, I am aware of a sound, an aura that I can equate with the sound of a particular piece of music. Bringing these two things together is what fascinates me.'"

84. Apart from being an utterly distinctive pianist, late in life the Canadian Glenn Gould (1925 - 82) did an appreciable amount of creative work in radio production. One of the most highly regarded of such productions is _The Idea of North_, from the late 1960s. Gould's contrapuntal and polyphonic programme mixed a small group of people (who had never actually met) talking - as if in a live conversation with each other - about their experiences of (and

reflections upon) the physical, emotional and spiritual challenges and rewards of life in the Far Canadian North. The programme took the form of a journey North: the rumbling wheels of a train provided a "basso continuo", the programme ending with the triumphant last few minutes of Sibelius' *Symphony no 5 in E flat major, op. 82* . In the contextual notes which he wrote about the programme in 1967, Gould acknowledged how much this "ennobling" idea of the North might be seen as a myth, in the negative sense of the word (after all, the products - and mentality - of Madison Avenue could be transported quite easily to the Far North). Nevertheless, Gould was determined to examine "that condition of solitude which is neither exclusive to the north nor the prerogative of those who go north but which does perhaps appear, with all its ramifications, a bit more clearly to those who have made, if only in their imagination, the journey north." 'The Idea of North: An Introduction' in Page, T. (ed.) *The Glenn Gould Reader* Vintage Books/Random House, New York 1990 pp. 393-4. Not only did Gould develop such a positive myth of the North in radio production: he also recorded the piano music of Nordic composers as distinct as Sibelius and the Norwegian Fartein Valen. See the contextual discography.

85. Castles, F. G.. *The Social Democratic Image of Society* Routledge and Kegan Paul, London 1978. It is essential to remember that the various primitivistic quests of much Nordic art have taken place within a context of democratic modernity, where the values of citizenship have been paramount. Like so much of Garbarek's music, the social and artistic history of the Nordic countries suggests, at its best, that one does not have to subscribe to such a (frequently heard) false dualism as, for example, the idea that one either values "progress" or risks becoming a "reactionary". Much of the primitivistic poetry of Tomas Tranströmer, which Garbarek has read with special interest, addresses precisely such issues.

86. For historical background to the emergence and impact of such an "idea of North" see Mjöberg, J. 'Romanticism and Revival' in Wilson, D. M. (ed.) *The Northern World: The History and Heritage of Northern Europe ad 400-1100* Thames and Hudson, London 1980 and Tucker, M. 'Not the Land, but an Idea of a Land' in Freeman, J. (ed.) *Landscapes From A High Latitude: Icelandic Art 1909-1989* Lund Humphries, London 1989. William Morris travelled to Iceland with much enthusiasm in 1871 and 1873.

87. See Tucker 1922 op. cit. (*Dreaming*) Chapter Six.

88. Quoted from 'Risk and chance. Dagger and guitar' (1963: from material as early as 1946) in Shield, P. 'On reading Jorn', in Hansen, P. H. (ed.) *A bibliography of Asger Jorn's writings* Silkeborg Kunstmuseum, Silkeborg 1988 p.36. For a thorough study of Jorn's ideas, see Shield, P. *Comparative Vandalism: Asger Jorn and the artistic attitude to life* Borgen/Ashgate, Aldershot 1998.

89. Tucker 1984 op. cit. ('Jan Garbarek: The Poetics of Space') p. 20.

90. For an introduction to Kierkegaard, see Kierkegaard, S. *The Journals of Kierkegaard* (ed. & trans. A Dru) Fontana/Collins, London 1967; Oden, T. C. *Parables of Kierkegaard* Princeton University Press,

Princeton 1978 and Mullen, J. D. *Kierkegaard's Philosophy: Self-Deception and Cowardice in The Present Age* Mentor Books, New York 1981.

91. Hammarskjöld, D. *Markings* (trans. W. H. Auden and L. Sjöberg) Faber and Faber, London 1975 pp.79, 102 & 148. See also e.g. p. 80: "Autumn in Lappland. The warm rain-laden east wind rushes down the dried-up river bed. On its banks, yellowing birches tremble in the storm./The opening bars in the great hymn of extinction. Not a hymn to extinction or because of it. Not a hymn in spite of extinction. But a dying which is the hymn." For Hammarskjöld's commitment to the seer-like quality in modern art, and his enlightened patronage of art at the United Nations, see Lipsey, R. *An Art Of Our Own: The Spiritual In Twentieth-Century Art* Shambhala, Boston and Shaftesbury 1990 pp. 444-60.

92. See Tucker 1992 op.cit. (*Dreaming*) pp. 254-9.

93. See Bates, B. *The Wisdom Of The Wyrd* Rider/Random House, London 1996. This rewarding book blends a deeply researched perspective on the contemporary relevance of the spiritual wisdom of the pagan North with a sensitive awareness of the wisdom of both Taoism and Native American cultures, for example.

94. Mari Boine was to have sung her composition *Gula, Gula* (Hear the Voices of the Foremothers) when it featured on the 1990 **I Took Up The Runes**. However, circumstances made it impossible for her to be at the recording session. She can be heard singing *Gula Gula* "live" with the Jan Garbarek Quartet (featuring Eberhard Weber, Rainer Brüninghaus and Nana Vasconcelos), at a May 1989 concert at the Grieghallen, Bergen, on **Natt Jazz 20 År** (Grappa GRCD 103). **Twelve Moons** and **Visible World** both feature appearances by Mari Boine: together with the Telemark singer Agnes Buan Garnås, she toured with the Jan Garbarek Quartet (featuring Marilyn Mazur, drums, percussion) in the early-to-mid-1990s, including a November concert at the Barbican Hall, London which was part of the major *Tender Is the North* Festival of Nordic art which took place there in winter 1992. On Sami culture, see below and note 142. As Garbarek is aware, he is hardly the first non-Sami to take an interest in Sami music and culture. In 1970, for example, the Norwegian composer Folke Stromhølm (born 1941) composed his *Samisk Ouverture*, to be followed by the 1972 *Samiaednan(Samiland)*: see Herresthal, H. *Norwegische Musik von den Anfängen bis zur Gegenwart* Norsk Musikforlag, Oslo 1987 p. 94. In 1973 Swedish saxophonist Arne Domnérus and his colleagues (including Egil "Bop" Johansen) recorded *The Joik* (traditional, arranged by Esko Linnavalli) on **Scandinavian Design** (RCA YSPL 1-587). The session was recorded in Finland, where there has been a good deal of jazz-meets-*joik* activity for some time now: see the contextual discography.

95. See below. Klee and Kandinsky, Picasso and Matisse, Byzantine icons, Norwegian folk art and contemporary ceramics; the sculpture of fellow Norwegian Gunnar Torvund, Sami art, the pottery of Shoji Hamada and Bernard Leach and the rhythms of certain Indian mythological motifs also indicate something of the nature of the

interest of Garbarek (and his wife Vigdis) in art. Garbarek has long had an interest in Eastern philosophies and poetry: also important to him are the myths, poetry and imagery of so-called "tribal peoples", which have stimulated a good deal of both his music and the titles which he has given to various pieces. Munch and Widerberg, Hamsun and Hesse, Vesaas and (the late) Olav H. Hauge (whose poems supply the stimulus for some of the titles on Garbarek's 1998 recording **Rites**), Meister Eckhart and Carlos Castaneda, Pär Lagerkvist and Tomas Tranströmer, Rainer Maria Rilke and Jan Erik Vold are some of the many diverse figures who have stimulated Garbarek's imagination. In 1993 I asked Garbarek if he would consider writing a brief piece in honour of the painter and musician Alan Davie (born 1920) for a book which I was then editing about this exceptional Scottish polymath (whose world-bridging images have a good deal in common with the latter-day music of Garbarek). This Garbarek kindly did, with distinct pleasure. See Chapter Six.

96. For an introduction to Hamsun in the context of shamanic ideas and the North, see Tucker, M. 1992 op. cit. (*Dreaming*) pp. 144-7. In the summer of 1988 Garbarek recorded the rubato tone poem *Pan* (which he originally composed for a radio version of Hamsun's 1894 novel of that title) with violinist Arve Tellefsen: see Tellefsen, A. **Pan** (Norsk Plateproduksjon IDCD 3)). In 1998 Garbarek recorded the piece again, solo, and this time on soprano as well as tenor: see **Rites** (ECM 1685/86).

97. The Norwegian artist Christian Khrog (1852-1925) - whose belief that "All national art is bad, all good art is national" is very relevant in the context of the present chapter - believed that music should be written to the paintings of Munch, which were themselves music. Few have come as close to the world of Munch in music as has Garbarek: and given the development of Garbarek's music which is outlined in this chapter, one should remember that Edvard Munch is not just the painter of *The Scream* (1893): far from it. Munch is also the painter of *The Sun* (1911-16), the immense, affirmative mural which blazes out over the Oslo University Aula stage on which Garbarek played with George Russell in the late 1960s. See Tucker 1992 op. cit. (*Dreaming*) pp. 147-57. In Munch, the sublime - a key concept in the aesthetics of both Romanticism and Modernism - takes on strong shamanic overtones. See below.

98. Also worth noting here are the various projects of Laurie Johnson - particularly **Synthesis**, recently reissued, with other, related material, on Redial 557819-2 - and Lalo Schifrin: see **Firebird**. From a Scandinavian perspective, particularly important to note is pianist Bengt Hallberg's June 1965 recording **Collaboration** (Odeon E 062-34397), which brought solo piano, jazz trio and string quartet together in a stimulating variety of ways. Hallberg's observation on the sleeve is interesting: " I believe that the best of the current pop music - whatever that means - has a great advantage compared to modern jazz when it comes to development, contrasts, sound and intensity. If you listen closely, you'll soon discover that contemporay jazz has benefitted almost as much from pop as from the pure jazz tradition."

99. _Down Beat_ vol. 43 no. 2 , 29/1/76 p. 22.
100. Personal communication, July 1976.
101. Cook and Morton op. cit., first edition.
102. Personal communication, July 1998. Derived linguistically from the Latin _limen_ (threshold), the concept, or idea, of the liminal - that quality which can take one to (and perhaps across) various (often dangerous, or disorientating, but potentially rewarding) thresholds of experience is crucial to a shamanic concept of the arts. It is explored with particular insight in Livingston, P. _Ingmar Bergman and The Rituals of Art_ Cornell University Press, Ithaca and London 1982 pp. 92-100. The liminal individual, says Livingston, is a creature of crisis: a word which contains the ideas of opportunity and change.
103. _Euphoria_, from the 1941 collection _Ferry Song_. See _Selected Poems Of Gunnar Ekelöf_ (trans. M. Rukeyser and L. Sjöberg) Twayne Publishers Inc., New York 1967 pp. 33-4. It was Ekelöf himself who came up with the phrase "cloud visionary" (perhaps after Baudelaire's poem _The Stranger_).
104. _Down Beat_ vol. 45 no. 21, 21/12/78 p. 38.
105. The _ad libitum_ factor in Garbarek's music is crucial - as is Garbarek's unerring ability to choose an appropriate tempo for a piece. In recent years, especially, he has used a hand drum to help him determine the initial shaping of such matters. Personal communication, July 1994.
106. _The Edmonton Journal_ 15/10/87. For Garbarek, Tarkovsky's oeuvre is a natural extension of the work of Bergman, compelling on any number of levels. As a musician, Garbarek has admired in particular such moments as those in _Stalker_ (1979) when Stalker and his two companions break out from the confines of the bleak industrial world in which the film opens, and set out towards the liminal realm of the Zone - on a hand-pumped railway wagon. For several minutes, the soundtrack features nothing but the sound of the wagon's wheels turning on the track, as the imagery in the film gradually changes to that of a landscape (and from black and white to colour film). Personal communication, Spring 1988. For Garbarek's enthusiasm for the way in which Tarkovsky worked - and possible parallels between the director's and the saxophonist's ways of getting ostensibly small elements to set aspects of a larger picture in motion - see Hansen, E. 'Han skaper stillhet og renhet av musikk' (He creates stillness and purity out of music) _Fredriksstad Blad_, 25/4/87.
107. The Latin origins of these words are instructive: _religare_ (to bind in, to rule) and _spirare_ (to breathe).There may well be a good point in Freud's view that, for many, adherence to a religion involves a neurotic, sublimated defence mechanism against the inevitable pains and disappointments of life (inlcuding, ultimately, the fact of death). However, as Jung knew, such a perception does nothing to account for the truly generative, or creative, spiritual energy in humankind: the "breathing" energy essential to a fully realised life. Tarjei Vesaas is one post-Freudian author this century whose work illustrates very well the principle that, before one breathes out, so to speak, it is essential to breathe in. It is also, of course, essential to have pauses in this process: which is one reason why, although the technique of circular breathing

is available to Garbarek, he prefers the rhythms of breathing in *and* out, pausing, breathing in *and* out, etc. See Tucker 1996 op. cit. ('The Shamanic Spirit in Twentieth-Century Music') p. 94.

108. Rilke's magnificent *Duino Elegies* have been translated into English several times. Garbarek is familiar with the very fresh-sounding translation by David M. Young: *Duino Elegies* W. W. Norton & Company, New York 1978. The title of one of Garbarek's pieces on **Twelve Moons** - the somewhat Ayler-tinged lament *The Tall Tear Trees* - derives from Young's translation of the *Tenth Elegy*.

109. *Jazz Journal International* vol. 34. no. 2, February 1981 p.19.

110. *Oakland Tribune* 19/10/80; *Playboy* 1981 (precise date unavailable; ECM Archives, Munich).

111. *Audio* December 1980.

112. *Jazz Hot* October 1980.

113. Cook and Morton op. cit. (third edition) p. 480.

114. See Milhaud **L'Oeuvre Pour Orgue** (Fy FYCD 016 - a beautiful set of interpretations by George Baker, recorded in Chartres Cathedral). Olivier Messiaen - one of the many 20th-century composers whose work has interested and inspired Garbarek - has been the subject of several ECM productions e.g. Christopher Bowers-Broadbent's interpretation of **Meditations Sur Le Mystère de la Sainte Trinite** (ECM New Series 1494). For Garbarek's interest in 20th-century composition, see Chapter Five; and for a wide-ranging and thoroughly researched interpetation of the spiritual dimension in Messiaen, see Freeman, R. 'Trompette d'un Ange Secret: Olivier Messiaen and the Culture of Ecstasy', in Steer, M. (ed.) 1996 op. cit. (*Music and Mysticism*) part 2 pp. 81-124.

115. The Norwegian organist Johnsen (born 1945) has said: "Preparing and realising **Aftenland** was one of the most interesting experiences in my entire musical career. My exclusively classical education (altogether twelve years in Oslo, Munich, Copenhagen, New York and Paris) included improvisation, of course, both traditional and contemporary, but this was the first time I had the opportunity to discuss and realise complex musical ideas with a jazz musician. I have never practised jazz, but I am very fascinated by the mood of expression which is particularly found in improvised music and which is quite different from the composed one, especially in jazz. Most of the music on **Aftenland** is derived from approaching 'serial' and 'modal' techniques, although in a very sensitive 'tonal' way, mixed with elements difficult to explain with words [...] **Aftenland** can be classified neither as 'jazz' nor as 'classical' in the common understanding of the words. I am very glad to have been part of the project." ECM 'New Release' information sheet, ECM, Munich 1980. Nearly five and a half years before **Aftenland** was recorded, Swedish altoist Arne Domnérus and organist Gustav Lennart Sjökvist recorded the LP **Antiphone Blues** (Proprius PROP 7744) in Spanga Church. This is a very beautiful album, but with a much more "rooted" or traditional feeling than **Aftenland**. Apart from the pure improvisation of the title track, the programme features material from Ellington's Sacred Concerts, Afro-American spirituals, Swedish and Russian hymns, Robert Schumann

(arranged by Bengt Hallberg) and Vivaldi.

116. _Sweet Potato_ 6/11/85. Crucial here is the seeming taboo on death as a subject for discussion (and contemplation) in our ever-more "youth"-oriented world. See Ariès, P. _Western Attitudes To Death from The Middle Ages To The Present_ (trans. P. M. Ranum) Marion Boyars, London 1976 and the discussion of Heidegger and Castaneda on death in Tucker 1992 op. cit. (_Dreaming_) pp. 79-80.

117. _Manchester Evening News_ 16/1/89.

118. Schoier, I. _Pär Lagerkvist: En Biografi_ Bonniers, Stockholm 1987 p 521.

119. See Sjöberg, L. _Pär Lagerkvist_ Columbia University Press, New York 1976 pp. 7-9.

120. See Per Nørgård **Korvaerker** (Paula 17) - which also includes a piece by Art Brut artist Adolf Wolfli - and **Arne Nordheim** (Aurora NCDB 4933), which includes Nordheim's well-known _Floating_ (for orchestra).

121. See Wahlman, L. I. _Engelbrektsyrkan i Ord och Bild_ (Engelbrekt Church in Words and Pictures) Ernst Wessmans Bokforlag, Stockholm 1925.

122. _New Musical Express_ 15/1/83.

123. "My proverbial allergy to the sound and poetics of Garbarek" - _Compact: La Revue Du Disque Laser_ May 1987.

124. _Truth Barriers_ (trans. & with an Introduction by R. Bly) Sierra Club Books, San Francisco 1980. (_Sanningsbarriären_ was published in Sweden in 1978.) The title _The crossing place_ comes from Robin Fulton's translation, which Garbarek knew from his copy of _Tranströmer: A Special Issue_, Ironwood no. 13, Ironwood Press, Tuscon AZ 1979.

125. From the 1974 _Baltics_: see note 130. Such an oxymoron occurs quite frequently in Tranströmer's work. For an introduction to Tranströmer, see _Tranströmer: A Special Issue_ op. cit. passim; Fulton, R. 'Introduction' to _Tomas Tranströmer: Collected Poems_ Bloodaxe Books, Newcastle upon Tyne 1987 and Tucker, M. 1992 op. cit. (_Dreaming_) pp. 131-3.

126. _Below Freezing_, in _Truth Barriers_ op. cit. p. 32.

127. _Funchal_ in Tranströmer/Fulton op. cit. p 130. Available in slightly different translation in Tranströmer/Bly op. cit. p.39.

128. 'Introduction' to Tranströmer's _Night Vision_ (trans. R. Bly) London Magazine Editions, London 1972 pp. 8-9.

129. _The Journey's Formulae_ from the 1958 _Secrets On The Way_. Available in slightly different translation in Tranströmer/Fulton op. cit. pp. 49-50.

130. See _Baltics_ in Tranströmer/Fulton op. cit. pp.107 and 111; and _Schubertiana_ in Tranströmer/Bly (1980) p. 22. The **Gray Voice** recording is discussed briefly in the article which appeared in Norway's _Aftenposten_ paper when Tranströmer won the Nordic Council's Literature Prize in 1990. Tranströmer, whose work had been set to (very different) music before, by the Swedish new music group Harpans Kraft (The Power of the Harp) in 1974, is quoted as feeling strong enthusiasm for the **Gray Voice** record. See **Harpans Kraft**

(Caprice CAP 1070) and the article by Kari Bremnes on Tranströmer in *Aftenposten*, Oslo 22/1/90.

131. See Neumann, E. *Art and The Creative Unconscious* (trans. R. Mannheim) Harper Torchbooks/The Bollingen Library, Harper & Row Publishers, New York 1966 passim and Tucker 1992 op. cit. (*Dreaming*) pp. 18 & 97-9.

132. See the discussion in Gunnarsson, T. *Nordic Landscape Painting in the Nineteenth Century* (trans. N. Adler) Yale University Press, New Haven & London 1998 pp. 79-80. This superbly researched and illustrated book sheds considerable new light on various Nordic approaches to landscape painting, including the development of what Gunnarsson (Head of Collections at the National Museum, Stockholm) calls "the evocative landscape" of the 1890s and turn of the century.

133. See Tucker 1986 op. cit. ('Dreamer In A Landscape'); 'Not the Land, but an Idea of a Land' in Freeman, J. (ed.) *Landscapes from a High Latitude* Lund Humphries Ltd., London 1989; 1992 op. cit. (*Dreaming*) ch. 6 'Northern Lights', and 'Making the World: The Art of Frans Widerberg' in *Frans Widerberg: Bilder, En Reise* (Pictures, A Journey) Labyrinth Press, Oslo 1994.

134. *Wire Magazine* April 1987 p. 52. For a slightly earlier interpretation of Garbarek's work in the light of the Nordic shamanic tradition, see my *Jazz Journal International* vol. 39 no.1, January 1986 review of Garbarek's **Gray Voice** album (pp. 23- 4).

135. Ibid. (Sinker).

136. Eliade, M. *The Myth of the Eternal Return, or, Cosmos and History* (trans. W. R. Trask) Bollingen Series 46/Princeton University Press, Princeton 1974 pp. xiii-xiv.

137. Progoff, I. 'Waking Dream and Living Myth' in Campbell, J. (ed.) *Myths Dreams and Religion* Spring Publications, Inc., Dallas 1988 pp. 193-4. Bergman's comments are taken from a transcript of the interview supplied by Radio TV Reports Inc., Public Broadcast Laboratory, WNDT-TV, New York. See also *Bergman on Bergman* Secker and Warburg, London 1973. Here Bergman speaks of the "total dissolution of all notions of an other-worldly salvation" which he experienced in the early 1960s, and the growth instead of "a sense of the holiness - to put it clumsily - to be found in man himself. The only holiness which really exists. A holiness wholly of this world." p. 164. One can imagine that theologians and psychologists might care to debate the import of Bergman's words for some considerable time.

138. Ibid (Progoff) p.195.

139. *Genius Loci: Towards A Phenomenology of Architecture* Academy Editions, London 1980 p. 42. See also Norberg-Schulz's essay 'Snow' in *Winterland* De Norske Bokklubbene, Oslo 1993 pp. 36-9.

140. Borge, K. 'Garbarek Lokker' (Garbarek Calls) *VG*, Oslo 29/10/81. Garbarek's previous album-length involvement with Norwegian folk music - **Østerdalsmusikk** (MAI 7510) - was recorded in August 1975 with Torgrim Sollid (trumpet, percussion), Lars Martin Thomassen (trumpet, flugelhorn), Knut Riisnæs (tenor and soprano saxophone), Alf Erling Kjellmann (tenor saxophone) Erling Aksdal Jnr. (piano),

Bjørn Alterhaug (bass) and Ole Jacob Hanssen (drums). This is an extraordinarily beautiful and atmospheric album of collectively interpreted bridal marches, lullabies, cattle calls, "polska" dances and other folk melodies, sometimes played in time signatures as curious as $5^1\!/2\,/8$ time, according to Sollid's notes. Recorded for the politically committed, anti-EEC MAI label, its reissue in CD format is long overdue. Solothurmann 1995/7 op. cit. asks Garbarek if the use of Norwegian or Sami material by an urban musician like himself has connotations of a conservative or reactionary mentality, as it does (according to Soluthurnmann) in Switzerland, for example. Garbarek replies: "This is not the case with Norway. It doesn't have those connotations at all. Our folk music is really a 'recent discovery' if I could put it that way, beginning at the end of the last century and continuing into our own, when researchers went out into the valleys to find out about the culture there, the music and the painting and so on. And they found what I think must be a very old folk music, more or less conceived in those valleys because of their geographical location. It is difficult to get to them and people were living there for generations with little contact with the outside world. So you'll find a lot of 'blues' actually, what we call blue notes and untempered scales. The music is living, still, vividly in those valleys. When this music was brought to the cities it was not a conservative thing. It was rather revolutionary in fact." (p. 5) Garbarek's point is underscored by the political history of the farming and peasant class(es) in Norway, which has no trace of serfdom, as in Europe, and manifests, rather, a fundamental independence of spirit.

141. Tucker 1984 op. cit. pp. 18-19.
142. On the Alta project and protests see Libæk & Stenersen op. cit. (*A History of Norway*) p. 164. For an overview of the development of the Sami *joik* in recent times, see the 1988 **Samisk Musik i forvandling** (Caprice CAP 1351) which includes extensive, illustrated sleeve-notes, with English translation; Nils-Aslak Valkeapää **Juoigamat** (Finnlevy SFLP 8531), where the original one-and-a half version of *Aillohás* (which forms the thematic kernel of Garbarek's thirteen-and-a-half minute *He Comes From The North* on **Legend Of The Seven Dreams**) can be heard; and the range of music by Valkeapää, Esa Kotilainen, Seppo Paakkunainen and Mari Boine listed in the discography. For recent overviews of Sami history and cultural renaissance, see e. g. Ahlback, T. & Bergman, J. (eds.) *The Saami Shaman Drum* The Donner Institute for Research in Religious and Cultural History, Åbo/Almqvist & Wiksell, Stockholm 1991; Tucker 1992 op. cit. (*Dreaming*) pp. 338 - 41; Aarseth, B. *The Sami Past and Present* Norsk Folkemuseum 1993; Ullmann, L. 'A Modern Shaman: Nils-Aslak Valkeapää', *Listen to Norway* vol 1. no 2, Oslo 1993 pp.16-19; Various *Sami Contemporary Art*, De Norske Bokklubbene, Oslo 1994 (the catalogue for the exhibition in the 1994 Winter Olympics contextual events); Ullmann, L. 'Mari Boine: Inhabited by a Song', *Listen to Norway* vol. 2 no. 1, Oslo 1994 pp. 24-5; Graff, Ola 'The Impact of Sami Tradition', *Listen to Norway* vol. 5 no. 3, Oslo 1997 pp. 34-36.

143. Jim Pepper's *Witchi-Tai-To* was taught to Bobo Stenson by Don Cherry. Pepper (1941 - 92) recorded this traditional, peyote-induced vision chant as *Witchi-Tia-To* on his 1983 **Comin' and Goin'** (Antilles New Directions ANCD 8706). See Tucker 1996 op. cit. ('The Body Electric') pp. 81-3. The tune has featured often in Garbarek's live performances, sometimes - with the Garbarek/Stenson Quartet - in performances some half an hour and more long. In the early 1990s, when singers Mari Boine and Agnes Buen Garnås appeared with the Jan Garbarek Quartet, *Witchi-Tai-To* was played as a linked sequel to Mari Boine's *Du Lakha* (Near You), to stunning effect. Personally, I would like to have seen this coupling of songs recorded on the 1992 **Twelve Moons**, rather than the newly recorded version of *Witchi-Tai-To* which was presented. Lovely as this was - with the new, somewhat Native American-sounding rhythms perhaps conceived in homage to the late Pepper and his Kaw-Creek heritage - it added little to the (continued) impact of the 1973 recording, and eschewed the opportunities previously explored in the extended codas which the piece had often generated in live performance.

144. See Chapter Two and Tucker 1992 op. cit. (*Dreaming*) for an overview of the chief elements of shamanic consciousness. Such consciousness flows (freshly) underneath the surface of a good many ECM records: for an unusually direct example, see the 1994 release by Red Sun and Samul Nori - **Then Comes The White Tiger** (ECM 1499).

145. Given the history of Christian repression of the *joik* and the shaman's drum, it is somewhat ironic that the *joik*-inspired opening moments of Garbarek's *He Comes From The North* now introduce a weekly religious programme on Norwegian radio. In interviews, Garbarek has spoken of how wrong he feels it is to describe the *joik* - the purpose of which is to call into being the spirit or presence of the person or animal, for example, being *joiked* - as a simple or primitive form of music making.

146. For further discussion of this theme, see Tucker 1992 op. cit. (*Dreaming*) chapter 6 'Northern Lights'.

147. Schideler, R. *Voices Under The Ground: Themes and Images in the Poetry of Gunnar Ekelöf* University of California Press, Berkeley, Los Angeles & London 1973 p. 134. This is a valuable book, containing several of Ekelöf's essays in full, in English translation. See also the excellent, extensive Ekelöf, G. *Modus Vivendi: Selected Prose* (ed. & trans. E. Thygesen) Norvik Press, University of East Anglia 1996.

148. Ibid. (Schideler) p.133.

149. Ibid. p.137.

150. Mosnes, T. 'Europas Ledende' (Europe's Finest) *Dagbladet*, Oslo 22/1/83.

151. Ibid.

152. Moller, A. *Frans Widerberg:100 Pictures* J. M. Stenersen, Oslo 1980 pp.12 & 18 (English text, with an Introduction by Stein Mehren). For historical background on (and interpretation of) Widerberg, see Brun, H-J. & Ustvedt, Ø. *Frans Widerberg: Malerier 1956-96* (Paintings 1956-96, with English text) Grøndahl Dreyer, Oslo 1996 and the references in note 133 above.

153. As Linda Kohanov noted in her *Pulse* November 1989 review of

Rosensfole: " Although the music draws directly from the medieval story-songs of this icy northern land, **Rosensfole** is far from an aural museum piece. These two respected Norwegian artists have brought a highly expressive folk legacy into the 20th century, deftly crossing boundaries between traditional and modern sensibilities to create a timeless soundscape of mythic reflections." Originally released in Norway on Kirkelig Kulturverksted, **Rosensfole's** ECM release (described on the sleeve as produced by Jan Garbarek and Manfred Eicher) received positive reviews in a wide variety of magazines. In his _Dirty Linen_, Winter 1989/90 review, Cliff Furnald drew attention to "a sort of pseudo-medieval, pan-European style that echoes Mediterranean and Balkan sounds as much as Scandinavian roots". Furnald concluded: "If 'folk song' is to live and grow, then we need the likes of Garbarek on the frontline pushing it along." Writing in _Jazz Forum_ 1/1990, Roger Cotterell - author of one of the earliest, in-depth articles on the subject of folk-jazz fusions - suggested that some of the music had "the simple profundity of the blues". "The music", wrote Cotterell, "speaks timelessly, but in modern voice." Dybo 1996 op. cit. (_Åpne roms estetikk_) makes the point that, for all his use of folk tradition, Garbarek "does not represent any [particular] Norwegian folk music tradition" - ("ikke representerer noen norsk folkemusikk tradisjon." p. 130).

154. See Tucker, M. 'Through A Glass, Deeply', _Viktor B. Andersen's Maskinfabrik_ no. 22, Copenhagen 1998 pp. 17-31.
155. The music used was Garbarek's floating, Zen-like _Blank Space_, featuring Garbarek (soprano sax), Mehmet Ozan (guitar), Niels-Henning Ørsted Pedersen (bass), Marilyn Mazur (percussion) and the Ars Nova Choir. Recorded on Niels-Henning Ørsted Pedersen's 1991-2 **Uncharted Land,** it is among the best things either Garbarek or NHØP has recorded in the 1990s, with Pedersen's playing reminiscent of the spacious sensitivity he brought to the albums he appeared on in the 1970s with Paul Bley and John Tchicai. The curious, intriguing title of the piece may have derived from Tomas Tranströmer's poem 'Morning Birds', from the 1966 collection _Bells and Tracks_ . See Tranströmer/Fulton 1987 op. cit. pp. 74-5.
156. 'If You Ask Me', in Ekelöf/Rukeyser/Sjöberg 1967 op. cit. p. 40.
157. Rilke, R. M. 'To Music', in _An Unofficial Rilke_ (trans. M. Hamburger) Anvil Press Poetry, London 1981 p. 69.
158. 'Schubertania', in Tranströmer/Bly op. cit. p 23.

Inward: Niels-Henning Ørsted Pedersen
(Vienne, early 1990s) Tim Motion, Jazz Index

Travellers: Jan Garbarek, Eberhard Weber & Rainer Brüninghaus
(Town & Country Club/Forum, London November 1988)
Christian Him

Wayfarer

Together with the Swedish polymath August Strindberg (1849-1912), the Finnish poet Edith Södergran (1892-1923) was largely responsible for initiating poetic Modernism in the North. An extraordinary, Nietzschean poet, Södergran developed the sort of rhythmically free, yet lyrically focused language that was to have an especial influence on Gunnar Ekelöf: the Swedish visionary once described Södergran as "a Persian Princess living in Lapland".[1] Moving convincingly between reverie of earthly winter and forest, sea and summer, and the cosmic majesty of the crystal-clear vault of a Nordic night, Södergran is one of the great "yea-sayers" of the North. Identifying with Orpheus, and believing that "the inner fire" is the most important quality of mankind, she saw the poet's task as one of singing "pain's great hymn". In a particularly beautiful phrase, Södergran – who would die of the tuberculosis she contracted early in life from her father – once described herself as "a bonfire of joy on mirroring ice".[2]

There could hardly be more appropriate words with which to suggest the special resonance of Garbarek's art: that singing of "pain's great hymn" which, through the alchemy of those musical and psychological elements which might help one to revision such dualistic ideas as joy and sadness, "near" and "far", the "intimate" and the "infinite", deepens – extends – one's sense of *participation mystique* in life. Just as the imagination of Södergran can transport us from the leaf-strewn intimacy of a woodland walk to the transcendent majesty of the spaces that exist as much within us as without, so does the music of Jan Garbarek help us bridge worlds.

It is the bridging – and revisioning – of worlds (musical and spiritual, poetic and political) that so distinguishes the musical quest that Garbarek has undertaken for so many years. Steeped in the values of jazz, today Garbarek plays a variety of music which may seem ostensibly difficult to relate to the jazz mainstream. This he does with a variety of musicians, male and female, from various backgrounds around the world. Garbarek has no defining name or phrase for such music, other than "this is the music we play". And he has sometimes suggested to journalists that, should they manage to come up with a name for what that music is, they might let him know it.[3]

As the Norwegian author Tor Dybo has remarked, while Garbarek's music has made richly creative use of aspects of Norwegian folk tradition, Garbarek himself is not part of that tradition. Similarly, when questioned about his relation to the traditions which lie behind the Native American or Sami themes which he has played, Garbarek has always emphasised that he is not an expert in the traditions of those musics, but rather someone who has enjoyed playing particular themes, with particular musicians, at particular times: "These cross-cultural meetings, or however you want to describe them, always begin for me with a relationship to a particular musician. If there is some personal understanding and friendship, there is a good chance of making music together."[4]

Garbarek has made the same point about the Eastern-inflected work which he has played and recorded with such diverse masters of Indian music as L. Shankar and Zakir Hussain, Hariprasad Chaurasia and Trilok Gurtu.And one can say much the same about the various "scrious" or "art" music ventures with which Garbarek has been associated. These have included Keith Jarrett's **Luminessence** and **Arbour Zena**, and Garbarek's own arrangements for the *Låter* (Sounds) suite which he presented at the Kongsberg Festival in 1977 and the Montmartre Jazzhus, Copenhagen, in 1980; the suite for jazz quartet and strings which he premiered at the Grieg Hall, Bergen in 1982, with Palle Mikkelborg, who had assisted at the Montmartre in 1980, conducting; parts of Paul Giger's 1990-91 **Alpstein** and the vast majority of the 1993 **Officium** with the Hilliard Ensemble; Giya Kancheli's 1994 *Night Prayers* (recorded in 1995) and a fair portion of the 1995 **Visible World**, including the two-part title track. Just as he is a self-taught saxophonist, so is Garbarek (largely) self-taught in these areas: he took some instruction in Palestrina-like part writing in the late 1970s, but otherwise has relied upon his considerable ear and discriminating appreciation and knowledge of a good deal of "serious" or "art" music.[5]

While this is grounded in the nineteenth and twentieth centuries (with Chopin and Mahler, Schoenberg and Berg, Sibelius and Vaughan Williams, Bartók and Stockhausen, Penderecki and Takemitsu, for example, all of interest to him) Bach, Haydn and Mozart have been of scarcely less import. In fact, it was listening to Haydn and Mozart that confirmed Garbarek's belief that, by the 1970s, too much jazz had become either too cluttered, or too abstracted from matters of melody: of light and shade, and the textural and thematic distinctions of foreground and background.[6]

Recalling his feelings at this time, when he had expressed a preference for listening to folk music and ethnic music from all over the world rather than jazz, Garbarek commented thus in an important interview of the mid-1990s: "I had a feeling [in the late 1970s] that, for my own playing, jazz had reached a stage of too many abstractions removed from the source of the original folk music – the blues of Mississippi. I thought it might be time to look back and see what there was in the beginning and find out if there might be other paths to be taken. If we, as a new generation – as we were then – players with totally different backgrounds, looked to the sources and made our own steps from there, the music might grow in a new way. There might be a new branch."[7] Central to the development of that branch has been Garbarek's feeling that, while the blues had provided the roots for the great Afro-American innovators, Europeans or Scandinavians have their own blues, or blues equivalents: their own folk music.

As we have observed previously, what has come to fascinate Garbarek is the extent to which he has been able to intuit connections between aspects of Norwegian folk music (certain scales, or modal ideas, for example, often of what an equal-tempered system of classification would call a minor hue, and various melodic inflections that sound Turkish or Arabic) and the music of the Balkans; such connections then leading him further into the vast musics of Asia Minor and India. With regard to his own music, Garbarek's sense of the fructifying nature of such connections has been confirmed by musicians as diverse as the Greek composer and pianist Eleni Karaindrou and the Bulgarian kaval (flute) player and composer Theodosii Spassov.

When Karaindrou heard Garbarek for the first time, on the 1977 album **Places**, she felt a distinct Balkan quality in the music. This was to lead to her featuring Garbarek in the film soundtrack which she wrote for Theo Angelopoulos's 1986 The Beekeeper. As Karaindrou has recalled: "[..] when I wrote the theme for The Beekeeper, I understood very quickly that only Jan could provide the necessary colours. He was able to approach this composition without any folkloristic rhetoric and go directly to the essentials."[8] When I spoke to Theodosii Spassov about this aspect of Garbarek's work (in London in the summer of 1998, following an excellent concert which Spassov had given with his trio at the Bulgarian Embassy) Spassov suggested that, from his point of view, it was remarkable to see how the Norwegian qualities in Garbarek's music flowed to the Balkans and beyond, right down into the womb of India.[9]

I remember, nearly twenty years ago, Garbarek showing me what at the time was one of his favourite books: the Czechoslovakian photographer Josef Koudelka's album _Gypsies_ . These black and white, poignant portraits of daily life – of early childhood and death, music and dance, ritual and religion – were mostly taken in the separated Gypsy settlements in East Slovakia, during the period 1962-1968. It is a curious fact that a good part of Garbarek's sense of the connections between the music of his homeland and India simply reverses the direction of the current which, around 1000 AD, propelled the Gypsies from northern India into Europe. Crossing from Asia Minor by way of Crete and the Peloponnesus, the Gypsy tribes reached Europe by the early fourteenth century, and continued their dispersion westward and northward.[10]

As we have seen in an earlier chapter, for the Spanish poet and dramatist Lorca the foundations of deep song lay in this exodus. Would it be too much, then, to push the well-known connection that George Russell once made between Garbarek and Django Reinhardt and speak of a contemporary gypsy spirit in Garbarek? Not according to the Brighton-based saxophonist and band-leader Geoff Hearn, a passionate and accomplished musician who in recent years has led some of the finest contemporary groups in the south of England, such as Planet Earth and Akima.

Listening to the tenor themes and improvisations of music as distinct as Garbarek's 1988 _Voy Cantando_ (I Go Singing) and _Pan_ (where Garbarek is joined by Arve Tellefsen on violin and Kjetil Bjerkestrand on synthesiser) Geoff has spoken to me of what he hears as the unmistakeable Gypsy overtones in the music: "There's a tremendous sense of yearning in _Pan_, which is very Gypsy in spirit. It could be sentimental, in the negative sense, but it isn't. There's a lovely mixture of Romanticism with a folk quality; there's always some little twist, some rhythmic or harmonic tension, to keep the music on the edge, to keep the spirit moving. I'd call Jan Garbarek a great folk musician of today, a spiritual traveller of the world – and time. Take *Voy Cantando* , which is a good example of Garbarek's ability to travel in music. At the processional beginning, there's almost a touch of the Baroque; the Hispanic feel that emerges then brings Rodriguez to mind. There's a strong Islamic, or Arabic mood, a quarter-tone feeling in the following modulation, with pentatonic patterns underpinning the drone-driven improvisations (and some fine control of overblowing – of harmonics – by Garbarek). By the time the Spanish theme returns, and the piece ends, it feels like the musicians have come back from some sort of epic journey. The basis of the piece is relatively simple – but what the musicians [Garbarek, Weber and Brüninghaus] do with it is complex. Travelling, they've acquired knowledge. And they pass it on. That's also part of what I mean by a Gypsy spirit – the spirit that Don Cherry had, for example."[11]

If, for Lorca, deep song owed much to what he called the "lyrical channels" of Gypsy melody, such song was also, according to the poet, very close in spirit to what he called "the oldest Eastern verse" – by which Lorca meant Arabian and Persian poetry.[12] There are no lyrics on the 1992 **Madar**, recorded by Garbarek with the Tunisian oud master Anouar Brahem and Pakistani tabla virtuoso Ustad Shaukat Hussain. Nevertheless, this marvellous album would seem to contain as much of the spirit of Rumi – the much revered thirteenth-century Persian Sufi poet, whose work is often pregnant with musical metaphor – as it does of that Gypsy spirit which a musician like Geoff Hearn has remarked in Garbarek's wide-ranging, yet acutely focused art.

Madar might be called songlines for planet earth. The record followed a concert which Garbarek and Brahem had given with the African, Paris-domiciled drummer Manu Katché at the Frankfurt Jazz Festival: following Brahem's 1990 ECM debut album **Barzakh** Garbarek had expressed a desire to play and perhaps record with the oud virtuoso. Brahem, who holds the title of Director of the Music Ensemble of the City of Tunis, has long been committed to restoring the oud to its rightful place in his country's music, rescuing it from its recently diminished role as mere accompaniment to variety songs. A musician with wide-open ears, Brahem had long been aware of the music of ECM, and in particular the improvisational qualities of musicians like Garbarek and Keith Jarrett.

While living in Paris in the early 1980s, Brahem (born 1957) listened to a good deal of jazz. An encounter with Jarrett's ECM debut album **Facing You** was of especial importance: aspects of the pianist's modal improvisations reminded Brahem of Andalusian elements in the music of his native Tunisia and confirmed him in his desire to marry the Arabic-classical basis of his own music with judiciously selected elements from other, related musics. Steeped in the classical tradition of Arabic modes, Brahem has always claimed the right to draw upon the musics left in his country "by the colonialists, the occupiers" – thus giving himself access to the musics of Spain, Turkey, Morocco and France, for example. (While there are some lovely, transmuted echoes of Django Reinhardt on **Barzakh**, Spanish critics have remarked a striking command of flamenco elements in Brahem's work.)

Extremely well reviewed upon release, **Madar** is music of the (esoteric) mystical stream, brought into being by musicians from lands very different in terms of geography, politics and (to an extent) religion. It is music which hymns the naked, questing and devotional heart of life, in organic rhythms and phrase lengths now intimate, now extensive, and often soaked in the circling, ritual spirit of dance. And if a strong feeling of tradition informs the album, it is a feeling of tradition *made new*. Two Norwegian folk melodies, one – *Sull Lull* – more 'minor' in orientation than the other (*Joron*, also recorded by Garbarek on Niels-Henning Ørsted Pedersen's **Uncharted Land**) find their natural place within a programme of improvised originals, flowing out into new musical space over a variety of *maqam* rows, or modes: in music such as this, the rhythmically free improvisations, known in Arabic as *taqsim*, have a fixed tonality, but no time signature.[13]

Throughout, the interplay between all three musicians is magnificent, with Garbarek's sculpted tenor lines exhibiting a wondrous command (and diversity) of tone, emotional projection and rhythmic attack. Passages of broadly phrased jazz expression, poetically intense Arabic ornamentation and flowing, yet intricate Indian polyrhythm can rarely, if ever, have commingled so convincingly. As Josef Woodard noted in his May 1995 *Jazz Times* review: "[T]he distinctive ethnic imprints of the players weave together without forcing the cross-cultural issue or diluting the integrity of the parts [...] Garbarek's work, especially of late, is tantamount to an argument for universality. Here, Norway and the Middle East sound like neighbours with a common cause."[14]

Whether in philosophy, politics or the arts, arguments for universality are notoriously hard to justify, or substantiate. Commenting on Alan Lomax's observation that "Spanish *cante hondo*, Jewish cantellation, Indian ragas, Japanese geisha songs, and many Oriental song types are frequently heavily embellished and metrically free", Timothy Mitchell points out that, "Marvelous as it is to be able to account for [such] similarities [...] one must be able to account for the differences as well."[15] The point is well made. However, it is certainly the case that some musical elements, like certain modal (and pentatonic) scales, can be found in folk music around the world – as they can in an appreciable portion of Garbarek's music, from the late 1960s onwards. As we have seen, aspects of the 1988 *Voy Cantando* are pentatonic; so are parts of *Molde Canticle*, from 1990. And both *Witchi-Tai-To* and *Desireless*, from the first Garbarek/Stenson album, are (largely) pentatonic. With regard to the Indian connection in Garbarek's music, and his appearance on such albums as violinist L. Shankar's **Song For Everyone** and percussionist Zakir Hussain's **Making Music** (with the Eastern-oriented guitarist John McLaughlin), the violinist and composer John Mayer – who in the 1960s pioneered Indo-Jazz fusion music in Britain – has pointed out how tracks like *Let's Go Home* (from **Song For Everyone**) and the title track of **Making Music** both employ pentatonic scales (the first piece using only the ascending notes of Raga Bageshri and the latter Raga Deshkar).[16]

However, what Woodard's remark really points to is a universality of attitude, or approach, to music, rather than the question of the particular building blocks one might consider using to attain any such musical universality. As we know from language, if there were no structural or semantic difference built into the possibilities of expression, there would be no need for the life-blood of metaphor. As Garbarek himself might say, there is universality, and there is universality.

The idea of "world music" is often (rightly) viewed with suspicion by musicians who see in it little more than a simplistic (albeit effective) marketing device. However, it is certainly the case that, in recent years, the possibility of musicians from far corners of the world getting together to create meaningful music has increased exponentially. And so have the means for those musicians to learn about each other's work.[17]

Garbarek has spoken as follows about the issue of 'world music' today: "'World music' to me has at least two meanings. First of all the regular meaning – a music composed of ethnic elements from various parts of the world. But on the other hand, American pop music is the real world music. It's everywhere in the world and everybody listens to it whether they like it or not. Furthermore, for anyone living in Europe today, or any part of the globe where they have access to media information, there is a world music consisting of everything you hear. It's all there in the ether, in the air, all the waves. It's folk music from all over the world, classical, rock, pop, everything.There is no pure musical mind anymore which has known one source and stayed with that. Such a person hardly exists in our media-revolutionised world. So whatever we do is a transformation of this music of the media, from elevator music to concert hall music. It's a very, very wide span. It's a lot of information one has to take into consideration. Even if one tries to stay pure to something, that's not possible. You might make something you would not have made if you had not heard that piece of music in the elevator in 1987! You can theorize about these things, but everything is available. You can go into a shop ... and I did, and there in front of me was an album of music from Morocco. Large ensemble music. I didn't even know such an ensemble existed there. Well I bought it without listening and it was something very interesting. I bought it on impulse in a shop – in Tokyo! This is often how I choose my listening, almost randomly. I walk into some place and hear or see something. 'Let me take that'. Might be something worthwhile, it might not be. It will be there in me anyway."[18]

Rather than worry about how one might extract or extrapolate anything 'universal' from such a melange of possible influence and inspiration, Garbarek 'simply' composes and plays music that appeals to him. Nonetheless, it is undeniable that here is a musician whose work can strike the sort of note that, having absorbed much from the world, can carry high and wide around that self-same world. If Garbarek's extraordinary command of rhythm supplies the wings for such flight, the fuel for the journey comes, first and foremost, from Garbarek's sound.

As we have seen, Garbarek is a musician blessed with a uniquely resonant sound. Whether on tenor, soprano or wood flute, it is a sound which can be shot through with the Nordic *genius loci,* or spirit of place: now redolent of the still, twilight gloom of Northern forests, or the keening of winter storms across mountain plateaux;

now bringing to mind Ekelöf's "sunrise over the troll lake, the hot fragrant hill of wild strawberries in the midday sun, the bells in the forest and the clear, echoing voices around the lake in the evening".[19] However, just as there is much of the East in Ekelöf, so is there much of the Taoist and the Raga spirit in Garbarek and his sound. If his mellow flute often comes as near to the spirit of the reflections of Ruan Ji or Gao Shi as it does to those of Rumi or Tagore, Garbarek's soprano saxophone can at times sound uncannily close to the penetrating tones of the Indian shenai (a kind of double-reed oboe, which can be heard played by Charlie Mariano on Eberhard Weber's 1975 **Yellow Fields**). [20]

Like his sound, Garbarek's compositions can be full of the melancholy "cry" of the North. Reviewing the 1983 **Wayfarer**, Kris Larson went so far as to say that, "At times, Jan Garbarek's whole musical being is an outcry to God. And when he puts a saxophone to his lips, it is Psalm 22.2 [O my God, I cry in the daytime, but thou hearest not..] become sound."[21] However, if Garbarek's music often conveys such a sense of intense yearning, it also contains many irresistible moments of healing, participatory joy. Both qualities – yearning and joy – are in plentiful evidence in his playing on the 1979 **Magico** and **Folk Songs**, recorded with Charlie Haden and Egberto Gismonti, and Zakir Hussain's 1986 **Making Music**; while a sense of joy is very much to the fore in his contributions to Shankar's 1983 **Vision** and 1984 **Song For Everyone**. Such a quality of affirmation is equally present in the noble, rhythmically diversified, five-part *Molde Canticle* from the 1990 **I Took Up The Runes** as well as in a fair portion of the 1983 **Wayfarer** album.

If Garbarek is first and foremost an artist of the North, he is also, as some of the above-mentioned albums make evident, an artist who has drawn inspiration from – and played creative, new music with – improvisers from the four corners of the earth. This latter fact – the newness of the music which has resulted from such collaborations – has sometimes escaped the attention of critics.

Commenting on a concert which the trio of Charlie Haden, Egberto Gismonti and Garbarek gave at the Theatre de Champs Elysées in late 1979 or early 1980, the French writer Raoul Dengdett declared that the problem with this trio was that Garbarek exhibited no affinity at all with what Dengdett called "the Brazilian feeling".[22] On the one hand, the evidence of my own senses persuades me that

Dengdett is simply wrong here. The several concerts which I witnessed by this trio in 1980 and 1981 found Garbarek perfectly in tune "au feeling brésilien", whenever necessary. On the other hand, the point of the Haden/Garbarek/Gismonti trio was not to play American, Norwegian or Brazilian music in the hope of demonstrating each musician's ability to play the music of the others' countries with full historical "authenticity", as it were. The point of the trio was to make *creative* music. As the reviewer R. C. Smith once noted, "[Garbarek] has captured the spirit of improvisation, freed it of national idiom, and set it loose to roam the reaches of the globe."[23]

The Gypsy, or wandering, spirit in Garbarek is especially evident in parts of the 1983 quartet recording **Wayfarer**, the album which gives this chapter its title. Featuring Bill Frisell (electric guitar), Eberhard Weber (bass) and American drummer Michael DiPasqua, three-quarters of the group was thus the same as that which recorded the memorable **Paths, Prints** in December 1981, with the substitution of DiPasqua for Jon Christensen necessitated because of the latter's involvement with other touring and recording projects. As with the former album, much of **Wayfarer** projects a distinctly reflective, or poetic atmosphere. In sections of the title track, the see-saw, rocking grooves of *Pendulum* and the searing, Dada-esque evisceration of a ballad which is *Singsong*, the record also offers some of the most explosive, declamatory playing which Garbarek committed to vinyl in the 1980s.

The three-part *Wayfarer* epitomises the breadth of expression which is to be found both on this particular record and in Garbarek's music as a whole. The music moves from the distanced, eerie rubato ruminations of Part One, initially outlined in saxophone and guitar unison, to the spiralling, ecstatic affirmation of the fiercely swinging group celebration of Part Three: with lilting poignancy, a poised waltz section (referring to the pleasure park in the middle of Copenhagen, Garbarek has said that he wanted a sort of "Tivoli feeling" to this part) effects the musical and psychological transition between such extremes.[24]

As always with Garbarek, *Wayfarer* is rich in carefully considered dynamics. These are especially evident in the solo drum figures which, unusually, conclude the piece.[25] Introduced by a kicking, multi-voiced drum passage from DiPasqua and propelled by some strong, deeply grooved lines from Weber, Part Three features scorching, yet at the same time beautifully measured solos from both Garbarek and Frisell, before the music gradually fades into the meditative coda supplied by DiPasqua's spacious, broken-shuffle accents. Title and musical means thus combine to epitomise those twin notes of abstracted, spiritual meditation (the melancholy of introspection) and full-bodied, ecstatic affirmation (the euphoria of *participation mystique*) which so often distinguish Garbarek's art.

Contemporary as that art manifestly is – and as aware as Garbarek is of the media-revolutionised world – it is an art which contains but little of the hustle and the bustle, the noise and the aggression of today (the surreally off-centred *Singsong* is one of the few occasions when this is not the case). An unusually literate and intelligent man, Garbarek has always chosen the titles of his compositions with care. Traditionally, a wayfarer is someone who travels, not by car or plane, but by foot: and the dynamics of *Wayfarer* have more in common with the depth and the variety of the psychological insights in _Wayfarers_, Knut Hamsun's picaresque novel of 1920 (which begins with the impact of two travelling strangers, one of them a musician, upon a small Norwegian community) than it does with today's compressed and calculating TV narratives of so-called realism and digitalised special effects.[26] Similarly, the space that Garbarek sings into being on **Wayfarer** – whether on the lovely, liquid (and somewhat Weather Report-like) opening *Gesture*, parts of the title track, the haunting *Gentle*, or the magnificent meditation that is *Spor* (Tracks) – finds its poetic correspondence in the nature-inflected work of early twentieth-century poets like Rilke or Södergran, rather than the urban-driven rap rhythms of 1980s or 1990s America or Britain.

Contemporary – a term which has appeared more than once in this chapter – can be a notoriously misleading word. One of the shibboleths of the art world today is that, if new work is to be of any note, it must be somehow 'contemporary'. Often, this means little more than 'executed in the latest media'. So painting, for example, can suddenly become very 'uncontemporary' in some eyes, certainly when compared to a three-part video installation. But what happens when the current technology of the video installation is surpassed (as it inevitably will be) by even newer and more sophisticated media developments?

One thing that will certainly happen is that painters will continue to paint, their art informed by the sort of sense of time that can make them feel, now contemporaries of the cave painters of Lascaux, now contemporaries of Velazquez or Vermeer, Monet or Mondrian. In 1957 the British painter David Bomberg wrote as follows about this issue: "Whether the paintings or sculptures of the future are carried out in ferro-concrete, plastic, steel, wire, hydrogen, cosmic rays or helium, and oil paint, stone, bronze superseded as anachronisms, it is reality that man is yet subject to gravitational forces and still dependent on sustenance from nature and spiritual consciousness, an individual with individual characteristics to remain so for aeons of time."[27]

From this perspective, the question of the technology of 'contemporary' art pales into insignificance compared to the question of the nature of the themes, or the subject matter, addressed by that art – and *the depth of penetration of those themes* by the artist. What is impressive about Garbarek's art is the ability it has shown to embrace the 'contemporary' (technologically speaking, the synthesiser and sampler-fluent Garbarek is far indeed from being of a Luddite persuasion) while remaining sensitive to the ancient, archetypal resonance of both musical phrase and spiritual theme. A master of paraphrase, Garbarek has the uncanny knack, as Ian Carr has pointed out, of conjuring musical traces of "half-forgotten things from long ago" – in a contemporary setting.[28]

The dictionary definition of contemporary is, 'Living, existing, or occurring together in time [...] during the same period'. One's understanding of and approach to the term thus have a great deal to do with one's understanding of and approach to the question of time. Much art today has no sense of time within it beyond that of the journalistic deadline: its very contemporaneity is a guarantee of its ephemerality. In a wonderfully suggestive phrase, the film director Andrei Tarkovsky – one of Garbarek's (and Manfred Eicher's) chief elective affinities, as we have already remarked – once commented that it was essential, in film, to *allow time to live in the image*. The fascinating question is: what sort of time? And what sort of experience of time results from such patience? Exactly the same points apply to music, which is, of course, the ultimate art of time.[29]

If Garbarek is the sort of melodic singer of song whose work simultaneously arises from and transcends both its immediate geographical region and historical era, then it is important to reflect upon what this might signify, in terms of the experience of time, and hence "worlds of meaning", which that work may open up for the engaged listener. No matter what the harmonic or rhythmic context in which it unfolds, song manifests itself as melody. And, no matter how complex or simple it may be, melody is movement: its etymological roots lying in *melos*, Greek for 'limb'. As Stravinsky remind us in his <u>Poetics of Music</u>, melody – from the Greek *mélôdia* – is the intonation of the *melos*, which signifies a fragment, a part of a phrase.[30] Such simple semantic facts underline the key potential role of music as a multi-layered stimulus to the various journeys the self may come to take in life: perhaps to deeper and transformative aspects of its understanding of (and participation in) the mysteries of existence – and certainly to a deeper understanding of the word 'contemporary' than that so often peddled in today's art world.

Where, then, may the fragments of movement in *mélôdia* take us? And what sort of a sense of existence may they convey to us? Can Josef Woodard's belief that Garbarek's work "is tantamount to an argument for universality" carry any weight in today's Post-modern world? The fragments of Heraclitus declare, "Not I but the world says it: all is one".[31] However, for much of today's Post-modernist thought, such a synthesising idea of totality has long lost authority. Instead, contemporary theoreticians and practioners of the arts cultivate ideas of the *purely* fragmentary: the "all-too-human", the provisional, the flawed. And these are ideas which would often seem to arise from, and confirm, the sense that life, experienced as utterly profane, is now to be lived only within a completely *immediate* or 'contemporary' world.[32]

Despite – or rather, precisely because of – the recent plethora of such activity, one must ask: is the idea of totality (and with it, such ideas as the beautiful and the sacred which earlier this century so stirred a poet like Södergran) thereby to be swept aside for ever? Is the strength of Södergran's intuition that "It is not necessary to pray, one looks at the stars and has the feeling of wanting to sink down to the ground in worldless adoration" to be vitiated forever by nothing more than the glow of neon light?[33] To put the point another way, when one raises one's arm to point to the moon, is one now condemned to examining nothing but the state of one's own fingernails?

I, for one, hope not. It would be strange indeed if a particular, largely disillusioned experience of life – one rooted only in a particular

Western sense of (linear) time – should have the power to render nugatory the millenia upon millenia of spiritual aspirations and insights which preceded it. Today we may wish to claim, with withering certainty, that in contrast to the poets and mythologists of old, we *know* that the light of the moon is "only" reflected sunlight. However, from the psychological and spiritual point of view, why should we disappointed by such knowledge? It is hard to think of a more marvellous natural image, or metaphor, of the play of consciousness and the unconscious, near and far – of the energising richness of symbolic potentiality the world continues to offers us. Until the day each and every one of us becomes utterly 'contemporary', or robotic, the fruits of such potentiality can never be known to have been exhausted.

In this regard, it is helpful to consider the origins of the world 'symbol'. The etymological roots of the word imply a bringing together or binding of separate elements. Originally this was a technical term in Greek, signifying a token of remembrance. A host would present his or her guest with the so-called *tessera hospitalis* by breaking an object in two. One half was given to the guest, while the other part remained with the host. Later, should a descendant of the guest enter the house of the host, the two pieces could be fitted together again to form a whole, in a simple but profound act of recognition and remembrance.

What is art, at best, if not recognition and remembrance? Through art, said Auden, we break bread with the dead. And without any such activity, what is life but Macbeth's sad tale told by an idiot, full of sound and fury, signifying nothing? A key question which thus arises in what a good many would call today's post-Christian, mega-Capitalist world is whether or not the various fragments of our being may yet recognise themselves in any remembrance – or anticipation – of a potential whole. Is *everything* in life to be profaned, sundered beyond repair? And if it is not to be, where are what the humanist psychologist Abraham Maslow has called the "resacralising" resources of life to be found?[34]

When I have discusssed such matters with Garbarek, his response has always been that such resources can only be discovered within ourselves: for where else might the overall potentiality or the specific variables of spirituality be found? It may seem quite unnecessary to point out that, playing the saxophone, a musician like

Garbarek first breathes in, and then breathes out.[35] However, the point becomes more interesting when one reflects upon the origins of the word 'spirituality' in the Latin *spirare* – to breathe. Breathing in, breathing out; allowing time to live in the music, Garbarek is able both to *mediate* the experience of time *and allow time*, as it were, to mediate his understanding of and approach to the music – and meaning – that is melody. Music may be mathematics; but it is also a psychic language soaked in time – an open, immensely variable field of spiritually-charged potentiality.[36]

For the painter Ian McKeever, the bodily aspect of this potentiality is a crucial aspect of Garbarek's art, which McKeever has often fed into the lengthy and demanding process of making paintings: "I listen to music whilst I am working in the studio. Sometimes to the same piece over and over again, for weeks, or months even. There is something about such an engagement, the consistency, the repetition, that parallels the act of painting. For painting is a slow process, in which you are constantly going back over apparently known ground, but which in fact is increasingly unknown, mysterious. In the last few years I have played the *Four Last Songs* of Richard Strauss, the **Sun Bear Concerts** of Keith Jarrett and Jan Garbarek's **Dis**. With Garbarek, I am consumed by the body, the breath of the lungs, the living gesture that is our own body in the world: moving through the world; absorbing – making – the world."[37]

The language of body and breath (and heart and mind) which Jan Garbarek has developed – an essentially soul-full language – has the capacity to speak with equal, energising directness to Christian or Jew, Taoist, Hindu or Muslim, agnostic and atheist alike. And no matter how pared down it may at times appear to be, one of the most interesting things about that language is the expansive power-to weight ratio of its constituent parts, which are often coloured by distinctly non-European, or Eastern elements of tone and time.[38] In this regard, as in so many others, Garbarek's work is very much in line with key elements of the poetics of avant-garde Western Modernism this century. Often distinguished by a considerable reduction, or concentration, of its formal means, Modernism pursued the idea that, as the architect Mies van der Rohe once put it, "less" can be "more". As such, (artistic) Modernists were – and remain – critical of the surfeit of superficiality in the (social) modernity of industrialised culture. (In contrast, it is this very superficiality which so-called Post-modernism often seeks to celebrate.)

In Modernist poetics, one can often remark a turning towards the East, in search of a larger, deeper sense of the rhythms of existence than that present in what would often seen to be the prison house of industrialised mass production.Towards the end of _The Waste Land_ (1922), his penetrating, albeit problematic study of the spiritual aridity of a good deal of Western modernity, T. S. Eliot remarks of the various phrases and images from the past which he has woven into the five-part work: "These fragments I have shored against my ruins".[39] The final fragment which Eliot drew upon – and the last line of the poem – is the traditional ending to a Hindu _Upanishad_: "Shantih, shantih, shantih". As Eliot himself noted, this can be roughly translated as "The peace which passeth understanding".

Representing for the Hindu (approximately) what the New Testament represents for the Christian, the earliest of the _Upanishads_ were written down in Sanskrit between 800 and 400 B. C. As the scholar and translator Juan Mascaró noted, there is in these spiritual texts a noticeable reaction to the dictates of formalised religion and a celebration of the spirit that gives life as opposed to the letter of the law that kills it. Outlining such fundamental ideas – or insights – of the _Upanishads_ as their weariness with words, their emphasis upon the experience of creative joy and the fundamental intuition that the Divine, or Brahman, is within one – TAT TVAM ASI (Thou art That) – Mascaró suggests that the _Upanishads_ "can be called in truth Himalayas of the Soul."[40]

Naturally, I would not wish to make too much of any possible parallel between what Mascaró says here and George Russell's view that Garbarek "plays the Himalayas". Nevertheless, it is important to underline the extent to which Garbarek has been drawn to various aspects of Eastern poetics. In 1963 – the year he first played with musicians from outside Norway, when he jammed with the Josel Trio from Austria at the Molde Jazz Festival – the young Garbarek heard the sitar master Ravi Shankar in concert, in the Aula Hall at Oslo University. The concert, which was Garbarek's first encounter with Indian music, suggested how much other cultures had to offer, in both musical and spiritual terms.[41] Worlds began to open up, as they did following Don Cherry's first visit to Oslo in 1967, when the world-oriented trumpeter with a strong interest in Asian music and spirituality played with Garbarek at the Sogn Jazz Club. In 1970, Garbarek, Arild Andersen and Jon Christensen took part in a Norwegian TV programme with sitarist Bidal Llogh: the twenty-minute *Raga* reveals all participants shaping a range of serpentine lines with considerable dynamic finesse.[42]

While recording **Dis** in 1976, Garbarek – who has long appreciated the beauty of the end-blown shakukachi flute of Japan – immersed himself in another aspect of the East: the 17-syllable world of the Japanese *haiku*. Much in **Dis** can be listened to as a fascinating aural complement, or parallel, to the meditations contained within Basho's seventeenth-century masterpiece, <u>The Narrow Road To The Deep North</u>.[43] The atmospheric, Zen-inflected music of the late Toru Takemitsu (1930 – 96) has for many years been of considerable interest to Garbarek, from the austere beauty and dynamic contrasts of *November Steps* (1967) to the spacious, yet richly unfolding melodies of *A Flock Descends Into The Pentagonal Garden* (1977), for example. During the latter years of Takemitsu's lifetime, the feeling was mutual: the saxophonist treasures an inscribed manuscript which the jazz-loving Japanese composer once presented to him.[44]

A Zen-like sensitivity to factors of space and asymmetry can be discerned in a good deal of Garbarek's oeuvre. Exemplary here are his obbligati and solos on Jan Erik Vold's 1977 **Ingentings Bjeller** (Nothing's Bells); the variety of contributions he made (together with Collin Walcott, Steve Kuhn, Oscar Castro-Neves and old playing partner Arild Andersen) to David Darling's 1981 **Cycles** (and especially the suspenseful, searing solo he shapes on *Namasté*); his composition *Blank Space*, recorded on soprano with Niels-Henning Ørsted Pedersen on the latter's 1991-92 **Uncharted Land**, and the bamboo flute figures with which he framed the poetic reflections of his wife, Vigdis Garbarek, on her 1996 **Vägestykket** (Point of Hazard).

Garbarek's sensitivity to (and use of) various Indian factors of phrasing, sound and rhythm is no less remarkable. Trilok Gurtu, the exceptional, Bombay-born percussionist and band-leader, and master of all manner of polyrhythm, has played and recorded with the saxophonist on a significant number of occasions. These have included Garbarek's appearance on Gurtu's 1990-91 **Living Magic** album, and a most unusual – and excellent – 1993 concert in Santa Fe, New Mexico, when they played together in the sculpture garden of Native American artist Allan Hauser, during a festival in honour of Indigenous Peoples. The music featured Hauser on Indian flute, and his son Bob Haozous reading poems; three extraordinary singers, the Tuvan Sainkho Namchylak, Native-American Buffy Sainte-Marie, and the Sami Mari Boine, electric guitarist Roger Jacobs, and the Norwegian pianist and keyboard specialist Bugge Wesseltoft (who plays such a strong role on Garbarek's 1998 **Rites**).[45] Gurtu has also made two extensive tours with Garbarek: a 1985 European tour together with Shankar and the brilliant Brazilian percussionist Nana Vasconcelos, where this multi-national quartet played the music from Shankar's **Song For Everyone**, and a trio tour of Norway, again with Vasconcelos, in the late 1980s. (I was fortunate enough to hear the 1985 quartet at the WOMAD festival at Mersea Island. The interplay between all four musicians – at once rhythmically intricate and lyrically open – was simply stunning.) Gurtu considers Garbarek's command of the rhythmic complexities of Indian music "impeccable" – so deep, natural and assured that Gurtu has even wondered seriously if Garbarek might not have been Indian in a previous incarnation.[46]

Whatever one may think of such a suggestion, Gurtu's aesthetic judgement underlines the considerable extent to which Garbarek's musical sensibilities have been able to flourish in a variety of worlds which, not so many years ago, would have seemed totally 'alien' to a Western, "well-tempered" sensibility.[47] Along with the American-domiciled, but Austrian-born Joe Zawinul, Garbarek might fairly be called the great wayfarer, or "wandering soul", of today's European and Scandinavian jazz. Like T.S. Eliot, albeit without a trace of that poet's religious fundamentalism, or Gunnar Ekelöf, with his deep affinity for the ancient cultures of India, China and Japan, Garbarek has roamed far and wide – North, South, East, West – in search of that "easy commerce of the old and new [...] the complete consort dancing together" which to Eliot embodied the ultimate goal of his poetic (and spiritual) quest.[48]

Whether or not one wishes to share with Eliot the Christianity of his *Four Quartets*, it is hard not to agree with this poet that there are moments in life which are existentially – spiritually – special, and of an import one might only call holy. For Eliot, these were the moments so deeply immersed in time as to transmute one's experience of that dimension into intimations of *other* dimensions of existence: dimensions which open up mysteries far beyond the compass of (linear-driven) clock time – mysteries which take one, as Tomas Tranströmer has said, "upward into/the depths".[49] In such depths, we may come to *re-member* ourselves.

In his (seemingly) wryly titled 1992-93 album **Amuse Yourself,** Garbarek's compatriot, the tenor saxophonist and vocalist Bendik Hofseth, featured a track entitled *Lake of Memory*. With Arild Andersen supplying resonant, spacious bass punctuations, Hofseth's vocal (and very Garbarek-oriented saxophone) outlined the depths of experience and longing which can be stirred in the soul by a fragment of an old (and in this case, lullaby-like) melody heard on the radio. Drinking "the water, the flowing water", Hofseth and Andersen together fashion a poignant meditation on the streams of memory and meaning that may flow deep beneath the surface "noise" of so much of existence today.[50]

In similar vein, Tarjei Vesaas – an author blessed with the ability to intimate multi-layered metaphors in the most concrete of images – once meditated upon "the enormous network beneath the earth. Where lakes multiply into countless sources and finally into unimaginably small sources. Source upon source – while the thirsty stand thirsty behind the thirsty [...] The current never stops. As a great pulse never stops."[51] As we travel through life, is this not why at various times (and with various degrees of need) we look towards music – music that may both refresh and stimulate us, as it connects us again, to varying degree – with the larger currents, or pulse, of life?

At first sight, or hearing, the imagery of Hofseth's *Lake of Memory* might seem to conjure an anti-Platonic note. For, according to Plato, it was the drinking of the forgetful waters of Lethe – matter – by souls, as they approached birth, that led them to forget their true nature. However, the idea of memory, or anamnesis, which is crucial to Hofseth's piece is thoroughly Patonic. As the Platonic poet and thinker Kathleen Raine has pointed out, Jung's ideas of archetypes and the collective unconscious owe an obvious debt to the fundamental Platonic idea that the great task of the soul in its passage through this life is to remember the deeper aspects of itself, to intuit and come to study the beauty of that *terra incognita* which, in another existence, it once knew.[52]

In an extraordinary phrase, the Russian-Australian character Arkady in Bruce Chatwin's <u>The Songlines</u> suggests that "Music is a memory bank for finding one's way about the world."[53] Our current Western fixation upon the idea of time as flowing ceaselessly into something we choose to call the future may make such an idea seem, at best, quaintly nostalgic, at worst, severely limiting – especially to that idea of historically progressive (or avant-garde) innovation which has dominated so much artistic and political thinking this century. However, the notion that the resources contained in a memory bank will necessarily be limiting to any activity undertaken in the present is simply evidence of that childish, pathetic obsession with the self – seen solely in relation to the 'noise-ridden' and 'contemporary' present – which is all too evident in some areas of the arts today.[54]

As we have seen in previous chapters, a sense of primitivism – that approach to the poetics of creativity which seeks to recapture and make new something of the power of archetypal origins in art and life – informs a good deal of the work of Garbarek. Whether it be inflected by a Platonic sense of order or more ancient and shamanic ideas of ecstasy, in primitivism the idea of a "memory bank" – or "lake of memory" – is crucial.[55] This is so whether that bank or lake be accessed consciously or unconsciously, and whether it involves, as it were, the deposits accrued through various, far-flung generations or one's own life. In the latter instance, the idea of a creative return to childhood becomes crucial, as does the distinction between the childish and the child-like. If the former attitude is often limiting, if not highly destructive, to any concept of creativity that would seek to broaden and deepen the self's awareness of its potentialities, the latter has long been prized for its capacity to rekindle the magic of life, of *participation mystique*.

The Romantic poet and critic Charles Baudelaire once wrote that genius was "nothing more nor less than childhood recaptured at will – a childhood now equipped for self-expression with manhood's capacities and a power of analysis which enables it to order the mass of raw material which it has accumulated."[56] One of the most remarkable qualities in the music of Jan Garbarek is precisely this: the combination of child-like openness (and playful spontaneity) and adult courage (and synthesising discrimination) which it has increasingly come to manifest. As Garbarek's imagination has travelled far and wide across both continents and millenia, his music has re-membered much that is archetypal, as it has both drunk from and replenished, or made new, ancient sources of the inspiration of *mélôdia*. At times, Garbarek's music has approached that state of presence and potentiality which Eliot hymned in *Four Quartets*, and which Rilke – from a very different spiritual perspective – had earlier praised in his *Sonnets to Orpheus*. In the third of these sonnets, Rilke suggests nothing less than that "Song is Existence."[57]

What might Rilke have meant by this? "The rest may reason and welcome: 'tis we musicians know", asserts Robert Browning's Abbé Vogler.[58] What (and how) it is that musicians may know has long been a matter of debate. The anthropologist Claude Lévi-Strauss once observed that, "Since music is the only language with the contradictory attributes of being at once intelligible and untranslatable, the musical creator is a being comparable to the gods, and music itself the supreme mystery of the sciences of man."[59]

For Rilke, such mystery was best intimated in images. Music, the language that begins where other languages ends, was for this poet "the breathing of statues". The purest "heart-space" grown out of us, music remained always for Rilke that "innermost of us" which, seeking "the way out – holy departure", comes to surround us as "the most mastered distance", "the other side of air".[60] The spatial-temporal categories of past and future by which we organise so much of our sense of life would seem to have little if any application here. And what Rilke sought to express in his images of the ineffable would later be latent in the words which have come to be indelibly associated with ECM: "the most beautiful sound next to silence".[61]

Rilke's initial image of the breathing of statues may remind us of the original Greek meaning or interpretation of the word, music: the art of the Muse. Two key terms inform Greek discusion of that art: *ethos* and *pathos*. The first term, central to Plato's perception of the social role of music, signifies the idea (and ideal) of calmness and balance of mind, the personal and social reward consequent upon self-control. As opposed to the implicit stasis of *ethos*, the term *pathos* signifies those factors of movement and change which are the consequence of inspiration (literally: a breath from the gods). In his revisioning of the somewhat sanitized view of pagan Greece which had marked the Neo-classicism of eighteenth-century Europe, the poet-philosopher Nietzsche interpreted the creative interplay and (ultimately) healthy balance of *ethos* and *pathos* in terms of the figures of Apollo (God of Light, and associated with principles of lucidity and reason) and Dionysus (God of the chthonic, or earthly forces, and associated with the transformative energies of ecstasy).[62]

Underneath all the various philosophies, sociologies and psychologies of life and art which our century has spawned, the play of the forces of *ethos* and *pathos*, Apollo and Dionysus has remained as potent as ever. No other century, in fact, has had to contemplate the potential consequences of a destructive imbalance of these forces, or principles, to the extent that we have. And no other music has conjured the interplay of these forces with such refreshing impact as jazz. For many this century, jazz has been the great "open channel" in art, the music *par excellence* of crossings: geographical and racial, political and psychological, spiritual and poetic.

Speaking of the impact of jazz in America, Sonny Rollins – the magnificent tenorist whose work manifests a striking variety of approaches to the Apollinian and Dionysian principles, and the intelligence of whose musical spirit can at times (for all the difference in their approach to live performances) be clearly sensed in Garbarek – has underlined the politics that lie within poetics. For Rollins, jazz "was not just a music: it was a social force in this country, and it was talking about freeedom and people enjoying things for what they are and not having to worry about whether they were supposed to be black, white and all that stuff. Jazz has always been a music that had that kind of spirit [...] A lot of times, jazz means no barriers."[63] In terms of the impact of jazz outside America, Rollins' words could hardly be more relevant than they are to the music of Garbarek.

In 1992, Jan Garbarek was a recipient of the prestigious Paul Robeson Prize. The committee who awarded the prize cited, in particular, the contribution which the border-crossing nature of Garbarek's work had made to encouraging contact between different cultures, thus helping to combat racism. The award was conferred late in November, upon Garbarek's return to Oslo from a concert which he had just given at London's Barbican Centre as part of the major *Tender Is The North* season there (and where his compatriot, Frans Widerberg, had a major show in the Centre's Concourse Gallery, next to the concert hall in which Garbarek played). Here, Garbarek's regular quartet, with Eberhard Weber, Rainer Brüninghaus (born 1949) and Marilyn Mazur (born 1955), had been joined by the Telemark folk singer Agnes Buen Garnås and the Sami singer Mari Boine. Among other passages rich in song, the programme featured a beautiful combination of Mari Boine's *Du Lakha* (Near You) with the recently deceased Jim Pepper's *Witchi-Tai-To* (long a feature of Garbarek's concerts, and recorded on both the 1973 album of that title and the 1992 **Twelve Moons**).[64]

1992 was an appropriate year for Garbarek to receive the Paul Robeson Prize. Just three months before receiving the award, Garbarek had recorded **Madar**, one of his key border-crossing projects (as we have seen) with Anouar Brahem and Ustad Shaukat Hussain. Garbarek had first played with Hussain on another important and equally rewarding cross-cultural session, the May 1990 **Ragas and Sagas**. Released in the summer of 1992, this featured Garbarek and Hussain with the Pakistani musicians Ustad Fateh Ali Khan (vocal), Ustad Nazim Ali Khan (sarangi) and the Norwegian-domiciled Deepika Thathaal (voice), with North African drummer Manu Katché also featured on one track: *Saga*. Composed by Garbarek, and using the notes of Raga Asavari, the piece features the sort of suspended harmonies which introduce a note foreign to the traditions of Indian and Pakistani music. However, such a note finds its natural, story-telling place within the overall devotional context of music which respects tradition (the sound of the saranagi doubling with the voice on *Raga 1*, for example) even as, with the addition of Garbarek's sensitively turned soprano improvisations, it makes that tradition new.[65]

In September 1992 Garbarek had recorded **Twelve Moons**, the five-hundredth ECM album. Here, his regular working partners Weber, Brüninghaus and Mazur had been joined at times by Manu Katché and singers Agnes Buen Garnås and Mari Boine. While **Twelve Moons** was rich in Norwegian and Sami folk material, **Atmos**, the duo album which Garbarek recorded with double-bassist (and leader) Miroslav Vitous in February 1992 was soaked in the spirit of Slavic melody. All in all, therefore, 1992 furnished an extraordinary documentation of the extent of Garbarek's desire (and ability) to travel far and wide in – and through – music.

In a November 1992 interview with the Oslo-based critic and writer Roald Helgheim, Garbarek commented that, while he had never been the sort of person to be drawn to the front line of the barricades for any particular cause, he much appreciated the Robeson award, coming as it did in the name of someone who had been not only a great humanitarian, but a remarkable singer: "Over the past 10-15 years I've played with musicians from many different nations. It's been a painless process and we've never thought in categories like 'race'. I should really like to share the prize with all those I've played with [...] Music is a language everyone can understand, a sort of stress-less Esperanto, to put it simply. Whether I play with a tabla musician from India or a drummer from Oslo, we're part of the same family."[66]

After remarking how much he felt folk musics from around the world had in common, and how musicians from around the world were able to come together to create a sort of "neighbourhood" or "circle of friendship" while playing together in something of the spirit of such musics, Garbarek suggested that the recently-issued recording of **Ragas and Sagas** furnished an example of what he had been talking about: "The other musicians didn't have any English or Norwegian, and I didn't know any Urdu. We were able only to play together – and things went fine."[67]

Perhaps the most innovative – and provocative – of all such cross-cultural sessions in which Garbarek has participated to date involved four musicians who *do* share a common language with the saxophonist: English. In September 1993 Garbarek and the Hilliard Ensemble, England's specialists in early and avant-garde vocal music, recorded **Officium** at the beautiful Propstei Gerold in the Austrian mountains, an hour or so by car from Manfred Eicher's home town of Lindau.[68] One of the most extraordinary recordings of the decade, **Officium** is an exquisitely balanced blend of saxophone, voices – and centuries. In his sleeve-note to the album, tenor John Potter observed that, "When jazz began, at the beginning of this century, it had no name; nor did polyphony when it began around a thousand years earlier."[69] Potter continued: "These two nameless historical moments were points of departure for two of the most fundamental ideas in Western music: improvisation and composition. The origins of the performances on this record, which are neither wholly composed nor completely improvised, are to be found in those same forces that awoke a thousand years apart from each other."[70]

"What is this music?" asked Potter. He answered his own question thus: "We don't have a name for it: it is simply what happened when a saxophonist, a vocal quartet and a record producer met to make music together."[71] The idea for **Officium** had come to Manfred Eicher while he was in Iceland working on his film *Holozän*, based on the novel *Man in the Holocene* by Max Frisch – a study of what Eicher calls "the human tragedy of loneliness, of ageing, of encroaching isolation and the fear of losing one's memory", focused on one Herr Geiser (played in the film by Erland Josephson). Many years before, in the cathedral of Seville, Eicher had heard the *Officium defunctorum* (Offices for the Dead) of Christobal de Morales (c. 1500-1553). Driving through the lava fields of Iceland, Eicher heard the work again. As he explains in the sleeve-note to **Officium**: "During the work on the film in Iceland, I listened again and again to the *Tenebrae Responsories* by Gesualdo and the song of Jan Garbarek's saxophone. Morales suddenly appeared to me like the southern mainland over which the migratory bird from the north draws ever-widening circles. Before the basalt sea. No longer able to reconcile the intensity of the sounds with the figure of Geiser, I later decided on other music."[72]

Nevertheless, the vision remained, to bear fruit in **Officium**. As we shall see shortly, the result upset one or two historical purists. However, the measured, dynamically sensitive intensity which this unusual quintet brought to bear on its material – which ranged from medieval chant (reaching back to its pre-literate forms), early polyphony and Renaissance motets – had an enormous impact upon listeners, from various backgrounds, around the world. While **Officium** can hardly be called a jazz record in any conventional sense of the term, it is rich in the sort of improvisational qualities which will be familiar enough to anyone who has responded to the distant echoes of J. S. Bach's *Chorale Preludes* in Garbarek's sublimely balanced *Entering* from the 1977 **Places**, for example, or who has appreciated the mixture of folk-like simplicity and post-Romantic chromaticism on the 1979 **Aftenland**. A massive critical and commercial success, **Officium** has occasioned many live performances in Europe, Scandinavia and America.[73]

The material was chosen with Garbarek's possible contributions very much in mind: the music provides plenty of space for the saxophonist's customary excellence in matters of melodic paraphrase and dynamics. In his September 1994 *Time Out* review, Linton Chiswick suggested that the record constituted perhaps Garbarek's "most emphatic and ambitious artistic statement to date".[74] Be that as it may, the record certainly contains many moments of hushed, haunting beauty, from the opening, ascensional *Parce mihi domini* by Morales and (fourteenth century, Czechoslovakian) *Primo tempore* to the Gregorian *Regnantem sempiterna* and *Ave maria stella* of Guillaume Dufay (c. 1397-1474), for example. On the latter two numbers, Garbarek's spacious descant figures offer the sort of modulations which bring parts of **Aftenland** very much to mind: here, indeed, centuries speak to each other.

But what exactly is the nature – and the worth – of the language being spoken? While the vast majority of reviews of **Officium** were favourable – jazz critic Kenny Mathieson's estimate that here was music of "staggering beauty" may be taken as typical – some voices raised doubts about the project.[75] In Norway, one or two reviews raised the problem of 'kitsch', while in America a lengthy 1994 _Village Voice_ article pulled no punches. Surveying the recent popularity of medieval chant in the American music charts, Kyle Gann claimed that, on **Officium**, Garbarek's ("admittedly tasteful") saxophone "fills in for you the subjective response you might have had to the music if you had seriously listened to it. Garbarek, in the misbegotten vision of ECM head Manfred Eicher, has saved you the trouble. How can anyone listen to this disc, whose arbitrary alterations the long-dead composers are powerless to prevent, without thinking of the colorization of classic black-and-white films? This sentimentalized predigestion of medieval music brilliantly fits the zeitgeist of chant mania and suggests new, ever more nauseating directions."[76]

Strong words, these: but not necessarily wise words. Firstly, the existence of **Officium** does not stop anyone listening to other, saxophone-less versions of the material which is to be heard there. Secondly, when appeals are made to the authenticity of original material, it is well that those appeals are rooted in a proper understanding of the history to which they refer. In his sleeve-note to **Officium**, John Potter made plain the fact that the oldest material on the record, the pre-Gregorian chants, would have been part of a living (changing, developing) tradition: "Before Gregory and Charlemagne got their bureaucratic hands on them, these ancient songs had a life of their own, each monastery having its own living tradition."[77]

Further: to appeal to the helplessness of "long-dead composers" is to forget how much religious music itself has (in the modern jargon) appropriated previous music. As Gerardus van der Leeuw reminds us in his exemplary study _Sacred and Profane Beauty: the Holy in Art_ , "[M]any of our most beautiful psalm tunes were originally dance tunes [...] Luther composed his famous Christmas hymn, _'From Heaven High I Come To You'_, to an old riddle in verse, _'From foreign lands I come to you'_. The same development holds true for the hymn tunes which derived from Gregorian chant. Josquin Deprès, Obrecht, and Palestrina wrote Masses on secular themes [...] We must accustom ourselves to the fact that Handel's chorus, _'For unto us a child is born'_, was first written with a secular text: _'Modi voi non vo fidamit'_; the splendid spiritual cradle song from Bach's Christmas Oratorio, _'Schlafe, mein Liebster'_, was originally a song by which lust tried to tempt the young Hercules."[78]

Of course, the music on **Officium** does raise questions. Perhaps the most obvious one is that of historical context. If one wishes to draw upon something of the spiritual beauty and power of the past, can one simply jettison those aspects of the past which do not happen to fit into today's world-view? For example, how many of the many thousands who have bought and enjoyed **Officium** would want to take on board the old idea that the magical power of sung incantations is precisely that: magical, and hence to be treated with extreme caution? As late as 1316, van der Leeuw tells us, the Council of Cologne forbade the singing for anyone of the famous hymn of mourning *Media in vita in morte sumus*, unless special permissions were given: the song of death brought death.[79]

What all such arguments in favour of the inviolability of historical period and social fact overlook is what Joseph Campbell called the difference between "local" and "universal" elements of meaning in culture. Campbell spent the greater part of his working life writing about this theme from the mythological and spiritual viewpoint. In one well-researched volume after another, Campbell explored how the cultural forms of spirituality which are manifest in time are but some of the infinite "masks of God" which are necessary for human consciousness to begin to approach an understanding, or appreciation, of the true extent of the mysterious glory – or Divinity – of life.[80]

As even our profane world knows, you cannot look directly at the sun. Some form of protection, or shielding, from such primal, life-giving power is essential. And so it is with the ultimate ground, or root, of our being. Problems arise, of course, when one person, or culture, assumes its "mask" of meaning to be the only true one. To free oneself from such fanaticism, said Campbell, is to feel the liberating creative energy in the eternal play of the "local" and the "universal" elements of life.[81]

These are elements which history reveals to be in a more or less perpetual state of tension: at some moments "meaning" opens up; at other moments it closes down, or comes to ostensible "completion". What the music on **Officium** does is make the tension between closure and openness creative. And it does so by re-introducing into religious song the very element which had once been proscribed by Christianity as the voice of the Devil: the solo intrumental voice.

"Where flute players are, there can Christ never be" declaimed Chrysostom.[82] Because instrumental music has its roots in the cultic-ludic complex of ancient (shamanic) culture, it has often been troubling to Christians. "In place of the playing of tympani, let the singing of hymns resound" says Gregory of Nazianzus.[83] There are no tympani on **Officium**: instead, a saxophone. And what better instrument to reclaim – *and make new* – humanity's ancient heritage?

To speak of Garbarek's plaintively pitched saxophone on **Officium** as somehow "sentimentalising" the material upon which it improvises is thus to miss entirely the utterly radical nature of the project.[84] For here is music in which *ethos* and *pathos*, Apollo and Dionysus come to a new and subtly energising level of interplay: music in which relations of sound and silence, individual and group, the "local" and the "universal" are synthesised – sublimated – in a manner which suggests nothing so much as a quest for that *tessera hospitalis* which might set our fragmented self in potentially healing relation to an as yet unknown whole. As David Vernier wrote in a perceptive piece for <u>CD Review</u>, the refigured relation of form and tradition, freedom and improvisation that is **Officium** "was accomplished by musicians unafraid to reach out into an unknown region where music revered for its own sake would also serve as a catalyst for new creation."[85]

The music that is **Officium** epitomises the courage that Garbarek's work has exhibited for so many years. Talking once to the writer Tor Dybo about the way he (Garbarek) might classify or think about the many musical scales which he might draw upon in the course of various improvisations, Garbarek suggested that he did not think about such matters in terms of specific classifications or names. Rather, he thought of the world of scales as a large pool ('stor dam' in Norwegian) from which might emerge all kinds of possibilities.[86] The image has an unmistakeably Jungian ring to it, reminiscent of that 'lake of memory' of which Bendik Hofseth sings and plays in the tune of that title. Such Jungian overtones are no less discernible in Garbarek's remark that, no matter where we travel in life, we each have a forest deep inside of us.[87]

No matter how diverse the results of Garbarek's various explorations of forest, pool and lake may have been, two factors have always remained paramount. The first is that of quality. Whether it be a Norwegian folk melody or an Arabian mode, an Indian or Pakistani raga, a Gregorian chant or a Sami *joik*, Garbarek brings to music those qualities that are so evident in his stage-presence during the many concerts he gives: concentration, clarity, focus. As Manfred Eicher has said to me, Garbarek is always *present* in the music he plays. Such an ability to move within and across worlds, with empathetic discrimination, and to be able to handle different aspects of musical structure, mood and "meaning" – what psychologists call "affect" – is evidence of a strong and healthy personality, pursuing questions of the expansion and integration of musical and psychological – spiritual – meaning at an energising and inspiring level. Here we come to the second factor that has long distinguished Garbarek's work.

No matter how different the music that Garbarek has created may be, there is something that binds together such diverse recordings as, for example, **Madar** and **Officium**. That something is nothing less than the questing courage of the simultaneously naked and literate spirit of humanity which Joseph Campbell celebrated throughout his life and work. Unafraid, a wayfarer like Garbarek has the capacity to lead us far off the beaten track, deep into the regenerative heart of ourselves: to the place where, as Gunnar Ekelöf put it in his meditation *Euphoria* in the 1941 collection *Ferry Song*, all things are in all things, at once end and beginning. Here, as we break bread with the dead, "pain's great hymn" may sound with special resonance: the resonance that is Song become, however fleetingly, Existence.

Primo Tempore: Jan Garbarek & The Hilliard Ensemble
(The Barbican, December 1997) Christian Him

Notes to Chapter Five

1. Quoted in Södergran, E. _Complete Poems_ (trans. D. McDuff)
    Bloodaxe Books, Newcastle upon Tyne 1984 p. 50.
2. Ibid. p. 103 ('The Whirlpool of Madness', 1918). Given the theme of
    much of this chapter, it is interesting to note that Södergran wrote a
    poem entitled "The Gypsy Woman" (from her last collection _The
    Land That Is Not_. The title poem here opens with the beautiful line: 'I
    long for the land that is not'). See also Södergran, E.: _Love & Solitude.
    Selected Poems 1916-1923_ (bi-lingual edition, trans. S. Katchadourian)
    Fjord Press, Seattle 1992.
3. I am reminded of Ekelöf, who said that what he had written had been
    written _between_ the words, _between_ the lines, _between_ the meanings:
    'An Outsider's Way', in Ekelöf/Thygesen 1996 op. cit. (_Modus
    Vivendi_) p.156.
4. Press-release for **Madar**, ECM, Munich 1992. Ken Hyder hears a lot
    of warmth in the music that results from such meetings: "I think
    Garbarek's suffered a little from the Northern wasteland image. There
    is a wrongly received idea that Northern means cold, desolate
    landscapes, and therefore the music must also be cold, barren and
    distant. In my experience it is the opposite. The cold environment
    breeds a love of the warmth, need for friendship and co-operative
    effort to beat the hardships outside. This wrong-headed notion was
    reinforced in Jan Garbarek's case by the style of the recording. The
    ECM reverb sound has a propensity to make things appear colder,
    distanced and separate. But when I listen to what Garbarek is actually
    doing, it doesn't sound cold to me (and neither does Brazilian music,
    where they also use a lot of reverb in the studio). It's a case of the
    received image being at odds with what's really going down. Jan
    Garbarek is really a world folk musician in the same way that Don
    Cherry was. He seems to have the musical generosity of someone who
    feels comfortable within his own framework, and who can therefore
    reach out to others from a position of strength. If they have a
    Norwegian equivalent of the Scottish saying, 'We're a Jock Tamson's
    bairns' [we're all from a common stock – we're all brothers and sisters
    in humanity] Garbarek would probably subscribe to it." Personal
    communication, June 1998.
5. The rubato title track for strings, piano and bass (the last played by
    Charlie Haden, one of Garbarek's favourite musicians) on Keith
    Jarrett's October 1971 CBS recording **Expectations** had an especial
    impact upon Garbarek. He has always admired what he calls the
    flowing, organic quality in Jarrett's orchestral or string writing. In
    August 1998 Palle Mikkelborg commented to me about the distinctive
    qualities in Garbarek's own writing for strings. Mikkelborg first played
    with Garbarek at Sogn Jazz Club, Oslo in the late 1960s, and has
    subsequently played with him on many occasions. These have included
    working (and recording) with the Nordic Big Band of the early 1970s
    (which also included e.g. Juhani Aaltonen, Palle Danielsson, Terje
    Rypdal and Jon Christensen) and two ECM albums - Shankar's 1983
    Vision and Gary Peacock's 1987 **Guamba**. A great admirer of the

melodic qualities in Garbarek, of what he calls the magic in the saxophonist's phrasing, Mikkelborg played an important part in the realisation of both the 1980 *Låter* at Montmartre and the 1982 Bergen suite. Among other delights, including a setting of Garbarek's *Blue Sky*, the 1980 music featured a long, Miles Davis-like "rock-out", with an extensive, tough solo from Garbarek somewhat reminiscent (albeit in faster tempo) of that which he played on Terje Rypdal's *Keep It Like That - Tight* on the 1971 **Terje Rypdal**. The 1982 suite, played by the quartet of Garbarek himself, Bill Frisell, Eberhard Weber and Jon Christensen, with the strings of the Bergen Philharmonic conducted by Palle Mikkelborg, is simply lovely. The spacious string writing underlines the quality of "suspended" reflection, or reverie, in much of the music: while often sonorous in a manner reminiscent of both Mahler and Vaughan Williams, it is also - at times - strongly bitonal, giving a tart, Slavic edge to some driving passages for strings alone. Rapt readings of *Skygger*, *Spor*, *Still* and *Dansere* provide some of the many highlights. There are some pleasingly placed moments of Latinesque contrast: overall, considerable care is taken with transitional passages, with Weber's portamento role often crucial. My gratitude to Tom Bækkerud for making radio tapes of both the 1980 and 1982 music available to me.

6.   Solothurnmann 1995/97 op. cit p. 5.
7.   Ibid.
8.   Lake, S. 'Covering the waterfront: Eleni Karaindrou's music for films': sleeve-essay to **Music for Films** (ECM 1249).
9.   Personal communication, London July 1998. There are some interesting parallels between aspects of Spassov's music, as on the beautiful, 1995 **Beyond The Frontiers** for example, and parts of Garbarek's 1982 suite for jazz quartet and strings and 1998 **Rites**. See the contextual discography.
10.   *Gypsies* (with an essay by Willy Guy) Aperture Inc., New York 1975. For a comprehensive, superbly illustrated study of the relation of gypsy history and culture to flamenco, see Bois, M. *Le Flamenco* Marval 1994, distrib. Harmonia Mundi. See also Mitchell 1994 op. cit. (*Flamenco Deep Song*) and e.g. *Art Sud mediterranée* no. 11, Marseille 1996, special edition *les gitanes*. To be perfectly clear: in none of what follows am I suggesting that Garbarek plays flamenco music.
11.   Personal communication, April 1998. The Norwegian writer Hugo Lauritz Jenssen suggests another parallel or precedent, here: the legendary Norwegian violinist Ole Bull (1810-1880), whose breadth of repertoire leads Jenssen to call Bull a pioneer of "world music". 'Fra Telemark til Tbilisi' *DN-Magasinet*, Oslo 3/10/98.
12.   Lorca 1980 op. cit.(*Deep Song*) pp. 28 & 36.
13.   See Pacholczyk, J. F. 'Secular Classical Music in the Arabic Near East', in May, E. (ed) *Music of Many Cultures* University of California Press, Berkeley 1983 pp. 253-68.
14.   *Jazz Times* May 1995.
15.   Mitchell 1994 op. cit *(Flamenco Deep Song)* pp. 32-3.
16.   Personal communication, June 1998. I am grateful to Professor John Mayer for the considerable time he kindly gave to listening to and

commenting on a selection of Garbarek's Eastern-inflected work for me. Professor Mayer's own pioneering work in the Indo-Jazz fusion field has been reissued on CD: today, he leads a new and exciting band playing both old and new compositions in this field. See the contextual discography.

17. For a wide-ranging look at the implications of contemporary technology for music-making today, see Toop 1995 op. cit. (_Ocean Of Sound_).

18. Solothurnmann op. cit. p. 5.

19. Ekelöf/Schideler op. cit. p. 137.

20. See e.g. Ruan Ji _Songs of my Heart: the Chinese lyric poetry of Ruan Ji (AD 210-263)_ (trans. G. Hartill & Wu Fusheng) Wellsweep, London 1988; Shi Bo _Saisons: Poèmes des dynasties Tang et Song_ Editions Alternatives, Paris 1998 (which includes Gao Shi's beautiful 'Listening to the Flute at the Frontier', the first line of which is, in Shi Bo's French translation, "La neige pure danse dans le ciel du Nord"); _Unseen Rain: Quatrains of Rumi_ (trans. J. Moyne & C. Barks) Threshold Books, Putney, Vermont 1986, and Tagore, R. _Gitanjali (Song Offerings)_ (with an Introduction by W. B. Yeats), Papermac/Macmillan, London 1986 (first published 1912).

21. _Sweet Potato_ February 1-15 1984.

22. _Rock & Folk_ March 1980.

23. _Durham Herald-Sun_ 28/4/95.

24. Personal communication, Spring 1984.

25. When the Jan Garbarek Group, with David Torn, Eberhard Weber and Michael DiPasqua, played a full house at the Sallis Benney Theatre in Brighton Polytechnic in November 1984, their version of _Going Places_ ended with a subtly shaded drum feature from DiPasqua. An excellent drummer, able to combine drummer's and percussionist's roles with considerable grace, DiPasqua unfortunately had to leave music as a professional career, following an injury to his back.

26. _Wayfarers_ (trans. J. McFarlane) Condor/Souvenir Press, London 1980.

27. Quoted in Cork, R. _David Bomberg_ Tate Gallery Publications, London 1988 p. 45.

28. I think it was Hermann Hesse who once pointed out the curious fact, in order to live and create, one has to forget so much of what one experiences on a day-to-day basis, letting the unconscious help one sift things into some sort of qualitative sense of what is and is not important to remember. Of course, as Hesse certainly knew - and this chapter argues - it is also essential to human identity to _remember_ so many things in life. But to remember everything one experienced would be as hellish as to have no memory at all. The question thus arises: why do we forget and remember what we do?

29. Leeuw, G. van der _Sacred and Profane Beauty: the Holy in Art_ (trans. D. E. Green, with a Preface by Mircea Eliade) Holt, Rinehart and Winston, New York 1963 contains some excellent reflections on art and time. See e.g. p. 156, where Leeuw (following Kierkegaard) compares the element of time in painting and sculpture, music and poetry. See also Solothurnmann 1995/97 op. cit. for Garbarek's reflections on the role of time in his music, which conclude: "So, how

we can make our concept of time change is one of the more basic considerations of making music. It's a very difficult question." (p. 5.)

30. Stravinsky op. cit.(*Poetics of Music*) p. 39.

31. *Herakleitos And Diogenes* (trans. G. Davenport) Grey Fox Press, Bolinas, California 1979 p. 31 (fragment no. 118). Has the wisdom of Heraclitus (which has much to say to today's chaos theorists) ever been surpassed? One could meditate forever on Heraclitus' famous suggestion that, "One cannot step twice into the same river, for the water into which you first stepped has flowed on" (fragment 21). And it's hard to improve upon the Zen-like pithiness of fragment 53: "Hide our ignorance as we will, an evening of wine reveals it".

32. In 1997, tired of (if not sickened by) the profane tedium of so much art today - of the media-show that is the annual Turner Prize at the Tate Gallery, London, for example - several scholars and practitioners of art (poet and educator Peter Abbs, dancer Anna Carlisle and composer Jonathan Harvey) started a movement called *The New Metaphysical Art* at the University of Sussex, England. The movement, which includes Yehudi Menuhin, Arvo Pärt and Kathleen Raine among its patrons, has organised a variety of lectures and events and two successful conferences. Part of its manifesto states: "We are against the trivialization of art. Against the uncritical and endless use of parody and pastiche [..] We are against the reductive ethos, the crudely ideological and the merely historical [..] Art must begin again the broken conversation with eternity [..] To widen the circumference. To deepen the centre." In the autumn of 1998 the movement's programme included the session *Summoning the Spirit: Aspects of Revelation in Contemporary Jazz Music*, which featured tenor and soprano saxophonist Geoff Hearn and drummer Ken Hyder. See note 49 below.

33. Södergran op. cit. p. 154.

34. Maslow argues that psychology and psychiatry have for too long been dominated by the idea of sickness as a governing model for the understanding of human behaviour, its needs and aspirations. Essential as it is to treat, and attempt to understand, such sickness in people, we need to do so in the light of the examples which creative, self-realising (or "actualising") human beings provide of our capacity to realise or "actualise" ever-richer, or higher aspects of ourselves. See Maslow, A. H. *Towards A Psychology of Being* Van Nostrand Reinhold, New York and London 1968 and *The Farther Reaches of Human Nature* Pelican/Penguin, Harmondsworth 1973.

35. As already noted, the technique of circular breathing is available to Garbarek. It is important to remember how he prefers the rhythms of breathing with pauses - or breaks - in his phrasing, at appropriate points: and how, in often working out the tempi and rhythms of his compositions with the help of a small hand drum, factors of breath and bodily rhythms commingle. Personal communication, July 1994.

36. See Chapter Six and e.g. Berendt, J-E. *Nada Brahma: The World Is Sound* East West Publications, London and The Hague, 1987 and Hamel, P. M. *Through Music To The Self* The Compton Press, Tisbury 1978.

37. Personal communication, Spring 1998.

38. As we have seen, Garbarek's work has sometimes been described as minimalist. While it is the case that his own music has long been pared down to the essentials, and that he has participated in music which might be seen to approximate the description "minimalist" (e.g. the mesmeric *Karma Shadub* on violinist Paul Giger's 1990-1 **Alpstein**: see Chapter 6) I do not think the term gives anything like an accurate indication of the import and effect of the distilled range of elements (and consequent musical, psychological and spiritual creativity) in Garbarek's music. Certainly, any "minimalism" that there might be in Garbarek has little in common with the stripped-down "presences" and repetitive schema of such well-known minimalists as La Monte Young, Terry Riley, Steve Reich and Philip Glass. In Garbarek, the fundamental idea of tension and release, of psychologically rooted dynamics, of music as a narrative structure, remains of crucial importance. In much music of the so-called Minimalist school, such an idea is abandoned. See Mertens 1994 op. cit.(*American Minimal Music*) passim.

39. *Selected Poems* Faber and Faber Limited, London 1964 p. 67.

40. *The Upanishads* (trans. J. Mascaró) Penguin Books, London 1988 p. 43.

41. Garbarek has never played or recorded with Ravi Shankar, as has been stated in the jazz press. Nor did he ever play or record with the late Nusrat Fateh Ali Khan, as has also been suggested. For the supposed Ravi Shankar connection, see Morton, B. 'One Born With Wings', *The Wire* no. 64, June 1989 p. 33. Here we read that, "The most concrete outcome of Garbarek's exposure to Ravi Shankar's music was the 1984 album **Song For Everyone**, recorded with the great sitarist and released (inevitably) on ECM." This misinformation is repeated in Fordham 1996 op. cit. (*Shooting From The Hip*) p. 262.

42. The music can be heard at the National Jazz Archives, Norwegian Music Information Centre, Oslo. At times, Garbarek sounds as though he is playing the alto.

43. *The Narrow Road To The Deep North And Other Travel Sketches* (trans. Nobuyuki Yuasa) Penguin Books, Harmondsworth, 1979.

44. Takemitsu is a fascinating example of the creative play of the cross-currents of East-West in twentieth-century life and art. Debussy (himself deeply influenced by the East, as in the Javanese and Annamese music which he experienced in 1889) was one of Takemitsu's chief inspirations and elective affinities, together with Takemitsu's own native musical traditions, Zen, Japanese rock gardens - and much of the music of the post-Second World War Western avant garde. According to Christopher Small, in an excellent study of key aspects of Western music, "What Debussy did [..] was to liberate music from sequential logic [..in the music of Debussy..] We find ourselves much closer to the sonorous experience, in much more sensuous, tangible contact with sound, than in tonal-functional music. Nature (in this case the nature of sound) is treated with a lover's joy." (Small, C. *Music Society Education* John Calder, London 1977 p. 106.) Nature is treated thus in Takemitsu - as it is in Garbarek. For introductions to aspects of the poetics of Eastern spirituality and

creativity, see the references to Taoism in Chapter One, note 51 and the bibliographical references to Adam (1976), Coomaraswamy (1956) and Ross (1973).

45. Namchylak sang two keening, strongly shamanic - and improvised - numbers with the trio of Garbarek, Wesseltoft and Gurtu, inflected by the technique of "throat singing". The first of these moving invocations has been recorded by Namchylak as *Sehnsucht* on the 1991 **Tunguska-Guska** (where Grace Yoon, Iris Disse, Hartmut Geerken and Sunny Murray also appear) and as *Hymn* on the 1993 **Out of Tuva** (produced by Hector Zazou). The Santa Fe concert was the result of an idea by Norwegian poet and broadcaster Eric Bye, and Garbarek, based upon themes in the Norwegian TV programme *The Search for Mangas Colorados* which Bye put together, with Bob Haozous, and for which Garbarek supplied the music (some of which can be heard on **Visible World**). The concert ended with an extraordinary group performance, with Namchylak, Mari Boine and Sainte-Marie trading choruses over a strongly grooved riff, with obbligati from Garbarek. For an introduction to Namchylak and Mari Boine see Tucker 1996 op. cit. (*The Body Electric*) pp. 74-79. My gratitude to Knut Moe for making a video of this concert available to me.

46. Personal communication, May 1998. Gurtu speaks of Garbarek with great warmth.

47. For a fascinating study of the politics (and poetics) of this theme with regard to India, including a discussion of some jazz musicians - but not, unfortunately, Garbarek - see Farrell, G. *Indian Music And The West* Clarendon Press, Oxford 1997.

48. Eliot, T. S. *Four Quartets* Faber and Faber Limited, London 1974 p. 58.

49. Tranströmer 1980 op. cit.('Schubertania' in*Truth Barriers*) p. 23. On the idea of the holy - the mystery of the numinous - see Leeuw 1963 op. cit. and Otto, R. *The Idea of the Holy* (trans. J. Harvey) Oxford University Press, London 1923.

50. **Amuse Yourself** (Columbia 472 988 2). Wry as it may sound, the title track is in fact a very beautiful ballad. The record also contains a wonderful celebration of swing, *Swing City*, with a fine, meditative lyric by Hofseth interpeted by the composer himself and Junior Wells, with Nils-Einar Økland on Hardanger fiddle and Jon Christensen on drums added to the regular sextet (including guitarists Eivind Aarset and Knut Reiersrud) which features on the album.

51. Vesaas 1971 op. cit. ('The Rivers Beneath The Earth' in *The Boat In The Evening*) p.183.

52. Raine 1985 op. cit. ('The Use of the Beautiful' in *Defending Ancient Springs*) p. 171.

53. *The Songlines* Picador/Pan Books, London 1987 p. 120.

54. Of course, there is much that is interesting, even compelling in the avant garde today. My *Dreaming With Open Eyes* was an attempt to show how much spiritual value there may be in art which, at first glance, may seem devoid of precisely such a quality. Nevertheless, I share the reservations of *The New Metaphysical Art* movement at the

University of Sussex about much of the art which is being promoted as worthy of our attention today. Much as I am not overly keen on the idea of "movements", I welcome this movement's desire for art "Which is rooted in the body as it moves back to the primordial and forward to the spiritual". See note 32 above.

55. See Tucker 1992 op. cit. (_Dreaming With Open Eyes_) passim.

56. Baudelaire, C. _The Painter of Modern Life and Other Essays_ (trans. & ed. J. Mayer) Phaidon Press, London 1964 p. 8.

57. _Sonnets to Orpheus_ (trans. C. F. MacIntyre) University of California Press, Berkeley 1960 p.7 has "Song is Being" for Rilke's "Gesang ist Dasein", which - in Heideggerian terms, at least - is probably more accurate. Chatwin op. cit. p. 13 has "Song is Existence". At the risk of upsetting specialists, since this latter translation requires neither immediate nor extensive philosophical explication - certainly when compared to the use of 'Being' - I have used it here.

58. 'Abt Vogler (After He Has Been Extemporizing Upon The Musical Instrument Of His Invention)' in _Browning: A Selection by W. E. Williams_ Penguin, Harmondsworth 1964 p. 257.

59. Quoted and referenced (_The Raw and the Cooked_) in Storr, A. _Music and the Mind_ HarperCollins, London 1992 p. xi.

60. 'To Music' in _An Unofficial Rilke; Poems 1912-1926_ (trans. M. Hamburger) Anvil Press Poetry Ltd., London 1981 p. 69.

61. We touch here on extremely difficult (but essential, fascinating) ground. Garbarek has said, in somewhat Wittgensteinian manner, that the essential in life is that which cannot be put into words. ('Det essentielle er det du ikke kan si noe om': Jan Garbarek interviewed by Bjørn Stendahl, _Jazznytt_ no. 3 1984.) By the same token, is the essential in life that which one cannot express by _any_ form of communication - including music? Is it silence, above all, which takes one to the threshold of the holy (or the abyss)? See e.g. Leeuw 1963 op. cit. pp. 141-2, 227, 236. "Before the wholly other, one stands in silent reverence" (p. 236). But for Leeuw, music is able to indicate, or intimate, what he calls "numinous silence". (Ibid.)

62. See Nietzsche, F. _The Birth of Tragedy_ (trans. W. Haufmann) Vintage Books, New York 1967 and Otto, W. F. _Dionysus: Myth and Cult_ (trans. R. B. Palmer) Spring Publications, Dallas 1986. Written under the spell of Wagner (from which he was later to free himself) Nietzsche's 1872 study of the Dionysian and the Apollinian principles is subtitled 'Out of the Spirit of Music'. An early passage in the book reads: "In song and dance man expresses himself as a member of a higher community; he has forgotten how to walk and speak and is on the way towards flying into the air, dancing. His very gestures express enchantment. Just as the animals now talk, and the earth yields milk and honey, supernatural sounds emanate from him, too; he feels himself a god, he himself now walks about enchanted, in ecstasy, like the gods he saw walking in his dreams. He is no longer an artist, he has become a work of art: in these paroxysms of intoxication the artistic power of all nature reveals itself to the highest gratification of the primordial unity." (Nietzsche op. cit. p. 37.) In such extraordinary passages, Nietzsche goes to the core of the shamanic element in music,

in images which must surely also alert one to the potential dangers of such intoxication (one might say that a psycho-sociology of the problem of the "intoxicated" performer is already here). It is important to remember that for Jung, there was all the difference in the world between the destructive *inflation* of the ego to projective, mono-maniacal proportions and the healthy *integration* of the ego within the development of empathetic individuation. As Nietzsche knew, we need Dionsyus *and* Apollo, Apollo *and* Dionysus in ourselves.

63. Palmer op.cit. (*Sonny Rollins: The Cutting Edge*) p.26.
64. The appearance of the Jan Garbarek Group (with Rainer Brüninghaus, Eberhard Weber and Marilyn Mazur) at the Sallis Benney Theatre in the University of Brighton in November 1993 coincided with another Widerberg exhibition - this time of the Norwegian's striking watercolours - at the University of Brighton Gallery. It was a great pleasure to see Garbarek (and his wife, Vigdis) enjoying the work, and to be able to take Marilyn Mazur, herself a painter, around the exhibition. Marilyn responded immediately to Widerberg's language, and in particular, his use of the boldest of yellows.
65. Once again, I am grateful to Professor John Mayer for his observations.
66. Helgheim, R. 'Garbareks Robeson-pris', *Klassekampen*, Oslo 18/11/92. Of course, Garbarek is aware that that there are many levels of "understanding", in life as a whole as well as music. The use of the term 'Esperanto' as a metaphor may raise a question in some minds: the question of the value of what is being said within such a language as (some of) the music which Garbarek plays today. For example, in terms of sales, Garbarek's **Visible World** has been a very successful record. However, some critics have asked whether this record - the premise of which was to collect together some of the many pieces of music that Garbarek has made for film - is not a little too near the "easy listening" category for comfort. See e.g. Jenssen, H. L. 'Kunst - eller lydkulisse?' (Art - or background music?) *Dagens Naeringsliv*, Oslo 23/3/96. As Jenssen suggests, when you create film-oriented music like that on **Visible World**, there may be a very thin line between the result being melody of "transcendent beauty" - or simply functioning as pleasant background atmosphere. I think **Visible World** was a brave project, albeit flawed in places (such as the over-long development of the three-part *Distant Mountains*). There are some memorable compositions, particularly from the *Mangas Colorados* suite, and plenty of superb playing from Garbarek, especially on *Red Wind, The Creek* (with its soaring upper-register soprano lines in the bridge melody) and *Evening Land* (a long, episodic piece with Mari Boine, featuring both staggered, sampled percussion and - eventually - some extreme, high register tenor from Garbarek). There is also the opportunity, on *The Scythe*, to hear Garbarek play the Meraaker clarinet, which featured in the folk music of the Trøndelag area in Norway from *c.* 1770 to the 1930s. (See **Folkemusikk frå Trøndelag** GRAPPA GRCD 4069). One track, *Pygmy Lullaby*, has always struck me as something of a curiosity, in that its melody, developed in part

over a strongly rocking groove, does not sound much like anything from the Pygmy world that one can hear, for example, on **Echoes Of The Forest: Music of the Central African Pygmies** (Ellipsis Arts 4020). In Norway in the autumn of 1998 the issue of provenance was raised about the piece: was it "a traditional African melody", as stated on the sleeve, or in fact a melody from Samoa, on the other side of the world? The latter is apparently the case. The mistake occurred, perhaps, because of the attribution of the melody to Africa on the 1992 **World Mix** album by Deep Forest, where a sleeve-note speaks of "the ancestral wisdom of African chants" and the need to save the culture of the African Pygmies. Garbarek, who was introduced to the melody by his daughter Anja, may have read of the piece's provenance here. See Ronsen, A. 'Slurvete av Garbarek & ECM' (Careless of Garbarek & ECM) in _Dagbladet_, Oslo 15/9/98. If this is the case, it is a most unusual and isolated episode.

67. Ibid (Helgheim).

68. In October 1997 I visited Propstei Gerold, a small ensemble of buildings which, following a period of neglect in the 1940s, were beautifully restored in the mid-1960s, on the site of the original Romanesque church. The Franciscan-like simplicity of Propstei Gerold could not contrast more with the Baroque opulence of much of the Abbey Ottobueren, not much distance away in Southern Germany, where Keith Jarrett recorded the 1976 **Hymns, Spheres** and 1980 **Invocations** . At discreet (and discrete) moments, the plain white of the interiors at Propstei Gerold is set of by soft-coloured, but striking, primitivistic wall paintings by Ferdinand Gehr (1896 - 1996) - as in the wooden-roofed main hall, relatively small in dimensions, but harmoniously proportioned, in which **Officium** was recorded. Some eight hundred metres above sea level, Propstei Gerold has for many years been host to a successful variety of music concerts, including classical chamber music and contemporary jazz. The intitiative for this has come from Father P. Nathanael Wirth, who first came to Propstei Gerold in 1958. My gratitude to Betty Keller and Father Nathanael Wirth for the considerable kindness and consideration which they showed me during my visit to Propstei Gerold.

69. Sleeve-note to **Officium**

70. Ibid.

71. Ibid.

72. Sleeve-note to **Officium**.

73. Over a period of some three and a half years, I have heard **Officium** performed in King's College Chapel, Cambridge; the cathedrals of Salisbury, Canterbury and St. Paul's; and concerts halls in Birmingham (Symphony Hall) and London (the Royal Festival Hall and the Barbican). The spatial and dynamic aspects of the performance in a cathedral are striking, and the way in which the repertoire of the concerts has evolved, embracing both archaic and twentieth-century works, no less so. However, at the last concert I attended - at the Barbican, London in December 1997 - I had the distinct feeling that the concert would have been more rewarding had Garbarek "sat out" for more numbers than he did, thus increasing the contrasting, yet

complementary dynamic effect of his voice when heard in the full ensemble. In April 1998 the Hilliard Ensemble and Garbarek travelled to Propstei Gerold to record again.

74. _Time Out_ September 14-21 1994.
75. _The Wire_ October 1994.
76. 'Chant Chic', _Village Voice_ 18/10/94. _Down Beat_'s John Corbett suggested that "Garbarek is generally too high in the mix, overpowering the singers, and more often than not adds a syrupy, incongruous romanticism." _Down Beat_ November 1994. For a critical Norwegian review, sub-headlined "samarbeid med The Hilliard Ensemble har endt i musikalsk kitsch' (collaboration with the Hilliard Ensemble has resulted in musical kitsch) see Saetre, E. M. 'Garbareks stemmer' _Morgenbladet_, Oslo 4/8/94. See also Barker, J. 'Point of View', _American Record Guide_ March/April 1995, which begins with the warning: "Bad taste is abroad in the land." Barker underlines the dangers of anachronism - "the heavy-handed combination of totally disparate musical mentalities from totally different epochs or cultures". However, **Officium** (which Barker found the most genuinely interactive of the various time-crossing discs he discussed) is anything but heavy-handed. One wonders what Barker would make of the 1997 **Extempore** (LINN CKD 076) by Orlando Consort and Perfect Houseplants. Here, widely different textures and rhythms are deliberately juxtaposed, with any initial echoes of **Officium** dispelled through the introduction, for example, of drum-textured ostinato rhythms somewhat reminiscent of Carl Orff. **Extempore** could be seen as a Post-modernist response to the Modernist **Officium**: see my review in _Jazz Journal International_ July 1998 pp. 38-9. See also the 1993-97 recording by the Kronos Quartet: **Early Music (Lachrymae Antiquae)** Nonesuch 7759 76457 2.
77. Potter op. cit.
78. Leeuw op. cit. pp. 220-21.
79. Ibid. p. 216.
80. See the discussion of Campbell in Tucker 1992 op. cit. (_Dreaming With Open Eyes_) pp. 43-4, 103-4 and 332-4. For Campbell, there was all the difference in the world between holding onto ancient forms, in the spirit of either neurosis or academicism, and discovering _afresh_ those aspects of the trans-temporal realm which Campbell believed to be encoded in mythology, symbolism and art. Campbell spoke of the necessity of having the courage to let go of the fixed forms of the past. However, he did not mean to suggest by this that the archetypal energies and aspirations which had once fired those forms were now irrelevant to life. On the contrary: "When you have seen the radiance of eternity through all the forms of time, and it's a function of art to make that visible to you, then you have really ended life in the world as it is lived by those who think only in the historical terms. This is the function of mythology [..]". Quoted in Cousineau 1990 op. cit. (_The Hero's Journey: Joseph Campbell on His Life and Work_) p. 155. A key idea in Campbell is the distinction between the "tough-minded" mentality of those so-called "realists" who live only within the daily-driven round of historical time and socio-political events and the

"tender-minded" mentality of those creative spirits able to transcend the immediate frameworks of history, and move within that mytho-poeic sphere which might help one become ever more "transparent to the transcendent". For the poetic and political importance of Campbell's views here, see Tucker 1992 op. cit. (_Dreaming With Open Eyes_) passim. **Officium** is one of the finest "tender-minded" projects of recent years.

81. For Campbell, the "embodied" nature of art made it the great vehicle of such transformative energy. There was no contradiction in the idea of the sensuous summoning the spiritual: "The artist with a craft remains in touch with the world; the mystic can spin off and lose touch and frequently does. And so it seems to me that art is the higher form." This thought was inspired by a remark about the craft of art by Campbell's wife Jean, a dancer of distinction. Cousineau op. cit. p.139.

82. Leeuw op. cit. p. 227.

83. Ibid. p. 228. As Espen Mineur Saetre points out in his August 1994 _Morgenbladet_ review of **Officium**, the idea of bringing vocal church music and an instrumental voice together within the Western tradition is not new: Saetre cites Schutz's deployment of organ and voice. Nevertheless, the tensions (both implicit and explicit) within the words of Chrysostom and Gregory have been - and for many remain - very real.

84. In socio-political terms, the project would have been even more radical had a woman played the saxophone parts. However, see Chapter One for the Taoist-like tenderness - the anima - in Garbarek's music, a quality which transcends any idea of "gendered" creativity. While praising the record, my _Jazz Journal International_ review of November 1994 wondered why the Latin texts of **Officium** had not been translated (as such texts had on most previous New Series releases). In retrospect, I can appreciate that the lack of such translation could be seen to reinforce the radical nature of the project, focusing one's attention on the purely musical and spiritual aspects of the material. Nevertheless, I think this was a mistake, reducing the total potential experience of the record for many (including myself) and leaving ECM open to the charge (however unfair in reality) of intellectual snobbery. On the healing effect of Gregorian chant, see Goldman, J. _Healing Sounds: The Power of Harmonics_ Element, Shaftesbury 1994 pp. 51 & 75-76 and Steindl-Rast, D. (with S. Lebell) _The Music Of Silence: Entering The Sacred Space Of Monastic Experience_ HarperSanFrancisco 1995 (with CD **Chant** by the Benedictine Monks of Santo Domingo de Silos).

85. _CD Review_ October 1994. In late 1996, Garbarek took part in another radical project with voices, albeit one that only lasted some fifteen minutes. In connection with the Nobel Peace Prize ceremony in Oslo, it has become customary to have a celebratory musical concert. As part of the 1996 event at the National Theatre, Oslo Garbarek played soprano saxophone (on three numbers) with the Bulgarian women's choir which, founded in 1952, first came to the wider attention of Europe in the late-1970s and early 1980s as Le Mystère

des Voix Bulgaires. Garbarek has long appreciated the many qualities of this wonderful choir, with its very special, dynamically rich techniques of voice production (tones produced in the nose and the throat, supported by the startlingly clear resonance of overtones, with no tempering of intervals in the Western sense, and an assured, melismatic grasp of both the smallest and largest intervals). I am grateful to Jan Horne for making a video of this event available to me. Misha Alperin has worked and recorded with this choir: see contextual discography.

86. Dybo 1996 op. cit. pp. 73-4 and 133.
87. Garbarek expressed this thought to the artist Lea Andrews in November 1984, during the course of Andrews' research for his final year essay 'The Path: From Melancholy To Euphoria – Aspects of Nordic Creativity' which was submitted as part of his BA (Hons) degree in Fine Art at Brighton Polytechnic. Over the years, Garbarek has made similar remarks to myself. It is interesting to reflect upon how deeply the world of the "forest archetype" is present in Norway's remarkable stave churches: buildings which speak of earth and sky, consciousness and the unconscious, the pagan and the Christian, even East and West. See Lindholm, D. _Stave Churches in Norway: Dragon Myth and Christianity in Old Norwegian Architecture_ (trans. S. & A. Bittleston) Rudolf Steiner Press, London 1969.

GARBAREK
GISMONTI
HADEN

10 April	MANCHESTER	Royal Northern College of Music
11 April	LIVERPOOL	Everyman Theatre
12 April	LEEDS	Playhouse
13/14 April	LONDON	Shaw Theatre
15 April	NOTTINGHAM	Co-op Centre Hall

Magico Tour, Britain early 1980s

Mystic Vision. The Musician
Alan Davie
(1985 gouache, 60 x 73 cms. collection of the artist)

And The Tree's Heart Filled With Music

In March 1997 Jan Garbarek celebrated his fiftieth birthday. "A wanderer plays on muted strings when he reaches the age of two score years and ten", suggests the enigmatic Knud Pedersen in Knut Hamsun's _The Wanderer_.[1] However, while the music that Garbarek plays today is very different from the free-jazz explorations of his first quartet with Terje Rypdal, Arild Andersen and Jon Christensen, or the flowing modality of the Garbarek/Stenson and Keith Jarrett/Belonging quartets, it is no less potent for that. As the range of music on the 1998 double CD **Rites** (recorded in the month of Garbarek's fifty-first birthday) attests, the passing of the years has seen no dimunition of Garbarek's creativity: of his commitment to finding a path in music that is simultaneously fresh, yet shot through with ancient, archetypal aspects of feeling and form.[2]

That path has long taken Garbarek into different contexts and continents. Over the past decades, few musicians can have worked as hard, and in such different registers: Garbarek's first film commission, for example, came as early as 1970, for the Norwegian Pål Løkkerberg's _Exit_. Since then, he has had a steady flow of work in this field, together with various commissions for ballet and theatre music. Two of these areas of activity – film and ballet – are represented on the 1995 **Visible World**, while, as we have seen, the music on the 1979 **Aftenland**, one of Garbarek's most distinctive recordings, grew out of the improvisations which Garbarek supplied for Norwegian theatre director Edith Roger's production of Ibsen's _Brand_ in 1978. (He has also worked with Roger on music for Shakespeare's _A Midsummernight's Dream_ – interpreted in the early 1970s with Arild Andersen and Jon Christensen – and, in the mid-1980s, Ibsen's _Peer Gynt_. As with _Brand_, the music for _Peer Gynt_ was created by Garbarek alone). A married man, with a strong sense of family values – and an engaging sense of humour – Garbarek has somehow managed to combine all such work with an often-punishing touring schedule. And he has also found the time to write some of the most distinctive compositions in contemporary jazz.[3]

Often, visitors to jazz concerts are (understandably) unaware of just how much stamina – and patience – is required by musicians, in order to keep to a demanding touring schedule and arrive at the concert in time for a decent meal and a sound-check. With the Triptykon Trio in the early 1970s, for example, one particular Scandinavian tour combined school concerts and club appearances, resulting in some forty performances in a fortnight. In the mid-1970s, the touring schedule – and impact – of the Garbarek/Stenson Quartet in Scandinavia was at times such that people spoke (only half-jokingly) of a popularity a touch reminiscent of the Beatles. In the late 1980s, the Jan Garbarek Group, with Lars Jansson (keyboards), Eberhard Weber (bass), and Nana Vasconcelos (percussion), undertook an Arts Council Contemporary Music Network Tour in Britain, three weeks of concerts in America and Canada, and a wide range of concerts in Europe. By the mid-1990s, it was not untypical for a European tour of the Jan Garbarek Group, now with Rainer Brüninghaus (keyboards), Eberhard Weber (bass), and Marilyn Mazur (drums and percussion) to criss-cross Britain, Scandinavia and practically the whole of Europe, taking in some fifty-plus dates in a couple months.

Why work so hard? The obvious answer might be: if a living has to be made, why not make it a good one? However, to offer such a response would be to overlook a key factor in Garbarek's music: namely, the extent to which Garbarek is genuinely driven, as perhaps but one or two other musicians of his generation have been, to explore the manifold worlds that lie within improvised music.

Outside Norway, not many people know that the young Garbarek once played with Ray Charles, when the legendary singer's tenor player fell ill just before a late-1960s date in Oslo. And how many of Garbarek's legions of ECM fans could imagine him in the saxophone section of a punchy Oslo octet, contributing baritone – or bass sax – weightiness to a variety of highly danceable, Stax-like riffs? Yet this he did, when he was part of the ensemble which, together with singer Earl Wilson, recorded such soul classics as *Knock on Wood* and *Cold Sweat* on the 1970 **Live At The Studio** album.[4] Three further examples should suffice to indicate the catholic breadth of commitment which Garbarek has always brought to music.

In July 1969 Garbarek was part of a fine quartet, with Karin Krog, Arild Andersen and Jon Christensen, which made a pleasingly varied radio broadcast of both near- r'n' b and post-bop material (including Frank Foster's and Jon Hendricks' *Shiny Stockings*) with Swedish pianist and organist Berndt Egerbladh (who contributed the funky *The Beatmaker* to the date).[5] Two years later, Garbarek could be found, along with Arild Andersen and Jon Christensen, in the Dizzy Gillespie Workshop Big Band at the Kongsberg Jazz Festival, where the material included such bebop classics as *Manteca*, *Con Alma* and *Ray's Idea*. On July 18th of the same year, in the company of Terje Rypdal, Palle Danielsson and Jon Christensen, Garbarek recorded the atmospheric, dynamically provocative piece *Salamanderdans* with the Nordic Big Band, in Södertalje, Sweden. Among other Nordic luminaries, this aggregation featured Palle Mikkelborg and Juhani Aaltonen, Jesper Thilo and Heiki Sarmanto.[6]

Of course, Garbarek is not the musician – and the name – that he is today because of a talent for playing gospel and r'n'b charts, ballads and bebop, or even challenging big band music. The Garbarek of today is the person who has carved out a reputation for himself as one of the great melodists in jazz – and, indeed, music as a whole. Manfred Eicher has observed to me that, in his opinion, what Garbarek achieves in his finest improvisations is the equivalent in quality of any composition from the world of so-called "serious" or "art" music that one might care to name.[7] Remembering the time he spent in the Jan Garbarek Group of the late 1980s, the Swedish pianist Lars Jansson (born 1951) has spoken to me of what he felt to be the chamber music quality in the repertoire (much of which was drawn from the 1986 **All Those Born With Wings**). Jansson remembers "a very strong feeling of concentration and discipline in the music, which – despite the 'ethnic', or world-folkish aspects in much of what we played – often made me think of the qualities of string quartet music."[8]

In the early 1980s, the Norwegian classical violinist Arve Tellefsen commissioned a composition from Garbarek, which he has subsequently played often at his concerts. Titled *Peace*, it was played by Garbarek (on soprano and piano) as *4th Piece* on **All Those Born With Wings**.[9] For several years now, Tellefsen has invited Garbarek and his group (with Weber, Brüninghaus and Mazur) to appear at the Oslo Chamber Music Festival which he organises each summer. There could hardly be clearer testimony to the genre-crossing qualities of the refined, yet penetrating concept of both melody and group interaction which, over the years, a variety of Garbarek's groups have embraced with both discipline and distinction.

If the spirit of Apollo has often been foremost here, particularly in recent years, that does not mean that Dionysus has been exiled. Far from it, as the rollicking, cajun-like grooves of the 1998 *It's High Time* furnish particular and irresistible evidence.[10] The range of music on **Rites** – think only of the difference between the ostinato, bass- and piano-driven pulse of *Her Wild Ways*, the Taoist poise of *One Ying for every Yang* and the mellow, rolling affirmation of the multi-tracked modulations in *Where The Rivers Meet* – is testimony to Garbarek's continuing ability to offer listeners what he once called "a variety of rooms" into which they might travel while listening to his music.[11] For many years now, no matter how different those rooms (or moods) might be, the music that propels the engaged listener either towards or through them has been created with a maximum of economy.

The saxophonist Andy Sheppard recalls being backstage after a Garbarek concert in Britain in the late 1980s and hearing Garbarek answer, with great patience, a question which was something on the lines of, "why don't you play the sort of busier, more complicated or jazzy things that you used to?"[12] In an essay on 'Sibelius, Nielsen and the Symphonic Problem', the British composer Robert Simpson once observed of Sibelius how, in the chaste, modal beauty of the *Sixth Symphony*, "The great and progressive effort of will by which he [Sibelius] cut away all inessentials was itself a strengthening of the personality. The gestures may not be so large [as in such earlier work as the *Second Symphony*] but the glance is vastly more penetrating."[13] Whatever the emotional climate of the music he might choose to play now, the same can be said of Garbarek.

In 1990 the director Dorian Supin completed a film about the Estonian composer Arvo Pärt (born 1935). From the 1984 release **Fratres** onwards, Pärt's intensely focused, triad-based (or tintinnabuli) work has been recorded and presented on ECM.[14] It seemed only natural that, at a certain moment in Supin's film, the camera should take us into a studio session where Pärt, Garbarek and Manfred Eicher are seen working together. Over Pärt's simple repeated figures and sustained rubato chords, played on a Yamaha DX7, Garbarek sculpts the sort of distilled tenor melody that – to put the point as simply as possible – takes one towards that "other space" that has been the concern of so many poets of artistic practice, no matter what their particular discipline, this century.[15]

The capacity for melody, says Stravinsky in _Poetics of Music_, is a gift.[16] Writing about the ground-breaking, early-1970s Triptykon Trio of Garbarek, Arild Andersen and Edward Vesala, the writer and producer Steve Lake has spoken of the fact that, no matter how freely generated and improvised the music may have been, the playing of Garbarek already manifested that "songbird lyricism" for which he would later become so known.[17] The presence of Norwegian poet Jan Erik Vold on some of this trio's tours can only have helped the development of such lyricism: it is Vold who is the dedicatee of Garbarek's surreal soprano revisioning of _I'll Be Seeing You_ in his composition _J.E.V._ on the **Triptykon** album.[18]

Arild Andersen and Edward Vesala have each confirmed to me that, no matter how "free" the music became, one of the chief priorities of the Triptykon period was indeed to keep – and build upon – a sense of melody. This they often did through the challenging medium of the so-called "free ballad". Vesala is a master of creating and sustaining tension at slow tempi (hear the Zen-kissed cross-rhythms and textures he supplies on Tomasz Stanko's 1975 **Balladyna**, for example). Together with Andersen, he would create the sort of surreal trampoline that could propel Garbarek far out into space, while at other moments, Garbarek's rooted accents (perhaps on bass sax) might provide the sort of structural support that encouraged Andersen and Vesala to range far and wide.[19]

Garbarek's work has always been distinguished by the sort of subtly attuned group interaction that one finds on the **Triptykon** recording, as well as by that essential gift of a melodic sensibility that is able to flourish in a diversity of rhythmic settings. In conclusion to this examination of the "deep song" that is Garbarek's oeuvre, it is appropriate to recall several more of the many remarkable contexts wherein Garbarek has manifested the fruits of his belief that – as he put it in an interview of 1970 – no matter how extreme the expressive qualities one might wish to explore in a solo improvisation (fractured sound, or rhythmic and thematic paraphrase, for example), melody should never be neglected.[20]

In his study _Keith Jarrett: The Man and his Music_, Ian Carr rightly makes much of the many qualities of the Belonging Quartet of the 1970s, with Keith Jarrett, Garbarek, Palle Danielsson and Jon Christensen. For Carr, this quartet – which toured in Europe, America and Japan, and recorded two studio and two "live" albums – was one of the finest groups in jazz history. I agree. As Carr's analysis details, the mixture of Jarrett's gospel-soaked energy and hymnal lyricism, and Garbarek's literate jazz power and soulful reflection – the whole fired by a rhythm section which, while keeping a deep groove, was also able to conjure all kinds of cross-rhythms and rubato suspensions – resulted in some exceptional music. Finely balanced, yet exploratory tracks like *Belonging, Blossom, The Windup, 'Long As You Know You're Living Yours* and *Solstice,* from the first LP of April 1974; *Questar, My Song, Country* and *The Journey Home,* from the second studio recording of November 1977; *Chant of the Soil,* from the Village Vanguard, "live" **Nude Ants** of 1979, and the title track of **Personal Mountains,** the Tokyo "live" album from the same year, are all touchstones of contemporary jazz.[21]

So, in my view, are the three albums which the Jan Garbarek/ Bobo Stenson Quartet recorded in the 1970s, with the same rhythm section as the Belonging quartet: the November 1973 **Witchi-Tai-To,** November 1975 **Dansere** and September 1977 **Ingentings Bjeller** (the last with Jan Erik Vold). I never saw the Belonging Quartet live (although, thanks to the kindness of Jon Christensen, I have been able to enjoy the Spring 1974 German T.V. broadcast which the quartet gave shortly before recording **Belonging.** The programme reveals the immediate, special empathy which the quartet enjoyed: besides the material which would be recorded shortly on **Belonging,** the performance features *Mandala* – which would not be recorded until the **My Song** date of 1977). However, I count myself extremely fortunate to have heard the Garbarek/ Stenson Quartet, at something near its peak, in the summer of 1976 in Oslo.

Played with power and finesse, the music of this democratically open quartet could be both cool and (very) hot. The quartet had a sure sense of form – often, but not exclusively, modal – combined with an ability (and desire) to push form as far as possible. Deeply grounded in the Afro-American tradition, the music also projected a folk-like freshness and spiritual atmosphere which, it seemed, could only be Scandinavian (even though the quartet might be floating over the Indian fantasy-drones of a Carla Bley tune like *AIR (All India Radio),* grooving hard on McCoy Tyner's *Passion Dance* or digging deep, *à la* Pharoah Sanders, into the rubato reveries of Don Cherry's *Desireless).*

When **Witchi-Tai-To** came out in 1974, I remember playing it again and again, affected above all by the clarity and the depth, the questing melodic penetration and the rhythmic intensity in the music. Much as Garbarek was a main element here, I was equally impressed by the mobile, full-toned strength of Palle Danielsson (born 1946) and the shimmering, bar-slipping accents of Jon Christensen. And I was no less struck by the sensitive touch, lyrical taste and rhythmic power of pianist Bobo Stenson.

Born into a musical family in Västerås, Sweden in 1944, Stenson was playing seriously by the time he was twelve. Early influences included Wynton Kelly and Red Garland, as well as Bud Powell and Bobby Timmons, but McCoy Tyner and Bill Evans were to be Stenson's eventual favourites. An admirer of Jan Johansson – "the greatest ever in this country" according to Stenson – the young pianist came to Stockholm in the mid-1960s, called there by one of Sweden's potentially major, but tragic figures: tenor saxophonist Börje Fredriksson (1937 – 68). A distinctive player, whose combination of Coltrane-like authority and folk-inflected lyricism anticipates certain aspects of Garbarek's aesthetic, Fredriksson committed suicide. This was partly because of what musicians euphemistically call "personal problems", and partly because of an increasingly depressed feeling that people could not see beyond his origins in Coltrane to the originality that in fact lay within his own sound and phrasing.[22]

If Fredriksson confirmed Stenson's liking for Coltrane, so did Bernt Rosengren, with whom Stenson has subsequently played on many occasions – and whom he admires not just for his playing, but for the many years he has put into the organisational side of jazz in Sweden. At the same time, the continuing impact of cool school figures like Jan Johansson and Lars Gullin (Stenson was to play with the latter several times in the 1970s) kept a feeling for folk melody very much in his fingertips. By the time Stenson met Don Cherry in the late 1960s, when the trumpeter was often in Stockholm, he was entirely open to Cherry's various excursions into folk music from around the world. Among other numbers, Cherry taught Jim Pepper's peyote vision chant *Witchi-Tai-To* to Stenson, who later brought the piece into the Garbarek/Stenson repertoire – as he did McCoy Tyner's *Passion Dance*.[23]

From their extremely well-received debut at the Warsaw Jazz Festival in November 1973, through to their last appearances together in Bergen in 1979 (when they realised that, musically, they had begun to go their separate ways), the Garbarek/Stenson Quartet was one of the major groups of the decade, helping to establish all participants as considerable international figures.[24] At times, they worked intensively – and extensively – with the poet Jan Erik Vold. As I have remarked elsewhere in this book, their collaboration with this melodic-voiced, Zen-touched and jazz-loving artist on the 1977 **Ingentings Bjeller** (Nothing's Bells) is one of the finest of all poetry-meets jazz projects. It includes floating, enigmatic meditations from Vold, a spacious, limpid arrangement of some Satie by Stenson, multi-toned percussion from Christensen and deep, yet gliding bass melodies and root figures from Danielsson. The medium-slow *Slike Dine Dager Er* (So Are Your Days), which flows out of Stenson's Satie arrangement, contains one of Garbarek's finest-ever tenor solos: a lifetime's longing distilled into sixty three seconds of that "transcendental" melody that Stravinsky so prized.[25]

In the two decades or so that have passed since this recording – recently reissued on CD by Pan Records, Norway – the melodic aspect of Garbarek's work has become ever more apparent. One factor here is Garbarek's own development; another is the fact that, for most of those two decades, Eberhard Weber has played bass in every one of Garbarek's groups. As any one of the various solo and group projects which he has recorded for ECM will attest, Weber (born 1940) is one of the most remarkable melodists that jazz has ever seen. He also possesses a fine harmonic imagination, with a rhythmic dynamism to match. Together, he and Garbarek have shaped one of the great partnerships in jazz, refiguring the ways in which the simple and the complex, the melodic and the rhythmic might inform each other. As demonstrated by the fragile, haunting phrases of a composition like Weber's *The Last Stage of a Long Journey* (which the Garbarek group used to play in concert) or the almost Gregorian clarity and dignity of a track like *Part Three* of Weber's 1984 **Chorus** (on which Garbarek appears throughout), they are musicians who are consistently able to get to the heart of things.[26]

Manfred Eicher is fond of Valéry's remark: "Nothing is as mysterious as clarity". The truth of such an insight might be illustrated by any one of (literally) dozens of Garbarek performances over the years. One thinks of compositions like *Blue Sky* (with its lovely, airy melody set high above archetypal, affirmative major thirds) and *White Cloud* from the **Photo With ..** album, where John

Taylor's lyrically focused, rhythmically adroit contributions are so vital. Or one remembers the extraordinary, keening cries of the tenor and the minor-hued melody of the (synthesised) strings in *1st Piece*, the elegaic, abstracted meditations of *3rd Piece*, the rubato yearning of *4th Piece* and the desolate plangency of *6th Piece*, all from **All Those Born With Wings**. Further, chief candidates for consideration here include *Song Of Space* and *Close Enough For Jazz* from **Sart**, *Krusning* (Water Ripples) from **Dis**, *Tegn* (Sign) from **Aftenland**, *Kite Dance* and *Still*, from **Paths, Prints**, *He Comes From The North*, *Send Word* and *Mirror Stone*, from **Legend Of The Seven Dreams**, *Molde Canticle* from **I Took Up The Runes** (which <u>Wire</u> reviewer Mike Fish called Garbarek's *A Love Supreme*) and *Star* from the January 1991 album of that title.[27]

Any Garbarek enthusiast will have his or her own favourite moments of that "mysterious clarity" which this musician has long pursued with such refined intensity. In recent years, some of the most striking of all such moments, for me at least, have come from Garbarek's contributions to Miroslav Vitous's 1992 **Atmos** and Swiss violinist Paul Giger's **Alpstein** album of 1990-91. In particular, there is one piece on the latter album – the thirteen and a half-minute *Karma Shadub* – which, while not a Garbarek composition as such, epitomises the "deep song" that is Garbarek's art.

The duo performance of Giger and Garbarek on *Karma Shadub* is remarkable on several accounts. In the present context, what is especially noteworthy is the extent to which the magnificent tenor solo which Garbarek wraps over and around Giger's solo violin line is absolutely archetypal – in a double sense of the word. For here we can hear both a quintessential Garbarek solo, delivered in the classic dynamic arc of his fundamentally "arching" expression, and music which, from the psychological point of view, is about as archetypal as one might ever wish.

When I played this quietly – but insistently – driving music to the Swedish double-bassist Lars Danielsson, he was initially impressed by the sheer technical command of Giger's violin playing. (At the beginning of the piece Giger offers a solo outline of both the main "body" and the attendant harmonics of the ostensibly minimalist theme, with wrist-testing precision.) As Garbarek's tenor slowly eased – or rather, etched – its way into the picture, Danielsson became intrigued by the subtle but potent change in the emotional temperature of the music – by the alchemy the two voices had begun to create together.[28]

The piece stimulated a similar reaction from musician and lecturer Rod Paton when I played it to him. Subsequently, Rod has listened to *Karma Shadub* again and again. His comments on the music, offered in the spirit of both musicological and (Jungian) psychological analysis, are extremely interesting: "The aspects of psychic or mythic narrative which emerge in this piece are fascinating. The constant, unrelenting life-force which drives the music forward should not be confused with any standard idea of a 'minimalist' frame: the piece conjures a vast inner space with extraordinary concision, and offers an exemplary canvas of the potentiality of expression. The modality of the piece is Aeolian, based on the A of the pulsating life-beat of the initial violin note, but the music also operates on a lower level, dropping to the Dorian mode on G . It is on this mode that the saxophone enters, right into the root of Giger's chord, before then leaping up a fifth. It's like an energising anima spirit conjoining with the animus of the violin and enriching it. The saxophone envelops the violin with feeling, desire, passion, softness – wetness, even: all of the attributes a psychologist would associate with the image of the soul-bird. Eventually, the violin is abandoned to its solo fate – its aloness (all-one-ness) – and it returns (with exquisite poise, but not without some effort) to the unison A with which it began, climbing to the leading note (G sharp). This is the only time in the piece that we hear this tone, inducing thoughts about how we have chosen to define tonality (the opening A – 440hz – is the tuning note of European music) – and thus stimulating further thoughts about beginnings and endings, resolutions and transformations, in both music and life."[29]

Although the music is in Giger's name, the images of "vast inner space" and "soul-bird" which Rod Paton introduces here could not be more appropriate. For what is it that Jan Garbarek's melodic gift, his increasing concentration on the song-like essentials of melody and rhythm, have brought to music in such enriching measure, if not the twin factors of deep space and empathetic, world-bridging qualities of anima, or soul?

Space, vast space, said Gaston Bachelard, is the friend of being. But how do we come to understand, or experience it as such? By realising, said Bachelard, that in this life, we were meant to breathe freely.[30] Breathing freely, responding to the living pulse in the music that is the "deep song" of life, we open ourselves up to that potentially transformative state which Rilke celebrated in his poem *Moving Forward*, from the <u>*Book of Pictures*</u>. Feeling that he had come closer to the mystery of painting, to what language could not reach, Rilke spoke of how "the deep parts" of his life were pouring onward, " as if the river shores were opening out." With his senses, "as with the birds", the poet climbs "into the windy heaven, out of the oak", while, "in the ponds broken off from the sky", his feeling sinks, " as if standing on fishes".[31]

Simile, metaphor, image: all here deployed, not in that self-conscious (and often self-congratulatory) "language-commenting-on-language" manner of much writing today, but in the expansive, totalising spirit of shamanic *participation mystique*. Rimbaud, the explosive poet-*voyant* of the last century, believed that the flight of metaphor could change the world. And so, one must hope – in the spirit of Dizzy Gillespie or John Coltrane – might the magic of music. In a world threatened more and more by that nightmare which so-called primitive cultures have always been quick to recognise as the ultimate threat to their existence – loss of soul – the musician's potentially inspiring and ensouling role is as crucial today as it was to the shamans and their various communities, or tribes, of ten thousand years ago.[32]

In his collection <u>*Shaking The Pumpkin: Traditional Poetry Of The Indian North Americas*</u>, Jerome Rothenberg offers a lovely story – a peyote creation myth – of how the violin was born: "CEDAR, CEDAR was born./Born among stones and rocks [...] But CEDAR CEDAR didn't have a soul./Heavy was his heart. His heart was silent./Then Tahomatz the BIG BRAIN/sent Aimari the BIRD [..]/Aimari came singing: entered the tree/& became its pith./And the tree's heart filled with music./& CEDAR CEDAR sang. Quivered to caresses from the wind."[33] When Garbarek is asked, as he often is, for whom he writes or improvises the music he plays, his answer is always the same: the single, solitary listener. Today, there are many such listeners to his music. As Garbarek has "come singing" into people's lives, what else has he done but touch their souls? Lars Jansson still meets people – including musicians – who speak with special affection of the concert which the Jan Garbarek Group (with Jansson on piano and keyboards) gave at Copenhagen's Jazzhus Montmartre over a decade ago: a concert which left more than a few people in tears.[34]

Jan Erik Vold worked with Garbarek, off and on, for practically a decade. When I asked Vold recently what was so special about Garbarek, he replied: "The fact that he is an artist, first and foremost – that he has always had a vision of what it is that he wants to do in music. And he has been prepared to work very hard to realise that vision. He's had this special quality for a long time now. Thirty or more years ago, in fact, it was already there ... He's always been very self-directed – which means, among other things, knowing what it is that he *doesn't* want. Jan is not at all keen on the idea of re-union concerts or tours, for example. For those of us in Norway who knew him back in the 1960s, his fame today is no surprise. Through a deep belief in the possibilities of music, Jan's always been on the way to something special."[35]

In August 1998 Jan Garbarek received the highest honour of Norwegian culture: the Order of St. Olav, which was given to Garbarek at a level equivalent to a British knighthood. Although Arve Tellefsen had received the award some years earlier, this was the first time that a jazz musician had been so honoured. (Now that a precedent has been set, it would be nice to think that Karin Krog, who over the years has done such a considerable amount for Norwegian jazz, might receive similar recognition.) Naturally, such an honour speaks in the most resonant terms of the extent of Garbarek's contribution to music. But so too do the words – and the music – of all the many musicians who, one way or another, have come to acknowledge Garbarek as the major, innovative figure that he is in improvised music.[36]

Over the years, several musicians have paid explicit, recorded homage to Garbarek. In 1973 for example, on the solo **I'm Here** release on the Finnish Blue Master label, Edward Vesala recorded his forest-deep, shaman-touched *Homage To Jan Garbarek*. At the beginning of the 1980s, the Swedish-Norwegian Spring Quintet opened their eponymous album (which came with an encomium from George Russell) with a very different, much more urban tribute: saxophonist Stefan Grahn's driving, medium-up tempo *Til Jan G.* (To Jan G.)[37] Since then, Garbarek has been the recipient of a wide variety of indirect, but nonetheless unmistakeable tributes.

In Norway, the influence of Garbarek is especially evident today, not just because of the quality of the sound which he has achieved on the saxophone, but through his whole concept of making music with much more to it than "blowing on changes". The "singing" quality which Nils Petter Molvær once remarked in Garbarek's work on **Belonging** is evident in a good deal of contemporary Norwegian jazz: in musicians as diverse as Molvær himself and saxophonists Bendik Hofseth, Tore Brunborg and Karl Seglem, pianists Jon Balke and Jan Gunnar Hoff, and drummer Terje Isungset, for example. Recorded on Seglem's Nor-CD label, Isungset's 1997 **Reise** (Journey) is typical here. Together with trumpeters Arve Henrikesen, Per Jørgensen and Nils Peter Molvær, Isungset (who builds his own percussion instruments) shapes a mythically engaging journey though a suite of nine striking, Nordic-inflected compositions.[38]

Born the year (1961) that Garbarek chanced to hear Coltrane playing *Countdown* on the radio, the tenor saxophonist Karl Seglem has taken the sound of the saxophone that Garbarek opened up for subsequent generations, and the use of folk sources, into some potent (and moving) areas of expression. For Seglem, the Garbarek of the early and mid-1970s has been of especial importance: a combination of free yet disciplined energy and a "songbird lyricism" is very much apparent in Seglem's art. Regarding the latter quality, the beautifully paced and highly atmospheric tenor solo on the children's rhyme *So Ro Rela*, from the 1992-93 **Rit** (Rite) – where Seglem is joined by such characterful, contemporary musicians as Reidar Skår (keyboards, sampling), Berit Opheim (vocal) and Terje Isungset – is exemplary. Like the Isungeset recording, such a piece reveals how much Garbarek has encouraged Norwegian improvisers to explore their own heritage and imaginal resources, in a fresh variety of ways.[39]

Garbarek's influence can also be clearly felt in some of the many remarkable examples of cross-cultural music which have emerged recently in Norway. Examples might range from the 1994 **Saajve Dans** by Frode Fjellheim's Jazz Joik Ensemble and the 1997 **Song** by the Norwegian-South African group San to **'Mbara Boom**, the extraordinary meeting of the jazz trio of Tore Brunborg, Arild Andersen and Paolo Vinaccia with a Sicilian male choir which was recorded "live" at Oslo's Cosmopolite in March 1996.[40] And while I would not want to push the idea of Garbarek's influence too far, it seems to me that the atmosphere of exploratory and affirmative creativity which is evident today on such a distinguished Norwegian label as Kirkelig Kulturverksted (for which Garbarek originally recorded the 1988-89 **Rosensfole**) owes a good deal to the example of Garbarek and ECM. To offer only two examples: without Garbarek (and Manfred Eicher, and Jan Erik Vold) it is conceivable that Norwegians might not have been able to enjoy such arresting music on the Kirkelig Kulturverksted label as Kari Bremnes' **Løsrivelse** (Parting) – a haunting setting of various texts by Edvard Munch, with arrangements by Ketil Bjørnstad – and **"prøv å sette vinger på en stein"** (try to put wings on a stone), a poignant interpretation of the work of the much-loved Norwegian "poet of the forest" Hans Børli (1918-89) by (the late) Katja Medbøe (voice), Eivind Aarset (guitar), Per Jørgensen (trumpet), Edvard Askeland (bass) and Paolo Vinaccia (percussion).[41]

Outside Norway, Garbarek's influence is scarcely less evident. As evinced by much of a record like the 1992-94 **Flower In The Sky**, the fine Swedish saxophonist Jonas Knutsson (who has appeared on ECM with Ale Möller, Lena Willemark and Palle Danielsson) would seem to have lent a discriminating ear to various aspects of Garbarek's melodic and dynamic sense. Scotland's Tommy Smith, one of the most imaginative saxophonists and composers active today, has listened to various elements of Garbarek's art with both enthusiasm and an intelligence as well-honed as it is literate. He is one of the few musicians I can think of who is capable of taking such a Garbarek-inflected framework as the trio setting of *Folk Song* (not the 1979 Haden/Garbarek/Gismonti piece, but a Scottish melody) on the 1993 **Reminiscence** – and making the keening, mythopoeic qualities in the unfolding grandeur of the music very much his own. "When I first heard Garbarek", says Smith, "I was astonished by two things: his tenor saxophone sound and his use of space. What's also remarkable is his ability to make the soprano sing like the voice. Most other soprano players sound nasal in timbre: Garbarek sings like an angel. And I really like to hear and see the Garbarek Group live. It's such a beautifully polished show – simple, clear, yet magical like the Northern sky. I love the aura of mystery about Garbarek's band on stage."[42]

The idea of listening to Garbarek and being inspired to find one's own voice is central to Andy Sheppard's estimate of the Norwegian's importance. Like Nils Petter Molvær, Sheppard (born 1957) first encountered Garbarek through the 1974 album **Belonging**, when, in the mid-1970s, friend and pianist Geoff Williams sat him down and introduced Sheppard to what the saxophonist now describes as " a range of music that opened up both my ears and my life, really: Coltrane, Mingus, all the classic stuff – and Garbarek. Obviously, he's been enormously important. Not just to me, of course, but to many players who have come up in the last couple of decades. Like Coltrane, the influence can sometimes work the wrong way – trying too hard to sound like him. But that's not what the example of Garbarek should be about, not at all. He heard Coltrane, Ayler and all the other giants of that time – and had the strength to come up with something that was his own. He suggested an entirely new way of approaching the saxophone as an expressive, even poetic instrument. And he's still looking for ways to deepen, to extend, his own voice. That's the major influence, really, as I see it. The encouragement to go deep into yourself, and to try to find out what is really *your* voice, *your* contribution. And that's not a matter of ego – it's a matter of creativity. And it's a never-ending process."[43]

Sheppard's thoughts were echoed recently by his compatriot, the multi-instrumentalist and composer, John Surman. Like Garbarek, Surman (born 1944) is blessed with both an instantly recognisable sound and a surpassing melodic gift, which he expresses in ways related to, but in essence very different from Garbarek. (Think of how time is caressed through Surman's various uses of repeated patterns, or loops, or of the velvet elasticity of Surman's dynamic range, especially on bass clarinet.) Apart from an appearance together in a European Broadcasting Union Big Band project in the late 1960s, Surman does not recall playing with Garbarek very much at all. However, he sometimes used to appear opposite Garbarek at various festivals, especially during the period when The Trio (Surman himself, bassist Barre Phillips and drummer Stu Martin) was active. Nevertheless, Surman is very conscious of what Garbarek has meant for improvised music: "Like a lot of musicians, I've been aware of Jan for a long time. What can I say? The guy is a complete original. He opened up the whole field of expression for the saxophone, and created that sort of 'Northern landscape' area for others to explore if they wanted to. And then, think of his cross-cultural work, and the range of his compositions. He's both a great saxophonist and an outstanding musician – in the deepest sense of the word."[44]

"Songs", said Orpingalik, a Netsilik Inuit (or Eskimo), "are thoughts which are sung out with the breath when people let themselves be moved by a great force, and ordinary speech no longer suffices."[45] For Roald Helgheim, the Oslo-based Norwegian writer and critic who remembers seeing the Jan Garbarek Quartet win the Norwegian Amateur Jazz Championship in 1962, something of that force has always been in Garbarek's music. Helgheim, who has seen virtually all of Garbarek's working groups live at one time or another, considers that, throughout the years, the integrity of Garbarek's music has been its chief distinguishing factor: "I remember this handsome young man back in the early 1960s, winning the championship with music which was rather different from most of what was being played here at the time. And, ever since, Jan Garbarek has gone his own way. I may prefer certain periods of his work to others – I really liked the energy in the first quartet with Terje Rypdal, for example, and also the Garbarek/Stenson Quartet – but the point is, everything he has done, from the 1960s to now, has been done with total commitment, with integrity. Whether you think of the very special Northern quality he brought into music, the way in which he developed cross-cultural projects, or his collaborations with various singers, from Karin Krog right through to the Hilliard Ensemble – everything has been done in a spirit of real depth."[46]

The same point was made to me recently by Bernt Rosengren, the legendary Swedish tenor saxophonist who was such an inspiration to Garbarek in the early 1960s, and with whom he played in a variety of George Russell's ensembles in the mid-to-late 1960s: "You know, Jan and I didn't talk so much to each other, really. We played! Even then, you could hear that he was going to be special. He was so young, but he already had such good technique. And he was so free in his attitude: already a fine improviser, and very open to different ways in music. I've followed his music since and there have been some great groups. Some people have said that he 'went commercial' with the **Officium** record with the Hilliard Ensemble, but I don't think so. He's always meant what he played. And I like that record, it's very beautiful... Whatever changes the music has gone through, Jan has always remained true to himself."[47]

Music, said Rilke, might be imagined – or imaged – as that "heart space" grown out of us. But music also flows into us, expanding the inner dimensions of our being. It was music, said Gunnar Ekelöf, that had given him "the most and the best things" in life: the music that was built on silence.[48] In a 1934 essay *Under the Dog Star*, Ekelöf proclaimed his faith in mystery, saying that, "I believe in personal religiousness, free from dogma, rites, and gods. No one can force me to believe in anything but myself and what is in me."[49] But what was the most valuable thing within Ekelöf himself? Anticipating the beautiful insight of Tarjei Vesaas that life's deeper moments come when one listens for what one does not understand, Ekelöf wrote: "The only thing that has value for me is what I do not know. It is where my knowledge ends that I begin to live, that I begin to believe."[50]

Perhaps it was in music that Ekelöf – for whom a beautiful church bell meant more than a hymn or a sermon – felt the eternal tension between the (known, or experienced) part and the (mysterious, longed-for) whole of existence sublimated into something uplifting, rather than terrifying. Perhaps it was here that, as he once put the matter, the grief became small, and the joy great: where the many, mingled streams of life could flow with maximum, nourishing intensity.[51] As Ekelöf – like Rilke – knew, between the part and the whole stands death. If our death is not an event in the flow of our daily lives (it ends those lives) that is no reason why meditation on that event should not feed into a (potentially transformative) sense of the deeper, shape-shifting mystery, the mysterious totality of life.[52] Living, we die; dying, we are born. It is all a matter of consciousness – mediated by the great unconsciousness, the great mystery. And it is this mystery which flows through the work of Jan Garbarek: flows, as Ekelöf might have said, *between* the notes, *between* the phrases, *between* the meanings.

In 1943, four years before Jan Garbarek was born, the painter (and musician) Alan Davie (born 1920) wrote in his notebook: "The great works are made from life itself, stripped of superficiality and impurity; they are pure soul and joy, delicately like the delicateness of line across immense mountains."[53] In 1993 I asked Garbarek if he would consider contributing to a book which I was then editing about this extraordinary Scottish polymath, whose vibrant, musically-inflected painting and drawing Garbarek had come to know some years previously. Garbarek agreed to do so, immediately.

There are strong parallels between the two men's shamanically potent work. Both are immensely gifted improvisers, with a strong sense of composition. Both have produced work that is intensely personal, but which also summons the transpersonal. Both have shaped moments that, in our drearily rationalist and often overly theoretical times, speak sensuously of *life*. (Grey is all theory; but green, the Tree of Life, as Goethe said.) Both have produced work strongly redolent of the North, the Celtic, but which also turns towards the East.[54] And just as Davie had the courage to follow his inner voice, abandoning the gesturally free improvisation that brought him to fame in the 1950s and 1960s in order to cultivate a more mythically-oriented, world-ranging quality of composition in his imagery, so has Garbarek had the strength to move away from the (already well-shaped) "stream of consciousness" realms of his earliest achievements, in pursuit of far more melodically (and archetypally) inflected worlds.

What Garbarek wrote in homage to Alan Davie was short, but very much to the point:

> Your mind takes us fast
> and far
> through a borderless landscape
> of dream and symbol.[55]

What else is this landscape but the nourishing, shape-shifting heart of Garbarek's own work: the place where the streams of life might mingle, and the rivers meet? "Music", says Gerardus van der Leeuw in _Sacred and Profane Beauty: the Holy in Art_, "leads us into the depths of life, there where boundaries flee away."[56] Over the past decades, few musicians have sung those depths into the light of consciousness with more clarity and courage than Jan Garbarek.

The Universe Is Discovered Only At The Point Of Balance ...
Alan Davie
(c. 1989, brush drawing on paper, c. 42 x 30 cms. collection of the artist)

Jan Garbarek & Shankar
(Molde Jazz Festival 1985) Randi Hultin

Ralph Towner, John Abercrombie & Jan Garbarek
(Molde Jazz Festival 1977) Randi Hultin

Notes to Chapter Six

1. Hamsun, K. *The Wanderer (Under The Autumn Star & On Muted Strings)* (trans. O. & G. Stallybrass) Condor/Souvenir Press Ltd., London 1975 p. 273.

2. Garbarek has spoken of his search for the *ur*-tone, or primal sound, in the saxophone. See Dybo 1996 op. cit. pp. 137-38. (See also the recently reissued 1962 **Free Fall** by Jimmy Giuffre, Paul Bley and Steve Swallow, an extraordinary recording with titles like *Yggdrasill* and *Primordial Call* featuring some superbly expressive, dynamically volatile clarinet lines, and Diana Reeves' shamanically-inflected *Old Folks* and *Endangered Species* on her 1994 **Art and Survival**: see contextual discography.) In early 1997 Garbarek travelled to Northern India for three weeks, an event which would seem to have left its mark on at least some of the music presented on **Rites**. Here, Bugge Wesseltoft (who appeared on the 1990 **I Took Up The Runes**) contributes some striking passages of electronic textures and rhythm, especially on *Evenly They Danced* and the title track (which is presented twice, at the beginning and end of the album: firstly with Garbarek's soprano saxophone present, and secondly – and somewhat eerily – with it absent). See my review in *Jazz Journal International*, November 1998. Reviewed by John Fordham in October 1998, **Rites** was *The Guardian*'s (five star) CD of the week: *The Guardian*, 9/10/98. Garbarek experimented with electronically generated rhythm on a tour of the USA in June 1986, with drummer Kurt Wortman; following which, Billy Hart became the group's drummer for some German concerts in October and November 1986. Another musician who has had a relatively short stay in the Jan Garbarek group is guitarist Ross Traut, who played with the band in a European concert tour, including the Bracknell Festival, in summer 1983.

3. The interpretation of Garbarek's *Blue Sky* by keyboards player Håkon Graf and guitarist Jon Eberson (with bassist Terje Venaas, who played with Garbarek, briefly, in the early 1970s) on drummer Pål Thowsen's 1979 **Surprise** (NorDisc NORLP 403) is a relatively rare example of a recording of one of Garbarek's compositions by other musicians. Perhaps this is because the character of Garbarek is so intimately – and strongly – woven into those compositions. It is instructive to compare the two versions of *Blue Sky*: the 1978 Garbarek original exhibits more condensed rhythmic and dynamic tension, especially in the way the various melodic lines float across the rhythm. My thanks to Pål Thowsen (and Tor Hammerø) for making the **Surprise** album available to me.

   Dybo 1996 op. cit. p. 154 lists more of Garbarek's work in film and theatre. However, he excludes Garbarek's work with Jon Christensen and guitarist Knut Værnes on Stavros Doufexis' production of Aristophanes' *Lysistrata* at Amfiscenen, National Theatre, Oslo, 1981/2 season.

4. Besides Garbarek the ensemble featured Ditlef Eckhoff (trumpet), Knut Riisnæs (tenor saxophone); Calle Neumann (alto saxophone), Nipe Nyren (electric guitar), Geir Wentzel (organ), Sveinung Hovensjø

(electric bass) and Idar Nordberg (drums). Garbarek pumps out a good bass groove on *Cold Sweat*: perhaps something of this experience came back to him years later, when he played the funky bass saxophone lines in the latter stages of Shankar's *Psychic Elephant*, from the 1983 **Vision**. With its "growling" vocalising in the saxophone, his tenor solo on *All For You*, the opening number here, is a good example of how Garbarek's considerable knowledge of saxophone tradition and techniques has enabled him to draw upon archetypal means of expression, while setting such means in new light.

5. A fine musician, Egerbladh's 1995 **Night Pieces** – with Jan Allan (trumpet), Urban Hansson (soprano saxophone/flute), Mats Oberg (synthesiser); Palle Danielsson (bass) and Egil "Bop" Johansen (drums) – is a lovely record, proof positive that the lyricism of 1950s and 1960s Swedish jazz has the power to captivate today, in a variety of new textures and moods. Titles include *Lars (Lars Gullin in Memory)*, *Clouds in the Night* and *Arctic Night*.

6. At this time Garbarek also worked occasionally in a Scandinavian septet, which played, for example, at the Sogn Jazz Club. Besides Garbarek, the septet featured Palle Mikkelborg (trumpet); Calle Neumann (alto saxophone); Lennart Åberg (tenor saxophone); Heiki Sarmanto (piano); NHØP (bass) and Espen Rud (drums).

7. Personal communication, October 1997.

8. Personal communication, October 1998.

9. Tellefsen's interpretation of *Peace*, in an arrangement by Kjetil Bjerkestrand (keyboards), can be heard on **Intermezzo** (GRAPPA GRCD 4051).

10. I asked bassist Terje Venaas once what memories he had from the time he played with Garbarek: "His power, that's what I remember most. He has quite extraordinary power and control on the saxophone." Personal communication, Oslo *c.* spring 1982. **Rites** shows that power to be undiminished, and the control even greater. Venaas has made a fine record in the folk-jazz field, the 1993 **Toner Fra Romsdal** (Music from Romsdal) – with Ingeborg Hungnes (vocal), Bendik Hofseth (saxophone), Stian Carstensen (accordion) and Jon Christensen (drums). See contextual discography.

11. "I like to go into different rooms during a concert". Brodowski and Szprot 1984 op. cit. ('Mysterious Wayfarer') p 40. Garbarek talks here about his feeling for dynamics, in terms of both a solo (trying to avoid the clichés of climactic expression) and a concert as a whole.

12. Personal communication, October 1998.

13. Simpson, R. *Carl Nielsen: Symphonist* Kahn & Averill, London1979 (first published 1952) p. 193. This is a key essay: one of its central ideas – "Health is a rarer and better thing than sickness, and no-one who has it despises it" – is of especial relevance for much of today's art world.

14. See contextual discography and Hillier, P. *Arvo Pärt* Oxford University Press, Oxford & New York 1997.

15. *What Do You Know About Arvo Pärt?* (A Festi Telefilm, YleisradioTV 1; RM Arts co-production 1990). Dorian was responsible for the script, camerawork and direction of this unusual insight into Pärt's life

and work.
15. See Clark, T. A. 'Poetry And The Space Beyond' in _Poeisis: Aspects of Contemporary Poetic Activity_ The Fruitmarket Gallery, Edinburgh 1992 pp. 37-45. "The old Scottish name for a poet, 'makar', still retained this double sense of making, of fashioning not only a work but a world. To write a poem [or create a piece of music] is not just to make an object which will take its place among other objects but to introduce a structure which will reorder and revalue the existing physical and psychic facts. Whether the space beyond a poem, or around it, is hospitable or inhospitable, remote or contiguous, it is everywhere packed with energy." (p. 45.)
16. Stravinsky op. cit. (_Poetics of Music_) p. 39.
17. Sleeve-essay to **Triptykon** (ECM 1029). This essay gives an excellent picture of the Triptykon Trio.
18. Martin Davidson notes the relation to _I'll Be Seeing You_ in his October 1973 _Jazz Journal_ review of **Triptykon**. Vold has continued to work in the jazz and poetry field, often with pianist Egil Kapstad and Nisse Sandström, the fine Swedish saxophonist. In February 1988 he (Vold) made a particularly striking record with Chet Baker: **Blåmann! Blåmann!** – which also featured Philip Catherine (guitar), Egil Kapstad and Terje Venaas.
19. Vesala had worked with Andersen before their time together in the Triptykon Trio, with Juhani Aaltonen: see the August 1970 **Nana** (Blue Master BLU-LP 125) where the slow tempo/free ballad form is already present.The record contains a version of Andersen's _MY B_, shortly to be recorded on **Afric Pepperbird** as _MYB_. The **Afric Pepperbird** version is one minute fifty seconds, very much distilled when compared to the five-minute, five second recording on **Nana**. The Triptykon Trio worked extremely hard at their music. Edward Vesala recalls that they practised a lot before concerts, and that much time on tours (undertaken in the sort of Volkswagon bus that has become a mythical vehicle to several generations of musicians) was spent discussing the ways in which the music might evolve. These were open-minded musicians, aware of the worlds that lie within worlds: on one of their tours, in Frankfurt, Chick Corea sat in. Personal communication from Edward Vesala, June 1998.
20. Garbarek May 1970 op. cit. (_Jazznytt no. 2_).
21. Carr, I. 1991 op. cit. (_Keith Jarrett_) pp. 74-79 & 87-88. Because Carr deals so thoroughly with the Belonging band (comparing it to Jarrett's American quartet with Dewey Redman, Charlie Haden and Paul Motian for example) I have not felt it either appropriate or necessary to discuss the group in more detail than I do here.
22. Personal communication from Bobo Stenson, June 1998. Following Fredriksson's death, Stenson was entrusted with all his manuscripts: see e. g. the 1993 **Sister Majs Blouse [..] the music of Börje Fredriksson** (Mirrors MICD 002) with Bobo Stenson, Joakim Milder (tenor saxophone), Palle Danielsson (bass) and Fredrik Norén (drums). Fredriksson's slightly hard-edged, emotionally charged tenor can be heard on the memorial album **Börje Fredriksson** (Odeon E 054-34009). Here, Stenson (whose surname was then Stensson) plays piano

throughout, and Palle Danielsson (who played with Fredriksson from 1964 onwards) is also featured strongly. Recorded between 1966 and 1967 in a variety of locations, some of them "live", the selections on the record underline why it is that Stenson feels so strongly about Fredriksson's talent today: "He had everything – a master of music." Tracks like the medium-up-tempo, Coltranish *Blues for Bass* and *Summer in Stockholm*, the funky and relaxed *Go Go Miss Summar*, intricately phrased *Börjes Blues* and poetically compressed *Österländsk folkvisa* (Eastland folk song), *Adagio con expressione* and (especially) *Som et öde hus* (Like a ruined house) confirm what a loss to the jazz world Fredriksson's death was. Palle Danielsson has commented to me that Fredriksson "was searching for the roots, back into Swedish folk music." As far as Stenson knows, the young Garbarek was not aware of Fredriksson.

23. When Cherry came to Stockholm, he met several Swedish musicians who had been in Africa, and who educated Cherry about aspects of African music. One of these, Christer Bothén, presented Cherry with the doussn'gouni which he would play from then on. (Personal communication from Bobo Stenson, June 1998 and Palle Danielsson, October 1998.) For Cherry's playing with some of these musicians, see the 1973 **Eternal Now** and the 1981 Bengt Berger album **Bitter Funeral Beer**.

24. For detail on members of the quartet, and their common listening backgrounds (e.g. Coltrane and Davis) see Dybo 1996 op. cit. pp. 106-10. When the group travelled, they often listened to cassettes of folk music, a factor that also fed into the music of Rena Rama, the Swedish quartet that Stenson and Danielsson played in with Lennart Åberg and either Bengt Berger or Leroy Lowe on drums. (See contextual discography.) It takes nothing away from the brilliance of the Belonging Quartet to suggest that it must have been a little hard for Stenson to see the extent to which that quartet "took off" internationally. A generous-minded man, Stenson has nothing but praise for the Belonging Quartet. However, he confesses that there were times when he thought that "my own group, so to say" had been taken from him. One of the most heartening features of the jazz scene in recent years has been the extent to which Stenson has begun to get more and more of the recognition long due him, especially in his trio with Anders Jormin (bass) and Jon Christensen (drums). See contextual discography.

25. Stravinsky op. cit. suggests that, "If it is easy to define melody, it is much less easy to distinguish the characteristics that make a melody beautiful. The appraisal of a value is itself subject to appraisal. The only standard we possess in these matters depends on a fineness of culture that presupposes the perfection of taste. Nothing here is absolute except the relative." p. 41.

26. But they do this by subtle means. The British drummer John Marshall, who was the drummer in Eberhard Weber's Colours quartet (with Charlie Mariano and Rainer Brüninghaus) after Jon Christensen left in *c.* late 1976, has remarked to me that it was the different perspectives which everyone brought to it, the mixture of European and American

elements, that made playing the music so enjoyable. If the group played something with a Latin feel, for example, they would usually open up or subtly alter the beat so that the piece came out sounding "not quite Latin". "Openness" and "the in-the-gap experience" are terms, or phrases, which Marshall uses to characterise a good deal of the music recorded by Garbarek, Weber and Christensen on ECM. Personal communication, September 1998. In interview, Garbarek has often made the same point about the need for, and value of, different perspectives from the various players in a group.

27. _The Wire_ New Year 1991.
28. Personal communication, October 1997. Since 1985, Danielsson has worked off and on with Stenson and Christensen, and American saxophonist Dave Liebman, in his (Danielsson's) quartet Far North. See contextual discography.
29. Personal communication, June 1998.
30. Bachelard, G. _The Poetics of Space_ (trans. M. Jolas) Beacon Press, Boston 1969 p. 208. For Bachelard, it was essential to remember that "The _being-here_ is maintained by a being from elsewhere." (Ibid.)
31. Rilke, R. M. 'Moving Forward' in _Selected Poems_ (trans. & ed. R. Bly) Harper Colophon Books, Harper and Row, New York 1981 p. 101. See the discussion of Rilke in Tucker 1992 op. cit. (_Dreaming_) pp. 180-83.
32. On soul-loss in the modern world, see Tucker 1992 op. cit. (_Dreaming_) Chapter Four, and Hillman, J. _Anima: An Anatomy Of A Personified Notion_ Spring Books Inc., Dallas 1985.
33. 'How The Violin Was Born: A Peyote Account' in Rothenberg, J. (ed.) _Shaking The Pumpkin: Traditional Poetry Of The Indian North Americas_ Alfred Van Der Marck Editions, New York 1986 p. 308.
34. Personal communication, October 1998. Since his time with Garbarek, Jansson has kept very busy in music, making some fine trio records with Lars Danielsson and Anders Kjellberg, for example. See the contextual discography. In 1998 he took up an innovative post as Professor of Jazz at the Royal Academy of Music, Aarhus, Denmark 35. Personal communication, October 1998.
36. The American saxophonist Michael Brecker, who is sometimes suggested as being perhaps the most influential saxophonist of the last two decades, has warmly acknowledged the utterly distinctive quality and nature of Garbarek's approach. See Hammerø, T. 'Mannen Alle Har Skive Med' (The Man Everyone Has On Their Records) _Puls Furore_, no. 26, Oslo 23/10/96 p. 12. Over the years, Garbarek has received various important Norwegian cultural awards and has usually featured either at or very near the top of various polls in the international jazz press. In 1979, for example, he won the Harald Saeverud Prize and in 1995 he shared the Anders Jahres Culture Prize with singer Ingrid Bjoner. In 1976 Garbarek won _Down Beat_'s Talent Deserving Wider Recognition poll: he has consistently topped the various polls (for best group and record) in _Jazz Forum_. In March 1997 he was "artist of the week" on BBC Radio 3. In August 1998 Niels-Henning Ørsted Pedersen, who has been similarly successful in jazz polls, offered an interesting comparison of the achievement and

aesthetic of Garbarek with his own: "The whole idea of a 'Northern sound' has, unfortunately, become a little 'trendy' now, which I think is a pity. Because in the beginning it was something that emerged quite naturally, whether with members of an earlier generation like Lars Gullin or Jan Johansson, or Jan and myself, Palle [Mikkelborg] and Terje [Rypdal], for example. What Jan has achieved is, of course, remarkable. We played together in the 1960s – we grew up in jazz together, in a way. Now, I would say that what we do can be related, certainly – like on the **Uncharted Land** recording, for example. But I would say that what Jan does tends to cuts deeper than the music I play. His 'message', if I could put it like that, is more demanding, and so maybe more rewarding in the long run – it takes the listener farther 'out' (or 'in')." Personal communication, August 1998. This is a very interesting – and generous minded – observation, from a musician who, more than most, has absolutely no need to indulge in any false modesty. It raises an interesting question: how does one assess the stimulus or satisfaction offered by, say, the "cutting" shamanic reflections of records like **All Those Born With Wings** and **It's OK to listen to the gray voice** against the more sociable humanism of records such as NHØP's recent **Those Who Were** and **This Is All I Ask?** Fortunately, we can enjoy both modes of expression: and while I very much take NHØP's point, I would say that his moving tribute to Kenny Drew, for example, is as deep, in its own way, as anything that Garbarek has recorded. (See *Kenny* on **Scandinavian Wood** and the title track of **Those Who Were**.)

37. In 1998 Vesala wrote to me about his various experiences of playing with Garbarek. His letter ended with the comment, "Jan Garbarek is one of the finest persons I've ever met. I mean, also outside the music. If a person is good outside the music, he is also good in the music." Personal communication, June 1998. Vesala's estimation has been echoed – unsolicited – by every musician I have spoken to who has worked with Garbarek.

38. See contextual discography.

39. Personal communication from Karl Seglem, October 1998.

40. See contextual discography.

41. Of course, none of this is to detract from the integrity and importance of the vision and creative energy of producer Erik Hillestad at Kirkelig Kulturverksted. See contextual discography.

42. Personal communication October 1998. *Folk Song* is one of my favourite pieces of music from the last five or so years: Smith's command of the dynamics of musical 'narrative' is outstanding.

43. Personal communication, May 1998. On Sheppard's early years in jazz, see Parker, C. 'West Coast Strikes Back' *The Wire* issue 39, May 1987 pp. 30-33, where Sheppard speaks of playing as "singing through the saxophone." There are some interesting, albeit co-incidental parallels between aspects of the careers of Garbarek and Sheppard: since the mid-to-late 1980s Sheppard has played with George Russell, and in the 1990s he toured in a trio with Shankar and Nana Vasconcelos. Sheppard, it should be emphasised, has long been his own man in terms of his sound and overall approach to the saxophone.

44. Personal communication, October 1998.
45. _Eskimo Poems from Canada and Greenland_ (trans. T. Lowenstein, from material originally collected by K. Rasmussen) Allison & Busby, London 1973 p. xxiii.
46. Personal communication, October 1998.
47. Personal communication, October 1998. Of course, Rosengren himself has also remained true to himself in change, as evinced by his work in various groups of his own, or with Lars Gullin, Don Cherry, Maffy Falay and Salih Baysal, for example. With Turkish trumpeter and pianist Falay and his compatriot, violinist Baysal (the former "discovered" by Dizzy Gillespie during a U.S. state department tour of Turkey in 1956) Rosengren appeared in the early 1970s in the innovative and notable folk-jazz group Sevda (Turkish for 'love'), when he sometimes played the taragot (a kind of Rumanian folk instrument traditionally used for wedding ceremonies). Sevda also featured e. g. Gunnar Bergsten (baritone, Chinese flute) Tommy Koverhult (tenor, soprano), Björn Alke (bass) and Okay Temiz (drums). Bobo Stenson has played with Temiz, in the group Oriental Wind. See contextual discography.
48. 'An Outsider's Way' in Ekelöf/Thygesen 1996 op. cit. (_Modus Vivendi_) pp. 147-8. See also Leif Sjöberg's 'Introduction' to Ekelöf 1967 op. cit. (_Selected Poems_). Ekelöf's concept of music was wide, and often Taoist in orientation. See e.g. 'Prescription', ibid. This ends: "But do you want music:/Turn to the wilderness/and you will perhaps even hear the forest's gongs/if there is anything to you!" See also 'Like Ankle Rings, This Music': ibid. p. 36. There is much of the music of the forest's gongs in Garbarek – especially on **Ingentings Bjeller.**
49. Ekelöf/Thygsen op. cit. p. 85. I like to think that the concept of rites on Garbarek's **Rites** would have met with Ekelöf's approval.
50. Ibid. (Ekelöf) p. 84.
51. For Ekelöf on the part and the whole, see 'Diwan over the Prince of Emgión' in _Selected Poems_ (trans. W. H. Auden & L. Sjöberg) Penguin, Harmondsworth 1971 p. 21. Ekelöf's comment about church bells, sermons and hymns can be found in 'The Last Bell Toll', Ekelöf/Thygesen op.cit. p. 194. For Ekelöf, "The point of our lives [..] is not that we should be angels or devils but rather that we should be human beings on earth and that seems to be the hardest thing of all." 'Arthur Rimbaud, or the Battle against Reality', ibid. p. 101. Ekelöf believed in a sort of itinerant wisdom, often reminiscent of Heraclitus. I find many points of correspondence between Ekelöf and the French poet and singer Léo Ferré (1916-1993) – who set Rimbaud to music (as he did Baudelaire, for example). See the contextual discography and e.g. Belleret, R. _Léo Ferré: Une Vie D'Artiste_ Actes Sud/Leméac 1996. (On itinerant wisdom, see note 54 below.)
52. See Ekelöf, G. ' The Tale of Fatumeh' in Ekelöf op. cit. (_Selected Poems_) 1971 p. 94; Metzger, A. _Freedom and Death_ Human Context Books/Chaucer Publishing Co. Ltd., London 1973 pp. 1-14, and Rilke, R. M. _Duino Elegies_ (various editions and translations: see Chapter Four, note 108).
53. Tucker, M. (ed.) _Alan Davie: The Quest For The Miraculous_

University of Brighton Gallery/Barbican Art Gallery/Lund Humphries Ltd., London 1993 p.13 note 1. Davie's lovely spatial image is applicable to a good deal of Nordic jazz. Some years ago, Palle Mikkelborg was asked by George Russell to play the opening number on every night of Russell's concert tour. After a few nights, Mikkelborg asked Russell why he had been asked to do this, given that the band contained so many excellent (American) musicians. "Oh", said Russell, " American musicians might play the same note as you, Palle. But they wouldn't have the patience to wait for the echo of that note to come back to them." Personal communication from Palle Mikkelborg, August 1998.

54. On Goethe's perception, see _Faust_ and Eckerman, _Conversations with Goethe_ London 1883 pp. 258-59. In the preface to _The Blue Road_, a 'way book' about a journey to Labrador which he once undertook, the Scottish poet and thinker Kenneth White writes: "[..] I recall that in some of the old traditions they talk of the _itinerant_ mystic, and they say that if a man caught up in 'Western exile' wants to find his 'Orient', he has to go through a passage North. /Maybe the blue road is that passage North, among the blues of silent Labrador. /Maybe the idea is to go as far as possible – to the end of yourself – till you get into a territory where time turns into space, where things appear in all their nakedness and the wind blows anonomously./ Maybe." _The Blue Road_ Mainstream Publishing Company Ltd., Edinburgh 1993 p. 11. The relevance of these lines to the work of Garbarek – which, in recent years, White has listened to with considerable interest – should hardly need underlining. See also White's lines in his _Mémoires Pyrénéens_ : "trying to get in touch with the territory/ always the love for the locality/ outside all the localisms". PUP Vallongues, 1995 p. 27.

55. Ibid. p. 78. Frans Widerberg and Kenneth White also supplied tributes to Davie here.

56. Leeuw op. cit. p. 257. Zen, a spiritual tradition not investigated in Leeuw's text, would call this the movement towards _satori_, or ultimate enlightenment. In 'The Tale of Fatumeh' Ekelöf writes: "And only he will be welcome to the mystery/who seeks it within himself". Ekelöf 1971 op. cit. p. 123. As with the experience of music, as one moves 'inwards', so does one move 'outwards'. Herein lies the beauty and the power of the "deep song" in Garbarek's art. See Rilke/Bly 1981 op. cit. (_Selected Poems_) p.13: 'I live my life in growing orbits/which move out over the things of the world./ Perhaps I can never achieve the last,/but that will be my attempt. / I am circling around God, around the ancient tower,/and I still don't know if I am a falcon, or a storm,/or a great song.' (From _A Book for the Hours of Prayer_ 1899-1903).

Belonging: Keith Jarrett & Jan Garbarek, mid-1970s
Roberto Masotti

Tender Is The North
Reproduced with kind permission of Jazzwise
Christian Him

Discography

*(a) An **overview of the work of Jan Garbarek on record**,
arranged chronologically and listed under the year of recording:*

1966

Diverse Artists: *Jazz Jamboree* Muza XLP 0342 (Garbarek, tenor sax, and
Kurt Lindgren, bass, appear on one track: *Walkin'*)

George Russell: *The Essence of George Russell* Soul Note 121044-2
(recorded 1966-67)

Karin Krog: *Jazz Moments* Sonet SLP 1404 (Garbarek, tenor sax, appears
on two tracks, *All Of You* & *Dearly Beloved*, both reissued on the
1994 Karin Krog: *Jubilee: The Best of 30 Years* Verve 523 716-2)

1967

Georg Riedel: *Riedaiglia* Sveriges Radio RELP 1051

Jan Garbarek: *Til Vigdis* Norsk Jazzforbund NJF LP-1 (The title track, *Til
Vigdis*, was reissued on the 1984 Diverse Artists: *Norsk Jazz 1960-80*
Odin LP 09)

Egil Kapstad: *Syner* Norsk Jazzforum JF LP-1

George Russell: *Othello Ballet Suite* Soul Note 121 014-2

1968

Karin Krog: *Joy* Sonet SLP 1405 (The title track, *Mr Joy*, was reissued on
Norsk Jazz 1960-80 Odin LP 09)

Terje Rypdal: *Bleak House* Polydor 184189

1969

Jan Garbarek: *George Russell Presents The Esoteric Circle* Freedom FCD
41031

Diverse Artists: *Popofoni* Sonet SLP 1421/22 (recorded 1969-71)

George Russell: *Electronic Sonata For Souls Loved By Nature* Soul Note
121034-2

Jan Erik Vold: *Briskeby Blues* Karussell 551 055-2

1970

Earl Wilson: *Live At The Studio* Auto Grip 19701

George Russell Sextet: *Trip To Prillarguri* Soul Note 1121029-2

Jan Erik Vold/Jan Garbarek: *Hav* Philips 6507 002

Jan Garbarek Quartet: *Afric Pepperbird* ECM 1007

1971

Diverse Artists: *Svartkatten* TNBL 873

Jan Garbarek Quintet: *Sart* ECM 1015

George Russell Orchestra: *Listen To The Silence* Soul Note SN 1024

Diverse Artists: *From Europe With Jazz* MPS 2121437-0 (Garbarek, tenor sax, clarinet, flute, plays on *Salamanderdans*)
Terje Rypdal: *Terje Rypdal* ECM 1016

1972
Jan Garbarek/Arild Andersen/Edward Vesala Trio *Triptykon* ECM 1029

1973
Jan Erik Vold: *Trikkeskinner/Tre Små Ting* (single) Philips 6084 025
Art Lande/Jan Garbarek: *Red Lanta* ECM 1038
Jan Garbarek/Bobo Stenson Quartet: *Witchi-Tai-To* ECM 1041

1974
Diverse Artists: *NDR-Jazz Workshop 1974* NDR 0666 516
Keith Jarrett: *Belonging* ECM 1050
Keith Jarrett/Jan Garbarek: *Luminessence* ECM 1049
Ralph Towner: *Solstice* ECM 1060

1975
Torgrim Sollid/Erling Aksdal Jr et al: *Østerdalsmusikk* MAI 7510
Keith Jarrett: *Arbour Zena* ECM 1070
Jan Garbarek/Bobo Stenson Quartet: *Dansere* ECM 1075

1976
Jan Garbarek: *Dis* ECM 1093

1977
Ralph Towner/Solstice: *Sound And Shadows* ECM 1095
Kenny Wheeler: *Deer Wan* ECM 1102
Jan Erik Vold/Jan Garbarek/Bobo Stenson Quartet: *Ingentings Bjeller* PAN PACD 09
Keith Jarrett: *My Song* ECM 1115
Egberto Gismonti: *Sol Do Meio Dia* ECM 1116 (Garbarek, soprano sax, appears on *Café - Procissão Do Espirito*)
Jan Garbarek: *Places* ECM 1118
Gary Peacock: *December Poems* ECM 1119 (Garbarek, soprano & tenor sax, appears on *Winterlude* & *December Greenwings*)
Bill Connors: *Of Mist And Melting* ECM 1120

1978
Jan Garbarek Group: *Photo With ...* ECM 1135

1979
Diverse Artists: *NDR: Jazz Workshop 1979* NDR 0666 969
Keith Jarrett: *Personal Mountains* ECM 1382
Keith Jarrett: *Nude Ants* ECM 1171/72
Charlie Haden/Jan Garbarek/Egberto Gismonti: *Magico* ECM 1151
Charlie Haden/Jan Garbarek/Egberto Gismonti: *Folk Songs* ECM 1170
Jan Garbarek/Kjell Johnsen: *Aftenland* ECM 1169
1980

Jan Garbarek: *Eventyr* ECM 1200

1981
Gary Peacock: *Voice From The Past: Paradigm* ECM 1210
David Darling: *Cycles* ECM 1219
Jan Garbarek: *Paths, Prints* ECM 1223

1983
Jan Garbarek Group: *Wayfarer* ECM 1259
Shankar: *Vision* ECM 1261

1984
Shankar: *Song For Everyone* ECM 1286
Eberhard Weber: *Chorus* ECM 1288
Jan Garbarek Group: *It's OK to listen to the gray voice* ECM 1294
(1984 saw the release of *Jan Garbarek: Works* ECM 823 266 - 1, a
     compilation album drawn from *Afric Pepperbird, Triptykon, Dansere,
     Dis, Places, Folk Songs* and *Eventyr*)

1986
Eleni Karaindrou: *O Melissokomos* Minos Records MSM 646/647 (Some of
     Garbarek's appearances, tenor sax, were reissued on the 1991 Eleni
     Karaindrou: *Music For Films* ECM 1429)
Jan Garbarek: *All Those Born With Wings* ECM 1324
Zakir Hussain: *Making Music* ECM 1349

1987
Gary Peacock: *Guamba* ECM 1352

1988
Arve Tellefsen: *Pan* Norsk Plateproduksjon IDCD 3 (Garbarek, tenor sax,
     appears on *Pan*)
Jan Garbarek: *Legend Of The Seven Dreams* ECM 1381
Agnes Buen Garnås/Jan Garbarek: *Rosensfole* Kirkelig Kulturverksted
     FXCD 83 (recorded 1988-89; also released, under same title, with
     English sleevenote, on ECM 1402)

1989
Diverse Artists: *Natt Jazz 20 År 1992* Grappa GRCD 102 (Jan Garbarek
     Group, with Mari Boine, play *Gula Gula*, live recording, Grieghallen,
     Bergen May 1989. Recording released 1992)

1990
Jan Garbarek/Ustad Fateh Ali Khan et al: *Ragas and Sagas* ECM 1442
Jan Garbarek: *I Took Up The Runes* ECM 1419
Trilok Gurtu: *Living Magic* CMP CD 50 (recorded August 1990 & March
     1991: Garbarek, tenor & soprano sax, appears on *Baba* & *Once I
     Wished A Tree Upside Down*)
Paul Giger: *Alpstein* ECM 1426 (recorded 1990-91)

1991
Jan Garbarek/Miroslav Vitous/Peter Erskine: *Star* ECM 1444
Niels-Henning Ørsted Pedersen: *Uncharted Land* Pladecompagniet PCCD
    8045 (recorded October 1991 & March 1992; Garbarek, tenor and
    soprano sax, keyboard programming, appears on *Moving Pictures*,
    Nordavind, Joron & *Blank Space*)

1992
Miroslav Vitous/Jan Garbarek: *Atmos* ECM 1475
Jan Garbarek/Anouar Brahem/ Shaukat Husssain: *Madar* ECM 1515
Jan Garbarek Group: *Twelve Moons* ECM 1500
Vigdis Garbarek/Jan Garbarek: *Stemmer* music cassette NRK/Gylendal
    Norsk Forlag ISBN 82-05-20591-4 (texts by Vigdis Garbarek, with
    selections from various ECM albums by Jan Garbarek)

1993
Jan Garbarek/The Hilliard Ensemble: *Officium* ECM New Series 1525

1994
Jan Garbarek: *Trollsyn* Trollcd 9401 (promotional CD EP)
Giya Kancheli: *Caris Mere* ECM New Series 1568 (recorded April 1994 &
    January 1995; Garbarek, soprano sax, appears on *Night Prayers*)

1995
Jan Garbarek: *Visible World* ECM 1585

1996
Vigdis Garbarek: *Vågestykket* CD Lydbokforlaget ISBN 82-421-0583-9
    (texts by Vigdis Garbarek; Jan Garbarek, bamboo flute)

1998
Jan Garbarek: *Rites* (ECM 1685/6)

(b) **Contextual Recordings:**
*The following four sections are intended to give an indication
of the various historical contexts within which Garbarek's
work might be placed, should one so wish.*

(i) **Nordic & European Jazz**
Juhani Aaltonen/Otto Donner: *Strings* Love Records RCD 160
Lennart Åberg: *Partial Solar Eclipse* Japo 60023
Misha (Mikhail) Alperin/Arkady Shilkloper: *Wave Of Sorrow* ECM 1396
Misha Alperin: *Folk Dreams* JARO 4187 - 2
    North Story ECM 1596
Bjørn Alterhaug: *Moments* Arctic Records ARCX 2
    Constellations Odin NJ 44035 - 2
Arild Andersen: *Clouds In My Head* ECM 1059
    Shimri ECM 1082
    Green Shading Into Blue ECM 1127
    Lifelines ECM 1188

A Molde Concert ECM 1236
If You Look Far Enough ECM 1493
Sagn Kirkelig Kulturverksted FXCD 100 (also ECM 1435)
Arv Kirkelig Kulturverksted FXCD 133
Kristin Lavransdatter Kirkelig Kulturverksted FXCD 154
Hyperborean ECM 1631
Sommerbrisen Kirkelig Kulturverksted FXCD 198
Änglaspel: *Lappland* Dragon DRLP 112
Harry Arnold: *Big Band Classics 1957-58* Dragon DRLP 139/140
Azimuth: *Azimuth/The Touchstone/Départ* ECM 1546-48
    "How It Was Then .. Never Again" ECM 1538
Back Door: *Back Door* Warner Bros K 46231
Jon Balke/Magnetic North Orchestra: *Further* ECM 1517
Bardo State Orchestra: *The Ultimate Gift* Impetus IMP CD 19425
    Wheels Within Wheels Impetus IMP CD 19527
Bengt Berger: *Bitter Funeral Beer* (with a. o. Don Cherry) ECM 1179
B. C. J. O.: *Berlin Contemporary Jazz Orchestra* (conducted by Alexander
    von Schlippenbach) ECM 1409
Ketil Bjørnstad: *Leve Patagonia* Philips 834 713 - 2
    Water Stories ECM 1503
    The Sea ECM 1545
    The Sea 11 ECM 1633
Christer Bothén/Bengt Berger/Nicke Ström/Kjell Westling: *Spjärnsvallet* MNW 57P
Christer Bothén/Bolon Bata: *Mother Earth* Dragon DRLP 160
The Brass Brothers: *Brazzy Voices* In + Out Records IOR 77029-2
Willem Breuker: *The Message* Instant Composers Pool ICP 009
Tore Brunborg: *Tid* (with Bugge Wesseltoft, Anders Jormin, Jon Christensen,
    Norma Winstone) Curling Legs CLP CD 05
Rainer Brüninghaus: *Freigeweht* ECM 1187
    Continuum ECM 1266
Gavin Bryars: *After The Requiem* ECM New Series 1424
Ian Carr: *Old Heartland* MMC 1016
    Sounds & Sweet Airs (with John Taylor) Celestial Harmonies 13064 - 2
Philip Catherine: *Oscar* Igloo IGL 060
Lol Coxhill: *Fleas In Custard* Virgin Records C1515
Lars Danielsson: *Poems* (with Dave Liebman, soprano sax; Bobo Stenson,
    piano; Jon Christensen, drums) Dragon DRCD 209
    European Voices (with a. o. Nils Peter Molvær, Joakim Milder)
    Dragon DRCD 268
    Far North (personnel as Poems) Curling Legs CLP CD 13
Palle Danielsson: *Contra Post* Caprice CAP 21440
Johnny Dankworth: *Dankworth and the London Philharmonic Orchestra*
    Society SOC 963
Wolfgang Dauner: *Dream Talk* L + R Records LR 41.004
    Dauner/Weber/Karg/Braceful Calig CAL 30 603
    Get Up And Dauner: Masterpieces MPS 533 548 - 2
    Output ECM 1006
Alan Davie Music Workshop: *Suite for Prepared Piano & Drums* ADMW 002
    Phantom in the Room ADMW 004
    Tony Oxley/Alan Davie Duo ADMW 005

Deepika: *I Alt Slags Lys* Kirkelig Kulturverksted FXCD 118
Chano Dominguez: *Chano* Nuba 7756
    Hecho A Mano Nuba 7759
    En Directo (Solo Piano) Nuba 7760/1
Arne Domnérus: *Mobil: musik av Jan Johansson och Georg Riedel* Megafon
    MFLP S8
    Scandinavian Design RCA YSPL 1-587
    Antiphone Blues Proprius PROP 7744
    Vårat Gäng Sonet SLP 2647
    Blåtoner fra Troldhaugen (Fritt Etter Edvard Grieg) Kirkelig
    Kulturverksted FXCD 65
Otto Donner/UMO Jazz Orchestra: *Dalens Ande (The Spirit of the Valley)*
    Beta BECD 4025
Urszula Dudziak: *Future Talk* Inner City IC 1066
Cutting Edge: *Alle Tre* Curling Legs clp CD 19
Sidsel Endresen: *Exile* ECM 1524
Berndt Egerbladh: *Night Pieces* (with a. o. Jan Allan) Ladybird LBCD 0021
Bengt Ernryd: *Quartet 1964-65* Dragon LP 1
European Jazz Ensemble: *At The Philharmonic Cologne* M. A Music A 800-2
Maffy Falay/Sevda: *Jazz I Sverige '72* (with a. o. Bernt Rosengren, Salih
    Baysal, Okay Temiz) Caprice RIKS LP 31
    Live At Fregatten Sonet SNTF 665
Pierre Favre/Paul Motian/Freddy Studer/Nana Vasconcelos: *Singing Drums*
    ECM 1274
Pierre Favre: *Window Steps* ECM 1584
Svein Finnerud Trio: *Svein Finnerud Trio* Norsk Jazzforum JF-LP-2
    Plastic Sun Sonet SLPS 1406
    Thoughts Prisma Records (Hovikodden, Norway: no number)
    Travel Pillow Prisma Records FTCD 9401
Frode Fjellheim Jazz Joik Ensemble: *Saajve Dans* Idut ICD 943
Börje Fredriksson: *Börje Fredriksson 1937-1968* Odeon E 054 - 34009
    Progressive Movements Flash Music FC CD3
Paolo Fresu /Furio Di Castri: *Evening Song* Owl 7897672
Lille Frøen Saxofonkvartett: *(4 -Menn)* Odin LP 16
Michael Gibbs: *Michael Gibbs* Deram SML 1063
    Big Music Venture CDVE 27
Michael Gibbs with Joachim Kuhn: *Europeana: Jazzphony no 1* ACT 9220-2
Stephane Grappelli: *Young Django* (with Philip Catherine, Larry Coryell,
    Niels-Henning Ørsted Pedersen) MPS 815 672-2
Stephane Grappelli/Michel Petrucciani: *Flamingo* (with George Mraz & Roy
    Haynes) Dreyfus FDM 36 580-2
George Gruntz: *Jazz Goes Baroque* Philips BL 7645
    Theatre ECM 1265
Guttorm Guttormsen: *Soturnudi* MAI 7509
    Albufeira Ocatave OCLP 03
Lars Gullin: *"Fine Together"* Sonet SLPD - 2542
    1951-1960 - Decennium I Blåton Rosa Honung
    Records/QuadroMedia ROSACD 51
    Lars Gullin 1959-60 Artist ALP 30-114
    The EMI Years 1964-1976 EMI LG 1

Portrait Of My Pals Columbia 7924292
Barry Guy: *Study - Witch Gong Game 10/11* Maya MCD9402
Bengt Hallberg: *Collaboration* Odeon E 062-34397
Gunter Hampel: *The 8th July 1969* Birth/Natural Jazz nj 001
Tubby Hayes: *Late Spot At Scott's* Redial CD 558 183-2
    Down In The Village Redial CD 558 184-2
    100% Proof Fontana TL5410
    Mexican Green Fontana SFJL 911
    In Scandinavia Storyville STCD 8251
Joe Harriott: *Personal Portrait* EMI Columbia SCX 6249
    Memorial EMI One-Up OU 2011
    Free Form Redial 538184 2
    Abstract Redial 538183-2
Åke 'Stan' Hasselgård: *Swedish Pastry (with Wardell Gay & Benny*
    Goodman) 1948 Dragon DRLP 16
    Stockholm/New York 1945-48 Dragon DRLP 25
    Young Clarinet Dragon DRLP 163
Jonas Hellborg: *Elegant Punk* Day Eight Music DEM 004
André Hodeir: *Jazz Et Jazz* Philips PHM 200 - 073
Bendik Hofseth: *Amuse Yourself* Columbia 472 988 2
Dave Holland Quartet: *Conference Of The Birds* (with Anthony Braxton,
    Sam Rivers & Barry Altschul) ECM 1027
Dave Holland: *Emerald Tears* ECM 1109
Daniel Humair: *Surrounded 1964-1987* Flat & Sharp 597 292
Per Husby: *Dedications* Hot Club Records HCRCD 21
    Notes For Nature Odin NJ 4033 - 2
Ken Hyder's Talisker: *Land of Stone* Japo 60018
Ken Hyder: *In The Stone* (with Dave Brooks, Maggie Nichols & Talisker)
    Impetus IMP CD 19732
ICP 10'-Tet: *Tetterettet* Instant Composers Pool ICP 020
Terje Isungset: *Reise* NOR CD 9724
Italian Instabile Orchestra: *Skies of Europe* ECM 1543
Pedro Itturalde *Jazz Flamenco vols. 1 & 2* Blue Note 7243 8 53933 27
Rolf Jacobsen/Egil Kapstad: *Til Jorden* Zarepta ZA 34016
Sigurd Jansen: *Aurora Borealis* NOPA CD 2919
Lars Jansson Trio: *The Eternal Now* ton art 27
    Invisible Friends Imogena IGCD 055
The Jazz Couriers (with a. o. Ronnie Scott & Tubby Hayes): *In Concert*
    Music For Pleasure MFP 1072
Francois Jeanneau: *Ephemere* Owl 8272792
Bjørn Johansen: *Take One* Odin NJ 4021-2
Egil 'Bop' Johansen: *Samse Tak!* Four Leaf Records FLC 5013
Jan Johansson: *Folkvisor (Jazz på Svenska/Jazz på Ryska)* Megafon MFCD 0410
    300.000 Megafon MFCD 18
    Blues Heptagon HECD 018
    Ack Värmeland du sköna ROSACD 62
    Musik genom fyra sekler Heptagon HECD 002
Egil Kapstad: *Epilog: Bill Evans In Memoriam* NOPA CD 2901
Jonas Knutsson: *Flower In The Sky* ACT 2948-2
Göran Klinghagen: *A Hip Hop* (with Palle Danielsson, Jon Balke, Jon

Christensen) Dragon DRLP 121

Hans Koller: *Multiple Koller* L + R Records LR 41.003

Krzysztof Komeda: *Crazy Girl* (with a.o. Bernt Rosengren) Power Bros PB 00145
Astigmatic (with a.o. Zbigniew Namyslowski, Tomasz Stanko) Power Bros PB 00125
Ballet Etudes/Breakfast at Tiffany's Power Bros PB 00155
Memory of Bach Power Bros PB 00157
Nightime, Daytime Requiem Power Bros PB 00159
Moja Ballada Power Bros PB 00161

Karin Krog: *Jubilee: The Best of 30 Years* Verve 523 716 - 2
By Myself (with a. o. Egil Kapstad) Fontana Special 6426 031
Different Days, Different Ways (with a. o. Arild Andersen, Palle Danielsson) Philips FDX 202
Some Other Spring (with Dexter Gordon, Kenny Drew, Niels-Henning Ørsted Pedersen & Espen Rud) Storyville STCD 4045
Gershwin with Karin Krog (with a. o. Bjarne Nerem) Polydor 2382 045
We Could Be Flying (with a. o. Steve Kuhn) Polydor 23282 051
Cloud Line Blue (with John Surman) Polydor 2382 093
Hi-Fly (with a. o. Archie Shepp) Compendium/ Fidardo 2
Freestyle (with John Surman) Odin LP 17
The Malmo Sessions (with a. o. Nils Lindberg) RCA PL 40015
I Remember You (with Warne Marsh & Red Mitchell) Spotlite Records SPJLP 22
Two Of A Kind (with Bengt Hallberg) Four Leaf Records FLC 5063
Such Winters of Memory (with John Surman) ECM 1254
Nordic Quartet (with John Surman, Terje Rypdal, Vigleik Storaas) ECM 1553

Nils Landgren: *Gotland* (with Tomasz Stanko) ACT 9226 - 2
Swedish Folk Modern (with Esbjörn Svensson) ACT 9257 - 2

Nguyên Lê: *Tales From Vietnam* ACT 9225-2

Nils Lindberg: *Sax Appeal & Tri-Section* (with a.o. Lars Gullin & Rolf Billberg) Dragon DRCD 220
Saxes Galore/Brass Galore Bluebell ABCD 3004
Lapponian Suite (with a.o. Putte Wickman, Norrköping Symphony Orchestra, Gustaf Sjökvist, conductor) Bluebell ABCD 008

Jukka Linkola: *Crossings* (with Juhani Aaltonen & Helsinki Philharmonic Orchestra) Finlandia FAD 916

Lokomotiv Konkret: *A Voice Still Heard* Alice ALCD 003

Paco de Lucia: *El Duende Flamenco de Paco de Lucia* Philips 824 417 2
Interpreta Manuel de Falla Philips 836 032 2

Paco de Lucia/Al Di Meola/John McLaughlin: *The Guitar Trio* Verve 533 215 2

Lars Lystedt Quintet: *Blues After Dark: Live, Umea 1964* Dragon DRLP 15

David Mack: *New Directions* Columbia Lansdowne Series 33SX 1670

Albert Mangelsdorff: *Tension!* L + R Records LR 41.001
Now, Jazz Ramwong Pacific Jazz PJ- 10095
And His Friends MPS 15 210
Birds of Underground MPS 21 21746-9
The Wide Point MPS 68.071/15.396
Tromboneliness MPS 68.129/15.397
A Jazz Tune I Hope MPS 0068.212/15.528

Carlos Martins: *Passagem* ENJA ENJ 9073 2
Masqualero: *Masqualero* Odin LP 08
    Band A Part ECM 1319
    Aero ECM 1367
    Re-enter ECM 1437
John Mayer and Joe Harriott: *Indo-Jazz Fusions 1&2* Redial 538048-2
John Mayer's Indo-Jazz Fusions: *Asian Airs* Nimbus Records NI 5499
    Ragatal Nimbus Records NI 5569
Marilyn Mazur/Future Song: *Future Song* verABra vBr 2105 2
    Circular Chant Storyville STCD - 4200
John McLaughlin: *Extrapolation* Polydor 8415982
    The Mediterranean: Concerto for Guitar & Orchestra CBS MK 45578
Mezzoforte: *Surprise, Surprise* Steinar STE LPO2
Palle Mikkelborg/Kenneth Knudsen/Niels-Henning Ørsted Pedersen: *Heart To Heart* Storyville STCD - 4114
Palle Mikkelborg: *Anything But Grey* Columbia 471614 2
Joakim Milder: *Life in Life* Dragon DRLP 166
    Ways Dragon DRCD 231
Joakim Milder/Bobo Stenson/Palle Danielsson/Fredrik Norén: *Sister Majs Blouse (The Music of Börje Fredriksson)* Mirrors MICD 002
    Epilogue Mirrors MICD 007
Nils Petter Molvær: *Khmer* ECM 1560
Tete Montoliu: *Solo Piano* Timeless ti CD SJP 107/116
Moscow Art Trio: *Music* Jaro 4214 2
Eric Moseholm/Torben Kjar/Jesper Thorup/Birgit Bruel: *Jazz Pa Dansk* Exlibris EXL 20.004
Mount Everest Trio: *Waves From Albert Ayler* LIM 7503
Mujician: *Birdman* Cuneiform Rune 82
Zbygniew Namyslowski: *Lola* Decca LK 4644
    Zbigniew Namyslowski Quartet Muza SXL 0305
    Winobranie Power Bros 00121
    Kujaviak Goes Funky Power Bros 33859-2
    Zbigniew Namyslowski (with orchestra) Muza SX 1493
    Namyslovski Inner City IC 1048
    Secretly & Confidentially Koch Jazz 3-3808-2
Bjarne Nerem: *This Is Always* Gemini Records GMCD 47
Cæcilie Norby *My Corner Of The Sky* Blue Note 8534222
Fredrik Norén Band: *To Mr. J* Sonet SNTCD 1037
Northern Lights: *Stillness In The Solovski* Long Arms CDLA 98018
Opposite Corner: *Opposite Corner/Jazz I Sverige 1976* Caprice CAP 1117
Oriental Wind: *Bazaar* Sonet SNTF 894A
Out to Lunch: *Kullboksrytter* (with Sidsel Endresen, Norwegian String Quartet) Curling Legs CLP CD 15
Tony Oxley: *Ichnos* RCA Victor SF 8215
Evan Parker/Derek Bailey/Han Bennink: *The Topography of the Lungs* Incus 001
Evan Parker Electro-Acoustic Ensemble: *Towards The Margins* ECM New Series 1612
Niels-Henning Ørsted Pedersen/ Kenneth Knudsen: *Pictures* Steeplechase SCS 1068
Niels-Henning Ørsted Pedersen/Philip Catherine/Billy Hart: *Live At*

Montmartre Steeplechase SCS 1083
Niels-Henning Ørsted Pedersen: *The Eternal Traveller* Pablo OJCCD 966 - 2
    Scandinavian Wood Caprice CAP 21412
    Those Who Were Verve 533232 - 2
    This Is All I Ask Verve 539 695 - 2
Krzysztof Penderecki/Don Cherry: *Actions* Philips 6305 153
Esa Pethman: *The Modern Sound of Finland* RCA Victor LSP 10040
Dominique Pifarely/Francois Couturier: *Poros* ECM 1647
Courtney Pine *Journey To The Urge Within* Island ILPS 9846
    Modern Day Jazz Stories Antilles 5290282
Jean-Luc Ponty: *King Kong* Blue Note CDP 0777 7 89539 20
Michel Portal: *Turbulence* Harmonia Mundi HMC 905186
    Any Way Label Bleu LBLC 6544
Quatre (Franco d'Andrea/Daniel Humair/Enrico Rava/Miroslav Vitous):
    Earthcake Label Bleu LBCD 6539
Rena Rama: *Rena Rama (Jazz I Sverige 1973)* Caprice RIKS LP 49
    Landscapes Japo 60020
    Inside - Outside Caprice CAP 1182
Enrico Rava: *The Pilgrim And The Stars* ECM 1063
    String Band Soul Note CD 121114-2
    Carmen Label Bleu LBLC 6579
Django Reinhardt: *Swing de Paris* Charly (4CD) CD DIG 12
    The Best Of Django Reinhardt Blue Note CDP 7243 8 37138 2 0
Knut Reiersrud/Iver Kleive: *Bla Koral* Kirkelig Kulturverksted FXCD 106
Knut Reiersrud: *Tramp* Kirkelig Kulturverksted FXCD 129
    Klapp Kirkelig Kulturverksted FXCD 151
Vladimir Rezitsky (with a. o. Sainkho Namchylak, Ken Hyder): *Hot Sounds*
    From The Arctic Leo CD LR 218
Georg Riedel: *Jazz Ballet* Philips PHM 200-140
    Reflexioner (with Bengt Hallberg) Megafon MFLP S 23
Knut Riisnæs: *Flukt* Odin LP 05
    Knut Riisnæs/Jon Christensen/John Scofield/Palle Danielsson Odin NJ
    4042 - 2
Odd Riisnæs: *Speak Low* Taurus Records TRLP 825
    Thoughts Taurus Records TRCD 828
    Another Version Taurus Records TRCD 831
Aldo Romano/Louis Sclavis/Henri Texier: *Carnet De Routes* Label Bleu
    LBLC 6569
Gösta Rundqvist: *Until We Have Faces* Sittel SITCD 9212
Terje Rypdal: *What Comes After* ECM 1031
    Whenever I Seem To Be Far Away ECM 1045
    Odyssey ECM 1067/8
    After The Rain ECM 1083
    Waves ECM 1110
    Rypdal/Vitous/DeJohnette ECM 1125
    Descendre ECM 1144
    Chaser ECM 1303
    Blue ECM 1346
    If Mountains Could Sing ECM 1554
    Skywards ECM 1608

Bernt Rosengren: *Stockholm Dues* EMI Columbia SSX 1013
    Notes From Underground EMI Harvest E 154-34958/9
San: *Song* NOR-CD 9720
Heikki Sarmanto: *Everything Is It* EMI Odeon 5E 062-34640
    Suomi: A Symphonic Jazz Poem for Orchestra (featuring Juhani
    Aaltonen) Finlandia FACD 913
Alexander von Schlippenbach: *The Hidden Peak* FMP 0410
Manfred Schoof: *European Echoes* FMP 0010
Louis Sclavis: *Clarinettes* IDA Records ID 004 CD
    Chine IDA Records IDA 012 CD
    Chamber Music IDA Records IDA 022 CD
    Ceux Qui Veillent La Nuit Label Bleu LC 9743
    Rouge ECM 1458
    Les Violences De Rameau ECM 1588
Louis Sclavis/Dominique Pifarely: *Acoustic Quartet* ECM 1526
Ronnie Scott: *The Night is Scott And You're So Swingable* Redial 5588882
Karl Seglem: *Rit* NOR CD 9410
    Spir NOR CD 9830
Andy Sheppard: *Soft On The Inside* Antilles AN 8751
    In Co-Motion Antilles ANCD 8766
Andy Sheppard/Nana Vasconcelos/Steve Lodder: *Inclassificable* Label Bleu
    LBLC 6583
Andy Sheppard/Steve Lodder: *Moving Image* Verve 533 875 2
Andy Sheppard Group: *Learning to Wave* Provocateur PVC 1016
Dick Heckstall-Smith: *Celtic Steppes* 33 Records 33 Jazz 027 CD
Tommy Smith: *Peeping Tom* Blue Note CD BLT 1002
    Reminiscence Linn AKD 024
    Misty Morning And No Time Linn AKD 040
    Beasts Of Scotland Linn AKD 054
    Azure Linn AKD 059
Martial Solal/Niels-Henning Ørsted Pedersen: *Movability* MPS 5 D064-60207
Martial Solal/Didier Lockwood: *Solal/Lockwood* JMS 067 2
Martial Solal/Gary Peacock/Paul Motian: *Just Friends* FDM 36592 2
Søyr: *Søyr* (with a. o. Torgrim Sollid, Morten Lassem) MAI 7705
Spontaneous Music Ensemble: *Karyobin* Chronoscope CPE2001-2
Spring Quintet: *Spring Quintet* Polar PMC 330
Tomasz Stanko: *Music For K* Power Bros 00131
    Purple Sun Calig CAL 30610
    Peyotl, Witkacy Polonia CD 037/038
    Balladyna ECM 1071
    Bluish Polish Power Bros 00113
    Tales For A Girl, 12 Polonia CD 046
    Matka Joanna ECM 1544
    Litania - Music of Krzysztof Komeda ECM 1636
Bobo Stenson: *Underwear* (with Arild Andersen & Jon Christensen) ECM 1012
    Very Early (with Anders Jormin & Rune Carlsson) Dragon DRCD 304
    Reflections (with Jormin & Christensen) ECM 1516
    War Orphans (with Jormin & Christensen) ECM 1604
Jiri Stivin/Rudolf Dasek: *Tandem* Supraphon 1 15 1799
Red Sun/Samul Nori: *Then Comes The White Tiger* ECM 1499

Torbjørn Sunde (with a. o. Terje Rypdal): *Meridians* ACT 8263 2
John Surman: *How Many Clouds Can You See?* Deram 844882-2
    Westering Home FMR CD 16 - L795
    Morning Glory FMR CD 13 - L 495
    Upon Reflection ECM 1148
    The Amazing Adventures of Simon Simon ECM 1193
    Withholding Pattern ECM 1295
    Private City ECM 1336
    Road to Saint Ives ECM 1418
    A Biography Of The Rev. Absolom Dawe ECM 1529
    Proverbs and Songs ECM 1639
John Surman/John Warren: *The Brass Project* ECM 1478
Siri Svale Band: *Blackbird* Sonor Records SON CD 2001
Tamma: *Tamma* (with Don Cherry & Ed Blackwell) Odin NJ 4014-2
John Taylor with John Surman: *Ambleside Days* **ah** um 103
John Tchicai & Cadentia Nova Danica: *Afrodisiaca* MPS 15005
John Tchicai/Niels-Henning Ørsted Pedersen/Pierre Dørge: *Real Tchicai*
    Steeplechase SCS 1075
John Tchicai/Strange Brothers: *"Darktown Highlights"* Storyville SLP 1015
John Tchicai/Pierre Dørge: *Ball at Louisiana* Steeplechase SCS 1174
Henri Texier: *Le coffret JMS* JMS18696-2
Pål Thowsen/Jon Christensen/Terje Rypdal/Arild Andersen: *No Time for*
    Time Zarepta SLP 1437
Pål Thowsen: *Surprise* NorDisc NorLP 403
Radka Toneff: *Winter Poem* Verve 843 412-2
    Live in Hamburg Odin NJ 4044 2
UMO Jazz Orchestra: *Umo Jazz Orchestra* NAXOS 86010-2
The United Jazz + Rock Ensemble: *Live Opus Sechs* Mood Records 28.642
Michal Urbaniak & Urszula Dudziak: *Tribute to Komeda* MPS MC 21657
Michal Urbaniak: *Smiles Ahead* MPS 68.165/15.499
    Urbaniak Inner City IC 1036
Utla (Hakon Hogemo, Karl Seglem, Terje Isungset): *Brodd* NOR CD 9514
Various: *Jazz And Hot Dance In Norway 1920-946* Harlequin HQ 2029
    Jazz In Norway vol 1 1954-1955 RCA YNJL 1-801
    Jazz In Norway vol 2 1938-1943 RCA YNJL 1-703
    Jazz In Norway vol 3 1938-1943 RCA YNJL 1-718
    Jazz In Norway vol 4 Nostalgia 1922-1938 RCA YNJL 1- 735
    Metropol Jazz Norsk Grammofonkompani H 506 LP
    Norsk Jazz 1960 - 1980 Odin 09
    Club 7's Jubileumsplater: Club 7 1963-78 MAI 7812/13
    Jazz På Norsk Gemini GMCD 70
    Jazz From Norway Oris London Jazz Festival/Serious 1
    Jazz Meets The World MPS 29 22520-8
    Jazz Meets Europe MPS 531 847 - 2
    Jazz Meets Asia MPS 533 132 - 2
    Atmospheric Conditions Permitting: Radio Recordings Hessischer
    Rundfunk ECM 1549-50
    Document: The 80s. New Music from Russia Leo Records CD LR 801 - 808
    World Music Meeting Eigelstein Musikproduktion ES 2024
    Music In Sweden (with a. o. Arne Domnérus, Bernt Rosengren, Eje

Thelin, Björn Alke, Rena Rama, Opposite Corner) Caprice CAP 1131
Äventyr I Jazz och Folkmusik (with a.o. Bengt-Arne Wallin, Jan
Johansson, Georg Riedel) Caprice CAP 21475
Jazz Från Det Svenska 70-Talet Caprice LP 67/68
Sven Klangs Kvintett Dragon LP 9
The Down Beat Pollwinners In Europe MPS 15006
For Example: Workshop Freie Musik 1969-1978 FMP R1/2/3
Just Music ECM 1002
Edward Vesala: *Nana* Blue Master BLU - LP 125
I'm Here Blue Master Special SPEL 311
Nan Madol ECM 1077
Satu ECM 1088
Lumi ECM 1339
Ode To The Death Of Jazz ECM 1413
Invisible Storm ECM 1461
Nordic Gallery ECM 1541
Emil Viklicky: *Food Of Love* (with Julian Nicholas, Robert Balcar, Dave
Wickins) Melantrich MCD 014
Vienna Art Orchestra: *Blues For Brahms* Amadeo 839 105 - 2
Plays For Jean Cocteau Verve/Amadeo 529 290-2
20th Anniversary Verve/Amadeo 537 095 - 2
Paolo Vinaccia/Arild Andersen/Tore Brunborg/Il Coro di Neoneli: *Mbara
Boom* Sonet SCD 15117
Miroslav Vitous: *Mountain In The Clouds* Atlantic SD 1622
Majesty Music Arista AL 4099
First Meeting ECM 1145
Miroslav Vitous Group ECM 1185
Journey's End ECM 1242
Emergence ECM 1312
Bengt-Arne Wallin: *The Birth & Rebirth of Swedish Folk Jazz* ACT 9254 - 2
Bengt Arne Wallin/Nils Landgren: *Miles From Duke* Phono Suecia PS 28
Christian Wallumrød Trio: *No Birch* ECM 1628
Cleveland Watkiss: *Green Chimneys* Urban Jazz/Polydor CD 839 722 2
Trevor Watts/Moiré Music Drum Orchestra: *A Wider Embrace* ECM 1449
Eberhard Weber: *The Colours of Chloë* ECM 1042
Yellow Fields ECM 1066
The Following Morning ECM 1084
Silent Feet ECM 1107
Fluid Rustle ECM 1137
Little Movements ECM 1186
Later That Evening ECM 1231
Orchestra ECM 1374
Pendulum ECM 1518
Bobby Wellins: *Dreams Are Free* Vortex Records VS2
Birds Of Brazil Sungai BW 11
Nomad Hot House HHCD 1008
Lasse Werner/Bernt Rosengren: *Bombastica! 1959-60* Dragon DRCD 287
Mike Westbrook Concert Band: *Celebration* Deram SML 1013
Putte Wickman: *Happy New Year!* EMI Odeon E 062 - 34822
Barney Wilen: *Jazz Sur Seine* Philips 832 264-1

Joe Zawinul: *Joe Zawinul* Warner Jazz WE 889
  And The Austrian All Stars 1954-1957 RST Records RST - 91549 - 2
  The Rise & Fall Of The Third Stream/Money In The Pocket
  Rhino/Atlantic 8122-71675-2
  Zawinul Atlantic 7567 - 81375 - 2
  Dialects Columbia 489774 2
  Stories Of The Danube Philips 454 143 - 2
  My People Escapade ESC 03651-2
Monica Zetterlund: *Ett Lingonris Som Satts I Cocktailglass* RCA 74321
  32989 2
Monica Zetterlund/Bill Evans: *Waltz for Debby* Philips CD 510 268 - 2
Attila Zoller/ Hans Koller/Martial Solal: *Zo - Ko - So* SABA SB 15061

(ii) American & Other Jazz

Muhal Richard Abrams: *Levels and Degrees of Light* Delmark DD 413
Toshiko Akiyoshi-Lew Tabackin Big Band: *Tales Of A Courtesan (Oirantan)*
  RCA AFL1 0723
Gene Ammons: *Red Top: The Savoy Sessions* Savoy SV-0242
  Funky Prestige OJC-244 (P-7083)
  Boss Tenor Prestige PR 7180
Louis Armstrong & Duke Ellington: *The Complete Sessions* EMI Roulette
  LC 0542
Louis Armstrong: *Hot Five & Hot Seven 1925-1928 Masterpieces* Giants of
  Jazz CD 53001
Albert Ayler: *My Name is Albert Ayler* Fontana 688 603 ZL
  Spiritual Unity ESP/Fontana SFJL 933
  Bells - Prophecy ESP 101-2
  New York Eye And Ear Control (with Don Cherry, John Tchicai,
  Roswell Rudd, Sunny Murray) ESP 1016
  Vibrations (with a. o. Don Cherry) Freedom 28 41-2 U
  Music Is The Healing Force Of The Universe Impulse! AS 9191
Art Ensemble of Chicago: *Fanfare for the Warriors* Atlantic ATL 50 303
  Nice Guys ECM 1126
  Full Force ECM 1167
  Urban Bushmen ECM 1211/12
Gato Barbieri: *Togetherness* (featuring Don Cherry) Cicala BL 7068 J
  In Search of the Mystery ESP 1049
  Confluence (with Dollar Brand/Abdullah Ibrahim) Freedom FLP 41003
  Latino America Impulse! IMP 22362
Paul Bley: *The Fabulous Paul Bley Quartet* (with Ornette Coleman, Don
  Cherry, Charlie Haden, Billy Higgins) America AM 6120
  Barrage ESP 1008 - 2
  Paul Bley With Gary Peacock ECM 1003
  Paul Bley/NHØP Steeplechase SCS 1005
  Open, to love ECM 1023
  Japan Suite Improvising Artists Inc., IAI 37.38.49
  Time Will Tell (with Evan Parker & Barre Phillips) ECM 1537
Jane Ira Bloom *Art and Aviation* Arabesque Jazz AJ0107
Earl Bostic: *Jazz As I Feel It* King 846

Anouar Brahem/John Surman/Dave Holland: *Thimar* ECM 1641
Michael Brecker: *Michael Brecker* Impulse!/GRP 01132
Clifford Brown: *Memorial* (with Tadd Dameron Orchestra & The Swedish
    All Stars) Prestige OJC -017
Marion Brown: *Three For Shepp* Impulse! A-9139
    Porto Novo Polydor 583 724
    Afternoon Of A Georgia Faun ECM 1004
    Reed 'n Vibes (with Gunter Hampel) Improvising Artists 123 855 - 2
Dave Brubeck: *Time Out* Columbia CK 65122
    Time Further Out Columbia CK 64668
Don Cherry: *Complete Communion* (with a.o. Gato Barbieri) Blue Note 84226
    Symphony For Improvisers (with a.o. Pharoah Sanders) Blue Note
    BST 84247
    Eternal Rhythm (with a.o. Bernt Rosengren, Eje Thelin, Arild
    Andersen) MPS 15 204 ST
    Mu (with Ed Blackwell) Affinity CD Aff 774
    Brotherhood Suite: in Stockholm with Bernt Rosengren Group Flash
    Music FLCD 4
    Blue Lake (with Johnny Dyani & Okay Temiz) BYG YX 4022-3
    Organic Music Society Caprice RIKS DLP 1
    The Sonet Recordings(Eternal Now/Live in Ankara) Verve 533049-2
    Relativity Suite JCOA Records LP 1006
    Brown Rice A&M Jazz Heritage 397 001-2
    Music/Sangam (with Latif Khan) Europa Records JP 2009
    Hear & Now Atlantic SD 18217
    El Corazon (with Ed Blackwell) ECM 1230
    Dona Nostra (with a.o. Lennart Åberg & Bobo Stenson) ECM 1448
Ornette Coleman: *Beauty Is A Rare Thing: The Complete Atlantic
    Recordings* Atlantic/Rhino Records 8122 - 71410 - 2
    Town Hall, 1962 ESP/Fontana SFJL 923
    At The Golden Circle vols 1 & 2 Blue Note 4224/4225
    An Evening With Ornette Coleman Polydor 623 246/247
    Chappaqua Suite Columbia COL 480584 2
    Skies of America Columbia 65147
    Dancing In Your Head A & M Jazz CDA 0807
    In All Languages Caravan Of Dreams CDP85008
    Colors/Live from Leipzig (with Joachim Kuhn) Harmolodic 537 789 2
Billy Cobham: *Crosswinds* (with Michael & Randy Brecker) Atlantic K 50037
John Coltrane: *The Heavyweight Champion: The Complete Atlantic
    Recordings* Atlantic/Rhino Records 8122 - 71984 - 2
    The Complete 1961 Village Vanguard Recordings Impulse! IMPD4-232
    The Complete Africa/Brass Sessions Impulse! IMP 21682
    Coltrane Impulse! IMP 12152
    Ballads World Record Club T 670
    John Coltrane And Johnny Hartman Impulse! A 40
    Afro Blue Impressions Pablo 2PACD 2620-101
    Dear Old Stockholm Impulse! GRP 11202
    Crescent Impulse! MCAD 5889
    A Love Supreme MCA MCLD 19029
    New Thing At Newport (with Archie Shepp) HMV CLP 3551

Meditations Impulse! IMP 11992
First Meditations Impulse!/GRP 11182
Transition Impulse! 9195
Sun Ship Impulse! IMP 11672
*The Major Works of John Coltrane: Ascension/Om/Kulu Se
Mama/Selflessness* Impulse!/GRP 21132
Live In Seattle Impulse!GRP 21462
Live In Japan Impulse! GRP 41022
Live at the Village Vanguard Again! Impulse! IMP12132
Interstellar Space Impulse!GRP 11102
Expression Impulse! A 1920
Cosmic Music Impulse! 9148
Chick Corea: *Piano Improvisations Vol. 1* ECM 1014
Piano Improvisations Vol. 2 ECM 1020
Return To Forever ECM 1022
Trio Music: Live in Europe ECM 1310
Sonny Criss: *Saturday Morning* Xanadu 105
Anthony Davis/James Newton/Abdul Wadud: *I've Known Rivers*
Gramavision GR 8201
Miles Davis: *Birth Of The Cool* Capitol Jazz 7 92862 2
The Best Of The Capitol/Blue Note Years Blue Note CDP 7 98287 2
Walkin' Esquire 32-098
Relaxin' With the Miles Davis Quintet Prestige CA 98.428
Miles Davis/Gil Evans: *The Complete Columbia Studio Recordings*
Columbia/Sony 67397-S1
Miles Davis: *Milestones* CBS 460827 2
Kind of Blue Columbia Legacy CK 64935
Live in Stockholm 1960 Dragon DRLP 90/91
Copenhagen 1960 Royal Jazz RJ 501
The Complete Concert: 1964 CBS 471246 2 *ESP* CBS 467899 2
Highlights From The Plugged Nickel Columbia 481434 2
Miles Davis Quintet 1965-68 Columbia (6 CD set)
Filles de Kilimanjaro CBS 467088 2
Bitches Brew CBS 460602 2
In A Silent Way CBS 450982 2
At Fillmore Columbia/Sony COL 476909 2
Live Evil Columbia/Sony 485255 2
Aura (composer: Palle Mikkelborg) CBS 463351 2
Panthalassa: The Music of Miles Davis 1969-74 Columbia CK 67909
Bob Degen Trio: *Celebrations* (with Manfred Eicher, Fred Braceful) Calig
CAL 30 602
Jack DeJohnette: *Parallel Realities* MCA MCAD - 42313
Bill Dixon: *Intents And Purposes* RCA Black & White Series FXL1 7331
Eric Dolphy: *Out To Lunch* Blue Note BST 83163
Kenny Drew/Niels-Henning Ørsted Pedersen: *Duo* Steeplechase SCS 1002
Duo 2 Steeplechase SCS 1010
Duke Ellington: *The Blanton-Webster Band* RCA Bluebird 74321 13181 2
Back To Back: Duke Ellington and Johnny Hodges Play The Blues
Verve MG VS-6055
Three Suites Columbia 4679132

The Symphonic Ellington Reprise R - 6097
" ... *And His Mother Called Him Bill*" RCA NL 89166
The Far East Suite RCA Bluebird ND87640
New Orleans Suite Atlantic 7567-81376-2
Don Ellis: *How Time Passes* Barnaby/Candid BR - 5020
Peter Erskine/Palle Danielsson/John Taylor: *You Never Know* ECM 1497
    Time Being ECM 1532
    As It Is ECM 1594
Booker Ervin: *The Space Book* Prestige PR 7386
Bill Evans: *Everybody Digs Bill Evans* Riverside OJCCD 068-2
    The Village Vanguard Sessions Milestone 68 101
    Conversations With Myself Verve 821 984-2
Gil Evans: *Out Of The Cool* Impulse! IMP 11862
Bill Frisell: *In Line* ECM 1241
Kenny Garrett: *Pursuance: The Music of John Coltrane* Warner Bros 9362-46209-2
Stan Getz: *Stan Getz and Swedish All Stars featuring Bengt Hallberg* vol 2
    Metronome BLP 006
    West Coast Jazz Verve 2304 330
    Stockholm Sessions 1958 Dragon DRLP 157/158
    At Large Plus! vols 1 & 2 Jazz Unlimited JUCD 2001/2002
    Focus Verve 821 982-2
    The Girl From Ipanema: The Bossa Nova Years Verve 823611 2
    Sweet Rain Verve 815 954 2
    Captain Marvel Columbia CCL 468412 2
    Voyage Black Hawk BkH 51101 1
    People Time Gitanes/Emarcy 510 124 2
Stan Getz/Francy Boland: *Change Of Scenes* Verve Elite Edition 557 095-2
Dizzy Gillespie: *Bebop Enters Sweden* Dragon DRLP 34
    Gillespiana Verve 519 809 2
    Have Trumpet, Will Excite! Verve MV 2696
Dizzy Gillespie/Sonny Rollins/Sonny Stitt: *Sonny Side Up* Verve 521 426 2
Egberto Gismonti: *Amazonia* Carmo 9/517 716-2
    Solo ECM 1136
    ZigZag ECM 1582
Egberto Gismonti/Nana Vasconcelos: *Duas Vozes* ECM 1279
Jimmy Giuffre: *The Jimmy Giuffre 3* Atlantic 7567-90981-2
    Jimmy Giuffre 3, 1961 ECM 1438/39
    Free Fall Columbia Legacy CK 65446
Benny Golson: *Stockholm Sojourn* EMI Stateside SL 101150
Dexter Gordon: *Our Man In Paris* Blue Note CDP 46394 2
    One Flight Up Blue Note CDP 84176 2
    I Want More Steeplechase SCCD 36015
    Both Sides Of Midnight Black Lion BLCD 760103
    The Other Side of Round Midnight Blue Note CDP 7 46397 2
Trilok Gurtu: *The Glimpse* CMP CD 85
    Kathak Escapade ESC 03655
Charlie Haden/Christian Escoude: *Gitane* Disques Dreyfus FDM 36505 - 2
Coleman Hawkins: *The Essential Coleman Hawkins* Verve 2304 537
Coleman Hawkins/Ben Webster: *Blue Saxophones* Verve Super 2304 169

Graham Haynes: *The Griot's Footsteps* Verve 523 262 - 2
Joe Henderson: *The Blue Note Years* Blue Note CDP 95627 2
    Porgy and Bess Verve 523 262 2
Johnny Hodges: *And His Orchestra (1938-39 Recordings)* CBS Realm 52587
Billie Holiday: *Immortal Lady vol 1* Charly QBCD 13
    The Complete Commodore Recordings Commodore CMD 24012
Abdullah Ibrahim: *The Journey* Chiaroscuro CR 187
    The Mountain Kaz Records KAZ CD 7
Mark Isham/Art Lande: *We Begin* ECM 1338
Joseph Jarman: *As If It Were The Seasons* Delmark DD 417
Keith Jarrett: *Expectations* Columbia/Sony 467902 2
    Death And The Flower Impulse! MCD 29046
    Mysteries: The Impulse Years 1975-1976 Impulse! IMPD - 4 - 189
    Facing You ECM 1017
    Solo Concerts, Bremen, Lausanne ECM 1035/37
    The Köln Concert ECM 1064/65
    Hymns, Spheres 1086/87
    The Survivors' Suite ECM 1085
    Sun Bear Concerts ECM 1100
    Eyes Of The Heart ECM 1150
    Invocations/The Moth and The Flame ECM 1201/2
    Spirits ECM 1133/34
    Still Live ECM 1360/61
    Changeless ECM 1329
    At The Blue Note: The Complete Recordings ECM 1575-80
Elvin Jones: *Puttin' It Together* Blue Note CDP 7 84282 2
Jo Jones: *The Jo Jones Special* Jazztone J1242
Duke Jordan: *Flight to Denmark* Steeplechase SCS
Stan Kenton: *City of Glass* Capitol Jazz 7243 8 32084 2 5
Franklin Kiermyer: *Kairos* Evidence ECD 22144
Lee Konitz: *Lee Konitz Meets Jimmy Giuffre* Verve 527 780-2
Lee Konitz/John Pål Inderberg/Erling Aksdal Jr./ Bjørn Alterhaug: *Steps*
    Towards A Dream Odin NJ 4050-2
Art Lande: *Rubisa Patrol* ECM 1081
Yusef Lateef: *Live at Pep's* EMI His Master's Voice CSD 3547
Charles Lloyd: *Dream Weaver* Atlantic 588025
    In Europe Atlantic 588108
    Journey Within Atlantic 587101
    Fish Out of Water ECM 1398
    All My Relations ECM 1557
    Canto ECM 1635
Joe Lovano *Universal Language* Blue Note 07777 9983025
Herbie Mann: *The Wailing Dervishes* Atlantic SD 1497
Wynton Marsalis: *In This House, On This Morning* Columbia 474552 2
Warne Marsh: *Sax Of A Kind: Warne Marsh In Norway* (with a. o. Torgrim
    Sollid, Terje Bjørklund) Hot Club Records HCR 7
Pat Metheny: *Bright Size Life* ECM 1073
    Watercolors ECM 1097
Bingo Miki: *Scandinavian Suite* three blind mice TBM 1005
Charles Mingus: *The Black Saint And The Sinner Lady* Impulse! IMP 11742

Town Hall Concert: European Tour '64 Jazz Workshop OJCCD 042 2
Roscoe Mitchell Art Ensemble: *Sound* Delmark DE 408
    Congliptious Nessa Records n - 2
Hank Mobley: *Soul Station* Blue Note BST 84031
Louis Moholo Octet: *Spirits Rejoice!* Ogun OG 520
Brew Moore: *Brew's Stockholm Dew* Sonet SNTF 624
Lee Morgan: *Search For The New Land* Blue Note BLP 4169
Oliver Nelson: *The Blues And The Abstract Truth* Impulse! IMP 11542
Erkan Ogur: *Fretless* (with a. o. Philip Catherine, Bulent Ortacgil, Arto
    Tuncboyaciyan) Feuer und Eis FUEC 714
Old And New Dreams: *Old And New Dreams* (Don Cherry, Dewey
    Redman, Charlie Haden, Ed Blackwell) ECM 1154
    Playing ECM 1205
Opeye: *Moss 'Comes Silk: Avant-Shamanic Trance Jazz* Humming Bird CD 1
Charlie Parker: *Masterworks 1946-1947* Giants Of Jazz CD 53007
    Charlie Parker in Sweden XTRA 1010
    With Strings: The Master Takes Verve 523 984 2
Gary Peacock: *Voices* CBS/Sony SOPM 179
    Eastward Sony SRCS 9333
Art Pepper: *Living Legend* Contemporary S7633
Jim Pepper: *Comin' and Goin'* Antilles ANCD 8706
Oscar Pettiford: *Montmartre Blues* Black Lion BLCD 760124
Barre Phillips: *Mountainscapes* ECM 1076
    Three Day Moon ECM 1123
Sun Ra: *The Heliocentric Worlds Of Sun Ra vol 1* ESP 1014
    The Heliocentric Worlds Of Sun Ra vol 2 ESP 1017
    Space Is The Place Impulse! IMP 12492
Dianne Reeves: *Art And Survival* ERG/EMI 7243 8 28494 21
The Revolutionary Ensemble: *The People's Republic* Horizon AMLJ 708
Sam Rivers *Trio Live* Impulse! IMP 12682
    Contrasts ECM 1162
Max Roach: *Survivors* Soul Note SN 1093
Sonny Rollins: *Tenor Madness/Saxophone Colossus* Prestige CDJZD 002
    On Impulse! MCA Impulse! MCAD-5655
    Alfie Impulse! IMP 12242
    East Broadway Rundown Impulse! IMP 11612
    Sonny Rollins' Next Album Milestone OJCCD 312-2
    Horn Culture Milestone OJCCD 314-2
    The Solo Album Milestone M-9137
    Silver City: A Celebration Of 25 Years On Milestone Milestone
    2MCD - 2501 -2
    Global Warming Milestone MCD 9280 2
Ned Rothenberg: *The Crux* Leo Records CD LR 187
George Russell: *The Jazz Workshop* (with a.o. Bill Evans) Koch Jazz KOC
    CD 7850
    New York, NY & Jazz In The Space Age (with a.o. Paul Bley, Bill
    Evans) MCA Records MAPD 7031
    Jazz In The Space Age Chessmates/GRP 18262
    Stratusphunk Riverside OJCLP 232
    Ezz-Thetics (with a.o. Don Ellis, Eric Dolphy) Riverside OJCD 070-2

The Stratus Seekers (with a.o. Paul Plummer) Riverside RLP 412
The Outer View (with a.o. Sheila Jordan) Riverside OJCCD 616-2
At Beethoven Hall (with a.o. Don Cherry, Bertil Lövgren) MPS 539 084-2
Vertical Form VI Soul Note SN 1019
Electronic Sonata For Souls Loved by Nature - 1980 Soul Note
121009-2
The African Game Blue Note CDP 7 46335 2
So What Blue Note BT 85132
"It's about time" Label Bleu LBLC 6587
Pharoah Sanders *Tauhid* Impulse! GRP 11292
   Karma Impulse! IMPL 5038
   Journey To The One Theresa TRCD 108/9
Lalo Schifrin: *Firebird* EastWest Records 0630-10513-2
Tony Scott: *Music For Zen Meditation and Other Joys* Verve 521 444 - 2
Sextet of Orchestra USA: *Theatre Music of Kurt Weill* Bluebird ND 86285
Archie Shepp/Bill Dixon: *Quartet* Savoy MG 12178
Archie Shepp: *And The New York Contemporary Five/Bill Dixon 7-Tette*
   CBS Realm 52422
   And The New York Contemporary Five Polydor 623 235
   And The New York Contemporary Five vol 2 Storyville SLP 1009
   The House I Live In (with Lars Gullin) Steeplechase SCC 6013
   Four For Trane Impulse! IMPD 218
   Fire Music Impulse! IMP 11582
   Mama Too Tight Impulse! IMP 12482
   One For The Trane Polydor 583 732
   The Way Ahead Impulse IMP 12722
   Things Have Got To Change (with a. o. Joe Lee Wilson) Impulse! AS
   9212
   Bird Fire: Tribute To Charlie Parker West Wind 006
Wayne Shorter: *Night Dreamer* Blue Note CDP 7 84173 2
   JuJu Blue Note BST 84182
   Adam's Apple Blue Note CDP 7 46403 2
   Speak No Evil Blue Note BLP BST 84194
   Odyssey of Iska Blue Note CDP 7 84363 2
   Native Dancer Columbia 467095 2
Horace Silver: *The Best of Horace Silver* Blue Note BST 84325
Wadada Leo Smith: *Divine Love* ECM 1143
   Kulture Jazz ECM 1507
Sonny Stitt & Friends: *High High The Moon* Chess/GRP 18172
L. Subramaniam/Stephane Grappelli: *Conversations* Milestone 68166
Cecil Taylor: *In Transition* Blue Note BN LA 458-H2
   Air Barnaby/Candid Z 30562
   Live! At the Cafe Montmartre Debut/Fontana SFJL 928
   Unit Structures Blue Note BLP 4297
   Segments 11/Winged Serpent Soul Note SN 1089
David Torn: *Best Laid Plans* ECM 1284
   Cloud About Mercury ECM 1322
Lennie Tristano/Buddy DeFranco: *Crosscurrents* Capitol M -11060
McCoy Tyner: *The Real McCoy* Blue Note 4651226
   Remembering John Enja 6080 2

Blues for Coltrane Impulse! MCAD - 42122
The Turning Point Birdology 513 163 - 2
Tony Vacca/Tim Moran: *City Spirits* (with Don Cherry & Tim Wolf) Philo/Rounder PH 9007
Various: *Esquire Jazz Concert (Metropolitan Opera House 1944)* Giants of Jazz CD 53035
The Sound Of Jazz CBS 57036
Modern Jazz Concert: Six Compositions commissioned by the 1957 Brandeis University Festival of the Arts Columbia WL 127
Mirage: Avant-Garde & Third-Stream Jazz New World Records NW 216
Jazz Abstractions: John Lewis presents Contemporary Music Atlantic 588043
The Connection (music by Kenny Drew & Cecil Payne) Charlie Parker Records AJS 16
Les Années Blue Note: The Avant Garde 1963-1967 Blue Note 854194 2
The ESP Sampler ESP 1051
Gittin' To Know Y'All MPS 15038
Nana Vasconcelos: *Saudades* ECM 1147
Storytelling Hemisphere 7243 8 334 442 0
Collin Walcott: *Cloud Dance* ECM 1062
Collin Walcott/Don Cherry/Nana Vasconcelos: *Codona* ECM 1132
Codona 2 ECM 1177
Codona 3 ECM 1243
Mal Waldron: *One-Upmanship* (with a. o. Steve Lacy & Manfred Schoof) Enja 2092 2
Weather Report: *Weather Report* CBS 64521
I Sing The Body Electric Columbia 468207 2
Sweetnighter Columbia 485102 2
Mysterious Traveller Columbia 471860 2
Tale Spinnin' Columbia 476907 2
Black Market CBSCD 81325
Heavy Weather CBSCD 81775
Mr Gone CBS 82775
8.30 CBS 88455
Kenny Werner: *Unprotected Music* Double-Time Records DTRCD 139
Kenny Wheeler: *Gnu High* ECM 1069
Around Six ECM 1156
Music For Large And Small Ensembles ECM 1415/16
Joe Lee Wilson: *Without A Song* Inner City IC 1064
What Would It be Without You Survival Records SR 110
Secrets Of The Sun Inner City IC 1042
The Shadow Agharta PCCY-00153
Lester Young: *The "Kansas City" Sessions* Commodore CMD 14022
Lester Young Trio Verve 521650-2
Lester Young With The Oscar Peterson Trio Verve 521451-2
The Zawinul Syndicate: *The Immigrants* Columbia CK 40969
Black Water Columbia 465344 2
Lost Tribes Columbia CK 46057
World Tour ESC Records ESC/EFA 03656-2

(iii) *traditional/improvised/song/poetry/speech*

Mikhail Alperin/Arkady Schilkloper/Sergey Starostin: *Prayer* Silex Y225039
Vicente Amigo: *Poeta* (with a. o. Miguel Rose) CBS/Sony COL 487502 2
Angelite: *Mountain Tale* JARO 4212 - 2
Balkana: *The Music of Bulgaria* Hannibal HND 1335
Amira Baraka: *New Music, New Poetry* India Navigation IN 1048
Arve Moen Bergset/Annbjorg Lien/ Steinar Ofsdal: *Bukkene Bruse* Grappa
    GRCD 4053
Jens Bjørneboe: *Våpenløs: Jens Bjørneboe leser egne dikt* (with Arne
    Domnérus Sextet) Pan Records PACD 07
Carla Bley/Paul Haines: *Escalator Over the Hill* JCOA 839 312-2
Mari Boine: *Gula, Gula* Real World CDR W13
    Goaskinviellja/Ørnebror LEAN MBCD 62 (also released on Verve)
    Møte I Moskva (with Allians) RCA/BMG 74321 10 1762
    Leahkastin Sonet MBCD 94
    Eallin Antilles 533 799 - 2
    Balvvoslatina (Room of Worship) Antilles 5591232
Kari Bremnes: *Løsrivelse* (texts by Edvard Munch, arrangements by Ketil
    Bjørnstad) Kirkelig Kulturverksted FXCD 123
Bukkene Bruse: *Åre* Grappa GRCD 4100
Voix Bulgaires: *Le Mystère des Voix Bulgaires* CAD 603
    Le Mystère des Voix Bulgaires vol 2 CAD 801
Eric Bye: *Langt Nord I Livet* Kirkelig Kulturverksted FXCD 144
Ry Cooder & V. M. Bhatt *A Meeting By The River* WLACS29
Danza Fuego *Flamenco Poetry: Tribute to Federico Garcia Lorca* EUCD 1449
Elise Einarsdotter/Lena Willemark: *Senses* Caprice CAP 21442
Brian Eno/David Byrne: *My Life In The Bush Of Ghosts* EGCD 48
Agnes Buen Garnås: *Draumkvedet* Kirkelig Kulturverksted FXCD 50
Léo Ferré: *Les Poetes vols 1-3* Barclay 847 171 - 2
    Les Loubards EPM FDC 1008
Jon Fosse/Karl Seglem *Prosa* NORCD9616
Serge Gainsbourg: *du jazz dans le ravin* Philips/Mercury 522629 - 2
Glenn Gould: *Glenn Gould's Solitude Trilogy* CBC Records PSCD 2003-3
Olav H. Hauge: *Mange års røynsle med pil og boge* Det Norske Samlaget 2
    music cassette ISBN 82 - 521 - 2790 - 8
Andre Jaume/Christian Gorelli/Bernard Gueit/Remi Charmasson/ Hakim
    Hamadouche: *Iliade* CELP C 37
Nusrat Fateh Ali Khan: *Mustt Mustt* Real World 0777 7862212 3
Harpans Kraft: *Harpans Kraft* Caprice CAP 1070
Hedningarna: *Trä* Silence Records SRCD 4721
Langston Hughes: *Weary Blues* Verve 841 660 - 2
Ingeborg Hugnes/Terje Venaas: *Toner Fra Romsdal* (Odin NJ 4047 - 2)
Tony Hymas: *Oyaté* nato VG 662 669003
Henry Kaiser & David Lindley/Various: *The Sweet Sunny North* Shanachie 4057
    The Sweet Sunny North vol 2 Shanachie 64061 (both volumes feature
    extensive documentation of traditional and developing folk music in
    Norway, including performances by eg Ailu Gaup, Kirsten Bråten
    Berg, Tone Hulbækmo, The Brass Brothers, Farmer's Market and Knut
    Reiersrud)

Hölderlin: *Gedichte gelesen von Bruno Ganz* ECM New Series 1285
Holliger: *Scardanelli-Zyklus* ECM New Series 1472/73
Yoshikazu Iwamoto: *Flute Shakuhachi* Musique Du Monde 92543 2
Anna-Kaisa Liedes: *Oi Miksi* Riverboat Records TUGCD 1009
Michael Mantler: *Cerco Un Paese Innocente* (with Mona Larsen & The
    Danish Radio Big Band: music to the poetry of Giuseppe Ungaretti)
    ECM 1556
Master Musicians of Joujouka: *Joujouka Black Eyes* le coeur du monde SR 87
Katja Medbøe *prøv å sette vinger på en stein* Kirkelig Kulturverksted FXCD 1921
Yehudi Menuhin/Ravi Shankar: *West meets East* HMV ASD 2294
Stephan Micus: *Implosions* ECM/JAPO 829 201-2
    Wings Over Water ECM/JAPO 831 058-2
    Koan ECM SP 230 5804
    The Music Of Stones ECM 1384
    Athos: A Journey To The Holy Mountain ECM 1551
R. Carlos Nakai & Wind Travelin' Band *Island of Bows* Canyon CR7018
Sainkho Namchylak: *Sainkho: Out of Tuva* CramWorld craw 6
    Tunguska-Guska (with Grace Toon, Iris Disse & Sunny Murray)
    Schneeball 01049 -6
    When The Sun Is Out You Don't See Stars FMP CD 38
    Lost Rivers FMP CD42
    Letters Leo CD LR 190
    Amulet (with Ned Rothenberg) Leo CD LR 231
Kenneth Patchen: *Reads with Jazz in Canada* Folkways Records FL 9718
Ole Paus/Mari Boine/Kari Bremnes: *Salmer På Veien Hjem* Kirkelig
    Kulturverksted FXCD 105
Valentina Ponomareva/Ken Hyder/Tim Hodgkinson: *The Goose* Megaphone
    004/Woof 014
Michael Riessler: *Honig Und Asche* ENJA ENJ-9303 2
Nitin Sawhney: *Displacing the Priest* Outcaste Records Caste CD 2
Ravi Shankar: *East Greets East: Ravi Shankar in Japan* Deutsche
    Grammophon 2531 381
Shankar: *Who's To Know* ECM 1195
Shakti: *Shakti with John McLaughlin* Columbia 467905 2
    A Handful Of Beauty Sony SRCS 9381
    Natural Elements CBS 82329
Taraf de Haidouks: *Dumbala Dumba* Craw 21
Theodosii Spassov: *Beyond The Frontiers* Gega New GD194
Stan Tracey: *Jazz Suite Inspired By Under Milk Wood* Steam TAA 271
Tomas Tranströmer: *Östersjöar* Bokbandet music cassette BOK 09
Nils-Aslak Valkeapää: *Juoigamat* Finnlevy SFLP 8531
    Beaivi, Áhčážán DAT CD 10 (4 CD, with Esa Kotilainen)
    Beaivi, Áhčážán DAT CD 4 (with Esa Kotilainen)
    Dálveleaikkat/Winter Games DAT CD 17 (with Esa Kotilainen, Johan
    Anders Bær, Seppo Paakkunainen)
Various: *The Nonesuch Explorer - Music from Distant Corners of the World*
    Nonesuch H7-11
    Echos Du Paradis: Sufi Soul Network 29982
    The World Of Traditional Music Ocora (6 CD set) 560061-6
    Chants Chamaniques Et Narratifs De L'Artique Siberien Musique du

Monde 92564-2

Deep In The Heart Of Tuva Ellipsis Arts CD 4080

Folk Music from Telemark Grappa GRCD 4066

Folk Music from Trøndelag Grappa GRCD 4069

Samisk Musik i forvandling Caprice CAP 1351 (with English text)

Beyond the River: Seasonal Songs of Latvia EMI Hemisphere 7243 4 93341 20

Beyond The Blues: American Negro Poetry Argo PLP 1071

Poetry and Jazz in Concert Argo DA 26

Tarjei Vesaas: *Les eigne Texter - Dikt og Prosa 1953-1970* Det Norske Samlaget music cassette ISBN 82 - 521 - 2747 - 9

Jan Erik Vold/Chet Baker: *Blåmann! Blåmann!* Hot Club Records HCRCD 50

Jan Erik Vold: *Sannheten om trikken er at den brenner* (with a. o. Nisse Sandström, Knut Reiersrud, Egil Kapstad) Hot Club Records HCRCD 70

Lena Willemark/Elise Einarsdotter: *Secrets of Living* Caprice CAP 21377

Lena Willemark/Ale Moller: *Nordan* ECM 1536

Agram ECM 1610

Hector Zazou: *Sahara Blue* Crammed Discs MTM 32

Songs From The Cold Seas Columbia 477585 2

(iv) **Aspects of Composed Music 1890s - Now**

Aho: *Symphony no 10/Rejoicing of the Deep Waters* (Osme Vanska, conductor; Lahti Symphony Orchestra) BIS CD 856

Hugo Alfvén: *Swedish Rhapsodies 1-3/A Legend of the Skerries/ Elegy* (Icelandic Symphony Orchestra, Petri Sakari, conductor) CHANDOS CHAN 9313

Louis Andriessen: *De Tijd* (incl. Schoenberg Ensemble, Netherlands Chamber Choir) Elektra Nonesuch 7559 79291-2

Barber/Ives/Copland/Cowell/Creston: *Adagio for Strings/Symphony no 3/Quiet City/Hymn and Fuguing Tune no 10/A Rumor* (The Academy of St. Martin-In-The-Fields, Nevill Mariner, conductor) Argo ZRG 845

Barry, John: *The Beyondness of Things* (English Chamber Orchestra) London 460 009 2

Bartók: *Suite no 2, Rumanian Folk Dances, Transylvanian Dances, Hungarian Sketches* (Budapest Symphony Orchestra, conductor Miklos Erdelyi) Hungaraton LPX 11355

Bjørklund: *Music For Strings* (Marianne Thorsen, violin; Bjarne Fiskum, conductor, The Trondheim Soloists; the Chilingirian String Quartet) Hemera HCD 2923

Buck: *Landscapes* (Svend Aaquist, conductor; Danish Chamber Players) dacapo 8. 224034

Cage: *Music of Changes* (Herbert Henck, Piano) Wergo WER 60099 - 50

In a Landscape (Stephen Drury, Keyboards) Catalyst 09026 61980 2

Giger: *Chartres* (Paul Giger, violin) ECM New Series 1386

Gorecki: *Symphony no 3* (Dawn Upshaw, soprano; London Sinfonietta, David Zimmerman, conductor) Elektra Nonesuch 7559 - 79282 - 2

Grieg: *The Complete Piano Music, Vol 11: Lyric Pieces, Books 5-7* (Eva

Knardahl, piano) BIS CD-105

Lyric Pieces (Selection) (Einar Steen-Nøkleberg, piano) NAXOS 8.554051

Songs: Lieder (Anne Sofie Von Otter, mezzo-soprano; Bengt Forsberg, piano) Deutsche Grammophon CD 437 521- 2

Peer Gynt (Ernst-Senff-Chor, chorus master; Jeffrey Tate, conductor; Berlin Philharmoniker) EMI CDC 7 54119 2

Hindemith, Britten, Penderecki: *Lachrymae (Trauermusik; Lachrymae op 48a; Konzert fur Viola und Kammerorchester)* (Kim Kashkashian, viola; Stuttgart Kammerorchester, Dennis Russell Davies, conductor) ECM New Series 1506

Hovhaness: *Mysterious Mountain/And God Created Great Whales/Celestial Fantasy* .. (Seattle Symphony, conductor Gerard Schwarz) Delos DE 3157

Lady Of Light/Avak, The Healer (Royal Philharmonic Orchestra, conductor Alan Hovhaness) Crystal Records CD 806

Spirit Murmur (The Shanghai Quartet) Delos DE 3162

Ives: *A Set Of Pieces* (including *The Unanswered Question*) (Orpheus Chamber Orchestra) Deutsche Grammophon 439 869 - 2

Janson: *Interlude/String Quartet/Wings/Cradle Song* (Christian Eggen, conductor; Royal Philharmonic Orchestra; The Norwegian String Quartet; Jazz Ensemble including Tore Brunborg/Palle Mikkelborg/Rune Klakegg/Arild Andersen/Jon Christensen; Elin Rosseland, soprano) NCD 4918

Johnson: *The Musical Worlds of Laurie Johnson (Symphony/Synthesis, The Wind in the Willows, Hedda Suite)* (London Jazz Orchestra, London Philharmomic Orchestra, London Studio Symphony Orchestra; Laurie Johnson and Jack Parnell, conductors) Redial CD 557 819 2

Langaard: *Music of the Spheres/Four Tone Pictures* (Gitta-Maria Sjöberg, soprano; Jesper Grove Jorgensen, chorus master; Gennady Rozhdestvensky, conductor; Danish National Radio Symphony) Chandos CHAN 9517

Ligeti: *Lux Aeterna/Volumina/String Quartet no 2/Etude no 1* (North German Radio Chorus, Hamburg, director Helmut Franz; La Salle Quartet; Gerd Zacher, organ) Deutsche Grammophon 2543 818

Lundsten: *Nordisk Natursymfoni nr 1/"Stromkarlen"* HMV 4 E 061 - 34785

Lutoslawski: *Trois Poemes d'Henri Michaux/Postludium/String Quartet* (Polish Radio Choir, Krakau, director Witold Lutoslawski; Polish Radio Symphony Orchestra, conductor Jan Krenz) Wergo WER 60019

Mahler: *Symphony no 3* (Norma Proctor, contralto, Ambrosian Singers, Wandsworth School Boys' Choir, London Symphony Orchestra, conductor Jascha Horenstein) Unicorn UKCD 2006/7

Symphony no 4 (Judith Raskin, soprano; The Cleveland Orchestra, conductor George Szell) CBS Maestro MYK 44713

Symphony no 9 (Berlin Philharmonic Orchestra, conductor Sir John Barbirolli) EMI/Classics For Pleasure CFP 41 - 4426 3

Kindertotenlieder/Ruckert Lieder/ Lieder Eines Fahrenden Gesellen (Janet Baker, mezzo-soprano; Halle Orchestra/New Philharmonia Orchestra, conductor Sir John Barbirolli) EMI CDC 7 47793 2

Song of the Earth (Christa Ludwig, alto, Rene Kollo, tenor, Berlin Philharmoniker, conductor Herbert von Karajan) Deutsche Grammophon/Galleria 419 058-2

Mahler/Uri Caine: *Urlicht/Primal Light* New Edition, Winter and Winter 910 004 - 2

Messiaen: *Turangalîla-Symphonie* (Yvonne Loriod, piano; Jeanne Loriod, ondes martenot; Myung-Whun Chung, conductor; Orchestre de la Bastille) Deutsche Grammophon 431 781 - 2

   Meditations Sur Le Mystère de La Sainte Trinité (Christopher Bowers-Broadbent, organ) ECM New Series 1494

   Seven Haiku (with Schoenberg: *Chamber Symphony, op 9, 3 Pieces for Orchestra*) (Yvonne Loriod, piano, Strassbourg Percussion Ensemble, Domaine Musical Orchestra, conductor Pierre Boulez) Everest 3192

Milhaud: *L'Oeuvre Pour Orgue* (George Baker, organ) FYCD 016

Nielsen: *Symphonies no 4 "The Inextinguishable" & no 5* (National Symphony Orchestra of Iceland, Adrian Leaper, conductor)

Nono, Furrer, Kurtag, Rihm: *Hommage à Andrei Tarkovsky* (Various works: Ensemble Anton Webern, Claudio Abbado director; Arnold Schoenberg Chor, Erwin Ortner, chorus master) Deutsche Grammophon 437 840 - 2

Nordheim: *Arne Nordheim (Evening Land; Floating; Solitaire)* (Elisabeth Søderstrøm, soprano; Miltiades Caridis, conductor; Oslo Philharmonic Orchestra) Aurora NCDB 4933

Nørgård: *Korvaerker* (including *Aftonland*) Da Camera, director Erling Kullberg) Paula 17

O' Suilleabhain: *Oilean/Island* Venture CDVE 40

Olsen: *Six Old Village Songs from Lom/Adagio/Variations over a Norwegian Folk-tune* (and other works; Arve Tellefsen, violin, Oslo Philharmonic Orchestra, conductor Mariss Jansons, Kjell Baekkelund, piano) Philips 410 445 - 1

Pärt: *Tabula Rasa (Fratres; Cantus; Fratres; Tabula Rasa*; Gidon Kramer, violin; Keith Jarrett, piano; Staatsorchester Stuttgart, Denis Russell Davies, conductor; the 12 cellists of the Berlin Philharmonic Orchestra; Tatjana Grindenko, violin; Alfred Schnittke, prepared piano; Lithuanian Chamber Orchestra, Saulus Sondeckis, conductor) ECM New Series 1275

Paakkunainen: *Symphony no 1/Suite for Symphony Orchestra, improvising group and a joik soloist* (Nils-Aslak Valkeapää, Johan Anders Bær, Karelia Group/Studio Orchestra, conductor Paul Magi) DAT CD 11

Rautavaara: *Cantus Arcticus: Music of Rautavaara(Cantus Arcticus/String Quartet no 4/Symphony no 5*; Leipzig Radio Symphony Orchestra, Maz Pommer, conductor; Sirius String Quartet) Catalyst 09026 62671 2

   Violin Concerto/Isle of Bliss/Angels and Visitations (Elmar Oliviera, violin; Helsinki Philharmonic Orchestra, Leif Segerstam, conductor) Ondine ODE 881-2

Reich: *Octet/Music for a Large Ensemble/Violin Phase* (Steve Reich, piano, Shem Guibbory, violin, plus ensemble) ECM New Series 1168

Rypdal: *Undisonus (for Violin & Orchestra)/Ineo (for Choir & Chamber Orchestra)* (Terje Tønnesen, violin, Royal Philharmonic Orchestra, London, conductor Christian Eggen; Grex Vocalists, director Carl

Hogset, The Rainbow Orchestra) ECM 1389

Sæverud: *Complete Piano Music volume 2* (*op 21, 22, 24, 25*; Einar Henning Smebye, piano) Victoria VCD 19085

Sinfonia Dolorosa (with David Monrad-Johansen *Pan* & Knut Nystedt *The Burnt Sacrifice*; Bergen Symphony Orchestra & Chorus, conductor Karsten Andersen) Philips 6507 007

Samkopf: *Mårådalen Walk* (Kjell Samkopf, treated sounds) HEMERA HCD 2907

Sandvold: *Introduction & Passsacaglia in B minor/Variations on a Norwegian Folk Tune* (with Arne Eggen: *Ciacona in G minor*; Kjell Johnsen, organ, Engelbrektskyrkan, Stockholm) Ansgar Grammofon MC - ANS - 30 - 30

Schoenberg/Webern/Berg: *5 Pieces for Orchestra/5 Pieces for Orchestra/3 Pieces for Orchestra* (London Symphony Orchestra, conductor Antal Dorati) Mercury 432 006 - 2

Schoenberg: *Piano Works* (*op 11, 19, 23, 25, 33a, 33b; Piano Concerto op 42; Fantasy op 47 & others*; Glenn Gould, piano} Sony SM2K 664

Ravi Shankar/Philip Glass: *Passages* Private Music 260947

Schwitters: *Ursonate* Wergo WER 6304-2 286 304-2

Sibelius: *Symphonies nos 2 & 6* (Anthony Collins, conductor, London Symphony Orchestra) Beular 2PD 8

Symphonies nos 3 & 6 (Sir Alexander Gibson, conductor, Scottish National Orchestra)

Symphony no 5 (original & final versions) (Osmo Vanska, conductor, Lahti Symphony Orchestra) BIS CD 863

Pohjola's Daughter/Tapiola/ Rakastava (Neeme Jarvi, conductor, The Gothenburg Symphony Orchestra) BIS CD 312

Songs (Tom Krause, baritone, Pentti Koskimies, piano) Decca LXT 6314

Wilhelm Stenhammer: *Symphony no 2/Excelsior! (Overture)* (Royal Scottish National Orchestra, Peter Sundkvist, conductor) NAXOS 8.553888

Stockhausen: *Gesange der Jünglinge* Deutsche Grammophon 138811

Kontakte/Refrain (Aloys Kontarsky, piano, wood blocks; Christoph Castel, percussion; Karlheinz Stockhausen, celesta, percussion, supervision)

From The Seven Days (Peter Eotvos, Herbert Henck, Michael Vetter, Karlheinz Stockhausen) Deutsche Grammophon 2561 301

Michael's Reise ECM New Series 1406

Stravinsky: *Le Sacre de Printemps* (Columbia Symphony Orchestra, conductor Igor Stravinsky) CBS 72054

Firebird Suite/Four Norwegian Moods (with Liadov *The Enchanted Lake, Eight Russian Folk Songs* etc; Bergen Philharmonic Orchestra, conductor Dmitri Kitajenko) Virgin Classics 7243 5 61322 21

The Firebird/The Song of the Nightingale/Tango/Scherzo à la Russe (London Symphony Orchestra, conductor Antal Dorati) Mercury 432 012-2

Szymanowski: *The Complete Music for Violin & Piano* (Detlef Hahn, violin; Mark Fielding, piano) ASV Quicksilver CD QS 6215)

Symphony no 3 "Song of the Night" (with *Symphony no 4/Concert Overture*, Polish State Philharmonic Orchestra, Katowice, Karol

Stryja, conductor) NAXOS 8.553684

Harnasie/Mandragora/Etude (Polish State Philharmonic Chorus & Orchestra, Katowice, Karol Stryja, conductor) NAXOS 8.553686

Takemitsu: *November Steps* (Katsuya Yokoyama, shakuhachi; Kunshi Isuruta, biwa; Bernard Haitink, conductor; Royal Concertgebouw Orchestra, Amsterdam) Philips 426 667-2 (with Messiaen's *Et Exspecto Resurrectionem*)

Quatrain/Stanza 1/Sacrifice/ Ring/ Valeria/ A Flock Descends Into The Pentagonal Garden (Seji Ozawa, Hiroshi Wakasugi, conductors; Tashi Quartet; Boston Symphony Orchestra) Deutsche Grammophon 423 253-2

A Way A Lone (Tokyo String Quartet; with works by Barber & Britten) RCA Victor 09026 - 61387 - 2

Tippett: *A Child of Our Time* (Sheila Armstrong, Felicity Palmer, Philip Langridge, John Shirley-Quick; Brighton Festival Chorus; Royal Philharmonic Orchestra, conductor Andre Previn) RPO Records CDRPO 7012

Tormis: *Forgotten Peoples* (Estonian Philharmonic Chamber Choir, Tonu Kaljuste, conductor) ECM New Series 1459/60

Toby Twining Music: *Shaman* Catalyst 0926 61981 2

Tuur: *Crystallisatio* (Tonu Kaljuste, conductor; Tallinn Chamber Orchestra, Estonian Philharmonic Chamber Choir) ECM New Series 1590

Tveitt: *Suite no 1 from A Hundred Folktunes from Hardanger/Harp Concerto no 2/Nykken* (Turid Kniejski, harp; Per Dreir, conductor; Royal Philharmonic Orchestra) SIMAX PSC 3108

Valen: *Piano Sonata no 2* (with works by Morawetz, Anhalt, Hetu, Pentland; Glenn Gould, piano) Sony/Glenn Gould Edition SMK 52677

The Complete Symphonies (Bergen Philharmonic Orchestra, Aldo Ceccato, conductor) SIMAX PSC 3101

Symphonic Poems and Orchestral Songs Simax PSC3115

Valkeapää: *Goase Dušše (The Bird Symphony)* DAT CD 15

Various: *Estonian Experience* Finlandia 0630 - 122442

Various: *Northern Lights - Music From Scandinavia* Finlandia 4509 99524-2

Northern Landscapes: Pastoral Music of Sweden, Denmark, Norway and Finland CBC Records SMCD 5157

Aurora Borealis: Music from Norway (Arnestad, Fongaard, Janson, Nordheim, Persen, Soderlind, Thommessen) Unicorn RHS 357/8

Norwegian Contemporary Music (Janson, Thoresen, Thommessen, Hegdal, Bull, Asheim, Wallin) Aurora ACD 4992

The Solitary Saxophone (works by Berio, Scelsi, Takemitsu, Stockhausen; Claude Delangle, saxophone) BIS CD 640

Vasks: *Message/Cantabile/Cor Anglais Concerto/Musica Dolorosa/Lauda* (Riga Philharmonic Orchestra, Valdis Zarins, conductor) Conifer Records CDCF 236

Vaughan Williams: *Job: A Masque for Dancing* (London Symphony Orchestra, conductor Sir Adrian Boult) HMV ASD 2673

Vaughan Williams/Benjamin Britten et al: *Elegies* (Kim Kashkashian, viola, Robert Levin, piano) ECM New Series 1316

Briskeby Blues: *Jan Erik Vold 1993*
photo Arve Kjersheim
Reproduced with kind permission of JazzNytt

Terje Rypdal
ECM

Arild Andersen
ECM

Miroslav Vitous
Wolfgang Kraus

Anouar Brahem
ECM

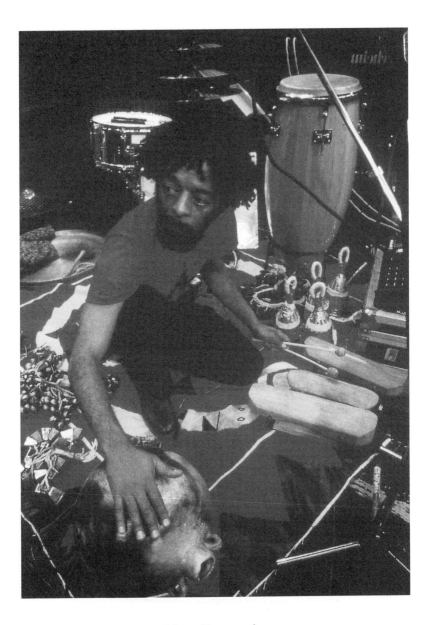

Nana Vasconcelos
(Logan Hall, 1987) Christian Him

Marilyn Mazur (Royal Festival Hall, 1993)
Christian Him

Bibliography

Aarseth, Bjørn: *The Sami - Past And Present* Norsk Folkemuseum, Oslo 1993

Abraham, Gerald (ed.): *Sibelius, A Symposium* Oxford University Press, Oxford 1947

Adam, Michael: *Wandering In Eden: Three Ways to the East Within Us* Wildwood House, London 1976

Adorno, Theodor: *Prisms* (trans. Samuel & Shierry Weber) Neville Spearman, London 1967
Philosophy of Modern Music (trans. A. G. Mitchell & W. V. Bloomster) Sheed & Ward, London 1973

Ahlbäck, Tore & Bergman, Jan (eds.): *The Saami Shaman Drum* The Donner Institute For Research In Religious and Cultural History, Åbo 1991

Alison, J & Brown, C. (eds.): *Border Crossings: Fourteen Scandinavian Artists* Barbican Art Gallery, London 1992

Alperin, Mikhail (Misha): 'Garbareks musikk er musikalsk naturvern', *Bergens Tidende* July 29, 1990

Angell, Olav/Vold, Jan Eric/Økland, Einar (eds.) *Jazz I Norge* Gyldendal, Oslo 1975

Angell, Olav & Vold, Jan Erik: 'Intervju med Karin Krog' ibid pp. 79-83

Andersen, Svein: 'Lyrisk urkraft', *Nordlys*, Tromso June 27, 1987

Angilette, Elizabeth: *Philosopher at the Keyboard: Glenn Gould* The Scarecrow Press, Inc., Metuchen, N.J., & London 1992

Apostolos-Cappadona, Diane (ed.) *Art, Creativity and the Sacred* Continuum, New York 1996

Babbitt, Milton: 'Who Cares If You Listen?', in Girvetz, Harry & Ross, Ralph (eds.): *Literature and the Arts: The Moral Issues* Wadsworth Publishing Company, Inc., Belmont 1971 pp.24-29

Bachelard, Gaston: *On Poetic Imagination and Reverie* (trans. & ed. Colette Gaudin) Spring Publications Inc., Dallas, Texas 1987

Baggenaes, Roland: 'Dexter Gordon - an interview', *Coda* June 1972 vol 10 no 7 pp. 2-5
'Mal Waldron', *Coda* February 1977 issue 153 pp. 2-3

Bailey, Derek: *Improvisation: its nature and practice in music* Moorland Publishing, Ashbourne /Incus Records, London 1980

Barker, John: 'Point of View' *American Record Guide* March/April 1995

Barrett, William: *What Is Existentialism?* Evergreen/Grove Press Inc., New York 1965
Irrational Man: A Study In Existential Philosophy Heinemann, London 1972

Bashō: *The Narrow Road To The Deep North And Other Travel Sketches* (trans. Nobuyuki Yuasa) Penguin Books Ltd,, Harmondsworth 1975
On Love And Barley: Haiku Of Bashō (trans. Lucien Stryk) Penguin Books, London 1985

Bates, Brian: *The Wisdom Of The Wyrd* Rider, London 1996

Beckett, Samuel: *Poems In English* Calder and Boyars, London 1968

Benestad, Finn & Schjeldrup-Ebbe, Dag: *Edvard Grieg: The Man and the Artist* (trans. William H. Halvorsen & Leland B. Sateren) University of Nebraska Press/Alan Sutton, Gloucester 1988

Bengston, Jim: *Empty Landscape* Labyrinth Press, Oslo 1996

Bergh, Johs: 'Portrett: Jon Christensen', *Jazznytt* 6, Oslo 1981 pp.4-8

Bergh, Johs & Evensmo, Jan: *Jazz Tenor Saxophone In Norway 1917-1959* Norwegian Jazz Archives, Oslo 1996

Bergman, Ingmar: *The Magic Lantern: An Autobiography* (trans. Joan Tate) Hamish Hamilton, London 1988
Images: My Life in Film (trans. Marianne Ruuth) Bloomsbury, London 1994

Berendt, Joachim-Ernst: 'Teutonic Tour: Through Asia With The Albert Mangelsdorff Quintet', *Down Beat* September 10 1964 vol 31 no 25 pp.13-15
'Albert Mangelsdorff', *Down Beat* February 10, 1977 vol 44 no 3 pp.16, 41 & 44
'A New Kind of Musician', *Jazz Forum* no 70 2/1981 pp.52-55
The Jazz Book - From New Orleans to Jazz Rock and Beyond Paladin/Granada Publishing, London 1983
'Glosses on a Philosophy of Jazz' in Berendt (ed.) *The Story of Jazz* Barrie and Jenkins Limited, London 1978
Nada Brahma: The World Is Sound. Music and the Landscape of Consciousness East West Publications, London & The Hague 1988

Bernstein, Leonard: *The Unanswered Question: Six Talks at Harvard* Harvard University Press, Cambridge, Massachusetts & London 1976

Blackford, Chris: 'He comes from the North', *Rubberneck* November 6, 1989 pp. 4-8

Blumenthal, Bob: 'George Russell: Stratus Seeker', *Down Beat* October 1993 vol 50 no 10 pp. 24-26

Blyth, R. H. *The Genius Of Haiku: Readings from R. H. Blyth on poetry, life, and Zen* The British Haiku Society 1994

Borgeaud, Pierre-Yves: 'Le plus beau son après le silence', *L'Hebdomadaire* (Switzerland) November 1994

Bouchard, Fred: 'Miroslav Vitous: Both Sides Of The Bass', *Down Beat* September 1994 vol 51 no 9 pp.18-20 & 63

Bourne, Michael: 'Jan Garbarek's Scandinavian Design', *Down Beat* July 1986 pp. 26-28

Bream, Julian: 'Toru Takemitsu: An Appreciation' *Avant magazine* issue 3 Autumn 1997 p. 9 (first appeared in *Guitar Review*)

Brembeck, Reinhardt J. 'Manfred Eicher: Seeker of Sound', *Inter Nations* (Germany) 1/1997 pp. 40-43

Britt, Stan: *Long Tall Dexter: A Critical Musical Biography Of Dexter Gordon* Quartet Books, London 1989

Brodowski, P./Szprot, J.: 'Jan Garbarek: Mysterious Wayfarer', *Jazz Forum* JF 86, 1984:1 pp. 38-44
'Music with Integrity: Manfred Eicher talks to JF's Pavel Brodowski' ibid pp. 46-50

Brown, Marion: *Recollections* JAS, Frankfurt am Main 1984

Budds, Michael: *Jazz In The Sixties: The Expansion of Musical Resources and Techniques* University of Iowa Press, Iowa City 1978

Cage, John: *Silence* The M. I. T. Press, Cambridge, Massachusetts & London 1971

Campbell, James (ed.) *The Picador Book of Blues and Jazz* Picador, London 1995

Carney, Raymond: *Speaking The Language Of Desire: The Films Of Carl Dreyer* Cambridge University Press, Cambridge 1989

Carr, Ian; Fairweather, Digby; Priestley, Brian: *Jazz: The Essential Companion* Grafton Books, London 1987 (reissued/revised edition *Jazz:The Rough Guide,* Rough Guides Ltd, London 1995)

Carr, Ian: *Music Outside: Contemporary Jazz in Britain* Latimer New Dimensions, London 1973
Miles Davis: A Critical Biography Quartet Books, London 1982
Keith Jarrett: The Man and His Music Grafton Books, London 1991

Cassirer, Ernst: *Language And Myth* (trans. Susanne K. Langer)

Dover Publications Inc., New York 1953

Castles, Francis G.: *The Social Democratic Image of Society*
Routledge & Kegan Paul, London 1978

Chatwin, Bruce: *The Songlines* Picador/Pan Books, London 1987

Chung-yuan, Chang: *Creativity and Taoism* Wildwood House,
London 1975

Clark, Thomas A.: 'Poetry And The Space Beyond' in Murray, G.
(ed.) *Poeisis: Aspects Of Contemporary Poetic Activity* The
FruitMarket Gallery, Edinburgh 1992

Cocki, Jay: 'Sounds From a White Room', *Time Magazine* April 27,
1981

Cole, Bill: *John Coltrane* Schirmer Books/Macmillan, New York 1976

Connor, Steven: *Postmodernist Culture: An Introduction to Theories
of the Contemporary* Basil Blackwell Ltd., Oxford 1991

Conrad, Charles: 'Charles Lloyd: Tonight, I Feel Your Freedom',
Down Beat July 1997 vol 64 no 7 pp. 30-32 (includes review
of Jan Garbarek Group concert at Tallinn's Jazzkaar Festival)

Cooke, Mervyn: *The Chronicle Of Jazz* Thames and Hudson Ltd,
London 1997

Cook, Richard: 'Before and after silence: an interview with Manfred
Eicher', *Wire* issue 58/59 New Year 1989 pp. 50-53
'Thrills and chills', *The Sunday Times* March 8, 1992
'Polyphonic Perversity: The Facts' *The Independent* April 26,
1996

Cook, Richard/Morton, Brian: *The Penguin Guide To Jazz On CD*
Penguin Books Ltd., London 1996 (third, revised edition)

Coomaraswamy, Ananda K. : *Christian and Oriental Philosophy of
Art* Dover Publications, New York 1956

Cotterrell, Roger: 'Back to the folkways' in Cotterrell, Roger (ed.)
Jazz Now Quartet Books, London 1976

Cousineau, Phil (ed.): *The Hero's Journey: Joseph Campbell on his
Life and Work* Harper and Row Publishers, San Francisco 1990

Crawford, John C. & Crawford, Dorothy L. : *Expressionism In
Twentieth-Century Music* Indiana University Press,
Bloomington & Indianapolis 1993

Cuddihy, Michael (ed.): *Ironwood 13: Tranströmer, A Special Issue*
Ironwood Press, Tuscon 1979

Daliot, Yisrael: 'Bela Bartók in Norway', *Listen to Norway* no 1 vol
4 Oslo 1994 pp. 8-11 (includes Arne Nordheim & Lasse
Thoresen on Bartók)

Davies, Laurence: *Paths To Modern Music* Barrie & Jenkins Ltd.,
London 1971

Day, Steve: *Two Full Ears: Listening to Improvised Music* Soundworld, Chelmsford 1998 (contains 17-track CD)

Dean, Roger: *New Structures In Jazz And Improvised Music Since 1960* Open University Press, Milton Keynes 1992

Dermoncourt, Betrand: 'Jan Garbarek' *Octopus*, France Autumn 1996

Derry, T. K. : *A History Of Scandinavia* George Allen & Unwin, London 1979

Devereux, Richard; Green, Lynne & Clark, Thomas A.: *In Stillness and In Silence* Usher Gallery, Lincoln 1994

Dilberto, John: 'Bill Frisell: Guitars & Scatterations', *Down Beat* May 1989 vol 56 no 5 pp.16-19

Dittman, R. : *Eros and Psyche: Strindberg and Munch in the 1890s* UMI Research Press, Anne Arbor 1982

Documenta X, 1997 Kassel: *the book: politics poetics* Gantz Verlag 1997

Donoghue, Denis: *The Arts Without Mystery* The British Broadcasting Corporation, London 1983

Dunlop, Ian: 'Edvard Munch, Barnett Newman, And Mark Rothko: The Search For The Sublime', *Arts Magazine* February 1979, vol 53 no 6 pp.128-130

Dybo, Tor: 'Garbarek And The Nordic Sound', *Nordic Sounds* 3/95 pp.12-14
   Jan Garbarek - Det åpne roms estetikk Pax, Oslo 1996

Dyer, Geoff: *But Beautiful: A Book about Jazz* Jonathan Cape, London 1991
   'Tradition, Influence and Innovation'(Afterforeword to *But Beautiful*) in Campbell (ed.) 1995 op. cit.

Eisenberg, Evan: *The Recording Angel: Music, Records And Culture From Aristotle To Zappa* Picador/Pan Books Ltd., London 1987

Ekelöf, Gunnar: *Selected Poems of Gunnar Ekelöf* (trans.Muriel Rukeyser & Leif Sjöberg) Twayne Publishers Inc., New York 1967
   Songs Of Something Else (trans. Leonard Nathan & James Larson) Princeton University Press, Princeton 1982
   Modus Vivendi: Selected Prose (trans. Erik Thygesen) Norvik Press, University of East Anglia, Norwich 1996

Eliade, Mircea: *Shamanism: Archaic Techniques of Ecstasy* (trans. Willard R. Trask) Bollingen Series 76/Princeton University Press, Princeton 1974
   'The Sacred and the Modern Artist', *Criterion*, Divinity School, University of Chicago 1965 vol. 4 pt. 2 (available in

Apostolos-Cappadona ed., 1996 op. cit.)

Farrell, Gerry: *Indian Music and the West* Clarendon Press, Oxford 1997

Feigin, Leo (ed.): *Russian Jazz: New Identity* Quartet Books Limited, London 1985

Flaherty, Gloria: *Shamanism And The Eighteenth Century* Princeton University Press, Princeton 1992

Friedrich, Otto: *Glenn Gould: A Life And Variations* Lime Tree, London 1990

Fordham, John: 'Blowing across the borders', *The Guardian* February 23, 1993
'Jan's New Habit', *The Guardian* September 9, 1994
'The sax man cometh', *The Guardian* November 25, 1996
Shooting From The Hip: Changing tunes in Jazz Kyle Cathie Limited, London 1996

Fox, Charles: 'Economy drive', *New Statesman* February 13, 1987

Fraser, J. T. (ed.): *The Voices Of Time* Allen Lane, The Penguin Press, London 1968

Furseth, Ingrid: 'Oslo: Ledende Jazzby', *A Magasinet (Aftenposten)* nr. 52 , Oslo December 30, 1978

Gadamer, Hans-Georg: *The Relevance Of The Beautiful and Other Essays* (trans. Nicholas Walker) Cambridge University Press, Cambridge 1991

Garbarek, Jan: Sleeve-note to *Popofoni* (Sonet 1421/1422)
'Amoeba Refutation', letter to *Down Beat* July 13, 1978 vol 45 no. 13 p. 9
'Tribute to Alan Davie' in Tucker, Michael (ed.) *Alan Davie: The Quest For The Miraculous* University of Brighton/Barbican Art Gallery/Lund Humphries Ltd., London 1993

Garbarek, Vigdis: *Veien Til Deg Selv* Gyldendal Norsk Forlag, Oslo 1992
Vågestykket Gyldendal Norsk Forlag, Oslo 1996

Gilbert, Mark: 'Joe Zawinul: Interview', *Jazz Journal International* vol. 51 no. 5, May 1998 pp.12-13

Gioia, Ted: *The Imperfect Art: Reflections On Jazz And Modern Culture* Oxford University Press, New York, Oxford 1988

Goddard, Chris: *Jazz Away From Home* Paddington Press Ltd., New York & London 1979

Godwin, Joscelyn (ed.): *Music, Mysticism And Magic: A Sourcebook* Arkana/ Routledge and Kegan Paul Ltd., London 1987

Gohnson, Geir: 'Love and Death [Arne Nordheim]' *Listen to Norway* no 2 vol 5 Oslo 1997 pp. 6-11

Goldman, Jonathan: *Healing Sounds: The Power of Harmonics*
Element Books Ltd, Shaftesbury 1994

Goldson, Elisabeth (ed.): *Seeing Jazz: Artists and Writers on Jazz*
Chronicle Books, San Francisco 1997

Graf, Ola: ' The Impact of Sami Tradition', *Listen to Norway* no 3
vol 5 Oslo 1997 pp. 34-36

Granholm, Åke (ed.) *Finnish Jazz* Finnish Music Information Music
Centre, Helsinki 1974

Greiner, Ulrich: 'Der Saxophonist Jan Garbarek: Hymnen an die
Nacht', *Die Zeit*, June 3, 1994

Gridley, Mark C.: *Jazz Styles* Prentice-Hall, Inc., Englewood Cliffs
1978

Grottum, Kåre: 'Folk Music & Jazz: Confrontation or
Cohabitation?', *Listen to Norway* no 1 vol 2 Oslo 1994
pp.18-21

Gundersen, Trygve Riiser: 'Vanskelig å vite hvor tonene slar ned',
Vårt Land, Oslo October 10, 1990

Gunnarsson, T. *Nordic Landscape Painting in the Nineteenth
Century* Yale University Press, New Haven and London 1998

Hadler, Mona: 'Jazz And The Visual Arts', *Arts Magazine* June 1983

Hall, Michael: *Leaving Home: A conducted tour of twentieth-century
music with Simon Rattle* Faber And Faber, London 1996

Hamel, Peter Michael: *Through Music To The Self* (trans. Peter
Lemesurier) Compton Press, Tisbury 1978

Hammarskjöld, Dag: *Markings* (trans. W. H. Auden & Leif Sjöberg)
Faber And Faber Ltd., London 1964

Hammerø, Tor: 'Mannen Alle Har Skive Med', *Puls Furore* no 26,
Oslo 23/10/96 p. 12

Hamsun, Knut: *Hunger* (trans. Robert Bly) Gerald Duckworth and
Company Ltd., London 1967
Mysteries (trans. Gerry Bothmer) Souvenir Press, London 1973
Pan (trans. James W. McFarlane) Souvenir Press, London 1974

Hansen, Espen: 'Han skaper stillhet og renhet av musikk',
Fredriksftad Blad, Norway April 25, 1987

Hansen, Jan E. : 'The Music - The Silence', *Listen to Norway* no 1
vol 2 Oslo 1994 pp. 2-3

Hansen, Jan E.: 'Joiks and Jokes', *Listen to Norway* no 2 vol 1 Oslo
1993 pp. 20-22

Hardman, Dale: 'Miroslav Vitous', *Down Beat* February 14, 1974
vol 41 no 3 pp.16 & 38

Harrison, Max: *A Jazz Retrospect* David & Charles/Crescendo,
Newton Abbott 1976

'Rational Anthems: George Russell' pts 1-3 *The Wire* 1983 issues 3 (Spring pp. 30-31), 4 (Summer pp. 20-21) & 5 (Autumn pp. 19-21)

Hauge, Olav H. : *Don't Give Me The Whole Truth: Selected Poems* (trans. Robin Fulton & James Greene, with Siv Hennum) Anvil Press Poetry, London 1985

Haugen, Paal-Helge: *Stone Fences* (trans. William Mishler & Roger Greenwald) University of Missouri Press, Columbia 1986

Hayes, Michael: *The Infinite Harmony: Musical Structures In Science And Theology* Weidenfeld and Nicolson, London 1994

Heffley, Mike: *The Music Of Anthony Braxton* Greenwood Press, Westport, Connecticut & London 1996

Heidegger, Martin: *Poetry, Language, Thought* (trans. Albert Hofstadter) Harper Colophon Books, New York 1975

Heidkamp, Konrad: 'Portrait: Manfred Eicher', *Lufthansa Bordbuch* no 6, 1995

Helgheim, Roald: 'Garbarek spesial', *Klassekampen*, Oslo April 22, 1987

'Garbareks Robeson-pris', *Klassekampen*, Oslo November 18, 1992

'Intervju med Jan Erik Vold', *Jazznytt* nr 4 Oslo 1993 pp. 7-16

'Den synlege musikken', *Klassekampen* , Oslo March 23, 1996

'I musikkens rom', *Klassekampen*, Oslo November 20, 1996

Hennessey, Mike: 'Don Cherry's Catholicity', *Down Beat* July 28, 1966 vol 33 no 15 pp. 14-15

Hentoff, Nat: 'Whose Art Form? Jazz At Mid-Century' in Hentoff, N. & McCarthy, Albert (eds.): *Jazz* Quartet Books, London 1977

Jazz Is W. H. Allen, London 1978

Herrestahl, Harald: *Norwegische Musik: von den Anfängen bis zur Gegenwart* Norsk Musikforlag, Oslo 1987 (2nd edition)

'1000 Years of Norwegian Church Music', *Listen to Norway* no 3 vol 3 Oslo 1995 pp. 6-14

Hillier, Paul: *Arvo Pärt* Oxford University Press, Oxford 1997

Hillman, James: *Anima: An Anatomy of a Personified Notion* Spring Publications Inc., Dallas 1985

The Thought Of The Heart Eranos Lectures 2, Spring Publications Inc., Dallas 1987

Hodeir, André: *The Worlds Of Jazz* (trans. Noel Burch) Evergreen, Grove Press Inc., New York 1972

Holbaek-Hanssen, Hilde: 'Alfred Janson: The "friendly" modernist',

Listen to Norway vol 1 no 1 Oslo 1993 pp. 30-31
'Kåre Kolberg: A Quiet Fighter', *Listen to Norway* vol 6 no 2 Oslo 1998 pp. 24-25

Holbrook, David: *Gustav Mahler And The Courage To Be* Vision Press, London 1975

Hölderlin, Friedrich: *Hymns and Fragments* (trans. Richard Sieburth) Princeton University Press, Princeton 1984

Horton, John: *Grieg* J. M. Dent & Sons Ltd., London 1979

Hovdenakk, Per/Rajka, Susanne/Bjerke, Øivind Storm: *Henie-Onstad Art Centre 1968-1993* Henie-Onstad Art Centre, Høvikodden 1994

Howard, Michael: *The Magic Of The Runes: Their Origins and Occult Power* The Aquarian Press, Wellinborough 1980

Howes, Frank: *Music And Its Meanings* University of London/The Athlone Press, 1958

Hultin, Randi: 'Jan Garbarek', *Jazz Forum* February 1973 pp. 49-51
'Jan Garbarek: a remarkable jazz personality', *Jazz Forum* no 40, February 1976 pp. 51-53
Jazzens Tegn Aschehoug, Oslo 1991
Born Under The Sign Of Jazz, Sanctuary, London 1998 (revised edition of *Jazzens Tegn*, translated Tim Challman, with CD)

Hunt, D. C. : 'Today's Jazz Artist: His Communication and Our Technological Age' in Rivelli, Pauline & Levin, Robert (eds.): *Giants Of Black Music* Da Capo Press, Inc., New York 1979

Ibsen, Henrik: *Brand* (trans. Michael Meyer) Eyre Methuen Ltd., London 1978
Peer Gynt (trans. Peter Watts) Penguin Books Ltd., Harmondsworth 1977

Iversen, Carl Morten: 'Torgrim Sollid: et møte med "fjelljazzens far"', *Jazznytt* 4.5, Oslo 1995 pp. 5-11

Jacobsen, Rolf: *The Silence Afterwards: Selected Poems* (trans. Roger Greenwald) Princeton University Press, Princeton 1985

James, Burnett: 'The Impressionism of Duke Ellington', in his *Essays On Jazz* The Jazz Book Club/Sidgwick and Jackson, London 1962 pp. 163-174

Jenssen, Hugo Lauritz: 'Kunst - eller lydkulisse?' *Dagens Naeringsliv*, Oslo March 23, 1996
'Fra Telematk til Tbilisi' *Dagens Naeringsliv (DN-Magasinet)* Oslo, October 3, 1998

Jerman, Gunnar (ed.): *A Cultural Odyssey: Focus on Norwegian Art* Index Publishing, Oslo 1997

Ji, Ruan: *Songs of my Heart* (trans. Graham Hartill & Wu Fusheng) Wellsweep Press, Leytonstone 1988

Job, Pierre: 'Terminus Nord', *Telerama* no 2076, France October 25, 1989

Johanssen, Terje (ed.): *20 Contemporary Norwegian Poets* Universitetsforlaget, Oslo 1984

Johansson, Anders: 'Samtale med Jan Garbarek' *Vår Musikk* , Oslo 1/74

Jonason, Bjørn & Saemundsson, Matthias Vidar: *Havamal: The Sayings of the Vikings* Gudrun Publishing, Reykjavik-Goteborg-Oslo 1995

Jones, Andrew: 'Jan Garbarek: In All Languages', *Jazzis* 4/5, 1991

Jones, Gwyn: *A History Of The Vikings* Oxford University Press, Oxford 1973

Jost, Ekkehard: *Free Jazz* Universal Edition, Graz 1974
'European Jazz Avant Garde: Where Will Emancipation Lead?', in Gebers, J. (ed.): *For Example: Workshop Freie Musik 1969-1978* FMP, Berlin 1978 pp. 54-65

Kagan, Andrew: *Paul Klee: Art and Music* Cornell University Press, Ithaca & London 1983

Kagge, Stein: 'Sax Appeal', *Scanorama*, November 1989 pp .58-61
'Norwegian Jazz: Glowing in the Ice', *Listen to Norway* no 1 vol 5 Oslo 1997 pp. 14-19

Khan, Sufi Inayat: *Music* Sufi Publishing Company, England/Samuel Weiser, Inc., USA 1977

Kent, Neil: *The Triumph of Light and Nature: Nordic Art 1740-1940* Thames and Hudson, London 1987
Light and Nature in Late-19th Century Nordic Art and Literature Uppsala 1990

Kemper, Peter; Ruedi, Peter; Muller, Lars; Lake, Steve: *ECM: Sleeves of Desire* Lars Muller Publishers, Baden 1996

Kernfeld, Barry (ed.): *The New Grove Dictionary Of Jazz* Macmillan Press Limited, London 1994

Kierkegaard, Søren: *The Journals of Kierkegaard 1834-1854* (trans. Alexander Dru) Collins/Fontana Books, London 1967

Knapp, Bettina L.: *Music, Archetype And The Writer: A Jungian View* The Pennsylvania State University Press, University Park and London 1988

Knox, Keith: 'Lament for Lars', *Jazz Journal International* vol 30 no 10 October 1977 pp. 14-15

Knox, Keith & Lindqvist, Gunnar: *Jazz Amour Affair: En Bok Om Lars Gullin* Svensk Musik, Stockholm 1986

Knox, Keith: 'Bernt Rosengren', *Jazz Forum* JF 106 3/1987 pp. 36-39

Kolberg, Kåre: Sleeve-note essay, *The Essence of George Russell* Soul Note CD 121044-2

Kristiansen, Steinar: 'Intervju med Jan Garbarek' *Jazznytt* Oslo 1996 pp. 3-11

Kusch, Eugen: *Ancient Art In Scandinavia* Hans Carl Nurnberg 1964

Kvaløy, Sigmund: Sleeve-note essay, *Othello Ballet Suite* Soul Note CD 121 014-2

Kvifte, Tellef: 'Jan Garbarek: Jazz, Ethnic Romanticism, World Music or Personal Expression?', *Nordic Sounds* 4/90 pp. 8-9

Lagerkvist, Pär: *Evening Land* (trans. W. H. Auden & Leif Sjöberg) Souvenir Press Ltd., London 1977

Lake, Steve: 'Jan Garbarek: Saga of Fire and Ice', *Down Beat* November 17, 1977 vol 44 no 19 pp. 16-17 & 46
'Music From The North', programme notes to *Norwegische Jazz Festival* , Gasteig & Loft, Germany November 25-27, 1989
'Covering the waterfront' sleeve-notes, *Music For Films* (ECM 1429)
'Triptykon/The Power Of Three' sleeve-notes, *Triptykon* (ECM 1029)

Lao-Tsu: *Tao Te Ching* (trans. Gia-Fu Feng & Jane English) Vintage Books, New York 1972

Lauten, Marit: 'Karin Krog - anno 1997', *Jazznytt* Oslo 1997 pp. 20-25

Layton, Robert: *Sibelius* J. M. Dent & Sons Ltd., London 1965

Leach, Bernard: *Beyond East and West: Memoirs, Portraits and Essays* Faber and Faber, London 1985

Lebrecht, Norman: *The Companion To 20th Century Music* Simon & Schuster Ltd., London 1992

Leeuw, Gerardus van der: *Sacred and Profane Beauty: the Holy in Art* Holt, Rinehart and Winston Inc., New York 1963

Lehman, David: *Signs Of The Times: Deconstruction and the Fall of Paul de Man* Andre Deutsch Ltd., London 1991

Levas, Santeri: *Sibelius, a personal portrait* (trans. Percy M. Young) J. M. Dent & Sons Ltd., London 1972

Levin, David Michael: *The Body's Recollection Of Being: Phenomenological Psychology And The Deconstruction Of Nihilism* Routledge and Kegan Paul, London 1985

Libæck, Ivar & Stenersen, Øivind *A History Of Norway: From the Ice Age To The Age Of Petroleum* (trans. J. Aase) Grøndahl Dreyer Oslo 1998

Lienert, Konrad R. 'Interview with Manfred Eicher', *Tages-Anzeiger*, Zurich (undated; supplied by ECM Records, Munich)

Lindemeyer, P. *Celebrating The Saxophone* Hearst Books, New York 1996

Lindholm, Dan: *Stave Churches In Norway: Dragon Myth and Christianity in Old Norwegian Architecture* (trans. Stella & Adam Bittleston) Rudolf Steiner Press, London 1969

Lipsey, Roger: *An Art Of Our Own: The Spiritual In Twentieth-Century Art* Shambhala, Boston & Shaftesbury 1988

Litweiler, John: 'The Legacy of Albert Ayler', *Down Beat* April 1, 1971 vol 38 no 7 pp. 14-15 & 29
The Freedom Principle: Jazz After 1958 William Morrow and Company Inc., New York 1984
Ornette Coleman: the harmolodic life Quartet Books Limited, London 1992

Livingston, Barry: 'The Norwegian Jazz Scene', *Coda* issue 224, February/March 1989 pp. 9-11

Livingston, Paisley: *Ingmar Bergman and the Rituals of Art* Cornell University Press, Ithaca & London 1982

Lock, Graham: *Forces In Motion: Anthony Braxton and the Meta-reality of Creative Music* Quartet Books, London 1988
Chasing The Vibration: Meetings with Creative Musicians Stride Publications, Exeter 1994

Lopez, Barry: *Arctic Dreams* Picador/Pan Books, London 1987

Lorca, Federico Garcia: *Deep Song and Other Prose* Marion Boyars, London 1980

Luzzi, Mario: 'Enrico Rava', *Coda* issue 160 April 1 1978 pp. 24-26

Machlis, Joseph: *Introduction to Contemporary Music* J. M. Dent & Son Ltd., London 1963

Magnusson, Sigurdur A. (ed. & trans.): *The Postwar Poetry of Iceland* University of Iowa Press, Iowa City 1982

Mandel, Howard: 'Don Cherry: The World In His Pocket', *Down Beat* July 13, 1978 vol 45 no 13 pp. 20-22 & 54-55
'Jan Garbarek: Sax Solitude and Northern Light', *Musician* February 1983 pp. 36-40 & 116

Marcussen, Tor: 'Jan Garbarek: Hitlistene er børsnoteringer' *Aftenposten*, Oslo April 21, 1987

Maré, Eric De: *Scandinavia* B. T. Batsford Ltd., London 1952

Mathieu, Bill: 'Atonality In Jazz', *Down Beat* May 10, 1962 vol 29 no 10 pp. 16-18

Mathieson, Kenny: 'Editions Of The Cool' *Wire* June 1993 pp. 18-20

Matthews, David: *Landscape Into Sound* The Claridge Press, St
    Albans 1992
May, Elizabeth (ed.): *Musics of Many Cultures* University of
    California Press, Berkeley, Los Angeles, London 1980
McRae, Barry: *The Jazz Cataclysm* A. S. Barnes and Co. Inc,,
    Cranbury/J. M. Dent & Sons Ltd., London 1967
    'Brilliant Action', *Jazz Journal* March 1974 p. 18
    'In Search Of The Mystery', *Jazz Journal* April 1974 p. 27
    'You Know, You Know' *Jazz Journal* June 1974 pp. 25 & 50
    'The Coleman Atlantics', *Jazz Journal* April 1975 pp. 14-16
    'Don Cherry - A Disappearing Jazz Giant?', *Jazz Journal*
    October 1975 pp. 8-9
McFarlane, J. W.: *Ibsen And The Temper Of Norwegian Literature*
    Octagon Books, New York 1979
Mehren, Stein: 'Man and the Transparency of the Earth in a Lasting
    Night' in Moller, Arvid (ed.): *Frans Widerberg: 100 Pictures* J.
    M. Stenersens Forlag, Oslo 1982
Mei, Elisabeth van der: 'Pharoah Sanders (a philosophical conversa-
    tion)', *Coda* June-July 1967 vol 8 no 2 pp. 2-6
Milkowski, Bill: 'Terje Rypdal: Sculptor In Sound', *Down Beat*
    October 1997 vol 54 no 10 pp. 20-22
Miller, Mark: 'Kenny Wheeler's Many Vehicles', *Down Beat* April
    1980 vol 47 no 4 pp. 22-24 & 69
Mitchell, Charles: 'Ralph Towner: A Chorus of Inner Voices', *Down
    Beat* June 19, 1975 vol 42 no 12 pp. 16-18 & 40-41
Mitchell, Timothy: *Flamenco Deep Song* Yale University Press, New
    Haven and London 1994
Montale, Eugenio: *Poet in Our Time* (trans. Alastair Hamilton)
    Marion Boyars Publishers Ltd., London 1976
Morton, Brian: 'One born with wings', *The Wire* issue 64 June 1989
    pp. 30-33
Mosnes, Terje: 'Musikk - alltid: Terje Mosnes intervjuer Jan
    Garbarek', *Lyd & Bilde* nr 3, Oslo 1979 pp. 16-18 & 52
    'Fra scenen og salen' (Interview with Jan Garbarek) in
    Mosnes, T. *Jazz I Molde: Festivaler gjennom 20 År* Nordvest,
    Ålesund 1980 pp. 30-34
    'Europas Ledende: Jan Garbarek intervjuet av Terje Mosnes'
    Dagbladet, Oslo January 22 1983
    'Norwegian Jazz - Something to do with Mountains?', *Listen
    to Norway* no 1 vol 2 Oslo 1994 pp. 32-37
    'Karin Krog: First Lady of Norwegian Jazz', *Listen to Norway*
    no 3 vol 2 Oslo 1994 pp. 26-27

'Garbarek stempler inn igjen', *Dagbladet*, Oslo March 9, 1996

'Jazz in the City of Roses' *Listen to Norway* no 3 vol 6 Oslo 1998 pp. 36-41

Murray, Graeme (ed.): *Poeisis: Aspects Of Contemporary Poetic Activity* The FruitMarket Gallery, Edinburgh 1992

Nansen, Fridtjof: *Sporting Days In Wild Norway: Pages From My Diary* Thornton Butterworth Ltd., London 1925

Nicholson, Stuart: *Jazz: The Modern Resurgence* Simon & Schuster, London 1990

Nietzsche, Friedrich: *Thus Spoke Zarathustra* (trans. R. J. Hollingdale) Penguin Books, Harmondsworth 1967

Nilsson, Per Anders: 'Jan Garbarek: Nordiskt Ljus', *Musikermagasinet*, Sweden August 1990 pp. 54-61

Nolan, Herb: 'Eberhard Weber', *Down Beat* August 12, 1976 vol 42 no 14 p. 40

'Egberto Gismonti', *Down Beat* September 7, 1978 vol 45 no 15 pp 24-25

Norberg-Schulz, Christian: *Genius Loci: Towards A Phenomenology of Architecture* Academy Editions, London 1980

Nordic Arts Centre: *1945-1980: Art In The Nordic Countries* Nordic Arts Centre, Helsinki 1985

Nørgåd, Per: 'Dear Mr. [Sibelius]' *Nordic Sounds* no 3, 1997 pp. 3-7

Novalis: *Hymns To The Night* (trans. Jeremy Reed) Enitharmon Press, Petersfield 1989

Nowakowski, Leonard: 'Ralph Towner: Acoustic Eclectic', *Down Beat* May 1983 vol 50 no 5 pp. 14-17

Offstein, Alan: 'ECM', *Coda* March/April 1973 vol 10 no 12 pp. 7-14

Økland, Einar: 'Intervju med Jon Christensen' in Angell/Vold/Okland (eds.) 1975 op. cit. pp. 113-117

'Intervju med Jan Garbarek' ibid pp. 118-123

Orvedal, Ivar: 'Grieg and all that Jazz', *Listen to Norway* no 1, vol 1 Oslo 1993 pp .44-49

'Terje Rypdal: Navigator', *Listen to Norway* no 1 vol 3 Oslo 1995 pp. 40-44

'Synleg myte', *Klassekampen*, Oslo March 30 1996

'Romantic Aesthete', *Listen to Norway* no 1 Oslo 1997 vol 5 pp. 6-11

Opstad, Gunvald: 'Jeg blir nok aldri noen Liv Ullmann' *Faedrelandsvennen* March 11 1983

Østenstad, Inger: 'Crossing Musical Borders', *Listen to Norway* no 3 vol 5 Oslo 1997 pp. 16-19

Øsvold, Sissel B.: 'Green Blues', *Listen to Norway* no 1 vol 5 Oslo 1997 pp. 12-13

Pekar, Harvey: 'Swing As An Element of Jazz', *Coda* August/September 1974 vol 11 no 11 pp. 10-12

Pessoa, Fernando: *The Surprise of Being: 25 Poems* (trans. James Greene & Clara De Azevedo Mafra) Angel Books, London 1986

Palmer, Richard: *Stan Getz* Apollo Press Ltd., London 1988
   Sonny Rollins: The Cutting Edge Eastnote/Hull University Press, Hull 1998

Parker, Chris: 'Spirit of the lore', *The Times* November 26, 1996

Poole, Roger: *Towards Deep Subjectivity* Allen Lane, London 1972

Poulsson, Poul: 'Intervju med Jan Garbarek', *Jazznytt* no.2 Oslo May 1970

Prendergast, Mark: 'Northern Soundscapes', *Hi-Fi Review* February 1989 pp. 98-101

Primack, Bret: 'Zbigniew Namyslovski', *Down Beat* November 2 1978 vol 45 no 18 pp .44-45

Raine, K. *Defending Ancient Springs* Gologonooza Press, Ipswich 1985

Rajka, Susanne: 'Norway in the 60s, Image of a Decade' in *The Nordic 60s: Upheaval and Confrontation* Nordic Arts Centre, Helsinki 1991 pp. 156-61

Rawles, Simon: 'Jan Garbarek: Tender Is The North', *Jazzwise* Issue 18, London December 1997/January 1998 pp. 6-7

Rey, Anne: 'Manfred Eicher, brouilleur de pistes', *Le Monde* 27/10/89

Rickards, Guy: *Jean Sibelius* Phaidon Ltd., London 1997

Riggins, Roger: 'George Russell', *Coda* no 162, 1978 pp. 10-11

Rilke, Rainer Maria: *Sonnets to Orpheus* (trans. C. F. MacIntyre) University of California Press, Berkeley 1960
   Where Silence Reigns: Selected Prose (trans. G. Craig Houston) New Directions, New York 1978
   Duino Elegies (trans. David Young) W. W. Norton & Company Inc., New York 1979
   Selected Poems (trans. Robert Bly) Harper & Row, New York 1981
   An Unofficial Rilke (trans. Michael Hamburger) Anvil Press Poetry Ltd., London 1981

Roalkvam, Terje: 'Øyet som hører: intervju med Per Kleiva', *Ballade*, special Nordheim edition, nrs 2/3 1981 pp. 56-57

Rosenberg, Ulf-E.: 'Idealet er lyden jeg har i hodet', *Stavanger Aftenblad* May 23, 1992

Rosenblum, Robert: *Modern Painting and the Northern Romantic Tradition* Thames and Hudson, London 1975

Ross, Nancy Wilson: *Hinduism, Buddhism, Zen* Faber and Faber, London 1973

Rothenberg, Jerome (ed.): *Technicians Of The Sacred: A Range of Poetries from Africa, America, Asia, Europe & Oceania* University of California Press, Berkeley & Los Angeles, London 1985 (revised edition)

Rousseau, Jean-Jacques: *Reveries of the Solitary Walker* Penguin Books, Harmondsworth 1981

Russell, George: *The Lydian Chromatic Concept Of Tonal Organisation* Concept Publishing Co., New York 1959
Sleeve-note, *Jazz In The Space Age* Chessmates/GRP 18262
'Where Do We Go From Here?' in Cerulli, Dom; Korall, Burt; Nasatir, Mort (eds.): *The Jazz Word* The Jazz Book Club/ Dennis Dobson, London 1963
Sleeve-note, *Electronic Souls Loved by Nature* Soul Note CD 121034-2

Quinke, Ralph: 'Jan Garbarek: Heisses Horn aus dem kuhlen Norden', *Sounds*, Germany, August 1974

Rutter, Fredrik: 'Music and Dance', *Listen to Norway* no 2 vol 5 Oslo 1997 pp. 12-19

Sætre, Espen Mineur: 'Garbareks Stemmer' *Morgenbladet*, Oslo August 8, 1994

Sæverud, Katrine: 'Arve Tellefsen - Crossover Artist Extraordinary', *Listen to Norway* no 1 vol 2 Oslo 1994 pp. 38-42

Schaeffer, John: *New Sounds* Virgin/W. H. Allen & Co., London 1990

Scherwin, Johan: 'Det skenbart ENKLA', *Tonfallet*, Sweden no 7 1993 pp. 13-15

Schlotel, Brian: *Grieg* Ariel Music/BBC Publications, London 1986

Schulz, Klaus: 'The Hans Koller Story', *Jazz Forum* no 70 2/1981 pp. 46-50

Shah, Idries: *The Sufis* Star/W. H. Allen, London 1977

Shaughnessy, Adrian: 'ECM', *EYE: The International Review of Graphic Design* no 16 Spring 1995

Simosko, Vladimir: 'Cross Cultures', *Coda* April 1975 pp. 2-5

Simpkins, Cuthbert O.: *Coltrane: A Biography* Herndon House Publishers, New York 1975

Simpson, Robert: *Carl Nielsen, Symphonist* Kahn & Averill/Stanmore Press Ltd., London 1979

Skovgaard, Ib: 'Den norske lyd: interview med saxofonisten Jan Garbarek', *MM* no 7, Denmark, October 1980 pp. 12-14

Small, Christopher: *Music, Society, Education* John Calder Ltd, London 1977

Smith, Arnold Jay: 'Jazz In Europe: The State Of The Art', *Down Beat* February 9, 1978 vol 45 no 3 pp. 18-19, 39-40

Smith, Bill: 'Albert Mangelsdorff', *Coda* issue 168, August 1979 pp. 4-10
Imagine The Sound: Photographs And Writings By Bill Smith Nightwood Editions, 1985

Södergran, Edith: *Complete Poems* (trans. David McDuff) Bloodaxe Books, Newcastle upon Tyne 1984

Solothurnmann, Jurg: 'Jan Garbarek & Co. - Jazz aus Norwegen', *Der Bund*, Switzerland, April 1972
'Jan Garbarek: a thinking improviser', *Jazz Forum* no 54, 4/1978 pp. 33-37
'Enrico Rava: Jazz is everywhere', *Jazz Forum* JF 92 1/1985 pp. 36-41
'Interview with Jan Garbarek', *Avant magazine* issue 1, Spring 1997 pp. 4-6 plus (anon.) career overview of Garbarek, pp. 7-8. (This substantial interview is also available as ECM publication *Jan Garbarek*: available from New Note, Electron House, Cray Avenue, Orpington, Kent BR5 3RJ)

D'Souza, Jerry: 'Ralph Towner: a lifetime in one concert', *Jazz Forum* JF 105 2/87 pp. 22-24

Steiner, George: *Real Presences: is there anything in what we say?* Faber and Faber, London 1989

Stendahl, Bjørn: 'Portrett: Arild Andersen', *Jazznytt* 4, Oslo 1981 pp. 4-8
'Portrett: Karin Krog', *Jazznytt* 5, Oslo 1981 pp. 4-8
'Det essentielle er det du ikke kan si noe om: Jan Garbarek intervjuet av Bjørn Stendahl', *Jazznytt* 3, Oslo 1984 pp. 4-11

Stendahl, Bjørn: *Jazz, hot & swing: Jazz i Norge 1920-1940* Norsk Jazzarkiv, Oslo 1987

Stendahl, B./Bergh. J.: *Sigarett Stomp: Jazz i Norge 1940-1950* Norsk Jazzarkiv, Oslo 1991
Cool, klover & dixie: Jazz i Norge 1950-1960 Norsk Jazzarkiv, Oslo 1997

Stockhausen, Karlheinz: *Towards A Cosmic Music* (ed. & trans. Tim Nevill) Element Books, Shaftesbury 1989

Stokke, Olga: 'Grenser gir frihet', *Aftenposten*, Oslo November 14, 1992

Stolberg, Christian: 'Schrei des Nordens', *Wom Journal* no 6, Germany 1996

Storr, Anthony: *Music and the Mind* HarperCollins, London 1992

Stravinsky, I. *Poetics of Music* (trans. A. Knodel & I. Dahl) Harvard University Press, Cambridge, Massachusetts & London 1995

Szwed, John F.: *Space Is The Place: The Life And Times Of Sun Ra* Payback Press, Edinburgh 1997

Sweet, Robert E.: *Music Universe, Music Mind: Revisiting the Creative Music Studio, Woodstock, New York* Arborville Publishing, Inc., Ann Arbor 1996

Tarkovsky, Andrey: *Sculpting In Time: Reflections on the Cinema* (trans. Kitty Hunter-Blair) Faber And Faber, London & Boston 1989 (revised edition)
Time within Time: The Diaries (trans.Kitty Hunter-Blair) Seagull Books, Calcutta 1991

Tarting, Christian & Jaume, André: 'Entretien Avec John Cage', *Jazz Magazine* January 1980 pp. 48-51 & 64-65

Tawaststjerna, Erik: *Sibelius Volume 111: 1914-1957* (trans. Robert Layton) Faber and Faber Limited, London 1997

Taylor, Arthur: *Notes And Tones: Musician-To-Musician Interviews* Quartet Books, London 1983

Taylor, Roger: *Art, An Enemy Of The People* The Harvester Press Ltd., Hassocks 1978

Theberge, Paul: *Any Sound You Can Imagine: Making Music/Consuming Technology* Wesleyan University Press, New England 1997

Thomas, J. C.: *Chasin' The Trane: The music and mystique of John Coltrane* Elm Tree Books/Hamish Hamilton, London 1976

Tippett, Michael: *Moving Into Aquarius* Paladin Books, Granada Publishing Ltd., St Albans 1974
'Art, Judgement and Belief: Towards the Condition of Music', in Abbs, Peter (ed.) *The Symbolic Order* The Falmer Press, Lewes 1989

Toop, David: 'Jan Garbarek', *The Sunday Times*, December 12, 1994
Ocean Of Sound Serpent's Tail, London & New York 1995

Tranströmer, Tomas: *Truth Barriers* (trans. Robert Bly) Sierra Club Books, San Francisco 1980
Collected Poems (trans. Robin Fulton) Bloodaxe Books, Newcastle upon Tyne 1987

Tucker, Michael: 'Countdown for Garbarek' *Melody Maker*, London February 19, 1977
'Jan Garbarek: Beyond the Nordic Ethos' *Jazz Journal International* vol 30 no 10 October 1977 pp. 6- 8 & 19

'Northern Lights: Jazz In Scandinavia', *PS (Primary Sources on the International Performing Arts)* no 2 London 1979 pp. 15-18

'Jan Garbarek: The Poetics of Space' *The Wire* issue 7, Summer 1984 pp. 17-21

'Dreamer In A Landscape' in *Frans Widerberg: A Retrospective Exhibition* Brighton Polytechnic Gallery/ Newcastle Polytechnic Gallery, Newcastle upon Tyne 1986

'Eberhard Weber', *Jazz Journal International* January 1987 vol 40 no 1 pp. 12-14

'Jan Garbarek' *Contemporary Music Network Tour*, Arts Council, London February 1987 (unpaginated programme notes)

'Not the Land, but an Idea of a Land', in Freeman, Julian (ed.) *Landscapes From A High Latitude: Icelandic Art 1909-1989* Lund Humphries, London 1989

'Music Man's Dream' in *Alan Davie* Lund Humphries Ltd., London 1992

Dreaming With Open Eyes: The Shamanic Spirit In Twentieth-Century Art And Culture Aquarian/HarperCollins, London 1992

'Hearing The Colours, Dancing The Heartspace', *Contemporary Art* vol 2 no 1 Winter 1993-94 pp. 36-7 and 39-41

Frans Widerberg: Bilder, En Reise/Pictures, A Journey Labyrinth Press, Oslo 1994

'The Body Electric: The Shamanic Spirit in Twentieth-Century Music' in Steer, Maxwell (ed.) *Contemporary Music Review* vol 14, part 1 (special 2-part edition, *Music and Mysticism*) Harwood Academic Publishers, The Netherlands 1996 pp.67-97

'Magnetic North', *Jazz From Norway* Oris London Jazz Festival/Serious, London 1996 (unpaginated programme notes)

'Critic's Choice: Frans Widerberg', *Contemporary Visual Arts* issue 15, London 1997 pp. 56-60

'Through A Glass, Deeply', *Victor B. Andersen's Maskinfabrik* nr 22, Copenhagen 1998 pp. 16-31

Ullmann, Linn: 'A Modern Shaman [Nils-Aslak Valkeapää]', *Listen to Norway* no 2 vol 1 Oslo 1993 pp. 16-19

'Mari Boine: Inhabited by a Song', *Listen to Norway* no 1 vol 2 Oslo 1994 pp. 24-25

Ullmann, Michael: 'Starting from Zero: ECM at 25', *Schwann Spectrum* Fall 1994 pp. 6-10

Underwood, Lee: 'Shankar', *Down Beat* November 2, 1978, vol 45 no 18 pp. 42-44

Vahasilta, Timo: 'Edward Vesala: a drummer from the north', *Jazz Forum* JF 92 1/1985 pp. 30-35

Vanhoefer, Markus: 'Die Qualitat der Stille', *Munchner Merkur*, Germany June 19 1996

Various: 'John Coltrane Remembered', *Down Beat* special Coltrane edition July 2 1979 vol 46 no 13
Winter Land: Norwegian Visions of Winter De Norske Bokklubbene, Oslo 1993
Sami Contemporary Art De Norske Bokklubbene, Oslo 1994

Verschaffel, Bert & Verminck, Mark (eds.): *Wordlessness* The Lilliput Press, Antwerp 1993

Vesaas, Tarjei: *The Great Cycle* (trans. Elizabeth Røkkan) The University of Wisconsin Press, Madison, Milwaukee & London 1967
Land of Hidden Fires (trans. Fritz König & Jerry Crisp) Wayne State University Press, Detroit 1973
The Seed (trans. Kenneth G. Chapman) Peter Owen, London 1966
The Birds (trans. Torbjørn Støverud) Peter Owen, London 1968
The Ice Palace (trans. Elizabeth Røkkan) Peter Owen, London 1966
The Boat In The Evening (trans. Elizabeth Røkkan) Peter Owen, London 1971

Vold, Jan Erik: *Entusiastiske Essays: Klippbok 1960-75* Gylendal Norsk Forlag, Oslo 1976

Wandrup, Fredrik: 'Jan Garbarek - jazzkonge i OBOS-idyll', *Dagbladet*, Oslo July 31, 1976
'Pop-musikken ma vike plassen: Jazz-bølgen er over oss', *Dagbladet*, Oslo August 27, 1976
'Jakten pa musikkens kilde', *Dagbladet*, Oslo October 14, 1990

Ward, J. P.: *Poetry And The Sociological Idea* The Harvester Press Ltd., Brighton 1981

Ward, Phil: 'Rock Feature: Editions Of Contemporary Music', *HI-FI ANSWERS* March 1988 pp. 87-89

Watson, Philip: 'Jan Garbarek [Greenwich concert review]', *The Guardian* November 21, 1988

Weinstein, Norman: 'John Coltrane: Sounding The African Cry For Paradise', *NARAS Journal* vol 3 no 2 Fall 1992 pp. 31-43

Weinstock, John M. & Rovinsky, Robert T. (eds.): *The Hero In Scandinavian Literature: From Peer Gynt To The Present* University of Texas Press, Austin and London 1975

Westin, Lars: 'Jazz in Sweden', *Jazz Forum* JF 106 3/1987 pp. 30-35

White, Andrew: 'The Coltrane Context', *Jazz Forum* JF 106 3/87 pp. 4-6

White, Kenneth: *The Bird Path: Collected Longer Poems* Mainstream Publishing, Edinburgh 1989

Handbook for The Diamond Country: Collected Shorter Poems 1960-1990 Mainstream Publishing, Edinburgh 1990

The Blue Road Mainstream Publishing, Edinburgh 1990

Coast To Coast: Interviews and Conversations 1985-1995 Open World/Mythic Horse Press, Glasgow 1996

On Scottish Ground: Selected Essays Polygon, Edinburgh 1998

Wiggins, Mark: 'Officium', *Gramophone* October 1994 pp. 23 & 25

Williams, Donald Lee: *Border Crossings: A Psychological Perspective on Carlos Castaneda's Path of Knowledge* Inner City Books, Toronto 1981

Williams, Martin: *The Jazz Tradition* Oxford University Press, New York 1970

Willis, Ben: *The Tao Of Art* Century Hutchinson Ltd., London 1987

Wilmer, Valerie: *As Serious As Your Life: The Story of the New Jazz* Quartet Books Ltd., London 1977

'Joe Harriott: Abstractionist', *Down Beat* September 10, 1964 vol 31 no 25 pp. 12 & 37

Wilson, Colin: *On Music* Pan Books Ltd., London 1967

Wilson, David M. (ed.): *The Northern World: The History And Heritage Of Northern Europe* Thames And Hudson Ltd., London 1980

Wilson, Pat: 'George Russell's Constant Quest', *Down Beat* April 27, 1972 vol 39 no 8 pp. 15 & 28-29

Woodard, Josef: 'Joe Zawinul: The Dialects of Jazz', *Down Beat* April 1988 vol 55 no 4 pp. 16-19

'Keith Jarrett: In Search Of The Perfect E Minor Chord' *Down Beat* February 1989 vol 56 no 2 pp. 16-19

'Don Cherry: Globetrotter In The Mainstream', *Down Beat* November 1989 vol 56 no 11, pp. 23-25

Wormdal, Celine: 'Jazzmusikeren kom til Ibsen', *Dagbladet*, Oslo June 10, 1978

Yanagi, Soetsu: *The Unknown Craftsman: A Japanese Insight Into Beauty* Kodansha International, New York 1978

'The Dharma Gate of Beauty', *The Eastern Buddhist*, New Series vol X11 no 2 October 1979

Yoell, John H.: *The Nordic Sound* Crescendo Publishing Co., Boston 1974

Zwerin, Mike: 'Le Jazz Triste', in Gillenson, L. W. & Simon, G. T. et al (eds.) *Esquire's World of Jazz* Thomas Y. Crowell Company, New York 1975 pp. 188-194
Close Enough for Jazz Quartet Books, London 1983
'Manfred Eicher: A Distinctive Jazz Sound', *International Herald Tribune* 23/2/83
'Manfred Eicher's Jazz: Aesthetic Socialism', *International Herald Tribune* 24/10/89
'Manfred Eicher's Ever-Widening Circles of Jazz', *International Herald Tribune* 20/10/94

Eberhard Weber, (Logan Hall, 1987)
Christian Him

upward into/the depths... (Royal Festival Hall, 1993)
Christian Him

Index

(pagination for recordings listed in bold refers to chief passages of reference)